Coaching, M...........................al
Consultancy

ONE WEEK LOAN

Coaching, Mentoring and Organizational Consultancy

SUPERVISION AND DEVELOPMENT

Peter Hawkins and Nick Smith

Open University Press

Open University Press
McGraw-Hill Education
McGraw-Hill House
Shoppenhangers Road
Maidenhead
Berkshire
England
SL6 2QL

email: enquiries@openup.co.uk
world wide web: www.openup.co.uk

and Two Penn Plaza, New York, NY 10121-2289, USA

First published 2006

A catalogue record of this book is available from the British Library

ISBN-10: 0335-218-156 (pb) 0335-218-164 (hb)
ISBN-13: 978-0-335-218-158 (pb) 9780-335-218-165 (pb)

Library of Congress Cataloguing-in-Publication Data
CIP data applied for

Typeset by BookEns Ltd, Royston, Herts.
Printed in Poland by OZGraf S.A. www.polskabook.pl

Dedicated to all those engaged in cultivating the leaders and the leadership necessary for meeting the challenges of our time.

One can change the condition of the mind of a person
who is repeating the same reflections over and over,
by giving him quite another direction, a direction
which would interest him more. What we must first
accomplish in life is to clear the reflections from
our own heart, reflections which hinder our way.

The Palace of Mirrors by Hazrat Inayat Khan

Contents

Preface

Welcome! We have written this book to be both a help and a challenge for you in exploring the foundations of coaching, mentoring and organizational consultancy. We will also explore the interactive nature and process of enabling others to practise these crafts through providing supervision and other forms of development. Our hope is that the inevitable monologue form of a book will transform quickly into an ongoing dialogue with you and your practice. Since all good dialogues require some preparation and also some self-disclosure, we will share our departure points and the essential assumptions which underpin our work. That way, you should be able to contextualize our writing and our practice and make it useful for yourselves.

In sitting down to write about the subject of supervision, we have reviewed the experiences we bring to the conversation. Both of us had practised as psychotherapists for some years, and had then retrained and become organizational consultants, where for the last 20 years a portion of our activity was as executive coaches and occasionally mentors to our clients. So here we have two middle-aged white men, with a particular set of views and experiences, in a mainly UK context, wanting to have a conversation with a broad range of people from across different cultures, with different skill sets, different levels of involvement in the subject, and with their own special questions to ask us. As we sit at the computer, we see a range of people with a range of needs staring back at us. This makes the task of speaking clearly a difficult one. At least in coaching or supervision, most of the time, we have one person in front of us and we can tune in to them and what they need from us. This current task is infinitely more challenging as we start to engage with you.

Whatever our involvement with coaching, mentoring and organizational consultancy, or the supervision of these practices, all of us have one thing in common. We all have a concern with how we facilitate personal change well and keep improving our skills as we go on. These concerns will therefore be at the core of our book and provide the energy for making this journey of enquiry together.

Whether we have just begun to think about the subject or whether we have been practising for years, we will all have experience of trying to bring about some personal change in our own lives. Here we ask you to pause and reflect on a change challenge you set yourself. What personal changes have you tried to make in your life recently? You may have decided to learn a new language, stop smoking, lose weight or stop behaving in particular ways that are upsetting to others (e.g. stop getting so angry with people close to you). One of the underlying issues that is common to all these significant changes is that they cannot be achieved in one day or at the first attempt. They all require ongoing and determined action in order to succeed.

Were you successful at your attempted change? What do you think made the difference between success and failure? Was anyone else instrumental in making the change happen, or discouraging you in your endeavour? Was there an important conversation that helped you through a difficult patch, or an attitude you met in another that made you believe you could never achieve your change? Since we are not alone in the world, our relationship with others is important. What was the quality of the relationship you had that helped or hindered the change you set about? By further reflecting on this attempted change, evaluate how committed you think you were to making it happen. If you had had to put all your savings into the scale, would you have risked it all on your achieving your goal? How certain were you that you wanted this change? Really?

The answers to these considerations are at the heart of this book. To do our jobs well we need to understand what makes personal change happen and what blocks it.

Although the subject matter that the coach, mentor or consultant works with may often be different to the examples of the personal change agenda we have described above, the key similarity is that we are working with someone who wants to, or needs to, change the ways that they are currently behaving in their business role. Some of the business issues may closely parallel the personal changes we have just explored. We might be helping a chief executive to develop her direct reports, rather than take decisions for them; or working with a chief finance officer to help him reward staff when they produce good work, rather than wait until they have done something wrong and then criticize them. Other coaching, mentoring or consultancy situations may involve specific business issues such as how to deal with disquiet in the boardroom over recent falls in the share price. Whether the focus is personal change or business change, the common link is the need for people to do things differently and frequently that involves challenging their habitualized ways of behaving, thinking and feeling.

From your experience of change in yourself and facilitating others, what do you see as the key blocks to making change happen and sustaining it afterwards? There are probably many factors that make a difference to whether change becomes successful. One of the fundamental practices that a highly effective person will have is that they will find ways of generating relevant data about themselves and their activity, such as regularly getting feedback on how things are going. They think about that information and decide how to experiment if a change of course is indicated. They are in fact learning something new, and this capacity makes a generative difference in adult success or lack thereof. Adult learning may seem to be a rarefied topic of interest only to educationalists but, as we can see, it is of vital importance to anyone involved in personal change. It is a subject that we will return to in this book in a number of ways. It follows that a number of experienced executive coaches, mentors and organizational consultants, when asked how they would describe their role, have said that they are 'enablers of learning' at work. This is a core insight into the nature and practice of our craft.

Our assumptions about the crafts of coaching, mentoring and consultancy

So for us, what we do is simple and straightforward, yet it takes a lifetime to explore and develop! In order to have a dialogue about the core practices of coaching, mentoring and consultancy, and explore the vital importance of supervision to these activities, we need to be up front about the foundations upon which our approaches to change are based. Let us look at how implicit conjectures generate our reality.

We all make assumptions all of the time – and often we don't examine them. If I ring the police because some youths are gathering at the end of the road, I am probably being driven by a set of assumptions: that young people, looking like they do, are out to cause trouble; that they are probably dealing drugs; and that I wouldn't be safe going up to them and asking them to move on. These assumptions may or may not be correct in that instance. That is not the point. The point here is that if we don't examine our assumptions, we mask the true nature of our behaviours. This book is based on a set of assumptions that we have distilled over the years from the range of our experiences. We do not believe our way is the only way of being a coach, mentor or consultant, but we know it has been effective in the type of work we do.

There are six areas of belief that underpin our view of coaching, mentoring and organizational consultancy and its supervision:

- the first is about the nature of people;
- the second describes the nature of 'transformational change' and its consequences for our practice;
- the third focuses upon the way in which the coach, mentor or consultant uses themselves in their work with clients;
- the fourth relates to the essential role and importance of 'supervision' in the practice of our craft;
- the fifth is concerned with coaching, mentoring and consultancy as craft skills;
- the last is about the nature of systems and how they impact on our practice.

We believe that making these assumptions explicit is a useful exercise.

Before you read in more detail about our assumptions, we invite you to sit down and answer the following:

- What are your core assumptions about people?
- How do people best learn?
- What is the nature and what are the optimal conditions for change?
- What role do our relationships play in helping or hindering personal/ professional development?
- What are the conditions for change that organizations have to generate to remain focused on 'what the future requires of them'?
- How much of what we see resides within the individuals concerned and how much in the relationship between them?

The nature of people

- A person is at root a meaning-creating individual, who finds the deepest expression of that meaning creation in relationship (with other people, nature or the challenges they face).

- A person is constantly offered the chance to mature as a human being through their engagement with the world around them, and this maturity and wisdom is worth striving for and is responsible for the most satisfying and enduring elements of human culture.

- A person naturally seeks a purpose in their life that aligns with their values, but events can disturb and obscure that search.

- A person therefore operates in multiple, interpenetrating 'worlds' at the same time. They participate in the physical world, while having a rich thought life. Overlaid on this they also have an emotional reality different but connected to the other two. Alongside and underneath these is a reality that energizes us towards our highest ideals. We are then able to operate should we so choose in the 'world' of meaning and purpose (based upon our highest ideals). That purpose would shape the 'world' of feeling and relationships and our ability to engage in the subtlety of our interaction with the world around us. The way we think is shaped by our emotional reality. Physically we are challenged to embody these qualities; to, in fact, be our values.[1]

Transformational change

- Personal change always has to begin with oneself and flow outwards.

- Personal change begins in the now and flows into future actions, as well as easing the influence of previous actions.

- Personal change that transforms is based upon 'learn/learn' cycles not 'win/lose' competition.

- Personal transformation occurs on, and aligns, multiple 'levels' at the same time (behaviour, mindset, emotions and purpose).

- Personal change that is sustainable broadens existing character, rather than eliminating previous 'bad' bits and inserting new better bits! We do not believe in moral 'spare part' surgery.

The use of the person to effect change

- In the form of coaching, mentoring and supervision that we practice, we take it as axiomatic that the person doing the coaching/supervising uses themselves as a key instrument of change. This means that they use their personality to help

---

[1] As Maslow noted, if bodily needs are not satisfied we cannot move up the 'chain' to enage in our purpose. It is therefore by no means a foregone conclusion that an individual will be able to operate in all four realities at the same time. It is part of the broad remit of the coach, mentor or supervisor to at least bear this alignment and development in mind.

in creating change, rather than trying to be a blank canvas. This is different from the 'analytic/therapeutic' stances taken by those who see change as coming through insight and transference.

- The ability to reflect on our process and outcomes, and to experiment with new ways of creating shift for people, are key capacities to develop in order to engage in continual learning of the craft.

Role of supervision

- Supervision supports self-reflection as a key practice in developing mature and wise practice.
- Supervision links professional development with educational, managerial and personally supportive activity.
- Although supervision uses many of the skills of coaching, mentoring and consultancy, its main difference is that it both creates shift in the relationship and shows up the process by which the shift occurs. In this way the supervisee can not only experience the process, but also see how to replicate it in their craft practice.

Coaching, mentoring and consultancy as crafts

- Coaching, mentoring and consultancy requires a personal developmental journey by the practitioner, as well as an ongoing development of interpersonal change skills.
- There are stages on this journey that are important to track and understand.
- Its core purpose is to enable ongoing learning, development and change in individuals and wider systems.

The nature of systems

- A client or supervisee is always part of a larger context of influence. At any one time we will have at least three clients – the person in front of us; that person's client; and their client's client.
- We have to work at one and the same time with the presenting issue, within its wider context and the larger system of which it is a part.
- We have to be aware that the influences in the system may flow from the individual out or from the outside external context – in, and most often in both ways at the same time.
- The nature of our world is that it is dialogical and relational and therefore much of what we see as personal in fact is constructed between people.

We encourage you to use this list of our assumptions as you go through the rest of the book, to enable you to have a dialogue with us about what you believe and an ongoing enquiry about what works best. When framing our assumptions, it is important to do so in such a way as to keep the possibility of change alive in our work with others. For example, if I see a person I am working with as driven by anger, greed or self-interest, then these assumptions close down the options for change for the other person. These negative assumptions will shape my interactions and the way I will try to intervene. They will almost inevitably set up challenge and resistance in the other person, because I am coming from a position of criticism and blame. A better outcome will result if I start from the point of belief that everybody is of good heart in whatever they do and problems, where they do occur, are caused by the way these good intentions are interrupted or expressed. In the second case the options for change are broader for me, and simply require me to work with someone who wants the best for the situation too. We are then trying to refine the behaviour between us, rather than altering deep-seated emotions and character traits in the other person.

So one of the assumptions we have adopted in our work is that people always want the best for the situation. Whether it is objectively true or not, from a practical point of view, seems irrelevant to us. If my task is to help create change and move stuck situations on, shutting down options for change is not helpful. By believing the best of others, I at least start with the possibility that they can change and that we are broadly 'on the same side'. If I believe that they are out to do me harm all that happens is I get into a fight and change only happens with great struggle.

So what does our coaching look like? If you speeded up a session, like running the fast forward button on a DVD, there would be moments when the coachee (or supervisee) would physically shift in their chair, and if you slowed things down at that point you might find that they had shifted not just their thinking about something, but their feelings about it and their understanding of its importance. This physical shift is frequently therefore a concrete indicator of shifts in emotion and understanding becoming embodied. This is one of the key elements of the style in which we coach – we try to create a 'shift in the room'. We are not particularly concerned with abstract intellectual insights or thinking about issues. We are focused instead upon 'what do I need to shift in my own practice here and now, in the room, in order that I can help my coachee shift their behaviour, in the room, so that they will be able to move their issue to a successful conclusion when they go back to work?' We are therefore working with a 'high impact' model of change, which we call 'systemic transformational coaching', that rests on the assumptions which we have outlined for you above.

If we had video clips that covered the scope of our endeavour in this book, we could look not just at one-to-one activities, but also highlight the interactions with teams and interventions at organizational level. The craft practice skills of systemic transformational coaching have to be able to address in an impactful way the creation of change not just in the individual, but also in a group or a large body of people. It is true that in any of those contexts, the common denominator is the individual who, when all is said and done, has to change in a way that does not backslide to an earlier default behaviour. But there are other principles that relate uniquely to the team or organizational change beyond the practice with an individual. We have to become adept at recognizing the mechanisms for effecting larger-scale change too.

This is where supervision and professional development are so important. In this book we will show why we believe that having supervision is fundamental to our continuing personal development. We believe it provides a protected and disciplined space in which we can reflect on particular client situations and relationships, explore the reactivity and patterns clients invoke in us and, by transforming these confusions live in supervision, profoundly benefit the client. For too long the themes of continuing development and supervision of coaches and consultants have been neglected, and we intend to make our strongest case for the benefits and cost-effectiveness of this provision. It is time that coaches, mentors and consultants walked their talk and put their own continuing development at the heart of their professional life. All this is in our view part of the craft that we will explore with you on our journey through this book.

The six areas of belief that we delineated above, we see as ways of aligning and bridging the theory, the skills and our actual practice in a way that provides a check on current ways of working, enables a review of best practice and helps us navigate our own journey of professional and personal development in a positive and supportive way. It will become clear that many of the skills used in coaching, mentoring and organizational consultancy are also useful for supervision. We have already noted that the supervision relationship is about both recognizing and confirming good practice and also about challenging and changing beliefs and practices that do not deliver what they should for the client, the organization and the individual. Therefore, the unique element in supervision practice is attention to the practice of the craft and one's role in its delivery.

A book like this, which sets out to explain the way in which particular things work, can seem by its nature to assume that everything is understandable and knowable. Our subject matter – people and their relationships – is not a topic that in reality can be fully understood or explained. It puts us in mind of a story Gregory Bateson told about Bertrand Russell, the great twentieth-century mathematician and philosopher, and his older collaborator A.N. Whitehead. Whitehead had become a distinguished Harvard professor, and invited his younger colleague Russell to lecture to the senior Harvard academics and their wives on the subject of 'quantum theory', which even in the 1930s was extremely complex. Russell sweated and laboured for an hour and a half explaining the theory. At the end of his lecture, amid the applause of the distinguished audience, Whitehead got up and, in his falsetto voice, thanked 'Professor Russell for his brilliant exposition of the subject. What I particularly admired,' continued Whitehead, 'is Professor Russell's ability to keep unobscured the vast darkness of the subject!' As Bateson remarked, at first glance, this was a very clever put-down by the older academic of his younger colleague. But when you think about it a bit more deeply, it is a real tribute and appreciation of Russell's understanding of the subject. Russell had managed both to describe and explain what was known about the theory – and make clear what was still not known at the same time. It is said that knowing what you don't know is the gateway to wisdom. As authors we aspire, like Russell in his lecture, to successfully clarify the things that we do know about change, but to keep unobscured the vast number of things about the subject yet to be understood.

We have great enthusiasm for systemic transformational coaching as a way of working, and hope that you become as excited and inspired by its potential as we are. Even if you decide to practise another form of coaching we hope that the extended discussion in this book will sharpen your thinking about what you do and will help you clarify why you do it.

At its best, this way of working joins head and heart in a practice we call 'fearless compassion'. 'Fearless' in that we are often the only people who are able to give the difficult feedback to our client – and without that fearlessness they will go on unaware and therefore not achieve what they tell us they want. 'Compassion' in that, if we do not hold to the best in the other and put ourselves in their shoes, we are simply another harping critic and as such do not deserve to be trusted and listened to. Fearlessness coupled with compassion will help to create the change that is required.

Acknowledgements

We would like first to thank all those who have coached, mentored and supervised us on the important fundamentals of life. Nick would especially like to appreciate: Warren Kenton, Keith Critchlow and Master Lam Kam Chuen; Peter would like to honour: Murshids Fazal, Inayat-Khan and Elias Amidon; his colleagues at the Centre for Supervision and Team Development, Joan Wilmot, Robin Shohet and Judy Ryde and his peer mentors at the western academy: John Crook, Malcolm Parlett, Peter Reason and Peter Tatham.

Much of the material on which this book is based has been developed over the last 30 years or more in work with coaching individuals, teams and organizations and more recently in the training courses we have been running in coaching supervision through the Bath Consultancy Group in partnership with the Centre for Supervision and Team Development. We would like to thank all those we have coached, mentored, consulted to, supervised and trained. They have been our best and constant teachers in continuing to develop our craft, and continue to provide us with fresh challenges and useful feedback.

Our thinking in this book builds crucially on the work pioneered and written with our colleagues, Robin Shohet, Judy Ryde and Joan Wilmot, at the Centre for Staff Team Development over the last 30 years. Central to that was the publication of *Supervision in the Helping Professions*, now in its third edition and being used in over 20 countries. Our colleagues in both organizations have brought great quality of challenge and support to our thinking, writing and practice in these crafts. Especially we would like to thank those who have developed some of the thinking with us including John Bristow, Gil Schwenk, Robin Coates, Keith Humphrey and Hilary Lines. They also commented on parts of the text, as did David Jarrett, Fiona Ellis, Danny Chesterman, Chris Smith, Jane Speller, Sue Pritchard, Peter Binns, Clinton Lucy and Laura Heath.

In preparing the text we have had enormous support from the administrative staff at the Bath Consultancy Group, especially Lesley Bees, Amber Fraser-Smith, Rosie Howarth and Rebecca Todd.

Finally we would once more like to thank our partners Judy Ryde and Gay Smith for their love, patience, colleagueship, support and their many important contributions to the writing of this book. We also thank our children for their support, as they also bore some of the burden of our unavailability.

1

Golden threads of practice

Why has there been such a dramatic increase in the need for coaches, mentors and consultants?

Golden threads

The key competencies, capabilities and capacities necessary for this common craft

Summary

We were working with a major international corporation that wanted to change how they were perceived. 'We want to be the most admired organization in our sector,' the CEO said. 'Please will you help us refresh our presentation to the world.' We did a great deal of research on how they were currently seen by their stakeholders and how their stakeholders wanted them to be different. Gradually we explored with the top team how the perception of the company was based on thousands of daily interactions that all the members of this organization had with the different stakeholders. 'We have to change how our staff behave, they need to be more customer-focused,' the CEO declared. 'How can being more customer-focused start right here in the top executive team?' we asked. 'How can you be the change you want?' 'We don't meet with the customer,' was his reply. 'That might be part of the problem,' we replied, 'for that will send a signal to your staff by itself. What about the customers of your leadership. Do they experience you as being customer-focused?'

There was a stunned silence. The CEO eventually broke the silence and started to regain his position by starting to tell the others how they should lead differently. I was exasperated and was thinking, 'here we go again' and 'why did I not listen when members of the company told me he was such a bully and would be impossible to work with' and 'I'd better stop this and tell him what he is doing wrong'. Luckily, years of supervision on our work helped me listen to my internal supervisor voice, which interrupted me and said, 'You are about to do to him what he is doing to the team and they are doing to the company.

You are here to interrupt the pattern, not replicate it.' I caught myself, took a deep breath and smiled at the CEO. He caught my eye and then to my surprise, he caught himself. 'Wait a minute, let me start again. I think we need to start right here in this team, with what you guys need different from me, so I am better at enabling you to get out there and lead differently.'

Direct feedback had never happened in this team. The human resources department had tried introducing a 360-degree anonymous feedback process, but it had not really impacted among all the other data and reports. (The top team were known as 'fortress floor 20', where all their carpeted offices were co-located above the rest of the corporate headquarters.) Now with live coaching and some simple structures, the team started to give some appreciative and challenging developmental feedback to each other. The CEO was supported in really listening and letting his colleagues know what he had heard. After the meeting he called one of us aside. 'Why did they not tell me all of that before?' he asked. 'I think you know the answer to that,' I replied. 'Do you think it is appropriate for you and me to have some regular coaching sessions?' he enquired. The real change had started to happen.

We open with this simple story, as it encapsulated so many of the lessons we have learnt about change in people, teams and organizations. Understanding of the wider system most often starts from the outside-in; listening to all the different people the system serves and making sense of the connecting patterns that start to indicate what is the required shift. But transformative change always starts in the opposite direction, from inside-out. Real change always starts with us and our relationship with those in the room in the moment.

Why has there been such a dramatic increase in the need for coaches, mentors and consultants?

There is an exponential increase at this time in coaching, mentoring and supervision. If we look back, mentoring has happened informally for a long time, although offering it as a discipline, rather than one person's informal support of another, has been a more recent development. Consultancy to help organizational change has been used by business for 40 years or more, but its links with personal learning and leadership development are more recent connections. Supervision of these practices has arisen as a response to the huge and unregulated growth in practice of the other three and has only come to prominence in this area in the last few years. (Hawkins & Schwenh 2006)

What is driving this increasing need for personal and team support? The answer is complex. When we reflect on the experience of our coachees and supervisees, we see a huge increase in the demands made upon them. Fewer people are doing more work in shorter time frames. Technology is fuelling a lot of these increasingly urgent demands, particularly in business, but really in all phases of our lives. The technology in many fields now gives us access to volumes of material we cannot hope to encompass. For example, coming to terms with the 15,000 tunes that are held on a 60GB Ipod; our ability to process and keep in mind the hundreds of emails a day we might receive on our Blackberry that seem to require to be answered day or night; or our effective retrieval of the myriad documents, articles and items that have been stored on our laptop in the last year. New technology is constantly finding faster ways of informing us of all sorts of things to do with our lives and our business interests. It does not yet have the capacity to prioritize however. It contributes information at a scale and speed that is completely out of relationship with the way human beings are currently able to process and digest information. This is one example of what is driving business people to get the help of another to clarify, prioritize and strategize their way through this mass of material and act effectively in the world.

When faced with the challenge of learning a new skill or developing an existing one, we have found it helpful to reflect on what the core crafts of that practice are. For someone who has experience, it is easy either to just get into a habit or routine without thinking too much about why and how, or get immersed in the detail and find it hard to see 'the wood for the trees'. For those just starting out, that sense of not seeing the wood for the trees comes from a slightly different place. When you first start to grapple with a new body of knowledge, it is very hard to recognize what is most significant and what are just embellishments to the practice.

So as we sit here at the computer screen wanting to engage you, our reader, with our enthusiasm for this important subject, we want to share our belief that beneath all the differences we can discern in the different activities of coaching, mentoring, team coaching, organizational coaching and consultancy, supervision etc., there are some really important common threads that ground what we do and how we do it.

Before we plunge together into the detail of the book, and examine more specifically the key facets of coaching, mentoring, organizational consulting and their supervision, we feel it would be helpful first to look at the 'golden threads' that run through all these different craft practices. Having an overview of the similarities that link them will also help us begin to appreciate the differences between them. At source we believe that these golden threads are few but powerful, and they make systemic transformational coaching and supervising an exciting, impactful and endlessly interesting activity for us.

We believe that all the practices we explore in this book are part of a unitary craft of enabling adult learning and development in real time connected to the challenges of work. Our working definition of the purpose of coaching, mentoring and organizational consultancy would be that it is 'a practice that embodies methods by which one person can ethically enable others to achieve desired changes in their behaviour and attitudes in order to serve most effectively the larger cause in which the individual, team and organization are engaged'.

The golden threads we will explore are like core craft skills that we, as the learning enablers, need to learn and develop as we practice. When a craftsman or craftswoman starts out as an apprentice, they learn new physical and mental techniques and, through practice, habituate these into their business activity. At a certain point, they find that they have embedded the new behaviours and that these new skills are secure in day-to-day practice. There follows a period in which they get a great deal of vital experience by applying these principles to a range of different jobs and start to learn not only how to do their task but also how to organize more complex contracts and how to manage the complications that inevitably arise when doing business.

So a craft is a practical art that creates an effective and aesthetically pleasing solution to a practical problem. In order to maintain standards, as well as ongoing development of skills, the individuals involved need to be supervised and managed. We have used this craft analogy, not because we feel coaching, mentoring, organizational consultancy and their supervision are currently set up like a craft, but because we believe that 'craft' is a model that holds many interesting challenges that could usefully influence how we might organize in the future. Looking at craft traditions gives us a model for how key lore, principles and technical knowledge can be accurately transmitted over time. For coaching, mentoring, organizational consultancy and supervision to be counted as crafts, in the way we understand the term, practitioners would need to have agreed:

- underlying principles of practice;
- how the maturity and effectiveness of a practitioner could be judged;
- what it takes to transit through the maturity levels (Torbert *et al.* 2004 Stoltenberg & Delworth 1987);
- what constitutes a hierarchy of experience (rather than everybody's experience being seen as relevant/important as everyone else's).

In turning 'the craft of coaching and supervision' into more than an illuminating metaphor, there is much still to agree before it can become a practical reality.

Golden threads

The 'golden threads' that we mention in the chapter title are the consistent and underlying themes that appear in all aspects of the work we are describing in this book. Each of these elements will be discussed at greater length in other sections of the book, so at this juncture we simply want to introduce them to you and explain why they are important from our perspective.

The seven golden threads that flow though all our work are:

1   There is always more than one client you need to serve. This is true even when you are coaching or mentoring an individual executive.
2   All real-time learning and development is relational. This means that the coach, the mentor, the consultant and the supervisor need to be always learning themselves. The relationship needs to shift for the individual to shift.
3   Robust dialogue that balances challenge and support is essential for relationships to develop and individuals to learn.
4   Learning is for life, not just for courses. The moment we stop learning is the time our effectiveness in our work starts to decrease.

5   Adult human beings learn best through experience, not by being taught or told. The work of the learning enabler is never to know better and never to know first, but to create the enabling conditions and experiences that create a transformational shift in the relationship and the individual.

6   Transformational change becomes systemic when we focus on the shift in the part of the system we are working directly with (individual, team, functions etc.), to jointly create the shift that is necessary in the wider system.

7   Supervision is essential for the coach, mentor or consultant to remain effective and continue to develop.

There is always more than one client, even if only one of them is in the room with you

We now formulate this multiple focus as the 'Law of Three Clients'. In doing this we have benefited from the work done by RELATE, the UK relationship counselling charity, which frames its client focus in the following way: the first client is the person in the room; the second is their partner; but the third client is the relationship to which the first two should be in service. We see the Law of Three Clients applying to coaching, mentoring, organizational consultancy and supervision in the following way:

- the first client is whoever is in the room (an individual, a team etc.);
- the second client is the organization or network of which they are part;
- the third client is the purpose of their joint endeavour, to which they are both in service – their clients, customers, stakeholders etc.

In supervision there is the supervisee, their clients and the organization they work for. The relationship between the supervisee and their client can also be seen as a client focus for the supervisor.

All real-time learning is relational

One other broad belief we hold is that it is in our interactions with others that our maturity is forged. So as a coach, mentor or organizational consultant, we are not just there to solve the problems the client has, but also to provide authentic feedback about the impact the person has, live in the room. This enables them to use themselves more effectively, not just in achieving their own goals, but also in the service of others. It helps the client increase their own capacity to support their staff, customers and clients in unfolding their best capabilities as required in each situation.

For our clients to learn we also need to be learning, not in parallel, but in and through the relationship. Like such writers as Attwood and Stolorow (1984), Stolorow and Attwood (1992), Hawkins and Shohet (1989, 2006), Gilbert and Evans (2000) and Shaw (2002) we believe that all learning and change happens in an intersubjective relationship. This means:

- the learning is always interpersonal;
- it requires both parties to be fully engaged and able to stand back and reflect;
- it is an inquiry in search of greater possibilities not a search for 'the truth';
- that new ways forward are co-created;
- any new understanding that emerges is always partial and requires further engagement to test the limits of its usefulness;
- it involves a transformation of the current relationship in the service of greater relational capability in work beyond the room.

As Nasrudin said when asked how come he had learnt so much: 'I just talk a lot and when I see several people nodding their head, I write down what I have said' (Hawkins 2005).

The importance of robust dialogue that balances support and challenge

Enabling people to change the way they behave can trigger ethical worries for some people. What is it, therefore, in the way we go about our business that addresses these ethical worries? '1984' is now well in the past, but that date still embodies Orwell's spectre of a state in which people are subtly, and not so subtly, controlled, so that they conform to the demands of those in charge and in power. There is therefore an ethical challenge to our practice of creating change and the purpose of coaching in general. What is our practice in the service of? Are we ultimately supporting an organization that only has its own interests at heart and, in so doing, needs to bend others to behaviours that undermine their integrity at a fundamental level? If one of the golden threads of systemic transformational coaching is that it has a method of reliably helping others create behaviour change, we need to be wary that it is not going to become a tool that can be used to coerce individuals and groups to someone else's will, a will they have no real chance of resisting, because it is dressed up in the clothes of 'performance, efficiency and benefit to the organization' or, more directly, impacts on whether they stay in their job. Facilitating the change people wish for conjures up at least the theoretical possibility of forcing or coercing someone to do or be something that is not 'them'. In fact we are not trying to change people, but want to create conditions that enable people to change themselves. So let us look at a couple of stories that illustrate the sort of clients we might be talking about.

Recently one of the authors started working with James, a senior executive in a global investment house. James is in his late forties and had joined the investment house from another sector. It is a well-paid job, and he brings skills to the job that are not found in great abundance in the sector. He has a strong awareness of the business needs of his organization rather than just his clients, and has management and people skills that the company needs, but does not necessarily always appreciate. James is part of a senior team reporting to an executive director. In working with the executive director and his team, we were asked to collaborate with James and a couple of his colleagues in order to 'make the team function better'. In this environment, 'not fitting in' is only one step away from being fired.

Here is another example: Julia is an experienced coach, with previous experience as a psychotherapist. She came for supervision because she wanted to look in more depth at her current practice, and because the 'market' was demanding that coaches have this quality check on their practice. In the first session she 'brought' some of her coaching clients that she was feeling stuck with. Although for a number of her clients her coaching was extremely helpful, for these few clients she has brought, she indicated that she would need to move out of her comfort zone of behaviours. 'My sessions lack bite,' she said, 'I really support my clients, but they don't move on.' As Julia's supervisor, the author was being indirectly requested to help her shift her practice away from one set of assumptions and beliefs (based in this case on non-directive and reflective principles) and onto a more directive and challenging style of working.

In both these situations, the authors are working with people who are under pressure to change. These pressures from their environment may be pushing them in ways they have not agreed to go.

The root of the issue is that personal change needs to be both adaptive to the person's environment and generative for the person in that environment. It needs to be worked out through relationship, rather than imposed by the will of another. We cannot practice our coaching, mentoring and organizational consulting by insisting, as an expert, on other people doing something *we* think is right. It only works through dialogue. The degree to which we can usefully challenge another is equal to the degree we have already established that we are alongside them and have experienced, in the room, what it feels like to be in their shoes. The use of dialogue means that both coach and coachee are fully engaged in the endeavour, and that it is only this level of commitment that allows for real, transformational change to occur. Merely telling someone what will be better for them at best only generates intellectual commitment in the other. From our experience this is not normally enough to make a real difference. The dialogue ensures that the whole of the other person is engaged with the issue and not just their business brain. Because we have two people fully present in the discussion, we are less likely to do damage to the client by unilaterally imposing ideas that don't sit well with them.

In working with our client therefore we realize that we need to be aware of what this process is in service of. Change for change's sake, 'driving' change for people's own good, or change for someone else's aggrandizement are obviously not goals that we think are ethical for coaches, mentors or organizational consultants. Robust dialogue, born out of fearless compassion is, we believe, an important way of protecting both organization need and individual integrity.

Learning is for life not just for courses

One of the most fundamental principles for us, in this more uncertain world, is that learning is a necessary ongoing life activity, not just a short cut to doing what we really want to do. Lifetime learning, however, requires an open mindset. To have an attitude of constant inquiry and interest in improving what we do, we need to be clear as to our answers to the questions, 'Why?' and 'What's the point?', when they are raised in relation to ongoing learning. This accent on learning is not just focused upon learning new facts, but is more importantly helping us to mature as people. This means not so much having answers, but generating even more compelling questions and learning to live with some degree of uncertainty. As has been noted by others, this developmental learning journey is one that needs to help us transform raw data into information, through which we distil knowledge that eventually gives us wisdom. So learning for us is a purposeful activity. It is not merely to gather more and more data and information, but to distil it and place the resulting knowledge within a context of wise practice. This process transforms therefore not just how we understand the outside world, but also gradually transforms our inner world, and integrates thoughts, feelings and action with a wise purpose.

It follows, for us, that if learning is to be carried out in the way we described above, we need to make sure it is not an activity divorced from other aspects of our life. We are personally committed to creating a context for real-time learning opportunities, which addresses change in the here-and-now, not in the future and only in the head. The primary belief in the importance of personal learning and, in particular for coaching, mentoring, organizational consultancy and their super-vision, leads us to find opportunities to create that learning in real time. Our belief, therefore, is that change starts in the room with the client, but is always in service of what is beyond the room. Because what happens in the room is connected to what needs to happen outside the room, it stops the activity becoming self-indulgent navel-gazing. Through holding the wider set of relationships in mind (e.g. with the client's client, the funding organization, the community of practice etc.) we create a robust 'edge' to the learning that develops.

In our view, change has to be seen in the context of personal development and the movement to maturity. We see this as the challenge of a human life, to engage with the world around us and learn its lessons in such a way that we can increasingly benefit others and create a positive contribution to our community, rather than having demanded and taken, and left the world a poorer place. For those of our readers who accept this assumption, certain things follow in both our practice and in the development of our craft.

The development theme is present in both the broad attitudes we take to our work and explains some of the models we choose to use. As we mentioned earlier, we do not believe that coaching can be learned on one course and then mechanically applied for as long as you want afterwards. Because of the centrality of the dialogue process, we continually learn as much about ourselves as the coachee does about him or herself. To accommodate and digest this learning is therefore a lifetime quest. The learning and maturation does not stop. We like the story told of Master Kano, the founder of modern judo, who after a lifetime of practice, and in his eighties, in the weeks before he died, called his senior students around him. His main instruction for them after his passing was that he would be buried with his white belt, the symbol of someone just beginning their study in the martial arts. Any practice that involves understanding ourselves and others will take a lifetime and we will never know everything. We also need the humility to acknowledge the vast darkness of the subject still left to understand, however much we know. That freshness and wonder and ability to see with unclouded inquiring eyes, seems to be summed up in the title of a book by Shunryu Suzuki – *Zen Mind, Beginner's Mind* (1973).

In our work as coaches therefore we have found that it is particularly valuable to use developmental models. These models make explicit the ways in which our personality matures, and how we can recognize these various stages in the journey to maturity and what the stages contribute to the life of an organization. They allow us to view present behaviours in a broader life context, and link the specific work around business issues with broader issues of personal maturity.

Transformational change

When we boil down the essence of the practice underpinning coaching and supervision, it is to have the skills to help others effect personal change. The change we are focused upon as business coaches is mainly change in behaviour, although such change inevitably also entails change in mindset, emotions and sometimes core purpose.

We perhaps need to make clear what we mean when we talk generally about 'behaviours'. We have occasionally found that the way we use the term confuses people. They think that we mean, by this term, a sole focus on the body and its movement, somehow denying the importance of the emotional and intellectual aspects that drive how we act in the world. The reason we talk about 'behaviours', in the way we do, is that we are interested in our work literally making a difference. That is, if after our work together somebody only thinks differently but their actions remain the same, we would see our work as having not been successful. The outcome that we most keenly measure is whether or not, in their daily business life, they still behave in the same ways they used to behave before we started our work together. If we can find and measure the ways in which the client is acting differently, then we need to know if these changes are getting the hoped-for results for the individual client. And following this, are these changes translating into a measurable benefit for the organization?

First and second order change

The process we just described is entirely dependent on having a methodology that can actually help people change difficult behaviours. From both professional and personal experience we know that trying to instigate change can be extremely difficult. So why are some things easy to change and others change-resistant? Certain changes can be easily managed and cause no pain, distress or difficulty. They are what Gregory Bateson (1973) called 'first order' changes.

First order changes are those that simply require more of something or less of something. Since the 'something' is there at the beginning, it does not significantly challenge any of our basic assumptions about how the world is. More of something or less of something is one issue. So more vegetables or less vegetables in our diet should not cause a major change issue, unless it knocks up against another deeply-held assumption about the right balance of meat and vegetables in a meal. Trying new foods can be a major issue for some people, but a fairly relaxed experiment for others. All those who have brought up young children know how difficult such a change can be. First order change itself should not be a problem; the difficulty is not knowing what first order change looks like. It is often difficult to know exactly what our specific, tacit assumptions are that underpin our current choices, and how they might therefore crash against a new challenge. Where there are no such clashes, change should be easy.

However, second order change provides a wholly different challenge. Second order change is triggered when you start to challenge major assumptions within your world view. If I demand that you stop eating meat or that you exercise regularly when you haven't done so before, you may intellectually agree and intend to change. However, if these changes challenge core assumptions which, while tacit (i.e. held strongly but beneath conscious awareness), deeply shape your way of being, then you may well find that for indefinable reasons you seem to never get round to making the changes!

Later in this chapter we will talk more about the issue of commitment as a precondition for change. It is vitally important for a coach or a supervisor to understand the difference between grounded commitment and its 'look-alike sister', intellectual commitment. It is very easy to be fooled, both as the changer and as the coach of change, by thinking intellectual commitment is enough. For second order change it is not.

Programmed to resist change
The reason why second order change is difficult is that we have a natural tendency to resist changes that take us outside our current experience and 'comfort zone'. We need to note that physiologically and emotionally we naturally monitor ourselves on a continual basis and make continuous small adjustments to keep ourselves in our comfort zone.

The experience of being in our comfort zone is generated when we do what we normally do, when what we do is good enough for our current purposes. We register our habitual patterns as 'normal'. It is relatively easy to gently push the envelope around this comfort zone, although not without challenge, as anyone who has tried to eat less has found. When the changes you are making start to push you well outside your comfort zone there are physical responses brought into play, just like the central heating thermostat, to stop you carrying on. The unfit person who suddenly decides on a regime of running and vigorous exercise will experience a strong 'push back' from their body, in the form of stitch, lack of breath, muscle cramps, profuse sweating and nausea, unless prepared for and supported appropriately. The same is true in trying to make changes at the emotional level, but the push back here may be in the form of panic, lack of confidence, avoidance or insecurity, when we move far outside our normal patterns of response.

From transformational change to systemic transformational change

In the fifth golden thread we outlined the importance of creating a transformational shift in the room, but if we combine this notion with the first golden thread of working in service of multiple clients, not just the ones that are in the room, we realize that we need to focus on the transformational shift in the room, which will, in turn, create the needed shift in the wider system.

In this book, after we explore our approach to coaching and mentoring of individuals (Chapters 2 and 3), we look at team coaching (Chapter 4), organizational coaching and consultancy (Chapter 5) and creating a coaching culture (Chapter 6). Whatever the level of the system we are working with, we are also focusing on the wider systemic context – the team the individual executive manages; the customers of the team; the stakeholders of the organization; those for whom the coaching culture is trying to create greater value.

Thus, in the story at the beginning of this chapter, the focus was not just on creating a transformational shift in the CEO's behaviour, but concentrating on the transformational shift in the relationship between the CEO and his team that would create the shift in the way they lead the organization, which would change the felt experience of the staff, which would turn the culture towards being customer-focused. Clearly one transformational shift in the room does not create a whole culture change by itself, but it can be pivotal.

It is important to recognize that, prior to focusing on the shift in the CEO, we as the practitioners had to focus on monitoring ourselves in order to see how we were part of the systemic pattern, and first had to change ourselves.

This need to start the change with ourselves is nicely encapsulated in a Nasrudin story (Hawkins 2005):

> *Giving Up Coffee*
> *A senior manager came to Nasrudin for some individual counselling and pleaded with him to help him give up coffee, because he was drinking it constantly throughout his working day.*
>
> *After some consideration, Nasrudin told him that he thought he could help him. He asked him to come back and see him in two months' time.*
>
> *The manager agreed to this appointment and duly returned two months later.*
>
> *Nasrudin looked him in the eye and said: 'Stop drinking coffee, you do not need it any more.'*
>
> *The manager was a little taken aback. 'Is that all?' he enquired incredulously.*
>
> *'Yes,' replied Nasrudin, 'you will find that your craving for coffee has completely gone.'*
>
> *'Well you could have said that to me when we first met, so why did I have to wait two months and come back and see you?'*
>
> *Nasrudin smiled and replied, 'I had to give up coffee first.'*

For the practitioner to be the instrument of change they need to have their own ongoing reflective space, in which they can reflect on their own practice. It is to this essential requirement for effective practice that we now turn.

Supervision is essential

Supervision has become a core aspect of many of the people professions from social work to counselling, and from psychology to nursing (Hawkins and Shohet 2006), but only recently have we seen the beginnings of research, books, papers and training in coaching and mentoring supervision. Currently we are in a period in the professional development of these crafts where advocacy of the importance of supervision is running ahead of its practice. (Hawkins & Schwenk 2006)

So what is the lack of practice due to? In talking to a wide range of coaches and mentors we have been offered a number of different explanations:

- Lack of clarity about what supervision involves;
- lack of good-quality trained supervisors;
- lack of commitment to personal development as it makes us vulnerable;
- lack of discipline among coaches;
- addiction to be in the role of the person enabling others, rather than receiving.

Probably, all of these have some degree of truth and a full answer needs to include these and other factors. In the absence of a body of good theories, training and practitioners, many coaches have turned to counsellors, psychologists and psychotherapists for supervision or supervisory models. While there is much we can learn from these and other people professions that have been practising quality supervision for longer than coaching, there are also dangers, as we outline in Chapter 8.

We define supervision as: 'The process by which a coach with the help of a supervisor can attend to understanding better both the client system and themselves as part of the client-coach system, and by so doing transform their work and develop their craft'.

We believe that coaching supervision has three elements:

- coaching the coach, mentor, or consultant on their work with clients in a way that provides an external perspective to ensure quality of practice (the qualitative function);
- mentoring the practitioner on their development in the profession (the developmental function);
- providing a safe and reflective space where the practitioner with the help of the supervisor can attend to their own support and how they resource themselves (the resourcing function).

In the second section of this book we devote Chapters 7–11 to the various aspects of developing and supervising coaches, mentors and consultants, on courses and in individual and group supervision.

The key competencies, capabilities and capacities necessary for this common craft

Each of the above golden threads requires a set of skills that the craftsperson needs to learn how to use, their acquired competencies, selectively at the right time for the right need, thus turning the competencies into capabilities. We will also stress throughout this book that competencies and capabilities are not enough by themselves. What is more essential for a master practitioner in any of these related crafts is highly developed personal capacities. In the third section, in Chapter 12, we outline the core skills that we believe are necessary for coaches, mentors, consultants and supervisors. In Chapters 13–15, we outline the core capacities that we believe are required from the people who practise all these crafts.

Summary

In laying out the threads that we see running through the practice of coaches, mentors, organizational consultants and supervisors, we have charted the overall map that shows the type of terrain we seek to occupy and the tools we use for our work. We have tried to articulate the golden threads of our practice across these roles and gained some clarity as to the elements that make them up.

1   There is always more than one client you need to be serving; this is true even when you are coaching or mentoring an individual executive.

2   All real-time learning and development is relational. This means that the coach, the mentor, the consultant and the supervisor need always to be learning themselves. The relationship needs to shift for the individual to shift.

3   Robust dialogue that balances challenge and support is essential for the relationship to develop and individuals to learn.

4   Learning is for life, not just for courses. The moment we stop learning is the time our effectiveness in our work starts to decrease.

5   Adult human beings learn best through experience, not by being taught or told. The work of the learning enabler is never to know better, and never know first, but to create the enabling conditions and the experiences that create a transformational shift, in the relationship and the individual.

6   Transformational change becomes systemic when we focus on the shift in the part of the system we are working directly with (individual, team, functions etc.) that is necessary for a shift in the wider system.

7   Supervision is essential for the coach, mentor or consultant to stay effective and continue to develop.

In the following chapters we will be taking a detailed look at these elements and exploring their implications for our practice. This overview has been offered to give a bird's-eye perspective of the landscape we will cover. Throughout the book we delve deeper into the similarities and also address the differences we see between these different roles in enabling learning, development and transformational change.

SECTION 1

Coaching, mentoring and
organizational consultancy

Introduction to Section 1

Having set out our underlying assumptions about the craft of enabling adult learning in individuals, groups and organisations, Section 1 starts to clarify the essence of each of the three ways of offering adult learning in the organisational context, namely coaching, mentoring and organizational consultancy. This section is therefore discussing and exploring what we see as the key elements of each of these three practices. In the final chapter we go on to explore the way in which one can generate a coaching culture that supports and develops personal and organizational learning and change. Before we look at the whole area of supervision later in the book, we focus on the crafts that are to be supervised, and make sure we have a clear understanding of the practices that we are supporting and developing.

In Chapter 2 we explore the practice of executive coaching and put that in the context of the type of coaching we feel is most appropriate for the organizational context. Transformational coaching has a focus and a set of practices that we believe make it highly effective both for coaches and clients and their organizations. We also look at some of the boundaries that define coaching from some of its near neighbours such as counselling.

Whereas coaching has a more specific and short to medium term focus, we see mentoring as both more individual in nature and dealing with the broad sweep of a person's development through their career. In Chapter 3, we clarify what we see as the essence of mentoring and how it differs from coaching. From this base, we explore the key models we use that give an important framework for working with life and career transitions, and link them with the Torbert model, which describes the maturational development stages of leaders, a critical element to address whether in coaching or in mentoring.

While Chapters 2 and 3 have concentrated upon the individual, Chapter 4 looks at the differences in craft practice between working with individuals and coaching teams. This chapter explores what good team functioning looks like and therefore what the focus might be when working with a group around organizational improvement. We discuss the use of the CLEAR process when working with such teams and explore the implications of working with different types of teams in organizations, such as virtual, project or account teams.

Chapter 5 changes the perspective once again by looking at the use of adult learning principles in the development of whole organizations. In the first few chapters we have moved from individual to team as the 'unit of practice. In this chapter we have to place the systemic aspects of organizational activity centre stage with a particular focus on integrating strategic change, culture change and collective leadership development. We discuss the nature of organizational coaching and how it is different to individual or group coaching. Not only has the work focus changed in this work but the need for the coach to work as part of a team is also much stronger, in order to manage the strong currents of parallel process and organizational culture. We can see a spectrum of coaching activity clarifying at this point in terms of both the clients we have (whether individual, group or organizational) and the way we work as either a single practitioner or as part of a larger coaching or consultancy team.

In the final chapter of this section, we explore the culture that is needed to make full use of coaching activity in an organization. Part of this focus is looking at the type of culture that is needed and the shift in mindset required to move from the purchase of coaching in crisis situations, and often for remedial issues, to the global use of coaching as a key leadership style in the creation of a development and learning culture in an organization. We also discuss one or two organizational tools, such as descriptor analysis, that we have found helpful in creating the sort of clarity necessary to deliver these shifts.

2
Coaching

Introduction

In Chapter 1 we described the growth of a wide-ranging new profession of work-related adult learning facilitators. The ranks of these include coaches, mentors, certain types of organizational consultants and their supervisors. In that chapter we also looked at some of the important common threads of belief and practice that underpin systemic transformational coaching, which we placed at the centre of the learning facilitator's practice.

The world we live and work in is evolving its complexity at ever accelerating rates and our human maturity and wisdom struggle to keep pace. The world is crying out for human beings to get their act together – literally 'to act together' – and, through dialogue, to arrive at new ways of facing the current complex challenges of the world and, through supporting each other, to arrive at new wisdom and a new level of human maturity.

In *The Rock*, T.S. Eliot wrote in the middle of the last century:

> Where is the wisdom we have lost in knowledge?
> Where is the knowledge we have lost in information.

Since that time, Eliot's concern has become more relevant and more urgent. We see the endeavours of coaching, mentoring and organizational consultancy as part of a larger field of endeavour. This larger endeavour is to create ways for enabling us to learn and unlearn, develop and mature – that is, to become wiser and more able to make a meaningful contribution to the world, in the face of an ever-increasing volume of demands and data. Coaching, mentoring and consultancy offer our clients the time and space to re-prioritize and refocus their efforts and the efforts of those they work with. Supervision becomes the means for these facilitators to have time to think and review their practice. If all this activity cannot in some way help us to make the wise choices for our businesses, our communities and ultimately the planet, then we are all in trouble. It is an important task to which we are contributing. It is important therefore that our skills are up to the challenge.

In this chapter we are going to explore more specifically the nature of coaching and introduce our two core models that build upon each other. Firstly we use the CLEAR model for establishing a straightforward coaching style that clarifies what is needed by the coachee and offers a structured approach to arrive at some agreed actions, but in a way that attends to the adult learning cycle of 'think, plan, do and review'. This structured approach alone does not however address the interconnections and complexities in modern business and organizational leadership. In the increasingly fast pace of business, the other element that has to be worked with is the speed at which we help people create the changes they need. To combine both elements in our work, we use the 'systemic transformational coaching model', which is more dynamic than CLEAR and focused on creating a shift for the coachee live in the room. CLEAR then becomes the background framework for fashioning the broad shape of the coaching intervention.

As we mentioned earlier, executive coaching is primarily about facilitating personal change through allowing clients to experiment with different behaviours. We are aware that this common element of facilitating personal change does not set coaching apart from its other sister practices. What in 'coaching' highlights its special qualities, and distinguishes it from mentoring or organizational consultancy? One of the problems we all face in working in the area of coaching, mentoring and consultancy is the lack of precision and agreement as to what the terms mean. How do we decide whether we are coaches, mentors or consultants? Does it really matter anyway? If it does, are there clearly distinctive activities to be carried out under each of these headings, or do they inevitably overlap to some degree? In what context might I call myself a coach rather than a mentor, and can I slip between each of these activities without separate training in each? An obvious but worthwhile place to start disentangling the knot is to look at current definitions used in the field.

Defining the terms

What is 'coaching'?

When we start to look at what people mean when they use the term 'coaching', it becomes immediately obvious that there is no single agreed definition. For such a new profession, coaching has produced a plethora of definitions and in Table 2.1 we give a sample of those currently used.

Table 2.1 Definitions of coaching

Definitions	Author
A process that enables learning and development to occur and thus performance to improve.	Parsloe (1999)
Unlocking a person's potential to maximize their own performance.	Whitmore (1996)
The overall purpose of coach-mentoring is to provide help and support for people in an increasingly competitive and pressurized world in order to help them. • Develop their skills • improve their performance • Maximize their potential • And to become the person they want to be.	CIPD coaching courses definition
Primarily a short-term intervention aimed at performance improvement or developing a particular competence.	Clutterbuck (2003)
A conversation, or series of conversations, one person has with another.	Starr (2003)
The art of facilitating the performance, learning and development of another.	Downey (2003)
Defines the verb 'coach' – 'tutor, train, give hints to, prime with facts'.	*Concise Oxford Dictionary*
A coach is a collaborative partner who works with the learner to help them achieve goals, solve problems, learn and develop.	Caplan (2003)
Meant to be a practical, goal-focused form of personal, one-on-one learning for busy executives and may be used to improve performance or executive behaviour, enhance a career or prevent derailment, and work through organizational issues or change initiatives. Essentially, coaches provide executives with feedback they would normally never get about personal performance, career and organizational issues.	Hall *et al.* (1999)
A collaborative, solution-focused, results-oriented and systematic process in which the coach facilitates the enhancement of work performance, life experience, self-directed learning and personal growth of the coachee.	Grant (2000)

So what does this tell us about the activity of coaching, in a way that might inform our practice as we start this developmental journey towards developing and implementing the skills required for supervision/coaching? What can we deduce from these different definitions?

The key outcomes that distinguish executive coaching seem to be the facilitation of:

- performance improvement – and therefore it is goal-focused, results-oriented and practical;
- adult learning;
- personal development/support/and unlocking of personal potential.

The activities that deliver these outcomes arise from a working relationship with an individual that:

- generates a collaborative partnership;
- allows clear, unvarnished feedback;
- has a short-term and practical focus.

In this respect, coaching aligns with its older sibling 'sports coaching', which also focuses upon performance improvement, personal development and unlocking the individual's potential. To do justice to existing definitions that are in accord with our own experience, our working hypothesis reads as follows:

> Coaching is the focused application of skills that deliver performance improvement to the individual's work in their organization, through robust support and challenge. The coaching process should yield learning and personal development for the executive, and help them to contribute more of their potential. This collaborative relationship will be short-term and practically focused, and will be marked by clear, strong feedback.

Such a definition begs a few questions though. What skills are we talking about? What will robust support and challenge look like and how will it create change for the individual? What does 'short-term' actually mean in the context of a particular client? These are some of the questions that will be answered in the later chapters of this book. Our interest in the following pages is to unpick the nature of the skills that are needed in coaching and to try to understand why they work and in what conditions.

Why have we seen such a growth in these services and professions? The Chartered Institute of Personnel Development (CIPD) guide *Coaching and Buying Coaching Services* (Jarvis 2004) provides a good analysis of the growth drivers (see Table 2.2).

Table 2.2 Growth drivers

Item	% of respondents reporting this item as a main objective
Improving individual performance	78
Dealing with underperformance	30
Improving productivity	28
Career planning/personal development	27
Growing future senior staff	26
Fostering a culture of learning and development	24
Motivating staff	21
Accelerating change in organization	16
Demonstrating the organization's commitment to staff	16
Improving staff retention	10
Reducing cost of sending staff to external courses	9
Helping staff to achieve better work-life balance	5
Satisfying demand for coaching from employees	2

Many of these purposes can also be applied to the growth in the other two professions we are considering, mentoring and consultancy. We would add two other critical factors not mentioned in Table 2.2, though:

- the movement to outsource all non-core functions, which puts more pressure on core staff;
- the recognition that the most difficult challenges in all organizations lie in the relationships between people, teams, functions and stakeholders.

Confusion about what 'coaching' involves

As coaching and mentoring have rapidly expanded, they have also become more complex, fragmented and confusing to the purchaser. The CIPD 2004 survey found that 81 per cent of respondents agreed with the statement: 'There is a great deal of confusion around what is meant by the term "coaching"'. Only half of the respondents thought they understood the difference between the various types of coaching on offer. The CIPD 2004 report goes on to show how this is further exacerbated by the professional fragmentation that includes:

- a number of competing professional bodies with different standards and approaches;
- a proliferation of terms and their usage;
- a wide variety of routes to becoming an accredited professional;
- a wide variety of training programmes from very short courses to doctorate-level qualifications.

Types of coaching

Building on earlier work by Witherspoon (2000), we now see a continuum of coaching that distinguishes four types, by their main focus (see Figure 2.1).

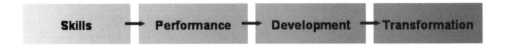

Figure 2.1   The coaching continuum

At one end of the continuum there is a focus on developing new skills in the coachee. These could be specific skills related to their role or job, such as sales skills, IT skills etc., or more general people management skills; how to appraise staff, or give and receive feedback. A lot of this sort of coaching would be offered in training courses.

Performance coaching is less focused on the acquisition of skills (inputs) and more centred on raising the coachee's level of performance (outputs and outcomes) in their current role. This is the sort of coaching typically offered by a manager or internal coach.

Development coaching is less focused on the current role and more centred on the coachee's longer-term development and thus has some aspects of mentoring (see Chapter 3). Besides helping the coachee develop competencies and capabilities, it will include more focus on the development of the whole person and their human capacities (see Chapter 13) and how they can use their current role to develop their capacity for future roles and challenges. Thus there is more focus on second order or double loop learning (Argyris and Schon 1978; Hawkins 1991), which focuses even more on second order learning and change. Whereas development learning will tend to focus on increasing the coachee's capacity within one level of life stage and action logic (see sections on the Hawkins and Torbert models in Chapter 3), transformation will be more involved with enabling the coachee to shift levels and transition from one level of functioning to a higher order level.

Donovan *et al.* (see Lincoln 2006) have developed a similar model which they term 'the spectrum of coaching', while adding two extra, intermediate stages, namely 'behaviour' between performance and development and 'transition' between development and transformation. Shaun Lincoln (2006) has used the spectrum of coaching to look at the choice of who delivers the coaching, be they a manager/coach, internal coach or external coach. He has researched these different forms of delivery in the coaching provided to further education colleges (see Figure 2.2).

Our belief, similar to Lincoln's, is that the manager/coach will tend to be more effective when focusing on skill and performance coaching, partly as they have an invested interest in the current job being done better and also because on the whole they will have had less in-depth coaching training. The internal coach who is 'off-line', but part of the same organization, will have more of an investment in the long-term development of the coachee and hopefully will have undertaken more

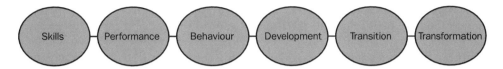

Figure 2.2 The spectrum of coaching

Source: Lincoln (2006)

in-depth coaching training and have some form of ongoing supervision and development themselves (see Chapter 6). This will make them more suitable for development coaching than the coach/manager. The external coach brings more of an outside perspective, with less internal investment or reference. They are not part of the culture of the organization, with its assumed behaviours and taken for granted belief systems and emotional climate. They are more likely to have greater in-depth training and experience in coaching in different contexts and at different levels of development, and therefore are more suitable for providing transformational coaching that impacts the whole organization.

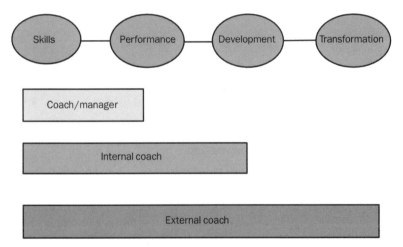

Figure 2.3 The coaching continuum: linked to types of coaches

This model is only intended to describe the general pattern, rather than prescribe what sort of coach should be used for each type of coaching. We believe any coach, with the right level of skills, could be transformational in relation to the person they are working with. If we need to link transformational coaching of individuals to the transformation of the organization then this needs the outside perspective of the external coach or consultant. The ability to coach at the higher levels will also depend on the maturity level of the coach in question. Technical experts (whether in finance, HR, or even sport) will tend to focus on skill development. Achievers will focus on performance and only those who have moved beyond achiever focus will have the internal space to focus on enabling higher order development and transformation in others.

Thus, to balance the model in Figure 2.3 above, we offer another pattern linking the type of coaching to the level of leadership development of the coach, using the Torbert model presented in Chapter 3 (see Figure 2.4). We will be returning to these classifications of the coaching continuum when we look at team and organizational coaching in Chapters 4 and 5. Having set the scene as to the type of coaching that is being offered, we now need to look at what we actually do in the sessions.

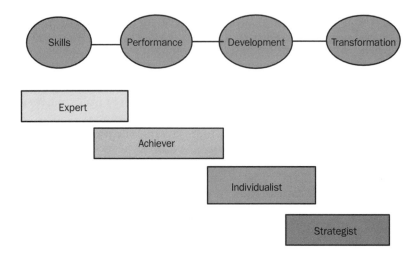

Figure 2.4   The coaching continuum: linked to Torbert levels

How do we shape a coaching intervention?

In the following sections we look at ways in which people have shaped both the flow within a session and across sessions. To illustrate this integrative approach, we will begin by presenting our phase model of coaching and then in more detail outline our model of systemic transformational coaching and show how it also includes aspects of performance improvement, problem solving, and learning and development.

The phases of coaching

The CLEAR model was developed by Peter Hawkins in the early 1980s and used to train both coaches and supervisors. It was then amended for the international 'Consulting with the Board' programme for PriceWaterhouseCoopers Global Partners between 1997 and 2003.

Contract   Coaching sessions start with establishing the client's desired outcomes, understanding which needs are to be covered and how the coach and the coaching process can be most valuable. Also, basic ground rules or roles need to be agreed by both parties.

Listen	By using active listening and catalytic interventions according to the Heron model, the coach helps the client to develop their understanding of the situation in which they want to effect a difference. The coach needs to let the coachee know that they have 'got their reality' – can understand and feel what it is like to be in their shoes. In addition, the coach can help the coachee hear themselves more fully, through mirroring, reframing and making new connections in what has been shared.
Explore	Appreciate the feelings the current situation has left the person with. Through questioning, reflection and generation of new insight and awareness with the client to create different options for handling the issue.
Action	Having explored the various dynamics within the situation and developed various options for handling it, the client chooses a way forward and agrees the first steps. At this point it is important to do a 'fast-forward rehearsal', to enact the future first step live in the room.
Review	Reviewing the actions that have been agreed. The coach also encourages feedback from the client on what was helpful about the coaching process, what was difficult and what they would like to be different in future coaching sessions (see Chapter 12). Agreeing how the planned action will be reviewed and future coaching sessions completes the work.

In Chapter 12 we will revisit this model and look at the detailed skills and competencies needed for each of the five stages. Also in Chapters 4 and 5 we will explore how this model can also be used to look at the processes of coaching teams and organizations.

There are a number of other very useful models of coaching phases that have been generated over recent years which usefully sit alongside the CLEAR model. Sir John Whitmore (1992, 1996) developed his GROW model which is widely used; James Flaherty (1999) offered a relational model; and Mary Beth O'Neill (2000) has built on action research (see Chapter 7) to develop a five-stage model of coaching.

GROW model (Whitmore 1996)

- *GOAL setting for the session as well as short and long term;*
- *REALITY checking to explore the current situation;*
- *OPTIONS and alternative strategies or courses of action;*
- *WHAT is to be done, WHEN by WHOM and the WILL to do it.*

Flaherty model (1999)

- *establish relationship;*
- *recognize opening;*

- *observe, assess;*
- *enrol client;*
- *coaching conversations.*

O'Neill model (2000)

- *CONTRACTING – find a way to be a partner;*
- *ACTION PLANNING – keep ownership with the partner;*
- *LIVE ACTION COACHING – strike when the iron is hot;*
- *DEBRIEFING – define a learning focus.*

As can be seen from the types of statements used, Whitmore's model – like the CLEAR model – focuses more on the phases of a particular session, whereas the Flaherty and O'Neill models concentrate on the phases of a whole coaching relationship.

Transformational coaching

We have adopted the term 'systemic transformational coaching' to distinguish our approach from those that focus on either skill or awareness or insight as the primary goals for progress.

From our years of experience in both coaching and supervising the coaching of others, in many different work settings, we have become increasingly aware that coaches and their clients are often frustrated when they recognize that, in spite of making clear progress in their sessions, these new insights often do not lead to the hoped for change back at work.

In our own practice we experimented with changing our focus from what needed to alter back at work to the transformation that needed to take place right here in the coaching room. Previously we used an action learning cycle that started with reflection on what needed to change, generated new understanding and awareness of what that entailed for the individual and then planned how such situations could be managed differently. The action stage was left for the client to carry out back at work (see Figure 2.5).

Now we aim to complete the full cycle of action learning in the coaching session. We ensure now that the action stage happens live in the room, at least once, followed by reflection and an agreement on how to implement the change back at work (see Figure 2.6).

After making this change we discovered that not only the energy of the sessions markedly increased, but more importantly the frequency of successful change back at work more than doubled. The same good result was achieved by our supervisees. This led us to coin this aphorism:

If the change does not happen in the coaching session it is unlikely to happen back at work.

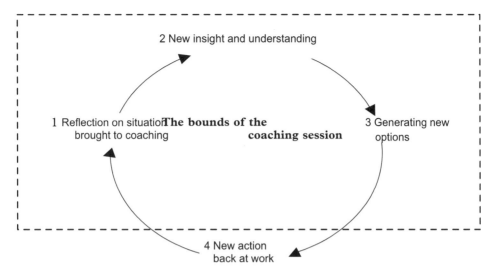

Figure 2.5 Performance coaching

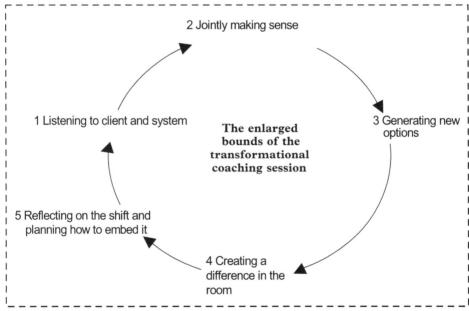

Figure 2.6 Transformational coaching

Gradually we refined this focus on creating the change live in the coaching session. We began to understand the mechanisms for creating this shift in the room. Many writers gave us important clues as to what needed to happen. For example, we adopted the stages of the Gestalt energy cycle (Zinker 1978) for the steps in creating an energetic shift in the coaching session. These stages are:

- raising awareness of a need for change;
- generating energy for and commitment to change;
- generating options for change;
- trying out the change;
- embodying the change;
- review;
- completion.

We adopted the concept of a 'felt shift' (Gendlin 1981) and expanded it to create a focus on the coachee experiencing a new way of handling a situation that was not just cognitive but resonated at a number of levels:

- in their language and way of talking about the issue;
- in their mindset and how they are framing the problem, issue or challenge;
- in their metaphors and how they are feeling about the situation;
- in their body and breathing and how they physically express themselves with the situation;
- in their emotional expression and engagement;
- in the way they are relating live to the coach in the room.

As coaches, working in a session, we look, listen and sense for a transformational shift that reverberates across all six of these levels. This is of central importance, since we know from experience that when the client achieves a transformational shift in the session, almost invariably a shift takes place back at their work.

Transformational learning

We will now show how the concept is attached to other key 'threads' that make up the core practice we are setting forth in this book. Although we want to keep extraneous theory to a minimum, the importance of transformational learning is a central tenet that underpins our approach. Influenced by the work of Paulo Freire, Jack Mezirow outlined the importance of creating transformational learning opportunities to assist adult learning. Mezirow suggests that for second order learning to occur, or as he puts it, 'for learners to change their "meaning schemes" (specific beliefs, attitudes and emotional reactions) they must engage in critical reflection on their experiences, which in turn leads to a perspective transformation' (1991: 167).

We would suggest that this perspective transformation is not just confined to Mezirow's focus of intellectual reflection. If emotional and other intelligences are engaged (see also the introduction to Section 3) in showing someone the lack of alignment between their current beliefs and the situation before them, then we believe this leads to perspective transformation. Mezirow states that the key catalysts for transformative learning are 'disorienting dilemmas', learning situations that do not fit one's perceived notions. Such disorienting dilemmas create emotional impact through dissonance and free the individual to generate new ways of interpreting experience. Mezirow concludes that 'transformational learning involves reflectively transforming the beliefs, attitudes, opinions and emotional reactions that constitute our meaning schemes' (1991: 167).

When we talk about transformational coaching, to what does the word 'transformational' refer? In adult learning, transformational relates to the shift in the adult learner, involving their beliefs and attitudes which underpin current ways of acting. We have already discussed the fact that any significant personal change requires a shift in the intellectual and emotional framework, which supports our existing view of the world. To create transformational learning for adults, this habitual framework has to be loosened in those domains where new beliefs or assumptions are required.

Systemic transformational coaching

As our practice in delivering, supervising and training transformational coaching developed, we considered the ways in which these practices link with how we enable organizations to shift in systemic and transformational ways (rather than just incrementally and transactionally). In a number of cases we focused on organizational transformation and used coaching for a number of senior managers as one of the interventions into the organization. Before we focused upon transformational coaching as a solution, we employed systemic cultural analysis to make sense of the prevailing patterns of behaviour, and mapped the systemic dynamics, cultural mindsets, emotional ground and motivational roots that characterized this organization. From this analysis we identified some key transformational shifts that needed to happen for the organization to make a major step change in its performance.

Applying this learning back in the coaching arena, we asked the question: '*To create the required shift in an organization, what needs to shift in this individual client today in this room, so that they can generate the change they want in the wider system?*' With this question at its heart, 'systemic transformational coaching' was born. We believe that it can be distinguished from other types of coaching, such as:

- skill coaching;
- performance coaching;
- development coaching.

The goal of systemic transformational coaching is to help clients transform how they think and feel about their issues in such a way that they will create a 'knock-on shift' in the wider organization and larger system in response to their coaching experience.

The craft of the coach is multi-layered, requiring high levels of attention and awareness and being open to using oneself in the service of what needs to change in the relevant system. The coach begins by listening intensely (see 'four-level listening' in Chapter 12) and responding with fearless compassion to the client in the room and their wider system outside. The coach is silently holding the questions:

- What is the shift that needs to happen in this wider system?
- What needs to shift in the relationship between this individual and the issue they are describing?
- For those shifts to occur what needs to shift right now in this individual?

The coach then shifts the focus back to the 'system that is live in the room' – themselves and their coachee and the relationship between them, all the while holding the following questions in mind:

- To be in service of those changes, what needs to shift in my relationship to this client right now?
- What do I need to alter in my being to help bring that about?

The coach holds these questions, not trying to work out an answer intellectually, but waiting for a felt sense of what is necessary for the intended transformative purposes.

Understanding of the coachee's situation starts with the larger view of the system of which they are a part. From here it moves down to the specifics at play in the present relationship. However, the change process moves differently. It always goes the other way round. It starts with the individual in the present moment, then reverberates through the relationship between coach and coachee, and then instigates a change in the coachee's relationship with their wider system.

In the listening phase we empathically enter the world of the other, discovering their felt reality, and begin to understand what it feels like to be in this particular situation. This phase requires the skills of 'matching' and the quality of 'presence'. In the shifting phase we need to allow the required shift to happen within ourselves and use the fullest range of emotional expression (Clynes 1989) to translate that shift into the relationship.

The transformational coach combines 'Authority, Presence and Impact' (API) by simultaneously demonstrating non-judgemental compassion for the other, while fearlessly naming any defensive processes like splitting, blaming or avoiding responsibility.

We would describe this metaphorically as the coach walking alongside the other, following the smoke till they both arrive at the fire at the heart of the conflict. With loving support, the coach fearlessly holds both their attentions on the source of the fire, for it is in the fire of conflict that new learning is jointly forged (Hawkins 1986).

Summary of requirements of systemic transformational coaching

Systemic transformational coaching requires the coach to be able to:

- create fast rapport with the client on both their personal and business agendas and create the link between the two;
- make interventions that enable the client to shift how they are thinking and feeling about the issue being explored in a way that leaves the coachee energized for action and will lead to a parallel shift in the wider organization, the whole system.

Thus, the coach needs to have a rich mixture of skills in:

- relationship and rapport building;
- matching and mismatching;
- understanding organizational systems dynamics;
- designing personal transformational interventions;
- using skilful framing and reframing;
- employing a wide repertoire of ways to engage emotionally with the client and the issues at stake.

As a further tool of our trade, we have enhanced the CLEAR model to incorporate the systemic transformational coaching approach. The questions in italics below are those that specifically address the transformational agenda.

Training coaches in a transformational approach, we have found that they begin by locating the transformational focus exclusively in the 'Explore' stage of the process. They see contracting as a prelude and the last two stages as a summary and coda. We aim to help them understand that a transformational coaching approach has to be centred in getting an embodied shift in the room from the beginning to the end of the session. Being transformational must inform and infuse every stage of the process.

Questions to guide the transformational coach

To illustrate this we have listed the questions we recommend for the performance-focused model of coaching. In italics we have added questions and interventions that provide a more transformational approach with an emphasis on creating the shift live in the room.

1 Contracting: starting with the end in mind and agreeing how you are going to get there together.

- How do you want to use your time?
- What do you most need to achieve in this session?
- How could I (or other group members) be most valuable to you?

- What in particular do you want us to focus on?
- *What would make this session a success, both for you and your organization?*
- *What do you want to have achieved or shifted before leaving here?*

2 Listening: facilitating the client in generating personal insight into the situation.

- Can you say more about that?
- Are there any people involved that you have not mentioned?
- How do other people – your boss, your colleagues, your team – see the situation?
- Let us see if I can summarize the issue ...
- *What I am hearing from what you have said is ...*
- *What I am sensing from listening to you is ...*
- *The connections I am making between what you have been sharing are ...*

3 Exploring 1: helping the client to understand the personal impact the situation is having on themselves.

- How are you feeling right now?
- Are there any feelings that you have not expressed?
- Does this person remind you of anyone? What is it you would like to say to that person?
- *What in you is standing in the way of you resolving this?*

Exploring 2: challenging the client to create new possibilities for future action in resolving the situation.

- Who might be of help to you that you have not yet consulted?
- Who has the information you need?
- Who has the skills you need?
- Who has the power to effect change in this situation?
- Can you think of four different ways of tackling this situation?
- *What is the wildest option you can think of for dealing with this situation?*
- *How would someone you admire deal with this situation?*

4 Action: supporting the client in committing to a way ahead and creating the next step.

- What are the pros and cons of each possible strategy?
- What is your long-term objective?
- What is the first step you need to take?
- When precisely are you going to do that?

- Who needs to be involved, consulted or informed?
- Is your plan realistic? What is the percentage chance of your succeeding?
- *What do you need to do right now to radically increase the percentage chance of success?*
- *Rehearse your opening line right now, as if I am the person you need to speak to.*

5 Review: taking stock and reinforcing ground covered and commitments made. Reviewing the process and how it could be improved. Planning the future review after the action has been tried.

- What have you decided to do next?
- What have you learned from this session?
- In what ways have you increased your own ability to handle similar situations?
- What did you find helpful about this coaching process?
- What did you find difficult about this coaching process?
- *What would you like to improve or do differently the next time you have coaching with me?*
- *When and where are you going to review this experimental plan you have just committed to?*
- *Are we going to have another coaching session, if so when and where?*

Making the coaching come alive

The questions we have set out above will not by themselves deliver what you, the coachee or the organization need. They simply help the coach frame interruptions to the patterns the coachee needs to change. They will generate the raw material from which a 'shift in the room' arises. In this chapter we are concentrating on the issues, methodologies and reasons for creating a shift in the room, since it is a central part of our transformational coaching method. We will also set out other supporting frameworks and methodologies such as API (the authority, presence and impact model), the Heron Intervention Styles (Heron 1975), Torbert Action Logics (Torbert et al. 2004) and others that help to frame a systemic view of work and suggest ways in which one can explore where blockages or strong supporting behaviours can be found and utilized in the cause of transformational change in Chapters 12 and 13.

Other approaches to transformational coaching

There are other approaches to transformational coaching, many of which draw on a psychotherapeutic underpinning. Iris Martin (1996, 2001) and her firm Creative Dimensions in Management Inc. describe themselves as corporate therapists, while seeing themselves as utilizing coaching, mentoring and consultancy approaches. Their very specific approach to transformational coaching/mentoring is in five phases:

- *Phase one: grounding in success* – 'each executive hero is led through a chronological review of past successes and a process for integrating them into a platform for accelerated growth. Then each hero builds the optimal environment for creating future success at work and home'.

- *Phase two: the stretch* – 'the hero is taught how to envision mastery in the arenas of work, family life, sports and health ... for each quadrant a stretch goal of 45 per cent over historical annual performance is mandatory'.

- *Phase three: the wall* – 'the wall consists of the negative beliefs, messages and experiences internalized in childhood ... the wall must be artfully overcome'.

- *Phase four: the hell* – 'the hero must then encounter their inner demons. Their old limited self is dying'.

- *Phase five: the win* – 'the hero, quite by surprise, finds themselves on the top of their own mountain ... They celebrate their successful transformation with their mentor, colleagues and family members'.

For our taste this approach is over-directive and rooted in an American heroic culture. For many executives it would appear overly psychological in its orientation. However, its approach is grounded in the fundamentals of understanding life transitions, which anthropologists have studied in many cultures (van Gennep 1960) and popularized as the transition curve (Kubler-Ross 1991). It provides some very useful approaches that can be incorporated into transformational mentoring when either the mentee and/or the whole organization are undertaking a major transition. We will explore this further in the next chapter, when we look at mentoring clients through transitions.

The differences between coaching and counselling

We are often asked questions about the boundary between coaching and counselling. Such questions are coloured by the fear of the trainee coach that they will inadvertently stray into areas of psychological and emotional complexity that they do not feel equipped to handle.

We believe that the first main difference between these two activities lies not in the areas they might explore but in the frame in which the exploration takes place. Coaching begins with a live work-related issue or challenge. In exploring this issue we may well have to explore some personal issues and patterns of the coachee, but the work should always lead back to its prime focus: how the coachee can better handle the issue or challenge that is rooted in the workplace.

This distinction does not hold for life coaching, where the focus is not on managing a work situation, but on how the individual manages their own life. Clearly, life coaching is much closer to counselling than executive coaching or other forms of work coaching. Counselling is more focused on the client's emotional responses to what is happening in their life; life coaching is focused on developing better ways of managing oneself and one's life.

The second main difference between coaching and counselling is well-articulated by Hall and Duval (2005) when they argue that coaching is based upon 'premises and principles of coaching as a modality that works with people who are healthy, have plenty of ego-strength, and whose basic attitude is that of a change-embracer, what Maslow called a self-actualizer'. Hall and Duval contrast this with therapy, which serves people who experience themselves as coming from a place of deficiency. They expect change to be both hard and painful.

The CIPD (2004) has produced a table showing the different emphases of coaching and counselling, which is reprinted in Table 2.3.

Table 2.3   Different emphases in counselling and coaching

Counselling	Coaching
Broader focus and greater depth	Narrower focus
Goal is to help people understand the root causes of long-standing performance problems/issues at work	The goal is to improve an individual's performance at work
A short-term intervention, but can last for longer time periods due to the breadth of issues to be addressed	Tends to be a short-term intervention
Counselling can be used to address psycho-social as well as performance issues	Coaching does not seek to resolve any underlying psychological problems. It assumes a person does not require a psychosocial intervention
The agenda is generally agreed by the individuals and the counsellor	The agenda is typically set by the individual, but in agreement/consultation with the organization
Other stakeholders are rarely involved	Other stakeholders (e.g. manager) are involved

Summary

In starting on our journey towards building the skill of supervision in coaching, mentoring and organizational consultancy, we have laid open what we see as the main skills of the systemic transformational coaching model. We have tried to not only discuss the major issues in practice, but also to give clear references as to how our thinking has evolved. It is always important to acknowledge the flow of ideas of which we are a part. Our intellectual mentors have been referenced, where we are aware of the legacy. In Chapter 3 we will build on these transformational coaching foundations and explore some of the concepts that although used in executive coaching and organizational consultancy are perhaps most important in the process of mentoring and the mentoring aspects of supervision.

3

Mentoring and working with transitions

Introduction

In this chapter we will first explore the nature and definition of mentoring and the differences between coaching and mentoring. Having shown how mentoring focuses on longer-term career development, we will offer two different models of career progression, our own model on stages in careers and Torbert's model of stages in leadership maturity. We then go on to explore how the mentor can help their mentees manage their personal and professional transitions.

What is mentoring?

The word 'mentor' originally comes from Greek mythology. We are told that before setting out on his epic journey, Ulysses entrusts the education of his son Telemachus to his old and faithful friend Mentor: 'For you, I have some good advice, if only you will accept it.' ... 'Oh stranger,' heedful Telemechas replied, 'indeed I will. You've counselled me with so much kindness now, like a father a son. I won't forget a word'. In following *Mentor's* advice to the letter, Telemachus ably supports his parents in their crisis and matures as a person in his own right.

Over the years, the term 'mentor' has gradually become associated with the idea of an older and/or more experienced person acting as a guide to a younger and/or less experienced person. The mentor is normally of the same profession or business as the mentee and has a more general guiding influence than a coach.

There are various definitions of mentoring that delineate the territory mentoring might cover. One of them is Clutterbuck and Megginson's pithy description. **Mentoring is 'off-line help by one person to another in making significant transitions in knowledge, work or thinking'** (1997). The mentor helps the mentee step 'outside the box of his or her job and personal circumstances, so they can look in at it together. It is like standing in front of the mirror with someone else, who can help you see things about you that have become too familiar for you to notice' (Clutterbuck and Megginson 1999: 17).

The CIPD (2004) veered away from trying to find a definition and instead looked at differences between mentoring and coaching by comparing and contrasting the focus and types of activities that characterize them, as shown in Table 3.1.

Table 3.1 Differences between mentoring and coaching

Mentoring	Coaching
Ongoing relationship that can last for a long period of time	Relationship generally has a set duration
Can be more informal and meetings can take place as and when the mentee needs some advice, guidance or support	Generally more structured in nature and meetings are scheduled on a regular basis
More long-term and takes a broader view of the person	Short term (sometimes time-bounded) and focused on specific development areas/issues
Mentor is usually more experienced and qualified than the 'mentee'. Often a senior person in the organization who can pass on knowledge, experience and open doors to otherwise out of reach opportunities	Coaching is generally not performed on the basis that the coach needs to have direct experience of their client's formal occupational role, unless the coaching is specific and skills-focused
Focus is on career and personal development	Focus is generally on development/issues at work
Agenda is set by the mentee, with the mentor providing support and guidance to prepare them for future roles	The agenda is focused on achieving specific, immediate goals
Mentoring revolves more around developing the mentee professionally	Coaching revolves more around specific development areas/issues

The key elements that occur regularly in the above table shape the CIPD definition of 'mentoring' as:

- entailing broader-ranging, longer-term conversations;
- dictated more by mentee's needs for future career development than specific issues in present job;
- mentor using their industry/sector experience to guide mentee's professional development.

This means that the role is less about creating precise and focused behaviour change and more about helping the mentee to construct a relevant larger picture that will animate their career choices into the future. As Table 3.1 shows, there is clear water between coaching and mentoring activities, when one looks at their different processes and outcomes. Where it becomes clouded again is the realization that many of the executives we are working with do not have clear and hermetically sealed needs that fit neatly into one side of the equation or the other. How does the mentor who has the industry experience respond when it becomes clear that to enable the mentee to move on, they will need to address a current performance issue? Or where the focus in coaching on current issues is begging a larger and more important question as to why the individual behaves or thinks in a particular way and its long-term value for them. In such moments the important thing to recognize is that a 'boundary' is being crossed, and that this needs to be acknowledged with the client. In discussion, the executive needs to look at the benefits and disadvantages that may accrue from them moving across that boundary with the mentor. A number of the skills that underpin coaching and mentoring are similar and others clearly different. Both coach/mentor and the executive need to make informed decisions about whether it is sensible to amalgamate these two roles for the purposes under discussion.

In our supervision work with supervisors, we have come across situations in which the supervisor is supervising a mentor working in a new organization, through a 'company start-up' contract, where the issues for the leaders of the firm were clearly not just lack of industry knowledge and business 'know-how', but were also about the need to change a number of their specific behaviours for the future survival of the business. As mentors, with a remit to provide professional experience, they were able to fulfil business needs, but frequently did not see beyond this to the need for behaviour change, and would not have known how to offer that if they had. We will look into the supervisory challenges of a situation like this in a later chapter, but for now it is simply worth noting that a lot of people see themselves as able to offer coaching, mentoring and consultancy, because of their ability to perform one of these functions through skill and experience. The reason we need clarity around these roles can be clearly pinpointed. It does not serve the client well, and ultimately does not serve the coach or mentor and the profession well, if they do not have the full range of skills with which to respond to their client's legitimate needs.

We know from experience that there has to be a degree of overlap between

Short-term issues, problems. goals and performance	Common ground of craft skills	Long-term professional and personal development

Coaching   Mentoring

Figure 3.1   The blend of coaching and mentoring

these two crafts, and that much of what is commonly termed 'executive coaching' is necessarily a blend of coaching and mentoring. As represented in Figure 3.1, in our view, both mentors and coaches need the required skills to be able to attend to the personal issues of change for their clients, as well as deal with the particular focus of their role.

Often a person will seek out mentoring at a time when they have come to a career transition and they want help from an 'elder' in successfully navigating the move from one stage of their career to the next. This could be a chief executive who wants to explore how to move into a career stage where they are no longer employed full-time, but have a portfolio career of non-executive directorships and advisory roles. It could be a young manager who has just been appointed a team leader for the first time and wants to explore how she develops her own style of team leadership and how she can coach others. The most common scenario is that of the successful manager in one functional area of the company, who is working towards becoming a senior executive, with organization-wide responsibility. Such a manager realizes that they will need to move beyond their technical function skills, and develop an ability to engage in broader business leadership.

If a mentor takes on their role as a consequence of their work history (i.e. their knowledge of the sector and the things that they have achieved over the course of their business career), they may feel ill-equipped to address broader issues with their mentee. Their business experience, we believe, needs to be leavened by some further training, which gives them the skills to help the mentee create the necessary personal change for moving forward. The tendency for the untrained mentor is to see the transition of the mentee solely through the lens of their own journey through a similar transition, and to give advice according to their own experience alone. Depending on the quality of support the mentor received through their own transition, their response may vary between:

- 'You will be fine, if you believe in yourself and demonstrate confidence.'
- 'Search out for allies and peers that can support you.'
- 'Find yourself a senior sponsor.'
- 'Get yourself on to a leadership course at a business school.'

Some, or all, of this advice may be useful, but will be of limited value because:

- the situation and psychology of the mentee will almost certainly be different to that of the mentor;
- advice-giving is nearly always less effective than skilfully facilitated exploration;
- successful transitions nearly always involve unlearning previous ways of behaving and thinking, as well as acquiring new ones;
- successful people in one phase of development are often unable to stand far enough back to help those trying to emulate their success;
- it is important to see the current transition in the context of the individual's long-term journey.

Successful managers, leaders, or non-executives do not necessarily therefore make the most effective mentors, although with the right interest and training their experience and organizational credibility can be great assets.

As we can see from the previous definitions of mentoring, it is a craft that focuses upon the aspects of transition. The transitions may be related to life stages, role changes, and/or sector focus. In this chapter we will go into some depth regarding the factors affecting professional transitions, exploring the Hawkins model (Hawkins 1998) and the personal transitions that map onto role changes clarified by the Torbert model (Torbert *et al.* 2004). We have already put in the disclaimer that there are very few totally discrete skills solely relevant to coaching, mentoring, or organizational consultancy. We believe that the Hawkins and Torbert models need to be understood by all practitioners, as well as their supervisors. As models, they are however crucial for the work of mentors.

Mapping life transitions

There are a number of models of adult development, leadership development and professional career stages that provide useful maps for exploring life transitions. In this chapter we are going to present our own model for the stages in professional careers. We will also delineate the model of the developmental stages of leadership that our colleague Bill Torbert generated. In Chapter 8 we will show how these and other models relate to the development stages of supervision.

Identifying stages in the professional career: the Hawkins model

We believe that all mentors need to have a good understanding of:

- adult development (see Chapter 7);
- the development stages in leadership; and also
- the typical professional career stages that people go through.

This model was first developed in 1998 for presentations to the senior managers of the newly-merged PricewaterhouseCoopers. It was entitled 'Taking Charge of your own Career'. Hawkins delineated the changes modern organizations have undergone. They no longer:

● employ people from school to retirement;

● provide straightforward ladders of career progression; or

● provide development supports to move from one stage to the next.

In recent years professional life has become a lot more complicated. To make progress you have to be much more self-managing, rather than being able to rely on the old support structures. You need to think of yourself as a one-person company, with your own:

● strategy;

● stakeholders;

● brand;

● ways of differentiating from others; and

● marketing approach.

In this evolving new world, careers do not progress up straight ladders, but take zig-zag and circuitous routes. To become a successful corporate leader, you need experience in front-line business units, corporate services, cross-cutting change teams and in different national and professional cultures. Sticking within the silo of a particular technical expertise, whether finance, marketing, sales or HR (i.e. in what is only one part of a complex business) could easily become a career cul-de-sac.

Every career path in this postmodern world could well be unique, but we still have a need for some maps and way-lines to shape an individual path. To support that need, a more generic map of career stages was developed, which could provide a wider framework for mapping an individual journey (see Table 3.2).

Table 3.2 The Hawkins model of career stages

Career stage	Core concern	Common age span
Experimentation	Who am I in the world of work?	16–35
Experience accumulation	Gaining credibility and track record and growing the curriculum vitae.	20–40
Full leadership	Making a difference in the world and leaving a legacy	30–60
Eldership	Enabling others, passing on the torch and stewardship	50–90

Hawkins elucidated this model in a letter to a young South African friend who was staying with him and who was looking for guidance about his future career direction.

Hans felt that he was at a crossroads. He was travelling after having become very disillusioned with the life he was leading. He felt that the vested interests in society and the senior people in the area he was working in were making it impossible to change the situation for the better. His disillusionment meant that he was now standing back criticizing, rather than attempting more skilful approaches to create necessary change. There was a strong sense in his questioning that others were not doing what they should and he felt doubtful about whether he himself had any valid contribution to make. Hawkins' letter became a vehicle for gently setting together the issue of his contribution to life with the realities of what he needed to concentrate on at different stages of his work life.

Dear Hans,

'Taking on leadership is giving up the right to blame others or make excuses.' I would like to share with you some thoughts on leadership. Why Leadership? Why you? Why now? Well I have been fascinated by leadership for many years. My fascination started when I was a lot younger than you are now. I wondered when I was young how individuals could make a positive difference in the world; how they could not only lead what was already set up and established but transform the current institutions into something new and different. We all have an inheritance, a pre-existing world that we are born into. This 'given' can be a burden; it can be a trap; but it can also be a springboard or a foundation. Now many people that I have met seem to me to spend their lives accepting this given and yet moaning or complaining about it. Ram Dass, an American academic dropout, who went east and became a spiritual teacher, has this marvellous line: 'It is amazing how many people sign up at the school of life and then spend their life complaining about the curriculum'. To take leadership is to stop moaning and to stop complaining about this 'given' and to engage with how you can take responsibility for transforming the 'given' into that which is 'fit for purpose'; 'fit for the coming times'.

A great starting question for discovering one's own leadership is: 'What is it that I can uniquely do that the world of tomorrow needs?' Both halves of this question are important and they can not be separated. You see I believe that everyone has an important contribution to make and everyone's contribution is unique. That means only they can make it. Most people I know, including myself, spend most of their life trying to find what their contribution is. Some people never find out, but some of those make their unique contribution without being aware that they have done so. A few fall into leadership very young. But do not envy them, for theirs is a hard path to sustain and many of them die early. I am thinking of Mozart, Keats, John Lennon or Jesus, but there are many examples.

For most of us there is a longer path that winds itself up the hill at an easier gradient. In trying to discern and communicate a pattern in this journey I have divided it up into four stages. But remember the map is not the territory and, as I said above, everybody's journey is unique and you cannot fit your life into anybody else's formula or model.

The first stage in the leadership journey is *experimentation*, where one's life is about finding out what you uniquely can do. Typically it involves a lot of trial and error. Trying things and feeling whether this feels right and is this something I can commit myself to.

The second stage is about *experience accumulation*. It only begins when you have made a commitment to a path, albeit a temporary one. Then within that path you can begin to master the discipline, discover your skill, grow your capabilities, begin to contribute and win acceptance and respect. In the past this phase was apprenticeship and even earlier it might have been about joining a guild. In the modern world this can be about growing the CV and the network address book of people who respect you enough to open doors for you.

It is not until the third stage that *full leadership* begins, and many do not get beyond the above stages. It starts when you stop asking questions such as: 'What do I need to do to fit in around here?' 'What will get me approval?' 'How do I get promoted?'. It starts when you begin to ask: 'What is the difference I want to make in the world?' What is the legacy I want to leave to those who come after me?'. Writers on leadership, like Covey and Bennis, write about how effective leaders move from focusing on inputs to focusing on outcomes, from focusing on doing things right to doing the right things. I want to go further and talk about the shift in focus from inputs to outputs, to outcomes, to leaving a legacy.

Certainly full leadership is not the end of the journey. Too much leadership writing accentuates the heroic or charismatic individual. It is important that we remember that leadership is never a solo activity. You cannot have leadership without at least three ingredients, a leader, a follower or co-leader and a shared endeavour. Take any one of these things away and leadership evaporates.

The final stage on this journey is *eldership*. This is when I learn to become less attached to the difference I will make and more to what is necessary and how I can enable others to meet that need. Our western society has forgotten about this final stage and has become somewhat fixated on the earlier stages. More communal and less individualistic societies have a great deal to teach us or remind us about this stage, if we can be humble enough to listen.

Why now? Well, having worked a lot over the last 20 years with large, global commercial companies, I am now returning to do more work on how to develop leadership capacity in the public sector. In today's world the public sector is far more complex than the private sector. Civil servants, local government executives, hospital leaders or school headteachers have many often conflicting customers or stakeholders. They also have diffuse products, and work processes that cannot be controlled mechanistically. The expectations of politicians and public service leaders are constantly growing. The public want them to make a real and noticeable difference to their lives and the world around them. Yet the world is more complex and intertwined than it has ever been and to make a difference in a complex system requires insight, humility and subtlety.

Why you? Well, by chance, good fortune or synchronicity, you have turned up on our doorstep at just this moment in time, not before or after. In the little contact we have had, I warm to your searching, your enquiring mind, your fresh engagement with the world around you. Yes, you are on a geographical journey, but also a personal quest. My hope is that, like you, I never stop travelling or questing. Using the ideas I talked about earlier I might portray my own personal challenge as moving from leadership to eldership. To me your challenge is focused more around exploring and experimentation at this present juncture. Each of us has to embrace the 'given', I don't think we have the option to take our ball back and not play. So the challenge at each moment is to choose how we are going to transform the given into that which is needed for those who come after us.

I do not hope that your journey is easy, but I do hope that it is engaging. I also hope that you may remember this watering hole fondly.

Peter

In this letter to Hans are condensed a number of iterations of discussion and challenge that would be present in the live mentoring conversation. The letter shows the importance of clarifying the specifics of the mentee's situation but also in painting the larger canvas on which their journey can be played out.

Mentoring an individual, in each of these stages, requires a different focus. For Hans it was how he creates a mindset that allows him to engage and experiment, to find the path he really wants to commit to and to see that in a broader context. In the *experimentation stage* generally, the individual needs help in reflecting on each job or role they try out to discover what fits, how they connect with the various activities of the role, what they enjoyed and what they learned. They also need to explore what did not work for them, what they felt out of tune with, and what they learnt from the difficulties.

Effective mentor interventions at this stage include:

- 'What do you want to try out next?'
- 'What do you enjoy and connect with in this job?'
- 'Where do you feel most engaged?'
- 'What do you most enjoy learning?'

In the stage of *experience accumulation*, the mentor or coach can help their client explore what they learn from every role, project or activity they engage with. In particular, how each new task or role provides the opportunity both to acquire new skill competencies and personal capacities. Each task/role change may affect how one is perceived by current stakeholders and future employers. For someone who has found their path, the challenge is more about how they engage with the in-depth understanding of their craft. But they also have to keep a 'weather eye' on what jobs they need to do and attend to the broader context and develop network contacts that allow them to understand the bigger picture within which they are now starting to operate.

Effective mentor questions at this stage include:

- 'What experience are you wishing to acquire?'
- 'How can you broaden your experience base?'
- 'To get promotion, what will those assessing you be looking for, and how can you acquire that capacity?'

The move from the phase of accumulation to *full leadership* requires a fundamental shift or 'metanoia' in life/work focus – from trying to impress and win approval from others, to taking one's own authority and making the best contribution one can to the world. The key learning focus here is how to integrate the question of 'purpose' into your life. Here a leader is faced with the question 'Why? To what end?', when they choose to take leadership. The extent that they find an answer to these challenges is the extent to which their leadership is seen as authoritative. We have coached a number of senior practitioners in professional firms, who were anxious to become partners. They were doing everything possible to prove their worth and meet the overt criteria to become a partner, in terms of winning new work, leading change initiatives, developing new methodology etc. However, they were turned down by the partner selection committee. The mentoring was focused on helping them realize that you do not become a leader by proving to someone else how good you are and asking them to confer leadership on you. Instead you need to step into leadership and act like a leader and then eventually others will start to recognize that you are a leader and respond to the leadership you are taking. You cannot become a leader through trying harder in the stage of accumulation.

We have also helped a number of professional firms develop the quality of feedback they give to aspiring partners in order to break the unhelpful 'try harder' mode which leads down a disappointment route. At one extreme, we had to help one large firm acknowledge that telling aspiring partners 'you lack the necessary gravitas' is unhelpful, particularly as the term has hidden prejudicial assumptions that 'proper' partners are middle-aged, white and male. In response to this pitfall we developed our model of authority, presence and impact, which allows selectors to identify aspirants with leadership potential (see Chapter 12).

Mentoring those who have arrived at the leadership phase requires a change in question. The mentor would more appropriately ask:

- 'What difference do you want to make in the world?'
- 'Where can you make your best and most unique contribution?'
- 'What would you be proud to have achieved by the time you retire?'
- 'As you look back from your deathbed, what would you have regretted not doing as a leader?'

There is a different but equally profound shift in the move from leader to *elder*. This is the shift from focusing on 'What can I achieve?' to 'What can I help others achieve?' For many this shift happens in the move from being a full-time leader in an organization, to moving into a third-age career with a portfolio of roles, such as non-executive positions on boards or being an adviser, consultant or even coach! Many more people are working well beyond 60, but many find it difficult to move from leader to elder. This is partly because we lack cultural role models to conceptualize the role of elder. We expect leaders to go on as leaders until they fail or die. It is also difficult for many individuals to give up taking direct control and asserting themselves. Many non-executive directors we have worked with act as back-seat chief executives, itching to get their hands back on the steering wheel!

Mentoring elders requires a different focus. The elder needs to be less focused on making a difference themselves, and more concentrated on how they can enable others to make a difference. In many ways, eldership requires the person to act as a mentor to others, and thus mentoring of elders is a form of mentoring the mentors.

Useful questions include:

- 'Who are the leaders of tomorrow that you can best support?'
- 'How do you think you can best enable those leaders to develop?'
- 'What is the wisdom and understanding that those leaders most need from you?'
- 'How can they best receive that from you?'

Mentors need to use such stage models for the transitions people will face in their careers, so that they do not just concentrate exclusively on the detail before them, but rather set it always in its broader context. The Hawkins model sketches out these transition steps in our work life. However, this model is not designed to show in detail what personal changes might need to be undertaken in order to fully develop oneself into a new stage on the career path. For this purpose, Torbert's work is specifically useful. He mapped the way in which a person's developmental maturity drives their style of leadership.

The Torbert model: developmental stages of leadership

We believe that the process of moving from 'experimentation' to 'eldership' in a business career is, in essence, a developmental journey. The lessons to be learned at each stage and for a successful transition are based on the individual's ability to be aware of, and handle, the increasing moral complexity of the choices facing them. Torbert has spent many years researching, testing and refining his model of levels of leadership development and the shifts they require in the individual (Torbert 2005). His descriptions build on the work of Loevinger and Blasi (1976) and others, who clarified the stages of adult development towards maturity. This particular interest is directed at the increasing complexity of the individual's moral choice in the maturational process. Torbert currently suggests *seven* definable stages of leadership development (Torbert's original developmental model showed eight steps).

His most recent work reflects the changes that he has made in refining these developmental stages. The old definitions also appear in Table 3.3 to make adjustment easier for people who have worked with the original ones.

Table 3.3 Seven stages of leading

Action logic	% sample profile	Torbert's previous definitions
—	—	Impulsive
Opportunist	5	Opportunist
Diplomat	12	Diplomat
Expert	38	Technician
Achiever	30	Achiever
Individualist	10	—
Strategist	4	Strategist
Alchemist	1	Magician
		Ironist

Many developmental psychologists agree that what differentiates leaders is shown by their preferred ways of acting under severe pressure or challenge. It shows their perception and interpretation of the situations they find themselves in. Their specific mode of responding to these pressures constitutes their internal 'action logic', and this is what discriminates different types of leaders. Torbert emphasizes how important it is for a leader to understand their own action logic and then explore how they can change it – through what he calls 'a voyage of personal understanding and development'. Such a journey not only transforms the capabilities of the individual, but can also transform the capabilities of an organization. Torbert's research with thousands of executives shows the positive impact of understanding their own action logic on their ability to lead. Research conducted over 25 years indicates that levels of corporate and individual performance vary significantly according to the prevailing range of action logics preferred by these leaders:

The research shows that three types of leader (Opportunists, Diplomats and Experts), some 55% of Torbert's sample, associate with below average corporate performance. They were significantly less effective at implementing organizational strategies than the 30% of the sample who measured as Achievers. Moreover, only the final 15% of managers in the sample (Individualists, Strategists, and Alchemists) showed consistent capacity to innovate and to successfully transform their organizations.

(Rooke and Torbert 2005: 68)

The opportunist

Focused upon	personal wins, and other people as opportunities to be exploited.
Characterized by	mistrust of others, egocentric behaviour, manipulation and ruthlessness of action.

Only about 5 per cent of leaders seen in Torbert's research came into this category. Their action logic is driven by a 'red in tooth and claw' view of life. They have a strong need to be in control, because they have to have what they want. They treat other people as pawns, as objects to be manipulated to get what they want or as competitors, who are seen to also operate with the same view of the world, whether they do or not.

Opportunists tend to regard their bad behaviour as legitimate in the cut and thrust of an eye-for-an-eye world. They reject feedback, externalize blame and retaliate harshly. Larry Ellison (CEO of Oracle) describes his early managerial style as 'management by ridicule': 'You've got to be good at intellectual intimidation and rhetorical bullying', he once told Matthew Symonds of the *Economist*. 'I'd excuse my behaviour by telling myself I was just having "an open and honest debate". The fact is, I just didn't know any better' (Rooke and Torbert 2005: 68).

The conventional action logics (of diplomat, expert and achiever) take social categories, norms and power structures for granted as constituting the very nature of a stable reality. We learn how to relate by gradually gaining increasing skill and control in one territory of experience after another. Developing skill in one pushes us to enter the next realm in sequence.

The diplomat

Focus upon	belonging, avoiding conflict, and gaining control over own behaviour, rather than other people or external events.
Characterized by	cooperating with group norms and performing daily roles well.

Around 12 per cent of the research population used a diplomat action logic. They have a much more benign effect in an organization, on a superficial level, than the opportunist, but without developmental support generate equally serious consequences if found at very senior levels. In a support role or in a team context, a diplomat leader provides the 'social glue' so vital to the sustainability of organizations over time. Their 'pleasing' focus is a relatively immature, and early, way station in the journey to personal wisdom and wholeness. The action logic is more associated with people when they start out in work, and research has shown that up to 80 per cent of all diplomats are at junior levels. The wish to be liked and to create harmony means that they naturally try to ignore conflict. Such a habit can be dangerous for a leader at senior level. The drive to 'pleasantness' means that they are terminally polite and friendly and find it almost impossible to give robust and challenging feedback to others. For the same reason diplomats find it very hard to initiate organizational change, since it rarely happens without conflict and upset of some kind.

One diplomat had made very good use of his action logic by pulling together fractious parts of a charitable enterprise. By getting the various team leaders to talk and feel heard, he established a group from a set of isolated individuals. The forming stage of this new group went well. But for the charity to get beyond feeling better and doing a series of unrelated 'good things' and to move on to perform as a focused and integrated whole, this management group needed to engage in difficult conversations with each other. The diplomat leader constantly defused these conversations and, when that did not work, began to have one-to-one meetings, rather than working from within the team. In the end the board decided to remove the diplomat and promote one of the team members, who was more able to encourage the necessary straight-talking among the staff.

The expert

Focused upon	developing control of the world of thought, by perfecting their knowledge both in professional and personal lives.
Characterized by	reliance on 'hard data', trying to develop watertight thinking, wanting continuous improvement, driving efficiency, doing what they know to be right.

Torbert's research has shown that experts make up the most common group at all levels of management, including executive management, forming almost 40 per cent of the managerial population. Some sectors have a strong culture based on this action logic – accountancy, investment analysts, market researchers, software engineers and technical consultants to name but a few. The individual expert can be an extremely good employee, provided that their craft discipline can be harnessed in a way that helps the organization. They are particularly likely to rise to senior positions in bureaucracies. Where the culture of the organization or the sector demands not just technical skill but emotional intelligence, their behaviour can be problematic. The strong chief accountant who struggles somewhat in a corporate role may have an 'expert' mindset.

The expert's style of management is often characterized by a certainty about what needs to be done by everyone around them. This drives out collaboration ('not all meetings are a waste of time – some are cancelled!') and is often expressed in the 'my way or the highway' attitude towards subordinates.

Emotional intelligence is neither desired nor appreciated. As Sun Micro-systems' CEO Scott McNealy put it: 'I don't do feelings; I'll leave that to Barry Manilow'. It comes as no surprise then, that after unsuccessfully pleading with him to scale back in the face of growing losses during the dot.com debacle of 2001 and 2002, nearly a dozen members of McNealey's senior management team left (Rooke and Torbert 2005: 70).

The expert works within a pattern of *thinking* (that is a particular view of the world or governing framework), which acquires a greater importance than behavioural norms. Problems tend to arise for the expert at times of change because they focus on doing things right – 'even if not the right things'. Experts tend to resist organizational change because it is difficult to get it right before you start.

Review of stages 1 to 3

These first three developmental stages have only limited viability as action logics for leaders of large or complex organizations. We have explained where each of them may create a temporary 'win'. Each of these three logics tries to avoid organizational change since prerequisites to such activity are:

- an ability to question, and reflect upon, what you are doing;
- to be open to personal change in behaviours; and
- a sensitivity to the real needs of others.

Each of these previous stages is driven by the needs of the leader, in some shape or form, not the needs of the organization or the stakeholders. Managers using these action logics can transform their ability to work into other modes of leading, but it is difficult for them to easily 'get' the need for such personal change.

The achiever

Focus upon	**deliverables, positive influence, and making it happen.**
Characterized by	**creating a positive work environment, open to feedback, sensitive to the needs of work relationships.**

Torbert's research shows that this logic is found in around 30 per cent of managers, who are able to both challenge their staff and support them and create a positive team and interdepartmental atmosphere. Achiever leaders can also reliably lead a team to implement new strategies over a one- to three-year period, balancing immediate and long-term objectives. For these reasons, achievers often find themselves clashing with experts. The dynamic often involves achievers aggressively challenging the basic assumptions that the expert works from. The expert subordinate finds the achiever boss hard to cope with, too, because the expert can clearly see the achiever's success in the business, even though they feel superior in their knowledge base.

The achiever is the first level on the developmental stages not to be driven primarily out of one area of experience, but seeks to integrate the three (*results, behaviour and thought*) in the service of overall system effectiveness. They will seek to create organizational climates in which such triangulation between ideas, behaviour and outcomes can take place. The achiever's ability to initiate and receive feedback supports their greater effectiveness within their own frame of reference. They still tend to operate within one frame of reference – for instance stockholder value or quality of products and services – but they will be more capable than experts of shifting to a different frame of reference, for instance, the chief executive who sees that her fixation on market share has been unhelpful and who begins to see the world in terms of customer satisfaction. Torbert describes the achiever leader as 'effectiveness and results oriented; the future is vivid and inspiring; feeling like an initiator rather than a pawn; tries hard to live up to his or her own standards; blind as to their own shadow; capable of choosing (but not creating) an ethical system' (Torbert *et al.* 2004: 86).

Whereas the leaders using conventional action logics appreciate similarity and stability, those using post-conventional action logics increasingly appreciate differences and participating in ongoing, creative transformation of the action logics they use.

Up to this point therefore, the leadership styles have been operating within a single frame of reference or view of the world. The post-conventional action logics are less and less formed by implicit frames that limit one's choice, and increasingly become explicit frames (like the theory of developmental action enquiry at the root of Torbert's work) that highlight the multiplicity of action logics and develops the freedom and the 'response-ability' to choose one's action logic on different occasions.

The individualist

Focus upon	recognizing and communicating with the different action logics, holding both present and historical contexts, awareness of conflicting emotions and dilemmas, difference and change rather than similarity and stability.
Characterized by	independent, creative work; focusing upon listening and finding patterns; starts to notice own 'shadow'; being experienced as something of a maverick.

The individualist action logic is seen in about 10 per cent of leaders. It recognizes that all the logics that we use are constructed, rather than God-given and true. They are partial constructions of oneself and the world. This seemingly abstract action logic provides an important service in organizations. Unlike the diplomat, who is trying to smooth things over and create a superficially harmonious atmosphere, the individualist is focused upon putting personalities and ways of relating into perspective and communicating effectively with those who have other action logics.

What sets the individualist apart from the achiever is their awareness of both sides of the dilemmas facing individuals or the organization, for example between someone's principles and their actions, between the organization's values and their implementation. This awareness creates a tension, which becomes the source of future creativity and a growing desire to develop further. Individualists are also likely to ignore rules that they think are irrelevant, which can make them a source of irritation to their colleagues with a conventional action logic.

The strategist

Focus upon	the importance of principle, contract, theory and judgement (not just rules, customs and exceptions) for making and maintaining good decisions; interweaves 'short-term goal' focus with 'longer-term developmental process' focus; the awareness that perception is shaped by one's action logic; playing a variety of roles.
Characterized by	creativity in conflict resolution; witty, existential humour; using double-loop learning; testing the limits of their organization's and their leader's constraints.

The strategist leader is relatively rare since they only account for about 4 per cent of leaders. We saw that the individualist is able to master communication with those who have very different assumptions and beliefs that drive the way they act, and can therefore create first order change – change in the degree to which things are done. The strategist goes one step further in their ability to create the common vision that appeals across different action logics, that encourages both personal and organizational transformation. This action logic can therefore create second order change – change in the type of things to be done.

Torbert et al. (2004) describe the strategist's skill as 'self-conscious reframing of mission, strategy and timing, listening to multiple voices of stakeholders and customers'. As discussed above, this is the first level that can initiate the deeper levels of learning that are necessary to strategic success without the attempt to coerce participants into a single frame of thinking that will inevitably kill the process. The strategist is able to see all ways of perceiving the world, all frames of reference, as potentially valid and is thus able to treat them with the respect necessary for deeper learning. Strategist leaders will always be open to the potential of the situation, to the ways in which the different perspectives of various stakeholders can be combined. They appreciate others' frames of reference and are continually looking for an appropriate frame of reference for the situation. They will be open to feedback from any source, whether clearly linked to their purpose or not. They will always be drawing people together to investigate difficult and challenging issues.

The ability to reframe situations and problems – to see them from different angles – can make the strategist appear untrustworthy to others. If insufficiently connected to some valid purpose, the strategist can indeed become manipulative, like Machiavelli. Thus the effective strategist will tend to have sources of support to reinforce and develop their sense of purpose. Such supports will often be outside the organization's boundaries, such as leaders on similar levels in comparable organizations.

The alchemist

Focus upon	the truth in the situation; many situations have multiple levels of activity and meaning; expressing multiple aspects of personality during the course of a day.
Characterized by	charismatic personality; extremely aware individuals who live by high moral standards; ability to catch the unique moments in the history of their organizations; embracing a sense of leisure and a fierce efficiency; creating symbols and metaphors that speak to people's hearts and minds; often engaged with multiple organizations and finding time for all.

The final action logic, for which Torbert has data and experience, is the alchemist. One per cent of the leaders studied fall into the alchemist category. What seems to set them apart from strategists is their ability to renew or reinvent themselves and their organizations in historically significant ways. Leaders who operate consistently beyond the strategist stage are extremely rare – Torbert quotes Pope John XXIII and Gandhi as examples. At this level, according to Torbert, the leader begins to let go of egocentricity and surrenders the attachment to being 'right'. The alchemist leader will not so much be consciously reframing situations in order to achieve outcomes but appears to be continually noting frames of reference arising – and then letting them go, the better to stay with the energy of the dance that emerges from the stillness of the present moment. As Torbert rather poetically states: 'A reframing spirit continually overcomes itself, awakening to its own presuppositions. A reframing mind continually listens into the dark of preverbal experience' (Torbert *et al.* 2004: 86).

The loss of attachment to self is an element of the meditative spiritual traditions and the personal cost of learning at this level can appear high. Many require near-death experiences or extreme personal crises to open the door to this level of leadership.

Nelson Mandela's behaviour at the 1995 Rugby World Cup final in Johannesburg may well have come from this level of leadership and illustrates clearly the capacity of the alchemist leader to create powerfully transformative symbols. The Springboks, the South African national rugby team, progressed to the World Cup final, which was staged at a venue that was seen as one of the bastions of white supremacy. Mandela attended the game. He walked onto the pitch wearing the Springbok's jersey, so hated by black South Africans, at the same time giving the clenched fist salute of the ANC, thereby appealing almost impossibly, both to black and white South Africans. As Tokyo Sexwale, ANC activist and premier of South Africa's Gauteng province said of him: 'Only Mandela could wear an enemy jersey. Only Mandela would go down there and be associated with the Springboks … All the years in the underground, denial, self-denial, away from home, in prison, it was worth it. That's all we wanted to see' (Rooke and Torbert 2005: 72).

Some important transition principles

Looking at Torbert's range of action logics, we can draw out one or two principles that are important to keep in mind when thinking about supporting people on a developmental journey.

- *Leaders can transform from one action logic to another.* This almost needs to be an article of faith for mentors, coaches and supervisors. Whatever the mindset of the person we are supporting as a mentor or supervisor, we have to believe that it is possible, for anyone who wishes it, to transform the action logic they currently have into a higher-level logic. The only thing that is demanded of them is the will and application to make this happen. Each type of transformation needs a different type of help to make the transition, which means that different methods of support are needed each time.

- *The search for new perspectives often manifests itself in personal transforma-tions.* We know from experience that it is impossible to transfer from one logic to another without engaging the whole of oneself in the process. Such a change of perspective as is required for an effective shift to another action logic is not achieved by a first order change. That means it is not about doing a bit more, or a bit less, of what you already do, nor by a relatively simple second order change, whereby bits of what you do are fundamentally changed (e.g. someone starts to do regular exercise from having formerly been a fully signed up couch potato). Second order change requires that we rethink some of our attitudes in order to create a difference. The kinds of transformational shifts Torbert is talking about can only be achieved if third order change or triple loop learning is embraced (Hawkins 1991). Such change is the product of challenging the overall pattern of the way we see things, not just aspects of it. This is why the transition to a new action logic demands, in T.S. Eliot's words, 'not less than everything' from us. In making that shift we see the world differently and therefore have the ability to behave in fundamentally different ways as a result.

- *External events can trigger and support transformation.* It is always important that as mentors, coaches or supervisors we don't see the world as dependent on our skills for its survival. Individuals have managed these kinds of personal transition before either mentors, coaches or supervisors were ever thought of and will probably do so after they have vanished back into the mists of time. What we are doing is assisting a process that could happen in other ways. One of the most significant ways in which a transformation can get sparked is by events conspiring to challenge the effectiveness of our current ways of being and doing. For example, the promotion to a new role may encourage a leader to expand their range of capabilities, however it might require fundamental rethinking of what truly matters and how it can be achieved so that the challenge is met with confidence and grace. In many cases the emergency that sparks off the need for mentoring is just such an unsettling event.

Mentoring people through transitions

Having described career stages and the different action logics and what they involve, it is important to reflect in more detail on the ways in which mentors, coaches and consultants can support the transition of leaders from one action logic to another and from one stage in their career to the next. Often in the transition process there are three recognizable stages (our approach draws on Van Gennep's 1960 study of rites de passage and Kubler-Ross's 1991 work on the transition curve) (see Figure 3.2).

The first stage, *unlearning*, is when the mentee begins to encounter the limits of their current way of being. They find themselves in a role or situation in which their past ways of operating no longer work so well for them. For some this is a time of frustration and loss of confidence, for having been previously very successful they now start to receive negative feedback. Others can cling desperately to their old skills and habits. The task of the mentor is to support their mentee in letting go and to courageously face the challenges and lessons with which life is currently providing them.

The second or *liminal* stage is where the mentee has left their previous way of operating but has not yet fully entered the next stage. The mentee will be experimenting with ways of operating in this new way and needs space to learn and reflect on these experiments. In this stage one can feel lost and confused and need a good deal of support and reassurance that this is a natural process that most people go through. There can be a tendency to want to retreat back to old ways of being or

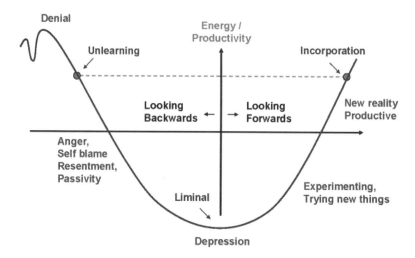

Figure 3.2   The transition curve

rush into an assumed and false confidence, rather than stay with the uncertainty and exploration.

The final stage is *incorporation*. This is the stage when the mentee starts to incorporate new ways of thinking, behaving and acting and make them both sustainable and their own. Recognition and appreciation of what has been established from the mentor is often most useful at this stage.

We will now explore more specifically how this applies to the shifts between the different Torbert and Hawkins stages. It will be clear at this point that only someone with an ability to work from a post-conventional action logic will be able to help with the transformation of those with a conventional action logic. People using conventional action logics, as we have already noted, cannot easily put themselves in another person's shoes to any sustainable degree.

From expert to achiever

This is the most commonly observed and practised action logic transition among business people and those in management and executive education. It is also the one most successfully addressed at present. The largest development bottleneck in organizations is in transforming those who have had expert success in their field, and who have on this basis been promoted into managerial duties that tear them away from the work they love. They experience tensions that need to be addressed.

Much of the work of training departments in large companies supports staff who experience transition stress. They offer programmes with titles such as 'Management by Objectives', 'Effective Delegation' and 'Managing People Performance'. They typically emphasize getting results through flexible strategies, rather than one right method used in one right way. The shift to achiever logic is epitomized by one of Stephen Covey's *Seven Habits of Highly Effective People* (1989), which states that we should 'always start with the end in mind'. He advises that we clarify the goal of achievement, and fashion what we need to do backwards from that the goal specification. This element of pragmatic ground-clearing makes sure that we do not lose the view of the wood in our fascination with every single tree between here and there.

From achiever to individualist

For mentors and coaches to reliably support the transformation of leaders from achiever to individualist requires an increase in their own ability to work with the unknown in an open, enquiring and experimental way. Where developing achievers focus upon results, developing individualists must encourage self-awareness and greater awareness of other world views. They also have to move from prescribed and rehearsed ways of communicating to being able to inquire about situations, without knowing the answer before they start. For the transformation to be successful, a leader needs to feel able to experiment with new ideas and ways of working.

To strategist and beyond

While the transformation to individualist is based upon developing a strong capacity for self-reflection and an ability to recognize the different views held in the organization as relative, supporting personal transformation of leaders to a strategist or alchemist requires the readiness to break out of current modes of thinking altogether. It needs the support of peers in a sustainable community of challenge. Life-altering events, such as a career or existential crisis or a new marriage, can sometimes be channelled to unfold their transformative power and open a door into strategist action logic.

The action logic needed to facilitate a transition shift

We have learned from experience that you cannot cognitively teach a person to comprehend the quality of consciousness of the developmental levels above their own, i.e. their current action logic will be blind to the essence of the action logics above. To help a person shift levels of consciousness, one has to confound their current level of being and thinking, by giving them a challenge which they recognize as important or intriguing but that cannot be achieved within their current mode of operating. This challenge acts as a form of a creative paradoxical double bind, which is meant to create a 'paradoxical seizure', fusing the old circuits of mind and forcing new connections to be created (Hawkins 1999). A good, and public, example of creating this type of 'seizure' is Mandela's arrival at the 1995 Rugby World Cup, which we have already cited.

This also raises the issue that it is impossible for us as mentors or coaches to help someone with the same action logic to move beyond it. In fact in our experience it appears that to facilitate such a leap; it takes a coach or mentor with the ability to function with an action logic two levels above the action logic of the leader they are trying to support. To only function at the next level above means that there is an inherent tension between the two logics that can trigger the innate resistance of both people. Thus in supervision of achievers who have been mentoring experts we have discovered in their enthusiasm for results and success for their mentees that they believe they become impatient with the expert's careful focus on doing things right and can start to urge them into just getting on with it. The expert can hear this as 'not understanding the technical difficulties' and even bullying.

The Torbert model of leadership development has a great deal to offer to mentors, executive coaches and their supervisors. It makes clear what the key elements of transition are for moving from one action logic to the next. The model works from an assumption that we are not imprisoned in our genetic coding and habit patterns but can change the way we do things and the way we see the world, if we are prepared to put in the time and effort that is truly needed. This is where mentors, coaches and supervisors come in. They can provide the support and challenge to help make these shifts a reality.

Summary

A strong awareness of the various developmental journeys we can make as we go through life lies at the heart of best practice for mentors. A mentor needs to know the psychology and details of the broad early development journeys that human beings go through. Early development seeks to create basic emotional and psychological maturity on the journey towards adulthood (see Erickson 1950). But more importantly they need to understand the stages of adult maturation and development, and how to enable others to move between one stage and the next. In this chapter we have provided two linked models on understanding both career stages and the stages in the maturation of leadership as useful maps to help mentors to enable the developmental journeys of their mentees. We have also talked about some of the skills useful for supporting life and career transitions.

It is our belief that mentors require many of the competencies, capabilities and capacities necessary for good coaching and coaches need some understanding of the work of mentoring, and in Chapters 12–15 we will outline these in more detail. We also believe, along with Torbert, Senge, Scharmer, Jaworski and Flowers (Senge et al. 2005), that cultivation of leadership in oneself and others is one of the most important tasks of our time. Leadership, however, does not just reside in leaders, but is a relational activity that requires working with others on a shared endeavour, in teams and organizations, and it is to ways of coaching and mentoring teams and organizations that we will turn in the next two chapters.

4

Team coaching

Introduction

> On another occasion Nasrudin was asked why it was that despite all the best efforts of the senior executives, all the different departments seemed to go in different directions. 'Well, that is easy,' replied Nasrudin, 'if they all headed in the same direction it would upset the balance, and the organization would topple over.'
>
> (Hawkins 2005: 90)

So far, we have explored the practice of coaching and mentoring individuals, an area that has been growing exponentially over the last 20 years. Equally important, but far less documented in the literature, is the coaching of teams, organizations and whole systems. In this chapter we will explore what is involved in coaching teams. For us teams are defined by the members having joint goals and some joint interdependency and accountability for outcomes. The coaching is therefore focused upon the end to which the team and its members are jointly in service.

We define team coaching as 'enabling a team to function at more than the sum of its parts, by clarifying its mission and improving its external and internal relationships'. It is different therefore from coaching team leaders on how to lead their teams, or coaching individuals in a group setting, although some of this chapter may be relevant to both those endeavours.

In the next chapter, we move on to explore how we might coach at the organizational level. This will lead us, in Chapter 6, to ways of developing a coaching culture within an organization.

Later in the book, we will also explore ways of supervising such team and organizational coaching and in particular the craft of providing systemic shadow consultancy to teams of consultants (see Chapter 11). But first let us consider the challenge of teams.

The challenge of teams

Peter Senge shares the following challenging observation: 'It is amazing how often you come across teams with an average intelligence of over 120, but the team functions at a collective intelligence of about 60' (personal communication). The truth of this was brought home to us time and again when we engaged in several research ventures on leadership development. Here are some quotes from the research in different organizational sectors:

> 'We know that about a third of local government performance is attributable to the collective leadership capability of the local authority, both members and chief officers, but we have no way of assessing that capability' and 'We know how to assess individual leaders, but not collective leadership groups.'
>
> Member of the Audit Commission

> 'In the three companies where I have been a senior executive the biggest development challenge has been how to develop the top team, when people are constantly leaving and joining.'
>
> FTsE 100 Chief Executive

> 'We have done a lot to develop individual leaders, but in many departments the top team functions at less than the sum of its parts.'
>
> Senior member of the Civil Service, Cabinet Office

> 'The quality of the executive team is one of the three most important factors in a growing business being successful.'
>
> Venture capitalist

We have long been interested in what makes some teams function as more than the sum of their parts, and some teams much less than the sum of their parts. In this chapter we will share what we have discovered, and provide some guidelines for how to develop teams to raise their collective performance.

The wisdom of crowds and the folly of teams

James Surowiecki in his fascinating book *The Wisdom of Crowds* (2005) gives numerous stories of how individual experts are less accurate than the averaged scores of a diverse group. From numerous studies he concludes: 'Ask a hundred people to answer a question or solve a problem, and the average answer will often be at least as good as the answer of the smartest member ... With most things the average is mediocrity. With decision-making, it's often excellence. You could say it's as if we've been programmed to be collectively smart' (p. 11). And, 'if you can assemble a diverse group of people who possess varying degrees of knowledge and insight, you are better off trusting it with major decisions rather than leaving them in the hands of one or two people, no matter how smart the people are' (p. 31).

However, he also explores at length studies of 'groupthink' and social conformity and how teams can become foolish through consensus thinking. He wants to discover the conditions which are necessary, for a team or crowd to be wise rather than foolish, and arrives at four basic conditions. There needs to be:

- *diversity of opinion* (each person should have some private information, even if it is an eccentric interpretation of the known facts);
- *independence* (people's opinions are not determined by the opinions of those around them);
- *decentralization* (people are able to specialize and draw upon local knowledge);
- *aggregation* (some mechanism for turning private judgements into a collective decision).

To understand why these basic conditions are so rare in organizations or corporate teams, we need to look at the factors that militate against their prevalence, and that lead to team conformity and foolishness. In our experience of working with teams across many sectors and in about 20 different countries we have discovered the following patterns of behaviour.

Organizations and teams tend to recruit and promote people who are most like existing members, which increasingly diminishes diversity. Organizational culture, which we sometimes define as 'what you stop noticing when you have worked somewhere for three months', has as one of its functions to 'create social cohesion', but in so doing further lessens the amount of independence and diversity.

Teams are keen to bond and many team-building events are geared to increase the 'togetherness of the team'. Some teams have members who are very anxious to please the top leader since they are the person who will influence their bonus and future promotion. Both of these factors further lower independence of thinking and diversity.

Teams often arrive at decisions by collective discussion that, while building consensus, also develops 'groupthink' with no mechanism for aggregating independent and decentralized thinking. We have discovered in recruitment that if the panel initially discusses the candidate together, the group will quickly cohere around a dominant reaction. If, on the other hand, they score the candidate against set criteria in private and then tabulate the results, a much richer picture of the candidate emerges.

So how do team coaches and organizational consultants best help organizations develop their leadership teams so that they are more than the sum of their parts? Let us first look into limiting assumptions often held about teams and their development and then the research into the characteristics of the most effective teams.

Limiting assumptions around team development

One of the reasons we feel that team coaching has not received its due attention up to now is that there are unhelpful assumptions held about the way we should work with teams. Table 4.1 represents a provocation to colleagues as to the challenges we see in working well with teams and the sort of mindset that has to be developed by the team members.

Table 4.1   Ten limiting mindsets in working with team development: a provocation

Limiting mindset	Antidote
1 Team building only needs to happen when the team first forms.	The best teams engage in lifelong learning and development.
2 Team development only needs to happen when things are getting difficult.	If the first time you address relationship issues is in the divorce court you have left it too late!
3 The performance of the team is the sum total of the team members' performance.	A team can perform at more than the sum of its parts or less than the sum of its parts. It is important to focus on the team added-value.
4 Team development is about relating better to each other.	Team development is also about how the team relates to all its stakeholders and how it is aligned to the wider organization's mission.
5 Team development is about the team having better meetings.	Team performance happens when the team, or sub-parts of it, engage with the team's stakeholders. The team meeting by itself is the training ground, not the match.
6 Team development only happens off-site in awaydays.	Team development can be assisted by off-site awaydays but the core development happens in the heat of working together.
7 Team development is about the team trusting each other.	Absolute trust between human beings is an unrealizable goal, particularly in work teams. A more useful goal is the team trusting each other *enough* to disclose their mistrust.

8	Conflict in teams is a bad thing.	Too much or too little conflict is unhelpful in a team. Great teams can creatively work through the conflictual needs in their wider system.
9	'We are not a team unless we work at the same things together.'	A team is defined by having a shared enterprise that can only be completed successfully by its members working positively together.
10	Team development is an end in itself.	Team development is only valuable when it is linked to improving the team'sbusiness performance.

If we manage to apply the antidote to these limiting mindsets we are well placed to look at developing effective teams.

Effective teams

Some of the best research on effective teams was carried out by Katzenbach and Smith (1993). They define a team as: 'a small number of people with complementary skills who are committed to a common purpose, set of performance goals, and approach for which they hold themselves mutually accountable'. They are very careful to distinguish such teams from what they term 'work groups'. The team, according to their description, is not just a group that comes together to report to the team leader on what each of them is doing, but a group that has specific purposes and tasks that can only be done jointly by the team, with mutual, as well as upward, accountability (see Table 4.2).

Table 4.2 Working groups and teams

Working group	Team
Strong, clearly focused leadership	Shared leadership roles
Individual accountability	Individual and mutual accountability
The group's purpose is the same as the broader organizational mission	Specific team purposes that the team itself delivers
Individual work products	Collective work products
Runs efficient meetings	Encourages open-ended discussion and active problem-solving meetings
Measures its effectiveness indirectly by its influence on others (e.g. financial performance of the business)	Measures performance directly by assessing collective work products
Discusses, decides and delegates	Discusses, decides, and does real work together

Katzenbach and Smith found that high-performing teams had the following characteristics in common:

- shared and owned purpose and objectives;
- shared specific performance goals;
- shared approach;
- mutually accountable;
- complementary skills (e.g. technical/functional; problem-solving/decision-making; interpersonal).

We have used these findings in our own research into what interrupts teams in working as more than the sum of their parts. We found the main interrupters were:

- *Lack of clarity of collective focus* – if a team has not clarified its collective focus, this will cause conflict in every aspect of its functioning.
- *'Either-or' solution debates* – we have not yet discovered a team that does not have some form of repeated 'either-or' debates like:
  - 'Should we grow organically or by acquisition?'
  - 'Should we centralize or decentralize?'
  - 'Should we confront this stakeholder or maintain our good relationship?'
  - 'Should we restructure (or not)?'

  Through working with this, we developed the 'law of either-or' (Hawkins 2005). It says that if you are having the same either-or debate for the third time you are asking the wrong question.
- *Accountability only occurs top down, not across the team* – in some teams, members only speak when it is their area of expertise or function that is being discussed and otherwise 'keep their head down'. Team meetings become serial reports to the boss.
- *Doing to each other what others do to us* – elsewhere we have termed this as 'parallel process'; the unconscious re-enactment of what we have experienced being done to us by others. One large consultancy firm we worked for played havoc with their internal meetings by always changing the timings at the last minute and then turning up late for each other. It took us some time before we realized that this was an unconscious re-enactment of how they were treated by their clients.
- *Aiming for agreement rather than commitment* – we have witnessed many teams who have apparently made a decision, which they were all going to carry out, only to find a month later that nothing had happened. We discovered that it was possible to predict when this was going to happen by taking notice of the non-verbal communication in the team meeting. The team members were voting with their hands saying yes, but their bodies and tones of voice were clearly saying otherwise. As with transformational coaching, if the shift in

commitment does not happen in the room it is not going to happen outside the room.

- *'Agenda-driven' rather than 'outcome-driven' meetings* – often it can feel as if the goal of some team meetings is to complete the agenda, rather than to create value.
- *Believing in effective team meetings = an effective team* – team meetings should enable effective teamwork during the rest of the time and not be an end in themselves. Teams are effective when they work in a joined-up way, even when they are working solo or in pairs or small groups.
- *Ignoring the 'smell of the dead fish'* – many teams have issues that affect everybody, but there is a tacit agreement that nobody should mention them. It is like a dead animal or fish under the table that everybody can smell, but nobody wants to deal with.

One of the key roles of a team coach is to interrupt these interruptions, but first they have to start by engaging the team in some form of mutual diagnosis of the critical areas that the team needs to focus on, to become more effective. For this we will use the CLEAR model again (see Chapter 2 for further discussion). In this chapter we will develop it for team coaching.

Coaching teams: the CLEAR process

When working as a consultant to teams, the role is very similar to being a team coach, where the client or coachee is the collective functioning and well-being of the team. As in individual coaching, we can use the CLEAR stages of Contracting, Listening, Exploring, Action and Review. Also, as in individual coaching, this flow is never just linear, since we cycle back into contracting before and after the listening phases and again throughout the repeated cycles of exploration and action.

C and L: contracting and listening

In team coaching the contracting and listening phases are more intertwined, and the team coach needs to operate several cycles where they listen and gradually contract. This often has three stages:

1   Initial exploratory discussions.
2   Some form of diagnosis.
3   Sharing the diagnosis and contracting the hoped-for outcomes from the change process.

Initial exploratory discussions

Often as a consultant one will be called in by a team leader and/or individuals, who have a specific brief to support the team's development. The work begins right from these initial discussions, but it is important not to confuse these early talks to some of the team members with a full contracting process with the whole team. Useful questions at this stage include:

- Why do you want help with team development now? Tell me some of the history that has led up to it.
- Why me/us? Who else are you talking to?
- Whose idea was it? Is everyone in agreement about it?
- Have you had help with team development before? What worked and what could have been better?
- What cannot be talked about in this team?
- How would you know that this development work had been successful?

Petrushka Clarkson (1995) has a useful notion that teams often come for help because they are either in danger, conflict, confusion or deficit, and depending on which of these are relevant, there are knee-jerk reactions that the consultant should avoid and more appropriate and considered responses that can help (see Table 4.3).

Table 4.3 Reactions and responses

Diagnosis	Consultant's knee-jerk reaction	Consultant's considered response
Danger	Teach Falsely reassure Rescue Contract unrealistically	Listen Acknowledge feelings Explore sources Explore nature Elicit emotional reality
Confusion	Get sucked into confusion Oversimplify Accept one frame of reference Fight Take sides	Restrain action Clarify issues Clarify roles Clarify authority Provide models and maps Explore options Assess impact/consequences
Conflict	Pathologize it Fear it Minimize it Ignore it Take sides	Learn its history Welcome and understand it Model conflict handling Value the differences Validate all parties Provide arena and referee
Deficit	Do it for them Work with solved problems Solve symptoms Give your favourite package Assume there should be a training solution	Establish what they have Find what worked before Find out what did not work Start where they are Establish needs and wants Provide relevant input

Source: Clarkson (1995)

Diagnosing team functioning

The diagnostic phase might take place when the consultant has individual semi-structured meetings with each member of the team, and/or sends out a questionnaire that asks each person for their perceptions on the team and what is needed. Also at this stage it can be useful to have additional conversations with some of the key stakeholders with whom the team interacts. Often, when working with a senior executive team, we will also interview the chair of the board and collect feedback from the tier of management that reports to this senior team. Sometimes we will also use diagnostic instruments and questionnaires, such as Belbin team role analysis (www.belbin.com/belbin-team-roles) or our own team effectiveness questionnaire (www.bathconsultancygroup.com) where each team member is asked to rate on a five-point scale their view of 15 aspects of team functioning, both how it is currently and what it needs to be for the team to succeed.

The data from these sources needs to be sorted and analysed – not to arrive at definitive conclusions about the team, but to develop emerging hypotheses and gain a sense of where it is most important for the team to focus.

To carry out this analysis we have developed a framework for addressing the various aspects of effective team functioning. Our model first divides the key aspects of effective functioning into four quadrants, using the axis of focus (from 'task' to 'purpose') and the axis of context (from 'inner focus' to 'outer focus') (see Figure 4.1).

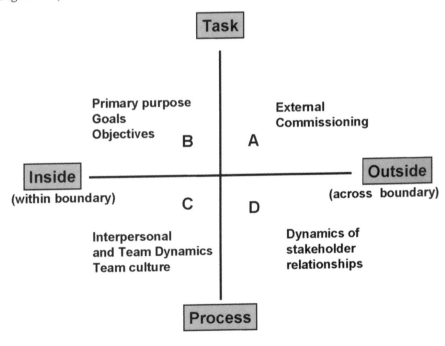

Figure 4.1 Team coaching model 1

Quadrant A: outer task focus

Similar to Katzenbach and Smith (1993), we believe it is essential for an effective team to have clarity of mission and purpose. This is located on the horizontal axis near the 'outer focus', in the sense that purpose, mission and higher order objectives will nearly always involve some dialogue and commissioning with external bodies. In the case of a senior executive team, they will need to agree their purpose with the board, the board with the shareholders, and so on.

Quadrant B: inner task focus

The effective team does not just rely on the commissioning given to it, but takes its agreed mission into collective ownership, works out how to succeed in delivering it and sets out an agreed timetable. It has a shared strategic work plan to which team members hold each other mutually accountable. As part of this process they need to decide what the issues are that the whole team needs to jointly own, what can be done by sub-groups of the team and what can be delegated to individual team members – with the team engaged in the roles of reviewing, supporting and challenging.

Quadrant C: internal process, relationships and culture

This comprises how the team functions and works together, the team roles and processes and the interpersonal relationships. It also includes the team culture, its habituated ways of doing things, its collective mindsets, its emotional climate and core motivations (for further material on organizational culture see Chapter 5).

Quadrant D: external relationships with key stakeholders

Teams often confuse being an effective team with what takes place in team meetings. We sometimes point out that what happens in meetings is like what happens on the training ground in sport – the game is not won or lost there. It is won in the quality of the myriad relationships which the team members have on behalf of the team with all the important stakeholders, not by focusing on the training pitch of team meetings. We have pioneered team 360° feedback processes, which are not focused on team members, but on how the team is collectively viewed by all its critical stakeholders, including of course its own team members. This kind of procedure enables the team to fine-tune its performance and improve its relationship with critical stakeholders (we will specify this process further in Chapter 6).

Each of the quadrants in our model is affected by a mixture of history, developmental stage of the team in its organizational environment and changes in the wider social context. Particular ways in which these influences bear on each other are shown in Figure 4.2.

Having used the team coaching model as a way of clarifying team functioning, we go on to use the CLEAR model as a way of structuring the intervention. Each of the quadrants offers different ways of intervening in each of the stages of the CLEAR model.

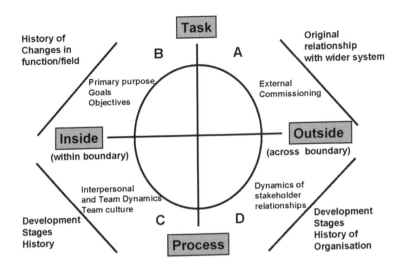

Figure 4.2   Team coaching model 2

C2: contracting the outcomes

Having carried out some form of diagnostic listening and analysis, it is important to find a way of playing this back to the whole team, in a way that engages them not in either swallowing whole or rejecting the feedback, but as co-diagnosers of its meaning. So instead of the team coach feeding the results back in the form of a beautifully crafted report that is so polished that no one can grasp hold of it, it is better to do so in a way which is full of hooks and intriguing entry points. The purpose is not just to 'tell it as it is' (necessary though that is), but also to create a real energy of engagement.

Having arrived at a shared view of the current state of the team and what is the required difference the team wants to create, we engage the team members in exploring what they want to achieve from the team development activity and, specifically, what success would look like. Sometimes we ask the team to work together to answer the following three questions:

- This event/process would be a success for us as a team if . . .
- This event/process would be a success for our organization if . . .
- This event/process would be a success for our clients/stakeholders if . . .

We then ask what they need both from each other and from us as consultants or facilitators of the team in order to achieve that success.

Successful contracting involves both 'starting with the end in mind' and the ability to ask intentionally naive questions, such as the ones used in the initial discussions above and in addition:

- What is the purpose of your meetings?
- What do you expect from one another?
- How would you know if this team coaching had been successful for you?
- What specifically would be happening differently?

Clear contracting is not only important for the success of team coaching, but it also models the way team members can contract among themselves, both about how they meet, but also how each person can be proactive in negotiating with the team their individual needs and those of their function.

E: explore

Once a clear contract for the team development and coaching has been established, the work moves on into the Explore stage of the CLEAR model, where the issues that have emerged in the contracting stage can be opened up and worked on. In this section we give examples of exploratory interventions for each of the four quadrants of the team development model. We would select from these depending on the needs of the particular team.

If, from the contracting stages, it becomes clear that there is a lack of clarity in the fundamental mission of the team, we would probably suggest a workshop with the team to clarify it and then also a joint meeting with the department responsible for commissioning the team's purpose, to clarify mutual expectations. When doing research on leadership challenges in the Civil Service, a number of people commented on how: 'the real leadership challenge lies at the interface between the politicians and the senior civil servants'. This is the 'commissioning interface' (quadrant A). If the team had a clear commission from the wider organization, but still lacked clarity of objectives, goals and plan, the explore stage would focus on turning the mission into clarity of team strategic plan (quadrant B).

Other teams may well need to focus on their internal relationships and team dynamics (quadrant C), while others on the relationships with their key stakeholders (quadrant D).

We will now give brief examples of how team coaching 'explores' interventions in each of the four quadrants.

Explore: quadrant A interventions ('team mission or commission')

In order to show what an 'explore' intervention would look like in this quadrant we need to see how we would get a team to clarify its mission.

When working with the formation of Capespan, from the merger of Outspan and Unifruco (Cape Fruit) in South Africa, we held team workshops for the board and senior executive teams to jointly co-create their mission. This ensured a great diversity of perspectives from executives and non-executives, from each of the legacy companies, and included board members who were fruit growers and therefore suppliers, executives who ran the core business in South Africa and also those who ran the international marketing entities. This wider attendance also ensured fuller ownership of the outcomes.

The mission of an organization, department or team is the overarching framework in which strategizing takes place. Our model of the organization mission is based on work by a number of key writers in the field (Binney *et al.* 2005; Senge *et al.* 2005). We introduced this model to Capespan by showing how its aspects interweave with each other and how we make best use of it as an exploratory tool (see Figure 4.3).

PURPOSE is WHY we are in business, our *raison d'etre* – the difference we wish to make in the world.

STRATEGY is WHAT we focus on, our core markets, competencies and geographies, also our unique value propositions and how we differentiate our organization from the competition.

CORE VALUES underpin HOW we do business, the principles and behaviours that distinguish how we relate within the business as well as to our customers and suppliers.

VISION is WHAT WE COULD BECOME if we were successful at fulfilling our purpose, focus our strategy and live in line with our core values.

Figure 4.3 The mission of an organization

We then invited the team members from both the board and executive team to complete the following statements.

1 The *primary purpose* of our organization is to . . .

2 The key *core values* of our organization that guide how things are done are . . .

3 *Strategy* – Our organization focuses on . . . its unique competencies that distinguish it from others in this field are . . .

4 *Vision* – If our organization was miraculously successful in achieving its purpose, carrying out its strategy and living out its core values, what we would see, hear and feel in two years time would be . . . .

The important thing about the answers that the team members generate is that they maximize the diversity of views; that each view builds on the others; and ends with a jointly created document.

Some boards we have worked with have preferred the executive team to produce their mission statement and then allow the non-executives to critically challenge and amplify what has been produced. In other settings the executive team and the board have worked separately on their mission statement, as well as their expectations and feedback to the other group. From these parallel explorations, a dialogue between the two groups was then facilitated to produce a third mission statement that is more than the sum of the two parts. This produces a good deal of learning for both groups.

Explore: quadrant B interventions ('from mission to plan')

For quadrant B, we would focus on turning the mission into a road map. Having arrived at a clear and truly agreed mission, the executive team at Capespan needed to turn this into a clear action plan. The key questions that we posed as team coaches at this stage were:

- How are we going to fulfil our purpose, in the area of our strategic focus, staying true to our core values, in a way that will move us towards our vision?
- What are the milestones and scorecard by which we can chart progress towards our goals?
- What are the key strategic activities that: we need to own as a whole team; we need to allocate to small sub-groups of the team or project teams; we need to allocate to individual team members?
- How do we have the team focus on business as usual and also focus on the core activities of making the merger successful?

Explore: quadrant C interventions ('team culture')

To intervene in quadrant C, we would focus upon the way the team relates and what blocks or supports getting to the agreed goals. Teams that work regularly and intensively together need to take regular time away from the pressures of front-line work in order to stand back and look at how they are individually and collectively functioning, and how they relate to the wider system in which they operate. This may take the form of an away-day, or a team development workshop, or sessions with an outside team coach, or it may be part of a larger organizational change and development programme.

Whichever way a team or group decides to manage their own dynamics, it is important to remember that the time to start focusing on what is happening in the process is when things are going well and not to wait until the group or team is in a crisis. When the levels of conflict, hurt and fear rise, it becomes much more difficult to see what is happening and to take the risk of making changes. However, for some teams it is only when they hit a crisis that they create the motivation to face what is happening, since sometimes 'crises create the heat in which new learning can be forged' (Hawkins 1986).

When working with one executive team in a large financial company, we asked the team members to complete the following questions separately and then share their answers:

- The unwritten rules of this group are ...
- What I find hard to admit about my work in this team is ...

- What I think we avoid talking about here is . . .
- What I hold back on saying about other people here is . . .
- The hidden agendas that this group carries are . . .
- We are at our best when . . .
- What interrupts us from being at our best is . . .

This was followed by each person receiving feedback from all the other team members on what they appreciated and found difficult about their contribution to the team. Then each person had the opportunity to say what they most appreciated and found most difficult about the team as a whole. This provides the beginnings of three lists – what the group values and needs to build on; what it wants to change; what is missing and needs to be introduced (see action stage, below).

In other teams we have also used more active exploration of team dynamics, such as sculpting the team or creating a team constellation. (For more information on team sculpting see Hawkins and Shohet 2006.) Interventions like this create more clarity and more open communication between team members and move this communication from neutral data to also include emotions and feelings.

Explore: quadrant D interventions ('dynamics of stakeholder relationships')

Intervening in quadrant D we focus on how the team relates to stakeholders across the various organizational boundaries. As in individual supervision, where mode 7 focuses on the wider, social and organizational context in which the work operates, it is also important to focus on the context that surrounds the boundary of the team.

As mentioned above, we have pioneered team 360-degree feedback processes, encouraging its critical stakeholders to state how they viewed the team, including its own team members, and these are discussed under 'evaluation' in Chapter 6. Where possible, as team coaches, we coach the team in engaging directly with inquiry conversations with their key stakeholders.

When working with a large venture capital and private equity company where we and our colleagues acted as coaches to all the company's teams, we asked each team to clarify their critical stakeholders. Then the teams collectively prioritized them and arranged for team members, either individually or in pairs, to go and interview representatives of those with the highest priority. The team members then brought their findings to an off-site team workshop ready to make a presentation. We then explained that we wanted them to role-play the stakeholders they interviewed, while the rest of the team role-played themselves, inviting the stakeholder into a team meeting to give feedback. This role-played feedback provided much richer data than they had prepared in the notes they thought they were going to present.

At the end of the feedback session, the team was expecting to thank the role-played stakeholder for their feedback and then leave the room. But at this point we moved towards the surprise second part of the process. We asked them while still in role to say what they would be talking about in the corridor, supposedly out of earshot, about the meeting in which they had just taken part. Then we asked the team playing themselves to do the same. This enactment provided second order feedback on the dynamic relationship between the two parties. Those role-playing the stakeholders made comments such as:

- 'They were being polite but they are not really going to do anything about what we said.'
- 'Did you notice how defensive they were?'
- 'I felt they were coming from different places.'
- 'That was a waste of time, they were not really listening.'

The team role-playing themselves would catch some of what Argyris and Schon (1978) call their 'defensive routines' with comments like:

- 'Well they would say things like that.'
- 'They clearly talked to a disgruntled client, I am sure that the others are not like that.'
- 'We should note the name of that staff member. They are clearly a troublemaker.'

Through this process the team are able to collect the key messages from the feedback and the key dynamics they noticed in the interaction. Doing this for all the different stakeholders provides the team with a rich field of data which allows them to explore what they need to do differently.

A: action

Moving on to the fourth phase of the CLEAR model, there are various ways of moving to action – a vital stage in the process. Having explored the ways in which the team has been responded to, and the impact of previous events on different aspects of team functioning, the team coach then has to help the team move from awareness into action. How are the team going to act differently and perform better?

Team development events can produce a lot of insight and energy, but unless this is focused on specific and prioritized new actions and behaviours, the new energy will soon dissipate. So the challenge for the coach is to deal with the material generated in a way that moves the group to committed actions quickly and surely. One way of effectively doing this is to use the three-way sort exercise.

Three-way sort (a good way of responding to material in quadrant B, C or D)
Initially we set up three flip charts, each one with a different title:

- What we need to hold on to and build on.

- What we need to stop doing.
- What we need to start doing.

We divide the team into three sub-teams and ask each sub-team to start at a different large sheet of paper or whiteboard. The first phase of this process is for each sub-team to brainstorm responses to the question in front of them. We then get them to put down their ideas, leaving some space between each idea. After five minutes each team moves to the next board to their right. The second phase of the process is to build on the ideas left by the previous team and make these more specific. At the second phase, the rule is that nobody can cross anything out, but everybody is encouraged to make more specific what is already there and add additional items. If, for example, the previous group has put 'communication', the second group would be asked to add their responses to the question 'communication between whom and about what?'

The third phase of the process involves the group moving on to their last board. Here once again the team members can add items that have not so far been included, but they need also to make more specific the items that are already there.

Finally, each group moves back to their original board, and having read what is there, prioritizes the issues. Alternatively, every team member can be given five stars and asked to allocate them, anywhere on any of the three boards, next to the priority issues that need action. They can allocate the five stars against issues in any way they want. This visual voting method quickly shows up how the team sees its priorities and directions for moving forward.

R: review

Finally, in order to complete the adult learning cycle, the team members need to review what they have learned, and what they will do differently in the future. Having contracted, listened, diagnosed, explored and planned action, the team focuses on building a review process. As in all learning and change cycles, the team should be prepared for the fact that they will discover more about their team culture and the systemic dynamics when they try to change things. They need to pre-empt the unavoidable disappointment that will arise when they discover the actions they plan at a team workshop will not work out the way they expected, once they are back in the ever-changing world of their work system.

Some teams positively build this process of tracking the progress into their regular meetings in a number of different ways:

- ensuring the mission statement is pinned up in the meeting room, and checking how the meeting decisions and meeting process align with the mission they agreed;
- having quick updates against the scorecard when they have a meeting;
- taking a key priority action area for review at each team session;
- reviewing the meeting in the light of their planned team improvements, and each person sharing what they think has been good about the meeting and

what they think could be even better next time;

- having the team coach attend their regular internal meetings of key events and provide live coaching.

Project teams

So far we have only talked about coaching management or executive teams, but team coaching is also very effective in supporting project teams, virtual teams and client account teams.

Deborah Ancona and her colleagues at MIT (Ancona *et al.* 2002) have carried out very useful studies of high-performing project teams. Their work showed that these teams share the following characteristics:

- high levels of external focus and activity;
- extensive ties in the organization and wider context;
- expandable tiers in its internal organization;
- flexible membership – both in the team and between the tiers;
- coordination within and between tiers.

They developed a three-phase model in the life of a project team:

- exploration;
- exploitation;
- exportation.

In the first phase, 'exploration', the team is combining its group-forming work with intense activity of members going outside their own area and scouting for ideas, resources and information that might suit their purpose. Many ambassadorial relationships with key stakeholders were formed to ensure effective sponsorship and support. The exploitation phase contains the creative activity work of the project team, where high levels of delegated tasks, flexible membership and coordination contribute significantly to success. Finally, in the exportation phase the work of the team has to be turned into action and the ambassadorial role is about selling their ideas, achieving agreement to moving forward and stimulating commitment to joint action from others.

Often a project team working on organizational change or a design or innovation team working on bringing out a new product or service can greatly benefit from having a team coach work alongside them. Such a coach needs to bring experience and skills in how to:

- build quickly a high-performing team (exploration);
- help it be focused on in its end goals (exploration);
- stimulate creativity, brainstorm and think outside the box (exploration);

- scenario plan (exploration);
- investigate and carry out action research cycles (exploration) (see Chapter 7);
- prototype and experiment possible ways forward (exploitation);
- redesign (exploitation);
- take their product to those who need to back it, support it, use it and get their commitment (exportation).

Virtual teams

In some of the large international companies where we are employed as team coaches, we have worked with project teams and account teams which operate virtually. Lipnack and Stamps (1996: 6–7) give a useful definition of virtual teams: 'A virtual team, like every team, is a group of people who interact through interdependent tasks guided by a common purpose. Unlike conventional teams, a virtual team works across space, time, cultures and organizational boundaries with links strengthened by webs of communication technologies'.

For a virtual team to work really well it needs some face-to-face time to build its ability to develop the relationships and sense of collective purpose. However, it is also important that the team coach is working live with the team when it is working virtually: joining teleconferences, web-based discussion groups or workrooms. A coaching web-based workroom and different forms of e-coaching can also be useful in such settings.

Professional services client account teams

We have also done extensive work with teams working on the same client accounts across the different professional services. These include teams of organizational consultants, lawyers, accountants, auditors, tax advisers, financial advisers and sometimes a mixture of different professionals coming from different advisory firms.

In this work our focus is to help the client account team provide a service to their shared client that is more than the sum of its parts, and where the team works to become more integrated than the client organization. Inevitably the account team can begin to take on some of the dynamics of their client organization and much of this team coaching is similar to team supervision, where one needs to focus both on the account team and the needs and dynamics of their client. We explore this more in Chapter 11 where we look at account team coaching and systemic shadow consultancy.

Conclusion

For teams to be wise rather than foolish, and function at a level that is more than the sum of their parts does not happen automatically. It needs working at on a regular basis. In sport there is a general recognition that a team of individual stars, thrown together, do not between them make a great team. High-quality team coaching, and time on the training ground, is essential for improving the team's success. Increasingly the same process is being recognized in the world of organizations. Only very recently the business world has understood that really good team coaches are not just people who were once experienced players, but are people who have undertaken specific training in team coaching and facilitation. They need to constantly upgrade their skills and receive regular supervision on their team coaching. Supervision on team coaching is particularly useful at the following points in the process:

- contracting;
- diagnosis and intervention design;
- reviewing a team workshop and planning how to sustain the momentum;
- regularly reviewing how the relationship is progressing.

At all these times all seven modes of supervision are relevant and nearly always necessary to ensure good-quality reflection (see Chapter 9).

5

Organizational coaching and consultancy

Introduction

The current world of consultancy

Mentoring and coaching organizations through transitions

The development trinity

Conclusion: the role of the organizational coach

Introduction

In Chapter 4 we explored the work of a team coach and made the point that we are focusing not upon the individuals in a team, but the group purpose held by its members, helping those members to be in service to that purpose. In this chapter we look at a form of coaching which focuses not on the team but on the whole system. Here the focus is not on the individuals or the teams but rather on helping individuals and teams deliver to the bigger purpose of the organization. This should not in any way be confused with working with the individuals, teams or departments within an organization.

This role we would term 'systemic transformational consultancy', because it has many of the same purposes as systemic transformational coaching. It is work, though, that can rarely be carried out by one person alone, but is more often carried out by a consultancy team. In Chapter 11 we will explore the necessary supervision for such a team.

Supervision needs to ensure that the team do not become embroiled in the dynamics of the organization, but can process their experience and make it available in order to enable the organization to more effectively see its own patterns and move forward.

The challenge of working at this scale is high, but the need for it continues to grow, as organizations face increasing challenges to develop and change at an ever-accelerating pace. For most organizations that we encounter, the number one challenge is to change and develop faster than their competitors, or at least as fast as the environment is changing around them. Whether in the private, public or voluntary sectors, organizations whose pace of change is slower than the changes in the demands of their environment become moribund and may soon cease to exist.

At the same time as facing the increasing rate of external change, the very nature of organizing has undergone some profound changes. Pettigrew and Massini (2003: 6–7) list some of the new characteristics of large commercial organizations such as:

- radical decentralization of profit responsibility to operating units, and reliance on internal contracting mechanisms;
- flattened organizational hierarchies;
- restricted head office roles, with top management focused on knowledge creation and dissemination;
- a shift from 'command and control' management styles, to 'facilitate and empower';
- highly elaborate formal and informal internal communication systems, lateral as well as hierarchical;
- extensive use of ad hoc interdivisional and interfunctional conferences, task forces and teams, rather than rigid organizational compartmentalization;
- the deliberate construction and use of internal labour markets for the dissemination of knowledge.

Coaching whole organizations is less common than coaching individuals and coaching teams. Yet in most organizations today the biggest challenges lie not in the individual people, nor in the teams, but in the connections between the various parts, levels and divisions of the organization. This can be in the lack of vertical connection, such as between boards and their executives; the top team and the middle managers; or it can be in the horizontal connections such as between marketing and production or the internal IT function and the front-line brokers.

In the first part of this chapter we need to explore the current world of organizational consultancy and define our own approach to organizational coaching and consultancy. This will then become the foundation for looking at how we work with the three interlocking elements of integrated change and development.

The current world of consultancy

We live in a time where it can seem as if everybody is a consultant in something – financial consultant, PR consultant, environmental consultant and many more. There are also nearly as many jokes about consultants as there are types of consultancy practice!

For many years the division of consultancy has been between 'expert' consultants, who sell solutions and 'facilitator' consultants, who help the client find their own solution. Both have had much criticism. Expert consultants are condemned for importing solutions without either understanding the context or working with the people within the setting in sufficient depth to help the client take things forward. Often, therefore, a solution created by an expert consultant fails to be implemented – and the consultant blames the managers in the organization and the managers blame the consultant. Facilitative consultants are caricatured as people who, when you ask them the time, borrow your watch, tell you the time and then charge you for the answer. In short, they are seen as simply playing back to the organization what the organization has already told them.

Beneath the jokes and caricatures, organizational managers are communicating that they need a form of organizational assistance that is not delivered by either of these two types of consultancy. There are, of course, occasions where what the 'expert' and the 'facilitative' consultant each have to offer are exactly what the client needs.

Building on the model of the coaching continuum that we used earlier (see Chapter 2), we can illustrate how different forms of consultancy focus on different organizational needs (see Figure 5.1). The technical consultant helps the organization develop organizational skills and competencies that they need and require for increased performance. This may be: new IT systems; HR processes; audit, accounting or tax procedures; or new forms of measuring performance. The organizational facilitator focuses on development, providing workshops, conferences and other enabled events where the organization can be helped to focus on its own development. What clients require on occasions though is a 'transformational partner' or 'organizational coach', who neither tells them what they already know or sells a pre-packaged solution, but who helps them realize more of their potential by 'walking alongside' and sharing their multiple experience as a guide, challenger and supporter.

The transformational consultant will partner the organization over time, helping it develop its strategy, its culture and its leadership, not just on paper in blueprint designs, but live in its work and relationships with all its key stakeholders.

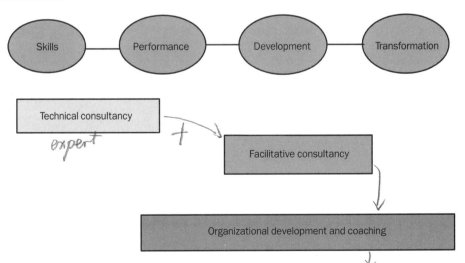

Figure 5.1   The organizational coaching continuum: linked to types of consultancy

Transformational consulting brings with it a whole range of important challenges, beyond those experienced by the technical or facilitative consultants:

- from being hired as an expert or facilitator to being engaged as a 'transformational partner' or organizational coach;
- from selling discrete projects, to being an ongoing consultancy partner over several years;
- from working with one function or level to working across all functions and levels within an organization;
- from working with one organization to working between organizations in a complex system;
- working in-depth with the individual, team, whole organization and wider system in a way that holds the connections;
- creating the shift in the room in a way that is linked to the needed shift in the wider system;
- working with the beliefs and mindsets to shift the heart and soul of an organization;
- from working conceptually to working experientially;
- from working with senior managers to working with the board;
- from working by oneself to work as part of a team.

In this book we concentrate on transformational consultancy, where the consultant – like the coach and mentor – is a real-time learning facilitator. We are excluding from this definition, therefore, consultants who trade on technical expertise, which they use to either fix the problem for the client or give technical advice. We also disregard for the purposes of this discussion those consultants who only facilitate internal organizational processes. For transformational consultancy, focusing on a two-way learning relationship is essential, and a transactional exchange of information and knowledge cannot suffice.

Transformational consultancy both builds on and develops the tradition of organizational development pioneered by such writers as Lewin (1952), Schein (1985), Burke (2002), Beckhard and Harris (1977) and Argyris and Schon (1978) in the USA and Trist and Murray (1990) and Miller (1993) in the UK.

Ed Schein (1985) defined Organizational Development (OD) as: 'all the activities engaged in by managers, employees, and helpers that are directed toward building and maintaining the health of the organization as a total system'. Reddin (1985) develops this: 'OD is operating on the interfaces to optimize the system'. This definition is useful because it distinguishes sharply organization development from management development which deals with the individual as the change target'. Warner Burke (2002) emphasizes the partnering aspect in his definition: 'respond to a felt need on the part of the client, involve directly and collaboratively the client in the planning and implementing of the intervention and lead to change in the organization's culture'.

We define transformational consultancy and organizational coaching as: 'Partnering an organization to transform and align its leadership, culture and strategy, so that it can shift the nature of how it is organized, its performance and the value it creates for all its stakeholders'.

Mentoring and coaching organizations through transitions

An organizational development consultant may be acting in a coaching role helping the whole organization face an immediate challenge, such as 'how do we restructure our organization to make it achieve a higher performance?' Often the development consultant is called in to help with or to mentor an organizational transition. Some of the transitions we have worked on with organizations include:

- moving from being owned privately to becoming a publicly listed FTSE 100 company;
- growing from a national to an international business;
- an architecture practice moving from 5 to 14 partners;
- a young university science business being 'spun-out' and becoming independent;
- a local government organization moving from a service provider centred organization to a strategic commissioning organization;
- two major companies merging;
- a large public service broadcaster rejuvenating its culture.

In all these very varied transitions, the role of the organizational development consultant has needed to combine coaching the organization on its change process, with mentoring the organization on how this transition is part of its longer development journey. Part of this role is to explore how this transition is being coloured and informed by previous transitions and change processes. Without this exploration, it is likely that the organization will be either replicating previous patterns unaware it is doing so, or acting out of reaction to past change efforts, which have not generated the desired outcomes.

Greg Dyke (2004: 210) writes about this process in the BBC, where we were brought in to help with their major culture transition process. One of the first tasks we coached and mentored in this process was a reflection on past changes:

> Having decided to back a culture change programme, the question was how to go about it. Over the years the BBC had been littered with the corpses of failed change programmes, which meant that staff were likely to be cynical and resistant to yet another initiative. So the Director of Television, Mark Thompson, and his Radio counterpart, Jenny Abramsky, both veterans of previous ventures, offered to look back, and see what lessons could be learnt. They found that too often the programmes had been run by external consultants, had been owned only by management and imposed on the

organization from the top, and they had been shot through with management jargon. As a result they'd tended to be short lived and had been resisted very effectively by an intelligent, articulate, and sceptical workforce. So we now knew what not to do. In particular, we knew that if we were to launch a change programme we had to see it through over a number of years.

The development trinity

In consulting to a company through organizational transitions, such as that attempted by the BBC and outlined above, we believe it is important to integrate and align three major change and development processes as shown in Figure 5.2. Each of these three aspects requires its own development logic and process, but for effective change it is important to ensure that the three are working in alignment. We will now look at each of the three change processes separately and at how they can be most effectively aligned.

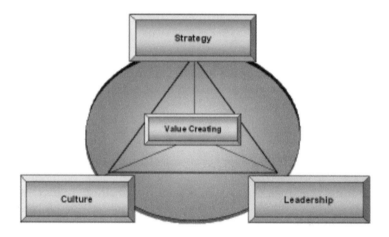

Figure 5.2   The development trinity

Strategy

Before we look at the importance of strategizing for making successful organizational transitions, and in particular at the role of the transformational organizational consultant, we need to check out current thinking on 'strategy'. The term 'strategy' is second only to 'leadership' in the vast literature that encompasses our field. For too long it has been dominated by theories that promulgate some of the following distortions:

● Strategy theorists have looked at organizations through a quasi-Darwinian lens. They see struggle abound within a 'survival of the fittest' competition for dominating their particular niche.

- They have focused on value appropriation by restricting competition and thereby sustaining and enhancing its profits.
- They have over-focused on creating shareholder value and under-focused on creating value for the other key enterprise stakeholders.
- They have emphasized short-term profit maximization without due regard to long-term sustainability.
- They have ignored critical unmeasured costs such as the costs to the natural environment and to human quality of life.

Our own work on strategy follows such eminent writers as Hamel and Prahalad (1996), Pettigrew *et al.* (2003), and particularly the late and great Sumantra Ghoshal and his co-writers Bartlett and Moran (see Birkinshaw and Piramal 2005). Ghoshal and Moran (2005), in their brilliant paper 'Towards a good theory of management' put forward a new view of strategy and we cite some of their core contentions:

'The goal of strategy is value creation, not value appropriation.'

'[The] new view of strategy [is] as a process of guided evolution, with managers as the guide of the process.'

'It is the process of expanding and accommodating the entrepreneurial judgement of people within a framework of organizational integration that allows individuals to use the accumulated resources of the company in the pursuit of new value creation opportunities.'

(Ghoshal and Moran 2005: 15–16)

These quotes contain and parallel our own definition of strategy: 'Strategy is discovering what you can uniquely do that the world of tomorrow needs and then pursuing it' (Hawkins 1995). We developed this one line definition because it connects:

- strategy and purpose;
- organizational competencies and external needs;
- current capabilities and future external requirements;
- discovery and action.

These are all important aspects of strategy that need to stay in dynamic connection. It is also important to realize that strategy is not the same as having a strategy statement, which might be a temporary articulation of what has been decided. Strategizing is not an event but an ongoing process of 'guided evolution', with 'managers as the guides'. The role of the organizational coach or consultant is to 'guide the guides'. Their task is to enable a more effective strategizing process that realizes and connects more of the potential of the organization to creating new value for its key stakeholders.

Ghoshal and Moran's (2005) emphasis on value creation rather than value appropriation is the cornerstone of their work of creating a socially responsible good theory of and for management. They describe a good theory as: 'One that both explains, as well or better than any alternative explanation and, at the same time, induces (as far as we can determine) behaviours and actions of people that lead to better economic, social, and moral outcomes, for them and for society' (p. 25).

It is important that organizations are clear for whom they are creating value. As a starting framework we ask companies to consider how they create value, and measure the value creation, for six major groups of stakeholders:

- investors and regulators;
- customers;
- suppliers and partners;
- staff;
- the communities in which they operate;
- the natural environment.

Each of these stakeholder groups can be seen as investing resources in the enterprise and legitimately expecting a return on that investment, without which they will withdraw that investment. The investment is of a different order in each case. Shareholders invest financial capital; customers a combination of money, loyalty and trust; suppliers and partners their own goods and services, but also their knowledge, their reputation and loyalty; staff their time and personal knowledge and resources; the community the social infrastructure in which the company operates and its social legitimacy; and the natural environment provides the natural resources that the company uses.

Ghoshal and Moran (2005: 16) illustrate the importance of thinking about staff as investors when they write about the new employment relationship where employees are not viewed as factors of production or strategic resources, but as 'volunteer investors':

> Just as shareholders invest financial capital in a company in the expectation of both income and capital growth, similarly employees invest their human capital in a company, with exactly the same expectations. The company's responsibility to employees, therefore, is both to ensure competitive remuneration and to continuously add value to them by enhancing their repertoire of useful knowledge and skills. The employee's obligation in this relationship is to continuously learn, in order to protect and improve their human capital, and to use their expertise and their entrepreneurial capabilities to create new value and thereby improve the company's competitiveness and performance.

In order to involve stakeholders in the organization, which creates the longer-term sustainability of the organization (in terms of capital investment, innovation and development, and useable resources) the modern organization needs to move from executives developing strategy, the board signing it off, the staff implementing it and the customers deciding whether they like it. The challenge is to move from strategy plans from the strategy department to more inclusive strategizing processes.

In order to create an inclusive strategizing process that also conforms to the needs of the adult learning cycle (Kolb 1984) there are seven steps to follow as illustrated in Figure 5.3.

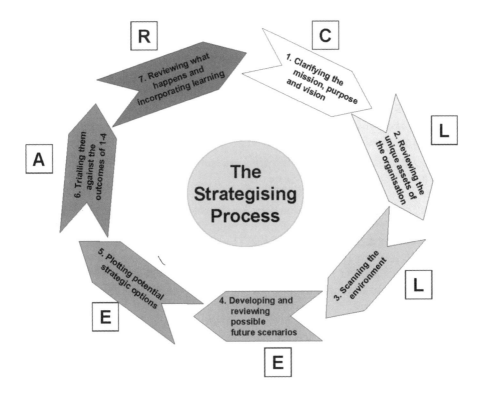

Figure 5.3 The strategizing process

Exploring this iterative process a bit more closely we see that it mirrors the CLEAR model that we have already discussed. There are seven steps to the process:

1 *Clarifying the mission, purpose and vision.* We need to start with the end in mind. This part therefore involves all stakeholders in creating the core intent and aspirations for the business and how these link to future success.

2 *Reviewing unique assets of the organization.* Listen to ourselves, to what the organization currently achieves and where the latent and unused resources and skills might be, as well as the ones that we do recognize and use. This includes

an appreciative inquiry into where the aspirational future is already beginning to happen in parts of the organization.

3   *Scanning the environment.* Listening outside the organization to what is going on in your sector, in business generally and what political, economic, social, technological, legal and environmental key trends (PESTLE) might have future impact on the organization and how your customers' needs are changing.

4   *Developing and reviewing possible future scenarios.* Explore all the possible ways these trends and the possible organizational directions might play out and prioritize the major themes you are discovering. The more widely this dialogue can be shared the better.

5   *Plotting potential strategic options.* Explore possible ways forward that incorporate as wide a range of possible scenarios into a robust strategic path for the organization, with evaluative feedback mechanisms that will keep the strategizing process alive.

6   *Trialling them against outcomes 1–4.* Having gained commitment to action, developing ways of trialling the strategic options agreed upon.

7   *Reviewing what happens and integrating the learning.* This is both the end of one cycle and the beginning of the next.

Once all the stakeholder groups have been involved at appropriate stages with the strategizing process, all the significant groups vital to the success of the organization should be actively engaged. They will start to become clear as to where they all need to end up. This immediately throws up the challenge, 'Is the way we do things around here the way that will get us where we need to go?'

If the answer to that challenging question comes back 'No!' even if only from one stakeholder group, then there are strong indications that the organization needs to check the efficacy of its ways of relating and connecting. As transformational consultants, we are holding the organization to its challenge of thinking, talking, relating and learning together in ever better ways in order to lead the organization forward.

It will become obvious as the strategizing process begins where staff and stakeholders habits of relating and connecting (i.e. the acting out of the organizational culture) are helping and where they are blocking the vital strategizing process. This is why culture is the second node of the transformational focus. By attending to the organization's culture, we are uncovering the current behaviours, mindsets, assumptions and values operating day to day. Having clarified what the current culture is, the transformational consultant not only encourages stakeholders to clarify what culture is needed to land the agreed changes for the organization, but also helps people to behave consistently from the start.

Culture

Let us first offer you a few quotes to illustrate aspects of this elusive animal:

> I came to see in my time at IBM that culture isn't just one aspect of the game – it is the game. In the end, an organization is nothing more than the collective capacity of people to create value.
>
> (Gerstner 2002)

> I made it clear to the staff that changing the culture of the BBC was on my agenda from day one.
>
> (Dyke 2004: 208)

> Culture is what you stop noticing and take for granted when you have worked somewhere for over three months.
>
> (Hawkins 1997)

> Culture resides in the habituated ways of connecting that an organization repeats.
>
> (Hawkins 1997)

Culture is a concept that is widely used and most people think they understand what it means – and yet it is subtle and elusive. This is because culture is not a thing that you can take out and measure, but a connecting pattern that pervades all aspects of an organization. Also it is very hard to recognize one's own culture, for as the Chinese say, 'The last one to know about the sea is the fish'. One's own culture becomes taken for granted and part of one's way of seeing the world. Many years ago we developed a model of organizational culture that builds on earlier work of Ed Schein (1985) and others (see Hawkins 1997), and illustrates the levels of culture within all organizations (see Figure 5.4).

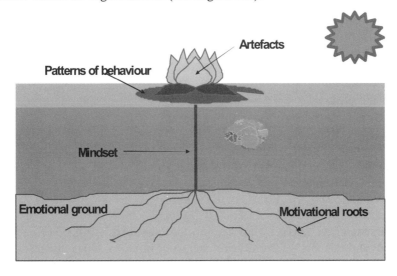

Figure 5.4 The Bath Consultancy Group model of culture

The Bath Consultancy Group model of culture

Before exploring the ways in which we can help transform organizational performance by developing appropriate relating and learning in the workplace, we need to explain briefly the elements of the model. We will run through the five discrete levels we see influencing an organization's culture as laid out in this model.

Artefacts

These are the day-to-day objects, environments, symbols and literature that are the manifestations of how the organization presents itself to the world. Rather like individuals, some are conscious of image, others concentrate on what they regard as more important matters. How we present physically should be aligned to the deeper levels of behaviour, mindset and values. Frequently it is not. To start to understand the organization's culture, look at the following clues:

- symbols of power and authority;
- dress codes;
- mission statements, values statements, strategy documents etc;
- objects displayed – photographs, certificates, artworks, other tangible indicators;
- layout of sites, workshops, offices.

Behaviour

The next level below artefacts is one that is often only observable for a while when we start working in a new organization. After that the general ways of behaving get subtly incorporated into our own default behaviours. The common patterns of behaviour in the organization that alert us to, and illustrate, the way in which things are done around here are:

- how people engage;
- how conflict is handled;
- how resources are allocated;
- how mistakes are handled;
- what is rewarded or given attention.

Are these behaviours, if carried on with, going to create the ways of relating that align to the new organizational goals?

Mindset

Behaviours are often driven by our assumptions about what is good or bad, correct or efficient and the way we frame problems – our mindset. Our mindset is our way of thinking that allows us to do our job without constantly having to work out the best way of tackling it. These assumptions are not obvious and therefore need to be uncovered through a variety of techniques. Look at asking the question 'What assumptions would I need to make to end up doing things this way?' These can be the commonly held organizational 'world view' which generates explicit ways of thinking and doing:

- habitual ways of thinking – usually valid for much of the organization's day-to-day business;
- taken for granted assumptions and ways of perceiving;
- organizational values-in-use etc.

Emotional ground
The emotional ground of an organization is partly created by the significant events in the life of that organization that have registered an emotional impact on staff and stakeholders. They are mostly emotional reactions that are not open to day-to-day awareness. For example, the impact on staff of an unsuccessful attempt to increase wages may not subsequently remain on the radar of conversation and thought among staff, but when the management need them to work overtime to complete an important order it might provoke a larger than life, negative response, out of proportion to the significance of the current event. The sort of things that might link in this unseen and unprocessed pool of reactions can be both positive and negative, such as:

- unprocessed reactions to major organizational changes;
- emotions imported from the organization's boundaries, e.g. from work with the client's customers and other stakeholders.

The emotional ground is also the emotional climate of the organization and the characteristic pattern of emotional expression that is used in its culture.

Motivational roots
At the most significant and deepest levels of influence on the organization and its ways of relating are the motivations, values and purpose that were involved in both setting up and continuing the organization. These motivational roots reflect our deeper reasons for caring about the organization, beyond meeting some of our own individual needs through it. One can look to recognize these roots in:

- the often forgotten passions that inspired the birth and later development of the organization;
- how people find meaning in their work;
- what connects the purpose of the organization with the purpose and motivation of the individuals within it.

This is a model of culture that acknowledges layers or levels of influence that exist, like a lasagne, with layer upon layer making up the one dish. In this model, culture becomes more functional for an organization as the layers align better with each other. As things happen in organizations, over time, these levels can easily be driven out of alignment. For instance, the original 'people values' (motivational roots) that inspired the founders of the hypothetical 'People First', to set up their training organization, may be out of alignment with the reactions of current staff to the partners having to sack one of the team leaders two years ago (emotional ground). Since the business started, the business environment they operate in has changed. It now requires more short, sharp interventions. There is less opportunity to work alongside clients in an ongoing, interactive way. This has meant a change in the way people need to think about their day-to-day jobs (mindset), especially the way in which they now have to sell. Such changes in thinking and attitude do not sit well with the principles held by the founders. Despite the changes demanded by the business, the way things are done socially in the company has changed little at a superficial level (patterns of behaviour). There are still staff meetings and a regular Friday lunchtime 'social'. Just recently they have moved from an old school building, where they started, to new city offices, and changed their logo and their brand to be more business friendly (artefacts), and therefore present a very different image to the world.

In this simple example one can see how, with good intent on everyone's part, it is quite easy to end up with the different levels of culture at odds with each other. If the organization then needs to create a major shift in how it delivers its new business strategy, this lack of alignment could very easily trip them up.

A more complex example, from our consulting experience, is the work Peter Hawkins did with British Aerospace at Filton, Bristol, in the 1980s. It clearly brings out the link between motivational roots, mindsets and patterns of behaviour. It also makes the extra point that for culture change to happen, it needs organizational unlearning before it is free to do things in a new way.

British Aerospace's site at Filton, like so many of the large aircraft manufacturing sites around Britain, had a culture that had been learned before and during the Second World War. In the world of aircraft production in the 1950s and 1960s there was an enormous demand for new and better planes. Companies were successful if they could be ahead of the competition in building the latest plane. The heroes were the designers and the engineers and of course the test pilots. Even in the late 1980s most of the managers had been their 'man and boy' and most had been brought up in a world of Biggles, Ginger and Airfix kits. There was a passion for designing and building innovative whole aeroplanes that united the site despite the union/management antagonism. This culture reached its peak in the construction of Concorde, which was not only the flagship product, but the cultural God.

The site was also very connected to its local community. Filton was the largest employer in Bristol and a very high percentage of its workforce was local. The opposition were seen as the other British Aerospace sites, rather international competitors, such as Boeing.

The challenges in the late 1980s was moving from building whole planes with the most high-tech functionality; to competing on price, reliability and effective process throughput. Filton was part of the wider Airbus consortium and aircraft assembly was happening across multiple sites and multiple countries, each dependent on the other for throughput. It was very hard to create streamlined processes when working with the 'competition', especially when there were intercultral and international issues.

The challenge for Filton was to move out of infatuation with gold-plated technical innovation and become passionate about competing in a commercially different world. But let us look at what happens when you try and create new learning in an old culture.

The company produced a video spelling out the doomsday scenario for Filton if it did not compete on the new terms: cost reduction, reliability, process efficiency etc. A copy was sent at Christmas to every employee. When we walked the site and talked to staff at different levels early the next year, there were three dominant reactions:

1 *Fatalism:* 'They have secret plans to close the site and there is nothing we can do about it.'

2 *Suspicion:* 'They are painting a bleak picture in order to scare the unions off demanding too much.'

3 *Denial:* 'Bristol would never let Filton close, it is too important for local employment.' 'We have the best designers and engineers in the world and British Aerospace would never want to lose that capability.'

New learning cannot be put into old bottles. To create or learn a new culture you first must unlearn the old, by breaking the frames through which new experience will be evaluated. When the Bath Consultancy Group carried out research into why change initiatives so often fail, the single major factor we found was that: 'Leaders, change agents and consultants tried to cascade a solution, before the majority of the organization had even bought into the problem'. We came up with the phrase: **'If they ain't bought the problem, they ain't going to buy the solution'.** People need a direct experience in order to learn this. Let us describe two direct unlearning experiences at British Aerospace in Filton. The first moment of unlearning was when we had worked together on trying to break down the functional silos and create more learning and better relationships across departments. The chief executive's exhortations and our workshops were not changing things. I said to him: 'The problem is you're the only one who is having the sleepless nights about the total functioning of the site. They are working their socks off, fixing operational problems in their functions. They just hear you and I making more demands. To shift their frame we have to transfer your sleepless night to them.' At the next executive team meeting he looked them all in the eye and told them that in two weeks time he wanted 50 per cent of their time managing corporate development rather than their own function. They had one week to come up with how they were going to manage their functions in two and a half days a week. This was to functional directors who were working excessive overtime firefighting operational problems. They immediately started kicking back, with 'How can I possibly ...?' questions. 'That is the challenge we all face,' he replied.

This broke the previous culture in which problems always came up the multiple levels of management and solutions always came back down.

The second unlearning intervention we will call 'sleepless in Seattle'. This is when the same chief executive worked more collaboratively to shift frames. He went with the main union shop stewards on a learning visit to Boeing. They travelled, hotelled and ate together for several days. This in itself was a previously unheard of experience. But the most effective unlearning was when the boss, who was the one who always previously had the answers, said: 'I want your help in discovering how we can make Filton better than Seattle, for I do not know how to do it.'

For Filton to transform its culture, it had to systemically transform its culture from the bottom level up, when previously it had tried to do so from the top level of artefacts down. It needed to start at the level of purpose and motivational routes, by mourning the death of building Concorde and the unity, passion and pride that brought with it. Only when this was acknowledged could a new pride and purpose be found for the organization in being able to be a world-class aircraft assembly site, focused on out-performing Boeing. Managers had to develop new mindsets, which were not about 'solving problems' for their staff, but coaching their teams and staff to solve their own problems, thus freeing up more of their time to create the improved connecting across the different functions.

Leadership

We started by looking at the importance of moving from 'developing strategy' to 'strategizing', which in turn supports and embodies dialogue, experimentation and learning review. We then explored the interrelated levels of influence that go to make up an organization's culture. To change that culture therefore requires both unlearning of old patterns and the learning of new ones. We also saw in the British Aerospace example the role of 'leading' rather than just 'commanding'. The third node of leadership is the other activity for creating successful organizational change. It has been said that after sex and gardening the next best-selling genre in books are publications on leadership. Much of the literature has derived from the USA, and is coloured by the American culture's fascination with the individual, the heroic and the pioneer. Many of the popular books, prior to the more recent change in emphasis, viewed leadership as:

- being located in individuals;
- solely at the top of the organization;
- heroic and 'strong';
- biased towards a masculine 'command and control' model;
- focused on ruthless turnaround.

This glorified what Ghoshal and others termed 'asshole management', derived from the comment by the business journalist Statford Sherman, who wrote: 'Jack Welch is the best CEO GE ever had. Jack Welch is an asshole' (quoted by Ghoshal in Bikinshaw and Piramal 2005).

This was part of a culture which glorified the celebrity CEO, who was praised for their tough ruthlessness and grim determination. Besides Jack Welch, there were many others of similar grim renown, such as Lee Iaccocca, Al Dunlop and Andy Grove in the USA. This ruthless image continues to this day in reality TV programmes like *The Apprentice* and *In the Dragon's Den* – but the scandals of Enron, Worldcom and others have made the general population less trusting of such tough hero figures.

More recently there has been the growth of other approaches to leadership, with emphasis on servant leadership, humility, feminine approaches, quietness, caring about the people and collective, distributed and trans-cultured leadership. Most coaches, mentors and consultants sooner or later are involved in developing leaders and so require a good understanding of what needs to be developed to help a leader to fulfil more of their potential.

What is leadership?

More definitions have been offered of leadership than perhaps any other subject on earth. All of them are contestable; many of them depend on which perspective you come from. But like a many-faceted diamond, every angle you look from diffuses light differently. Some definitions which reflect light in different ways include:

- leaders are created by followers;
- leadership is activity which mobilizes adaptation;
- leadership starts when you stop blaming others for things going wrong and take responsibility;
- we get the leadership we deserve.

Based on research across sectors and countries, we offer a model of the key aspects of integrated leadership, which we have used in the public, private and voluntary sectors. However, it is important to recognize that no individual can possibly encompass all the functions we highlight. Integrated leadership requires effective leadership team working across the board member/chief officer divide, across the corporate centre/operational divisions divide and across the divide between the organization and wider stakeholders (see Figure 5.5).

Leaders strategically creating value

Within this development triangle, developing leaders and leading is not about developing leaders *per se*, but about developing the collective capacity of leaders to guide the strategic evolution of the organization and steer the constant regeneration of the organization's culture.

It is also possible to view leading from the outcomes and benefits it produces and the way it creates value for all the key stakeholder groups (see above). In a research report on leaders and leadership development for the UK Society of Local Authority Chief Executives (SOLACE), we wrote about public sector leadership from the perspective of outcomes (Hawkins and Chesterman 2004):

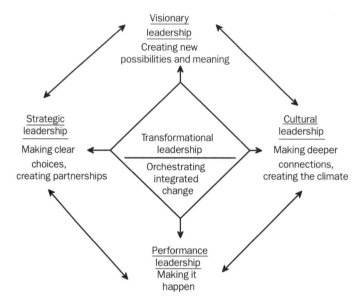

Figure 5.5 Aspects of integrated leadership

Whatever your perspective, one might infer successful leadership under the following conditions:

Citizens feel enjoined in creating the sort of community they want.

Local taxpayers experience a 'good enough' correlation between levels of service and the money they are prepared to pay for them.

Service users experience the level of choice and service quality that is consistent with their expectations.

Diverse stakeholders representing interest or place feel that their voice is heard and accounted for.

Adjacent agencies co-operate productively in the pursuit of both individual and collective purposes.

Local politicians experience local government as mediating successfully between individual and collective interests in a thriving democracy.

Regional and central government secure a 'good enough' fit between local variation and country/region wide strategy.

Regulators and inspectors discover a value chain that links and shows evidence for all these perspectives.

Given such a complexity of accountabilities and constituencies to service, it is not surprising that we often default to simpler models of leadership, which reduce the leadership challenge down to a set of behaviours for individual leaders. We do not argue that such models are of no use. They are. But individuals can never be omni-competent, and we maintain a fantasy if we act as if they can be.

As the research from Ashridge Management College put it:

> Valued leadership does not come from extraordinary people but from ordinary folk who remember what they know, recover their wits amidst the pressure of transitions and deal with what is immediate and present. It consists of doing ordinary things like connecting people, valuing them, protecting people from pressures above and around ... The findings demonstrate that new leaders are most successful when they stop thinking they can shape the future as they would like and face life as it is. Instead of trying to live up to some idealised picture of what leaders are, they make best use of what's in front of them. They become ordinary heroes.
>
> (Williams *et al.* 2004)

Leaders orchestrating culture change

Roberts (2004) writes about how for too many years we have overemphasized the role of leaders as strategists – and underemphasized the role of leaders as organizational designers. He provides a very useful model to assist leaders in the work of continuous organizational design. The model includes four key elements:

- people;
- architecture;
- routines, processes and procedures;
- culture.

He illustrates how performance comes from alignment or fit between strategy, organization and the environment and among the elements of organization (see Figure 5.6).

A core challenge for leaders is the significant difference in the speed and control you can have in changing some elements as opposed to others. The structure of the organization can be changed fairly speedily and with a high degree of control; whereas people and culture are much slower to change – and the ability to control the change from the top of the organization is limited. Thus all too often change processes create misalignments in the organizational design, as the structural and process changes run ahead of the cultural and people changes. Necessary complementarities are degraded.

A good example of this is the UK National Health Service (NHS), which over the last 20 years has become a seasoned expert in changing its architecture and its routines. There have been numerous large-scale reorganizations of strategic health authorities, primary care trusts, hospitals, as well as the introduction of new routines in performance targeting, national record-keeping, local commissioning, market mechanisms – to name but a few. However, the capacity to develop the

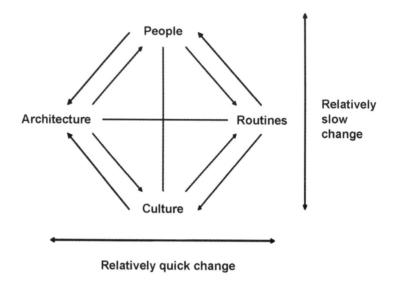

Figure 5.6   Organizational change

culture and the people working within the system has fallen way behind, which has led to most of the changes failing to live up to the expectations that accompanied their launch, and people still trying to adapt to the last change process when the next wave of change hits them from behind.

Leadership development

Both governments, public bodies and most large organizations have invested enormous amounts of money and time into developing their leadership capacity. There is already evidence that this enormous investment is not delivering the hoped-for benefits either in scale or speed. We believe that this is due to much of the development activity being based on paradigms of leadership and leadership development that are outdated and in some cases inappropriate.

The various development plans often view development of leadership as:

- being delivered to individuals;
- away from their work context;
- being able to be taught in the classroom;
- being delivered in block short courses;
- learning happening in separate sectors (e.g. schools, separate from health or local government and even separate from further and higher education).

The Bath Consultancy Group has carried out a number of research commissions on 'Best practice in leadership' and 'Leadership development'. In the private sector, the Group carried out research for PricewaterhouseCoopers, looking at how organizations could get the best return on investment in leadership development and exploring best practice internationally in some of the world's leading companies. A similar research process was conducted for the BBC (Abbotson and Ellis 2001).

In 2003 we researched for the Civil Service, reviewing their initiatives to improve individual and collective leading. For SOLACE (Society of Local Authority Chief Executives) we reviewed their scheme for continuous learning and looked at how to develop leadership capacity in local government.

From each of these studies we built up a picture of what best practice development of leaders and leading would look like in different contexts. We could not find a single organization that was executing best practice in all elements. But for each element there was an organization, or several organizations, that were being very effective and so there was much to be learned. The composite ideal organization would have ways of developing that:

- are based on a clear vision of leadership culture and capabilities needed for future success;
- are focused on developing leadership teams and not just individual leaders;
- develop individuals and teams within a context of integrated strategy and culture change;
- attend to the whole action learning cycle combining action, reflection, new thinking, informing new planning and rehearsal, leading to new action;
- provide real-time strategic challenges to leadership learning groups or teams that require them to relate in new ways and think outside the box;
- require leaders to work across sector boundaries in partnerships in a way that also reflects on the partnership working;
- create just-in-time learning where people receive learning as the need arises.

Based on this research, the Bath Consultancy Group has developed and tested an organizational diagnostic review process. This process reviews the future requirements for leading the organization and then assists the organization in developing their strategizing around this topic.

This process can help an organization review its leadership holistically in the light of future needs and focus on its collective leadership culture, as well as individual capabilities. Although the details of this process are not germane to our topic, it raises for us the fact that organizational consultancy or coaching needs to understand about not only the personal and career transitions of the individual (see Chapter 2), but also the organizational transitions of the group. Key to an effective transformational shift in an organization will be integrating activity between strategizing, connecting and leading. Each aspect of the transformational process needs to address the internal and external connections of the organizational system. Leading requires support both of those currently exercising it and also in bringing on new leaders. Developing leaders, we suggest, needs to be a topic clearly on the radar of the organizational consultant/coach. He or she needs to be pushing every opportunity that is offered in the organization, to exercise and deepen the activity of leading to the greater improvement and added value of the organization and the individuals in it, and seeing the everyday work and challenges of the organization as the seedbed of leadership development.

Conclusion: the role of the organizational coach

At the beginning of this chapter we talked about how dramatically the world of organizations has been changing, both in the commercial, public and the not-for-profit sectors. Our contention is that the world of organizational development consultancy has failed to keep apace with these changes since its pioneering work in the 70s and 80s. The last ten years has seen an enormous upsurge in the literature and training in individual coaching and mentoring, but a similar upsurge and rejuvenation is needed in the even more challenging field of organizational coaching and organization development consultancy.

We also contend that coaching an organization on its overall development is not something that can be carried out by an individual acting alone. Rather it requires a coaching team, working effectively together, and a team that receives regular shadow consultancy or team supervision from somebody one step removed from the face-to-face work with the client system. This person needs to be not only a trained supervisor and experienced organizational development consultant, but also somebody who has a systemic approach to understanding organizations as complex adaptive systems, where strategizing, evolving culture and developing leaders are recognized as continuous and intertwined processes. We will return to this subject in Chapter 11, when we explore 'systemic shadow consultancy'.

6

Creating a coaching culture

To What End?

The board of a large company was working on its mission statement.

'What is your fundamental purpose?' asked Nasrudin.

'Our mission is to create constantly increasing dividends for our shareholders,' the directors declared.

'To what end?' asked Nasrudin.

'So they make increased profits which they will want to reinvest in our company,' they said.

'To what end?' asked Nasrudin.

'So they make more profits,' they said, becoming somewhat irritated.

'To what end?' asked Nasrudin nonchalantly.

'So they re-invest and make more profits.'

Nasrudin pondered this for a while and thanked them for their explanations.

Later that week they had arranged to visit Nasrudin's house to work further on the mission statement. They found him in his garden stuffing oats into his donkey.

'What are you doing?' they asked. 'You are giving that poor beast so much food that it will not be able to go anywhere.'

'But it is not meant to go anywhere,' Nasrudin replied. 'Its purpose is to produce manure.'

'To what end?' they asked.

'Because without it I cannot grow enough oats in my small allotment to feed this greedy beast.'

(Hawkins 2005: 5)

Introduction

What are the needs that lead organizations to turn to coaching? Often it starts with them wanting to address concerns about individual performance at senior levels or the need to fast track certain leaders' development processes. It may then broaden out to address the development needs of all senior managers towards moving into more corporate roles, and/or the needs of higher potential staff in the organization. At these stages, coaching is most often commissioned by the human resources, training or organizational development departments of large organizations, who see coaching as a more cost-effective way of developing people management and leadership skills than classroom-based learning.

However, when an organization embarks on making coaching available to a larger percentage of its leadership and management populations, significant costs have to be taken into account, which raises strategic questions about return on investment (ROI). More critical questions begin to be asked, such as:

- How do we evaluate the return we are getting on this investment?
- Does all this investment just benefit the individuals, or does it provide organizational benefit?
- How do we make it part of the way we manage and lead on a day-to-day basis, rather than a separate activity?
- Coaching – to what end?

Increasingly, we are seeing organizations thinking more strategically about how coaching can add real value to their business. This often starts with managers considering the following questions:

- What are our key strategic priorities?
- What development does this require in our organizational culture?
- To achieve that development, what needs to shift in our individual and collective leadership and management style, and capability?
- How can coaching help make that difference?

This has led to a growing interest in how to 'create a coaching culture'. At the 2005 European Mentoring and Coaching Council conference in Zurich, this was one of the main themes. There were academic presentations on the subject, as well as presentations on how companies have developed in this direction, from such companies as Unilever, Tesco, HBoS, UBS and the BBC.

David Clutterbuck and David Megginson presented findings from their latest book *Making Coaching Work* (2005), where they use a number of case studies to show how companies have developed from training managers to do coaching, to building coaching into the way line managers manage on a day-to-day basis. They also show how this has been built into the fabric of the organization, by embedding coaching into many of the HR processes, such as job descriptions, performance management, reward etc.

What is a coaching culture?

Clutterbuck and Megginson (2005: 19) define a coaching culture as one where: 'Coaching is the predominant style of working together, and where a commitment to grow the organization is embedded in a parallel commitment to grow the people in the organization'. We consider this is a helpful starting place, but, as we will show later, not sufficiently broad.

Hardingham *et al.* (2004) enlarge the aspect of 'predominant style of working together' in their definition: 'a culture where people coach each other all the time as a natural part of meetings, reviews and one-to-one discussions'. This seems to describe a culture where there is much individual coaching, but later Hardingham *et al.* (2004: 187–8) widen their description to include more team activities, and they list the key characteristics of a coaching culture:

- the large number of cross-company teams, whose composition is based on individual interests and passions as well as on expertise;
- the leadership of those teams: the person with the most energy is the person who leads, irrespective of company position;
- the atmosphere of those teams, an atmosphere of openness and respect for and interest in everyone's views;
- a lot of coaching of staff by other members of staff;
- a habit of constant goal-setting about all aspects of the organization's life, from individual performance goals to goals of meetings to goals of conversations;
- the prevalence of strong relationships with a great deal of mutual recognition and respect;
- where there are only team bonuses, no individual ones;
- a lot of reviews with clients, exploring not just the overall delivery of a piece of work but also the performance of individuals.

The problem with such a list is that it conflates aspects of good managerial practice, a positive work environment and a number of coaching activities, which need separate deliberation.

Caplan's (2003: 4) model of 'coaching as an organizational culture' is somewhat similar, but has more emphasis on how coaching becomes part of both everyday management and also distributed leadership. This is summarized by Clutterbuck and Megginson (2005) as follows:

1 Everyone in the organization believes that learning is critical to individual and organizational success.

2 The leaders of the organizations use a non-directive leadership style, that is, they employ a coaching style with peers and subordinates.

3 Decision-making is developed as far as possible to those who are closest to having to implement the decisions. They are given freedom to take risks and set their own goals.

4 Managers view developing others and creating a learning environment as one of their major responsibilities.

5 Peers coach one another to share knowledge, to pass on expertise and to help one another, and also raise their own standards and general standards of professionalism.

6 Having a mentor or coach is viewed positively, and people are encouraged to seek mentoring or coaching support at various stages in their career and for various reasons.

Stages in developing a coaching culture

For any organization that is embarking on the road to developing a coaching culture, the first job before you even start is to ask some or all of these questions:

- What is the need to which coaching and a coaching culture is the answer?
- What would be the benefits of having a coaching culture?
- Where do we want to get to, that a coaching culture is an essential part of the journey?
- What will success look like and how will we evaluate the return on our investment in creating a coaching culture?

Later in this chapter we will address some of the possible answers to these questions as we explore the coaching culture value chain and how to evaluate the process from the end goal back.

Our own model of the stages in developing a coaching culture has expanded from both desk research of the relevant literature, our own review of the companies that we have worked with both on coaching and culture change and research carried out for CIPD (Hawkins & Schonk 2006). The model is descriptive rather than prescriptive, that is to say it describes the most common stages of development that organizations go through in establishing a coaching culture, rather than prescribing that all organizations must go through their development in this order (see Figure 6.1).

Figure 6.1   Stages in developing a coaching culture

Steps in the evolution of a coaching culture

These are:

1   The organization employs coaches for some of its executives.

2   The organization develops its own coaching and mentoring capacity.

3   The organization actively supports coaching endeavours.

4   Coaching becomes a norm for individuals, teams and the whole organization.

5   Coaching becomes embedded in the HR and performance management processes of the organization.

6   Coaching becomes the predominate style of managing throughout the organization.

7   Coaching becomes 'how we do business' with all our stakeholders.

The organization employs coaches or mentors for some of its executives

Most organizations first engage with coaching or mentoring when they discover that some of their executives have developmental needs that cannot be met through line management or internal HR provision. So they support the executives in having coaching or mentoring from either somebody externally or located elsewhere inside their own organization. This stage may start in an ad hoc way, but can develop into a major facility; companies like Unilever or GlaxoSmithKline have global approved lists of professional coaches who they have assessed, accredited and continue to support, and it is accepted practice that all executives will at some stage engage with a coach. This stage is often necessary before developing managers as coaches – as Kate Howsley, Kellogg's director of organizational effectiveness stringently put it: 'We concluded that to develop others, the coaches needed to be developed first' (quoted in Clutterbuck and Megginson 2005: 135).

   As we have said elsewhere in this book, being an effective coachee is a first step to becoming an effective coach.

The organization develops its own coaching and mentoring capacity

For many organizations, especially those in the public and not-for-profit sectors, establishing and maintaining a large panel of external professional coaches is financially prohibitive. Even for large successful commercial companies, once they proceed to extend coaching beyond the top levels, they usually start to develop an internal and less costly resource. Some start by equipping their internal development and HR staff with extra skills and training in coaching and mentoring. Others immediately go for developing line managers to either coach in their own teams and functions or to provide mentoring or coaching to other parts of the organization. The latter has the added benefit of increasing cross-company understanding for both sides of the relationship.

The organization actively supports coaching endeavours

Either of the first two developmental stages is vulnerable to a change in organizational leadership or climate, when new leaders may not understand or appreciate coaching and mentoring, or there is a need for cost savings and such activities are easy targets in tough, belt-tightening times. Stage 3 marks the beginning of establishing more permanent tent-pegs in the organizational fabric, with a chance of sustaining the coaching and mentoring tent when the winds of change start to blow strongly!

Such supports may include:

- top executives role-modelling by receiving coaching or mentoring and publicizing the fact;
- those who are doing the coaching being publicly endorsed through being given the time and resources to provide the service;
- internal coaching communities being established who meet regularly and review what is emerging as common patterns;
- the coaching communities being provided with ongoing supervision and continuing professional development (see Chapter 7).

Coaching becomes a norm for individuals, teams and the whole organization

At this stage coaching and mentoring no longer become provision-led, as a service marketed by the HR or development section, but a right that anyone can demand. They become part of the psychological employment covenant between the organization and the individual: the individual will always be able to access development opportunities and part of this development is the right to engage in coaching or mentoring both as an individual and as part of a team. At this stage the organization has entered into the new employment covenant that Ghoshal and others have advocated:

The company's responsibility to employees, therefore, is both to ensure competitive remuneration and to continuously add value to them by enhancing their repertoire of useful knowledge and skills. The employees' obligation in this relationship is to continuously learn, in order to protect and improve their human capital, and to use their expertise and their entrepreneurial capabilities to create new value and thereby improve the company's competitiveness and performance.

(Ghoshal and Moran, quoted in Birkinshaw and Piramal 2005: 16)

Coaching becomes embedded in the HR and performance management processes of the organization

At this stage, the organization builds receiving and providing of coaching and mentoring into its performance management and HR processes. This may be done in a variety of ways:

- all managers receive 360-degree feedback, which includes feedback on the coaching they provide and their coaching style;
- managers are scored and rewarded on the regularity and quality of the coaching they provide and the degree to which they have developed their staff's potential;
- teams have regular team effectiveness reviews, which include a review of the team coaching as well as the coaching style of the team leader (see Chapter 4).

Coaching becomes the predominate style of managing throughout the organization

At this stage coaching moves from being a separate activity, which is seen as time away from the day-to-day reality of work, to being part of how formal and informal management happens on a daily basis. There are many ways that one might see coaching becoming a general way of managing:

- team meetings might follow a coaching format using the CLEAR process or similar model (see Chapters 2 and 4);
- individuals, who are stuck with a problem, will seek out brief peer coaching from a colleague;
- performance reviews will have a coaching structure;
- relationship coaching will be used to resolve conflict.

Coaching becomes 'how we do business' with all our stakeholders

Finally, the organization can move on to utilize a coaching style not only in how it manages internally but also in how it engages with all its key stakeholders. At this stage the organization has a clear model for how it creates value for all its key stakeholders and how coaching and a coaching culture contribute to that value creation:

- *Coaching customers:* Clutterbuck and Megginson (2005) quote the example of British Airways training their check-in staff in coaching skills to support customers using the new self-check-in terminals.

- *Coaching partners and suppliers:* in our work with Capespan International, a global fruit company, we supported the company in moving from managing their fruit producers through contracting for quality and meeting targets with ever-higher standards, to coaching them in how to be more effective suppliers. We also supported them in how they could create this relationship at their interface with their retailer customers.

- *Coaching in the community:* we have worked with a number of organizations which have encouraged or indeed organized their high potential leaders to work with charity organizations in a coaching role. One very successful relationship developed between Shell and Centre Point, the young homelessness agency in central London, where some company managers have coached ex-offenders and others have mentored young entrepreneurs and their organizations through the Prince's Trust.

- *Using a coaching approach to create dialogue with investors:* we worked with one large financial company on how it carried out its twice-yearly roadshows to visit all its key investors and analysts, to share its half-year and full-year results. The style of the meetings changed from a slick presentation followed by critical questions and well-rehearsed political answers, to the company focusing on eliciting appreciations and concerns of the investors early in the meeting and addressing these through dialogue.

Other coaching models have recently presented the phases of developing a coaching culture. Clutterbuck and Megginson (2005) have offered great detail in their descriptions. They constructed a very useful questionnaire that helps organizations assess where they are in progressing towards their aim of a full coaching culture. They describe their stages as:

- *nascent* – an organization shows little or no commitment to creating a coaching culture;

- *tactical* – the organization has recognized the value of establishing a coaching culture, but there is little understanding of what that means and what will be involved;

- *strategic* – there has been considerable effort expended to educate managers and employees in the value of coaching and to give people the competence (and therefore confidence) to coach in a variety of situations;

- *embedded* – people at all levels are engaged in coaching, both formal and informal, with colleagues, both within the same function and across functions and levels.

Our own model concentrates more on the later stages of their process, and roughly maps onto it in the following way:

- *nascent* – our stage 1;
- *tactical* – our stages 1 and 2;

- *strategic* – our stages 3 and 4;
- *embedded* – our stages 5 and 6.

Coaching culture – to what end?

> When you create a culture of coaching, the result may not be directly measurable in dollars. But we have yet to find a company that can't benefit from more candor, less denial, richer communications, conscious development of talent, and disciplined leaders who show compassion for people.
>
> (Sherman and Freas 2004: 90)

Many of the arguments that have been put forward for creating a coaching culture are similar to the one Sherman and Freas published in the *Harvard Business Review* (Sherman and Freas 2004). They talk of the benefits a coaching culture can bring and of the problems it can help alleviate. They also appeal to a 'moral ought' – as if to say, if you are a decent person then, of course, you will want to have a coaching culture in your organization.

All these arguments can be very effective and persuade some individuals to engage further on the journey we have outlined here, particularly the people who have either had a very positive experience of coaching, or those for whom a coaching culture matches with their personal vision, values and corporate aspirations.

However, we have been engaged in cultural change efforts for over 20 years and have seen many similar endeavours to promote such things as learning organizations, total quality companies, empowered organizations, knowledge-sharing companies and many more. Our experience has led us to understand that any self-serving fashion in organizational development is doomed to be short-lived. *If the culture change endeavour becomes an end in itself, it will not be sustained beyond the energy of its enthusiastic creators.*

It is therefore important to ask, 'To what end is the coaching culture the means?' After clear answers have been generated, we must ensure that the coaching culture is well linked to the ends it serves and is evaluated from that perspective.

In Figure 6.2, we show the outputs that can derive from each stage of building the coaching culture. In the early stages of using external coaches, and training internal coaches, the main output to be expected is in increased leadership capacity and capability within those individuals being coached. A side benefit may also be the increase in leadership capacity and capability from those delivering the coaching.

As the organization builds up and supports its internal coaching community, in phases 3 and 4, there is more potential for delivering coaching beyond the top executives and senior managers to a much higher percentage of the workforce. This can ensure that there is a much higher level of distributed leadership, with those at lower levels taking more leadership responsibility.

In stages 5 and 6, where the organization is building coaching into its systems and organizational processes and establishing coaching as part of its culture, the expected outputs should include not only increased leadership capacity for individuals, but also for teams, functions and the whole organization.

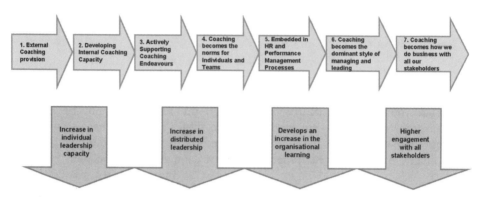

Figure 6.2   Developing a coaching culture – outputs

In the final stage, the organization should be experiencing much greater engagement with all its stakeholders.

So far we have considered the outputs that emerge from the coaching inputs, not the outcomes. Typically we find that there is a delay between the inputs and outputs and witnessing tangible outcomes. Often not until the second year of major investment in a coaching culture, with the organization having developed at least stages 1–4, are real returns observable in the organization's performance. To achieve real returns, in terms of creating greater value for all the stakeholders and increasing the financial returns to the investors, often entails the organization reaching stage 7. The difficulty can be that many organizations both in the private and public sectors have enormous pressure to deliver return on investment within one year. This can lead some organizations to cut their investment just before the point where the endeavour would produce sustainable value for them. Under-

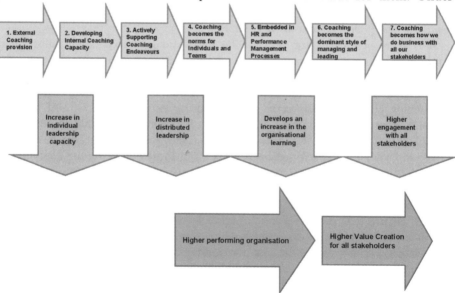

Figure 6.3   Developing a coaching culture – outcomes

standing the development pattern and its likely outputs and outcomes can help organizations make more sensible investment decisions, and create more realistic expectations of returns on that investment (see Figure 6.3).

This can be further supported by providing some form of ongoing evaluation that provides intermediate monitoring and evaluation of the outputs, and a barometer of the impact on stakeholder perceptions.

Evaluation

How an organization evaluates its coaching culture is likely to change as it progresses through the stages we described earlier (see Table 6.1).

Table 6.1   Stages of development

Stage	Likely evaluation method
1 The organization employs coaches for some of its executives.	Structured or informal feedback on providers by coachees.
2 The organization develops its own coaching and mentoring capacity.	Structured or informal feedback on internal coaches by coachees.
3 The organization actively supports coaching endeavours.	The above, plus formal reviews and assessment of coaches.
4 Coaching becomes a norm for individuals, teams and the whole organization.	The above, plus collecting comparative data on the effectiveness of coaching interventions across the organization.
5 Coaching becomes embedded in the processes in the HR and performance management processes of the organization.	The above, plus more emphasis on evaluating the performance outcomes in both teams and individuals from coaching.
6 Coaching becomes the predominant style of managing throughout the organization.	The above, plus 360-degree feedback and staff attitude surveys that are linked to evaluating the shift to the desired culture.
7 Coaching becomes 'how we do business' with all our stakeholders and is linked to our value creation mission.	The above, plus organizational feedback from key stakeholders on how the organization and its staff are perceived, linked to hard performance measures.

Most of the literature on evaluation, including Clutterbuck and Megginson's (2005) very thorough work, stops at level 5, where the evaluating focus is the behavioural changes in the organization's employees. Normally, this is done by measuring 'actual behaviour' against the 'espoused behaviour', as it has been formulated in the company's core values, leadership qualities, manager competencies etc. The danger is that even though the behaviours might be 'nice ones to have', the link between the espoused behaviours and organizational performance may be illusory, since at this stage we are evaluating *outputs* but not *outcomes*.

There is a salutary lesson from the car retail sector, where there was, for many years, a big emphasis on customer satisfaction, with dealerships putting a lot of effort into measuring this and trying to outperform their competitors in this area. However, later research showed there was very little correlation between high levels of customer satisfaction soon after purchase and the number of customers who bought their next car from the same dealer. It was only when the dealerships moved to measuring customer retention (outcome), rather than satisfaction (output), that they started to develop an evaluation system that could support value generation across both a wider stakeholder group, and over time.

The other evaluation trap is to measure short-term behaviour shifts and long-term financial performance and suggest that there is some causative link between them. To return to the quote earlier in the chapter: 'When you create a culture of coaching, the result may not be directly measurable in dollars. But we have yet to find a company that can't benefit from more candor, less denial, richer communications, conscious development of talent, and disciplined leaders who show compassion for people' (Sherman and Freas 2004: 90). To overcome this void – or canyon – between the short-term behavioural measures and long-term outcome measures (such as financial performance, analysts' ratings, customer and staff retention and attraction and similar measures) we have developed an organizational 360-degree feedback assessment tool, called 'descriptor analysis'. It enables the company to see how it is perceived by all its key stakeholders and how they would like to be able to perceive the organization.

Descriptor analysis

In many organizations we have asked the question: 'How do you connect the data you get from: your customer feedback; your staff attitude survey; your press analysis; regulator and company analysts' reports and investor feedback?' So far we have never had a fully satisfactory answer, but nearly all the senior executives whom we have asked found it an important question. One chief executive replied: 'If we could integrate all that feedback, we would have a powerful aerial view, which would transform our ability to steer our organization!' Unfortunately, in most organizations, the sales department manages the customer feedback, the marketing department manages the press analysis, the HR department manages the staff attitude survey, corporate affairs manages the investor feedback and the financial director manages the analysts' and regulatory reports.

Multiple stakeholder perceptions, when they are joined up, provide a valuable intermediate measure of change in organizational performance and value creation. We developed a methodology that can collect and integrate 360-degree feedback on the organization (and sometimes also its collective leadership) from a wide range of stakeholder positions.

The process (see Figure 6.4) begins with an analysis of:

a) all the descriptors (adjectives and descriptive phrases) in the organization's aspirational literature (annual reports, mission statements, visions, core value statements, CEO speeches, leadership competencies etc.);

b) all the descriptors used in the data currently collected from different stakeholders;

c) the key challenges, dilemmas and questions currently engaging the organization at a strategic level, garnered through group, team and individual interviews.

We then build a word search instrument that includes:

• 15 top descriptors from (a);

• 15 top used descriptors in (b);

• 15 descriptors from our word bank that reflect the key themes and dilemmas garnered from (c).

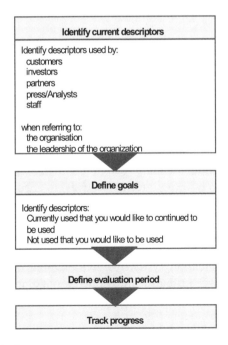

Figure 6.4   Descriptor analysis process

This word search is then included as part of a 360-degree feedback questionnaire sent to representatives of all the identified stakeholder groups, with the request that they underline three descriptors that they believe most accurately describe how they see the organization today, and circle three descriptors that they would like to be able to use to describe the organization in two or three years time. From this 'quick-to-collect' data, a quantified 'league table' can be produced of the most underlined descriptors that correspond to today's perception and of the most circled descriptors that represent the perception of what is expected in the future.

Sometimes we do a parallel word search on how the collective leadership of the organization is viewed. This can dramatically show what needs to shift in the leadership culture prior to achieving a shift in the organization in order that the perception of the organization moves toward that which is desired.

The outcome can then be built into an ongoing barometer that can be used to regularly review progress. This is done by building the ten highest underlined descriptors and the ten most circled descriptors into a shorter word search that can be integrated into all current stakeholder feedback mechanisms. One large British financial organization we worked with, some time ago, wanted to move from being currently seen as 'bureaucratic, British and institutional' to being 'leading, European and innovative'. They geared their culture change and leadership development processes to the goal of creating this shift, and gradually over the next three years they were able to see how each of their stakeholder groups were reporting a shift in how they perceived both the organization and its leadership, in the direction they had planned.

Conclusion

For an organization to develop a coaching culture is neither a quick nor easy process. However, the returns for systemically developing a culture where coaching is part of everyday relationships can transform not only the performance but the value creation of the organization. The journey will take a good deal of investment in time and money, and for this investment to be sustained over several years will probably require some form of ongoing measurement and evaluation process, not only of the outputs and increased capability, but also of the more tangible outcomes. Many leading global companies are on the journey from employing coaches, to training internal coaches, to ensuring that 'coaching is how we manage', and is built into the organizational processes and systems.

In this chapter we have mapped the developmental stages and shown the likely outputs and outcomes that can be expected at each stage, as well as ways of evaluating progress. Very few, if any, organizations have completed all seven stages and integrated an evaluation system to give ongoing feedback on organizational process. But then it will probably always be an ongoing journey and there is still much we can learn from our fellow travellers.

SECTION 2
Development and supervision

Introduction to Section 2

At the beginning of the book we outlined our belief that the coaching, mentoring, organizational consultancy and supervision all partake in the unitary craft of adult human development and in particular the craft of enabling real-time learning that simultaneously transforms an individual, team and organization and their work.

Coaches, mentors and organizational consultants are all developers of workers, managers and leaders, not as an end in itself, but in order that their client's clients and staff become more effective in their organizations and work endeavours. Managers and leaders have as one of their important functions the development of their staff – and therefore coaches, mentors and organizational consultants can be understood as 'developing the developers'.

In this section we start to look at the role, function and practice of supervisors and those that train coaches, mentors and consultants. We are therefore beginning to look at developing the developers of the developers. This development process needs to have both immediate impact, as well as attempting to have influence at both one step and two steps removed (see Figure 1).

The supervisor needs to be skilled at becoming aware of what they need to shift in themselves (1) to change the supervisory relationship (2) with their supervisee (the coach or mentor) so they in turn can create a shift in themselves (3) which will transform their relationship (4) with their client (coachee) (5) and this in turn will transform the client's relationship and impact on their organization (6) and its effectiveness in the wider world (7).

Thus we have both a unitary craft of development and different steps in the systemic chain of influence, which affects the contextual nature of the development practice.

In Chapter 7 we will first explore the core principles that apply to all forms of adult training and development and then show how these particularly apply to both the training and the continuing professional development of coaches, mentors and organizational consultants.

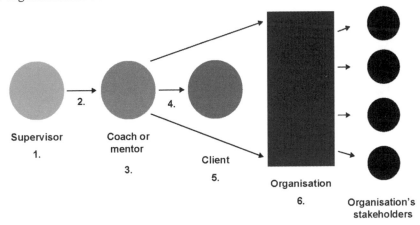

Figure 1　Chain of influence

We then set out our view of supervision as a core aspect of both basic training and lifetime continuing professional development for coaches, mentors and organizational consultants. We further develop our perspective on why and how the practice of supervision needs to change depending on the developmental context and level of the trainee's abilities.

We then step back, in Chapter 8, to look at the nature of supervision; its core functions; the various roles of the supervisor and how to get started in this particular development role.

Chapter 9 provides an in-depth articulation of our own 'seven-eyed process' model of supervision. It has been successfully used to train supervisors across many different people professions, in various countries, over the last 20 years. Here we present the models as particularly adapted for the fields of coaching, mentoring and organizational consultancy. (Those who want to explore a fuller version of this model as applied to the helping and therapeutic professions should read Hawkins and Shohet (2006)).

In Chapter 10, we explore how to adapt the practice of supervision from a one-to-one context to operating in supervision groups or peer groups. In Chapter 11, we build on this by describing how to practise a particular form of supervision – 'systemic shadow consultancy' – with teams of organizational consultants and professional advisers, who work with the same client organization.

7

Development of coaches

Finished Learning

An excited father came running up to Nasrudin waving a letter.

'I have just heard from my son that he has passed his MBA and finally finished all his learning.'

'Console yourself, sir,' began Nasrudin, 'I am sure that God in his infinite wisdom will soon send him some more.'

(Hawkins 2005: 43)

Introduction

Until recently many practising coaches, mentors and organizational coaches received little or no formal training. Age and experience were the main qualifications. Some had trained as organizational psychologists or undertaken a higher degree in organizational behaviour, but these were the minority. The majority had undertaken this work based on either a background in senior management or an earlier training in one of the psychological professions (psychology, counselling or psychotherapy). As discussed in Chapter 13 this has created the twin dangers of coaches either coming from a management background but lacking psychological sophistication or starting from a background of individualistic psychology, which fails to provide them with an in-depth appreciation of organizational realities.

Gradually we have seen the growth of training in each of these fields and, in just the last few years, there has been the emergence of masters and doctoral programmes in coaching and organization development and consultancy in Europe. These degrees have been underway slightly longer in North America.

This chapter explores what are the best development processes for coaches, mentors and consultants, both in basic training and continuing professional development, and the role of supervision in each stage of the developmental process.

Core principles of training and development

Based on the heritage of these different traditions as well as our experience in designing and delivering training in a wide range of professions, we would recommend that training for coaches, mentors and consultants should be based on the following principles:

1   Start (and end) with a focus on self-awareness, developed through experiential learning processes.

2   Teach theory only when experiential learning has already got underway.

3   Use 'just-in-time learning'. Learning is most effective when the learner has already recognized the need for that piece of learning and can apply the learning close to receiving it.

4   Develop the individual's 'authority, presence and impact' as articulated in our API model (see Chapter 13), through intensive feedback in small groups where the trainee undertakes coaching, mentoring or change work with their peers.

5   Teach basic skills and techniques in a way that brings things alive in the room, using demonstrations, illustrative stories, engagement and trainees reflecting on their lived experiences. Provide plenty of opportunity to practise and receive feedback.

6   Real-time learning. Learning is greatly enhanced when the learners address real issues that are current and unresolved, rather than case studies from the past. We refer to this as real-play as opposed to role-play.

7   After initial training, learners need a prolonged period of supervised practice before they return to create their own integration between self-awareness, skills, theory and their experience of practice.

8   A recognition that transformational learning requires unlearning as well as learning; and confounding our current patterns of behaviour and ways of seeing the world as well as comprehending new ways of being.

9   It is crucial that trainers and developers demonstrate a genuine belief and valuing of the learner's ability and potential and recognize that sooner or later they will exceed the teacher's capacity.

These principles, relating to the educational progression of learners, apply to any of the professions that focus on human relationships and where the use of oneself is the primary instrument of the work.

This progression means that first of all the beginner acquires competencies, then capabilities and throughout the processes is expanding their capacities.

Alongside the elaboration of continuing professional development there has been an enormous growth in mapping and defining the core competencies needed for a profession. This has been partly driven by the need to assess the skills of the learners for national or professional qualifications and a recognition that written examinations only attest to the ability to memorize and understand theory and do not examine the ability to use skills.

There has been much written about competencies and also their limitations. We have been influenced by Broussine (1998) and others in distinguishing between the 'three Cs' of *competencies, capabilities and capacities*:

- *competencies* we see as the ability to utilize a skill or use a tool;
- *capability* refers to the ability to use the tool or skill, at the right time, in the right way and in the right place;
- *capacity* is a human quality such as flexibility, warmth, engagement, imagination, etc., rather than a skill and has more to do with how you are rather than what you do.

This way of differentiating is discussed by Broussine (1998) in a paper looking at the role of chief executives in local government:

> The competence approach has a history: it holds a connotation, which can be interpreted as 'simplistic' and individualistic. The concept of acquiring a competence suggests a linear view of learning something which is pre-determined. My argument for the use of the concept of capacity is not only to do with the limitations of the concept of competence. The etymology of 'capacity' is the Latin word *capax* – 'able to hold much'. This has the implication, when related to managers' roles, of being able to hold complexity, ambiguity and paradox in the exercise of such roles. Thus 'the capacity to work with the political dimension' reflects the challenge inherent in working with sometimes difficult relations and being able to read intuitively the constantly changing political dynamic among a council's membership. The 'competence work with elected members' does not, I suggest, reflect the reality of the chief executive's role so well.

This important distinction between competence, capability and capacity can be linked back to our earlier model of the coaching continuum as in Figure 7.1.

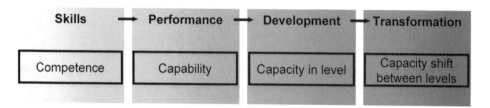

Figure 7.1 Coaching continuum: linked to competencies, capabilities, capacities

Development delivered through coaching, mentoring, consultancy, supervision or training can be focused on:

- skills in order to help people develop their competencies;
- performance to help people develop their capability of using their skills effectively and timely on the right choices;
- development to help people develop their capacity within their current level of being;
- transformation to help people shift to a higher order level of being.

These levels can also be linked to the levels of learning first articulated by Gregory Bateson (1973), and developed by many others such as Argyris and Schon (1978), Garratt (1987) and Hawkins (1991). Skill and performance focus mainly on the use of level 1 or single loop learning. Here we are learning to do more or less of the sort of things we currently do. Development and transformation, on the other hand, require level 2 or double loop learning. Double loop learning asks someone to shift significant portions of the way they view something and see it from another point of view. For example, if we were changing the accounting processes in our business, level 1 learning would be about fine-tuning what we currently do, making it more efficient. Level 2 learning would be looking at the effectiveness of the system and realizing that we need to redesign the accounting package. For the higher levels of transformation, level 3 or triple loop learning comes into play. Here we are looking at the purpose of the accounting process and maybe realize that we should think about the whole process from an entirely different point of view.

We will return to the competencies, capabilities and capacities needed for the crafts of coaching, mentoring, consultancy and supervision in Section 3 of this book.

Adult professional development with personal development at its heart

Many professional training courses are still fundamentally based on traditional educational approaches that emerge from pedagogy (i.e. the teaching/learning processes of children). We would argue, as we have done elsewhere (Hawkins

1986, 1991) that androgogy (i.e. the learning processes of adults) is very different from the learning processes of children (pedagogy).

Good adult learning practice recognizes that students are people with a great deal of already existent learning and life experience. We know that adult learning will be more effective if connected with the learner's already accumulated knowledge, which is rooted in and related to the life experiences people have undergone. Adults are even less able to learn from sitting in classrooms and being taught than children and need a more active learning process.

In recent work that we have carried out in the profession of teaching (Hawkins and Chesterman 2006) we have argued that at the core of professional development for teachers is the regular heartbeat of personal development. By developing our self we are developing our practice, by developing our personal capacities we are deepening our engagement with our clients and the effectiveness of our skills and capabilities. If continuing professional development is mainly focused on updating skills and techniques, then we become more and more transactional and lose the human quality and transformational aspects that are the ground of our work (see Figure 7.2).

We will explore more fully the nature of personal development in the final section of this book. We also believe that work has a spiritual dimension, and we will touch on this aspect when we consider what it might mean to get serious about 'polishing the professional mirror' (Chapter 16).

Figure 7.2 Continuing development

Action learning and action research

Kolb *et al.* (1971), Juch (1983), Revans (1982) and others have developed approaches to adult learning which demonstrate that learning is richest when it follows a cycle that incorporates several steps action, reflection on the action, new sense-making and theorizing, followed by planning new action. This process is sometimes referred to as the 'cycle of action learning' (Revans 1982) (see Figure 7.3).

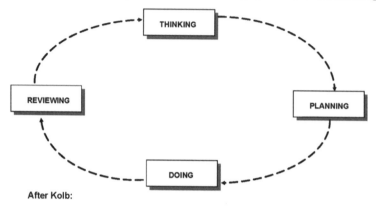

After Kolb:

Figure 7.3 Action learning cycle

We also need to bear in mind that different individuals have different learning styles, which affect where they are most comfortable starting on the learning cycle. Some people prefer to start with practical action and then reflect on what works and what does not. Others like to have the theory and explanation before planning to apply the model in action. Honey and Mumford (1992) have developed a number of methodologies for people to ascertain their learning styles. They show ways for students to explore how to both utilize their dominant preference and also to expand their repertoire of learning possibilities.

We have used Honey and Mumford's work to develop our own model of learning short cuts to help coachees and trainee coaches or consultants to become more aware of limiting learning patterns they can get drawn into or are drawn to as a personal default pattern. These need to be recognized before new learning can take place. There are five main limiting learning styles that we have identified (see also Figure 7.4):

1 *Firefighting or compulsive pragmatic activity.* This is the plan-do-plan-do trap where the motto is: 'If what you plan does not work, plan and do something different'. The learning stays at the level of trial and error.

2 *Post-mortemizing.* This is the do-reflect-do-reflect trap, where the motto is: 'Reflect on what went wrong and correct it'. The learning here is restricted to error correction.

3 *Navel-gazing and theorizing.* This is the reflect-theorize-reflect-theorize trap, where the motto is: 'Philosophize on how things could be better, but never risk putting your theories to the test'.

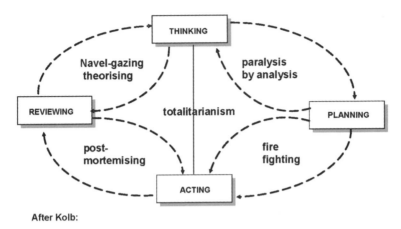

After Kolb:

Figure 7.4 Learning cycle short circuits

4 *Paralysis by analysis.* This is the analyse-plan-analyse some more trap, where the motto is: 'Think before you jump, plan how to do it and think a bit more'. Learning is limited by the fear of getting it wrong or taking a risk.

5 *Totalitarian response.* This is the theorize-do trap, where the motto is: 'Work it out in theory and then impose it on them'.

Action learning groups

Revan's (1982) genius was to recognize that this process of breaking out of limiting learning styles was often most effective when undertaken with peer fellow learners, rather than with so-called experts. Peers more easily generate a climate of experimentation, allowing a spirit of inquiry, support and challenge to facilitate this process.

This discovery led to the development of action learning, which Gaunt and Kendal (1985) define as: 'a method of problem solving for managers, which also offers scope for personal learning and development. The manager prepares for taking action on the job and at the same time learns about him/herself as a manager and as a person'.

Reg Revans, who was the first exponent of action learning as currently understood, first used the technique with Coal Board managers just after the Second World War. Since then, action learning has grown to be recognized as an effective way of enabling managers to develop both professionally and personally. It has been extensively researched, practised and written about in many aspects of adult and management learning by Mike Pedler (1996), David Casey (1993), and Hawkins and Maclean (1991).

Action research

In parallel to the development of action learning we have seen the development of action research, for example Reason and Bradbury in their *Handbook of Action*

Research (2000). In action research there is more emphasis on not just learning for one's own benefit, but also producing learning outcomes for others. This is how our colleague Peter Reason summarizes action research:

> Action research has a long history, going back to social scientists' attempts to help solve practical problems in wartime situations in both Europe and America. Many trace its origins to the work of Kurt Lewin in the 1940's to design social experiments that could take place in natural settings, and who is credited with the phrase 'Nothing is as practical as a good theory'. While many of the original forms of action research espoused participation, power was often held tightly by researchers. More recent developments place emphasis on a full integration of action and reflection and on increased collaboration between all those involved in the inquiry project, so that the knowledge developed in the inquiry process is directly relevant to the issues being studied. Thus action research is conducted *by*, *with* and *for* those engaged in the situation to be studied.
>
> It is important to understand action research as an *orientation to inquiry* rather than as a methodology. A recent text describes action research as '...a participatory, democratic process concerned with developing practical knowing in the pursuit of worthwhile human purposes ... It seeks to bring together action and reflection, theory and practice, in participation with others, in the pursuit of practical solutions to issues of pressing concern to people, and more generally the flourishing of individual persons and their communities'.
>
> (Reason and Bradbury 2000: 1)

Action research practices are articulated in many different ways. One, which we have found helpful, is to consider three interdependent strategies of inquiry. Good action research will strive to stimulate enquiry at each of these levels and to create connections between levels:

- *First-person research practices* address the ability of individual researchers to foster an inquiring approach to their own lives, to act awarely and choicefully and to assess effects in the outside world while acting. First-person inquiry skills for the basis of reflective practice and are essential for those who would provide leadership in any social enterprise.

- *Second-person action research/practices* such as cooperative inquiry address our ability to inquire face to face with others into issues of mutual concern, usually in small groups.

- *Third-person research/practice* includes a range of practices which draw together the views of large groups of people, members of 'whole systems', to create dialogue in a wider community of inquiry involving persons who cannot be known to each other face to face. It can be argued that at this level the research aims to create an informed 'social movement', part of a wider political process.

Unlearning

We contend that as humans get older, development needs to incorporate more and more 'unlearning' as well as learning (Hawkins 1999, 2005). The poet and novelist Ben Okri writes 'It is not what you have experienced that makes you greater, but what you have faced, what you have transcended, what you have unlearned' (Okri 1997: 61).

So what is unlearning? Bo Hedberg (1981) defines this concept in the following way: 'Unlearning is the process through which learners discard knowledge'. But to really understand 'unlearning', we need to turn to the spiritual teachers and traditions, where 'unlearning' has been reflected on and practised for thousands of years. Krishnamurti, the Indian philosopher, spiritual teacher and mentor of David Bohm wrote:

> Can you think of something that is not knowable? You can only think of something that you know. But there is an extraordinary perversion taking place in the world at the present time. We think we shall understand if we have more information, more books, more facts, more printed matter ... Obviously, knowledge and learning are an impediment to the understanding of the new, the timeless, the eternal ... With most of us, knowledge and learning have become an addiction and we think that through knowing we shall become creative.
>
> (Krishnamurti 1954: 154–5)

Hazrat Inayat Khan, the Indian musician and Sufi mystic who brought a form of universalist Sufism to the west in the early twentieth century wrote:

> But how does one unlearn? What one has learnt is in oneself. One can do it by becoming wiser. The more wise one becomes, the more one is able to contradict one's own ideas. The less wisdom one has, the more one holds to one's ideas. In the wisest person there is the willingness to submit to others. And the most foolish person is always ready to stand firm to support his own ideas.
>
> (Khan 1972: 108)

We would argue that unlearning is particularly important when one is attempting to move from one level of functioning to another. In Chapter 2 we describe in detail the Torbert model of leadership maturation. In discussion with Bill Torbert we have explored the difficulty that individuals often have in moving from one level of leadership to another, particularly when they have been extremely successful through utilizing their current style and way of making sense of the world. We propose that movement from one dominant mode of making sense of the world to the next does not happen through intellectually *comprehending* the next level of leadership, but rather through *confounding* one's current level of appreciation. Transitions especially benefit from a process of *unlearning* rather than learning in the traditional way.

At the behavioural level, unlearning can occur through confronting certain behaviours through direct feedback in order to bring them into awareness, or by interrupting repetitive habits to break a pattern.

At the level of belief or mindset, unlearning might happen through a process of enquiry into the assumptions behind the person's statement. This can be done through opening up their 'either-or frames' with which they divide their options (see Chapter 9, mode 2) or by reframing what is stated, opening an unexpected perspective, which in turn opens further ways of responding; we may challenge a contradiction or use other means of bringing 'taken for granted' mindsets into exploration.

At the level of emotional states, unlearning can happen through bringing a frozen cycle of feeling to completion, either through catharsis or action; through bringing a feeling into awareness and acceptance – noticing a feeling opens doors so that it can move through you; by shifting to another emotional rhythm like suddenly laughing at your sadness when you can see your situation differently; or we can sometimes facilitate a move from attachment to resentment to determination to move on. In Chapter 12 we will explore in greater detail how we might go about expanding our range of emotional expression.

At the level of purpose, unlearning involves a process of 'metanoia' – a turning around from one direction to another. Metanoia means a realigning of one's life direction; a moment of conversion or enlightenment, as if coming out of a closed room into a new area of open spaciousness. This happens at the same time as having a sense of compassion for oneself and one's current position.

Applying the principles to basic training

We have designed training for coaches, mentors, consultants and supervisors, which applies these principles and fulfils a set of criteria for valid training programmes. These criteria are that:

1   It recognizes that participants already have a range of natural capacities, learnt competencies and acquired capabilities.

2   The training should be seen as building on, and extending, their current range of skills and capabilities, while making them more aware of their own strengths and development areas.

3   The participants should be learning at least as much from each other as from the trainers.

4   The participants should be learning from working with each other, in three different positions, e.g. coach, client and observer.

5   When in the 'client position', they should bring real issues that are current and unresolved for them.

6   When teaching a framework, the explanation should take the shortest amount of time possible and then participants should have the opportunity to apply the framework to their own realities straight away.

7   Support and encouragement for acquiring new skills and capabilities and developing capacities need to be balanced by challenge and confounding habituated patterns that need to be unlearnt.

To illustrate what this is like in practice here are two short vignettes of typical moments in our training programmes.

Teaching the Heron model

One of the models we regularly teach is John Heron's (1975) model of 'six category interventions' (the model will be explored further in Chapter 12). It maps all possible helping interventions, whether they are used in a one-to-one or a group setting under one of the headings shown in Figure 7.5.

Having introduced the model with illustrations in about ten minutes, the trainer asks each participant to identify their preferred intervention style and go to one of the boards, placed around the room, with the name of that style. Meeting with other participants, who also share that preference, they identify in a few minutes the three advantages of that style, which they agree on as a group.

We then invite the groups to go to the board with the style that they consider the biggest challenge. At this board we ask them to discuss what they would need to learn to become confident and competent in this style of intervening. This links back into their small learning group, where we encourage everybody to experiment with using the less familiar intervention styles.

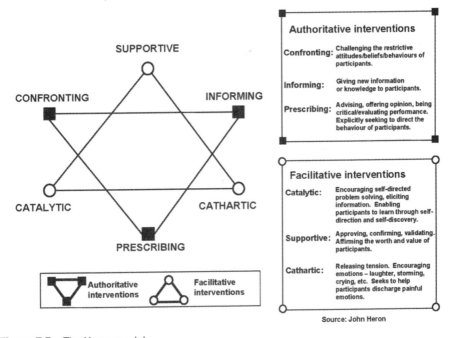

Figure 7.5   The Heron model

In the plenary this exercise is followed by live coaching by one of the tutors in the group using all six methods of intervening. We break the coaching to ask the wider group for suggestions of suitable alternative interventions. Some group members on the sidelines have the opportunity to work out possible next interventions for the coach to then try out.

Practicum groups

We spent many years both facilitating action learning groups and using small groups for people to practise and develop their coaching skills, using each other as clients. Eventually we decided to integrate both these approaches and develop a learning mechanism that would both help participants acquire the essence of systemic transformational coaching (see Chapter 2) and also develop their capacities of 'authority, presence and impact' (API, see Chapter 13). To illustrate this integrated process, we give an account of utilizing practicum groups in training for senior partners in one of the large professional services firms.

The programme was designed so that the majority of the time would be spent in small learning groups of five people, working with one of the experienced facilitators. The group started with sharing their 360-degree feedback – and their own assessment of their strengths and development challenges. We then asked the group what they wanted to experiment with, as well as receive more live feedback about, while in this group. These elements formed the basis for a group contract, and individual learning goals could be formulated within that contract.

The majority of the learning group time over the next two days was devoted to structured rounds of 'transformational coaching' on real situations brought by the participants. We referred to these as 'real play', both to distinguish it from role-play, to which many had an aversion, and also to accentuate the sense of being able to experiment with how people deal with real challenging work situations.

Each of the five group members had a chance to be in each of the following roles: the *consultant/adviser* brings a real, current, challenging case situation; the *coach* aims, in about 45 minutes, to create a shift in how the consultant is thinking, feeling and acting in relation to their case; the *shadow coaches* have responsibility for monitoring some aspect of the coaching process, e.g. the CLEAR model, Heron interventions etc., and help the coach raise their effectiveness in the frequent 'time outs' that are called in the coaching session.

In transformational coaching, the intention is not for the person bringing the issue or case to leave with a new insight or a 'must-do action list'; but rather to have experienced a 'felt shift' in the session, starting to think, feel and act differently about the situation they are concerned with. Our research shows that the chance of learning and change being transferred back into the live situation, is much higher when this felt shift occurs than when people simply leave with good intentions (see Figure 7.6).

In these small groups, we need to work with a systemic understanding of 'parallel process'. By this we mean that the job of the shadow coach is to shift the coach, so they shift how they are relating to the consultant, so the consultant shifts

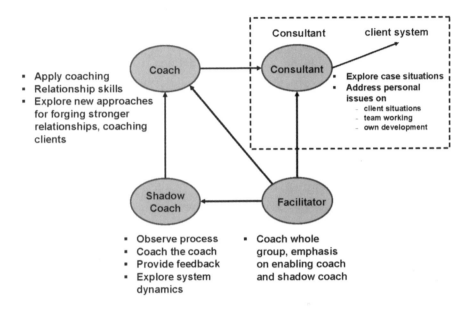

Figure 7.6 Roles in the practicum group

and changes how they are relating to the client, so we can be fairly confident the client system will shift beneficially.

Using a 'systems approach' means that an intervention for change at any point in the system ripples through the whole, generating change on all levels – provided the initial point of intervention has been chosen for maximum effect or minimum resistance to change.

Applying the principles to continuing professional development

Development of a coach, mentor or consultant does not end with either finishing a formal training or even with being accredited by a professional body. Learning is for life and we know that someone in the people professions, who has stopped learning, has stopped doing good quality work. It is when we think we know how to do the work that we start to replace curiosity with repetition, exploration with dogma and appropriate humility with pedantry. In the last 20 years we have seen the enormous growth of what is most often called continuing professional development. This has been fuelled by the rapid changes and developments in all professions, with the consequence that one's initial training is soon out of date. In the people professions professional development has also been driven by the recognition of how important it is to maintain and enhance oneself as the main instrument of one's practice.

A professional concert pianist told us in conversation that for every hour of performance he rehearsed for ten hours. He then asked us what that ratio was in our profession! Rehearsal time was negligible, so that it made for an almost immeasurable percentage of time at work. So in the next section we will explore different approaches to continuing professional development.

Definitions and models of continuing professional development

The mostly widely cited definition of continuing professional development in the literature is that of Tomlinson (1993) who defined it as: 'the systematic maintenance, improvement and broadening of knowledge and skills, and the development of personal qualities necessary for the execution of professional, managerial and technical duties throughout one's working life'. This definition has been adopted by several professional bodies (see Table 7.1 below), and was built on by Madden and Mitchell (1993) who emphasize the contextual nature of continuing professional development and its relation to the interests of a number of stakeholders: 'the maintenance and enhancement of the knowledge, expertise and competence of professionals throughout their careers according to a plan formulated with regard to the needs of the professional, *the employer, the professions and society*'.

Mike Broussine (1998) has done a good deal of work in this area, particularly for the public sector. He produced a table of professional definitions of continuing professional development (see Table 7.1).

Another key writer on continuing professional development is Rapkins (1996) who distinguished between two quite different models of continuing professional development policy and practice. She differentiates them according to their underlying motivation and came up with the *sanctions model* and the *benefits model*. Rapkins noticed that 'old and established' professional bodies (including regulatory bodies) tend to adopt a sanctions model in their continuing professional

Table 7.1   Definitions of continuing professional development by a sample of professional bodies (Broussine 1998)

Body	Definition
CIPFA	A systematic and planned approach to the maintenance, enhancement and development of knowledge, skills and expertise that continues throughout a professional's career and is to the mutual benefit of the individual, the employer, the professional body and society as a whole.
RTPI, RICS, Institution of Electrical Engineers	The systematic maintenance, improvement and broadening of knowledge and skill and the development of personal qualities necessary for the execution of professional and technical duties throughout the practitioner's [an engineer's (IEE)] working life.
The Law Society	CPD enables solicitors to 1) learn new professional and management skills; 2) develop existing areas of expertise and skill; 3) meet the changing demands of clients and society; 4) improve the efficiency and effectiveness of the profession; 5) plan their career development.
CIPD	*CPD is systematic, ongoing, self directed learning.*
Institute of Management	*The process of planned, continuing development of individuals throughout their career.*

development schemes, and use compulsion as one of their ways of getting staff to take up continuing professional development. In contrast 'new and/or developing' bodies (largely non-regulatory) tend to adopt the benefits model, and rely on voluntarism in members' participation.

Characteristics of good practice

Table 7.2   Characteristics of good continuing professional development practice (Rapkins 1996)

Steps	Characteristic
Professional body	• Existence of a continuing professional development coordinator/manager, accessible and knowledgeable • Continuum of education between pre- and post-qualification
Organization of continuing professional development policy	• Clear policy statement • Clear aims for continuing professional development • Planned and systematic approach to continuing professional development emphasized
Form of continuing professional development provision	• Recognition of a wide range of activities • Work-based continuing professional development recognized • Continuing professional development provision available through professional body • Provision accessible to all and inexpensive
Promotion and marketing	• To employers as well as professionals • To potential providers • Emphasis on partnership between professionals, employers, providers and professional body
Monitoring and evaluation	• Where necessary, then by quota • Emphasis on individual professional identifying needs for continuing professional development and evaluating learning activities

The role of supervision in basic training and in continuing professional development

Supervision and supervision skills are at the core of all good training in the people professions. From the very start of training in coaching, mentoring and consultancy, the trainees should be working with each other, in pairs, threes and small learning groups. The trainer needs to utilize supervisory skills to set a learning climate, which is 'more like a sand pit in which we can play, than a law court in which we judge' (Hawkins and Shohet 2006). This means that trainers also need to model giving and receiving feedback, which is clear, owned, balanced and specific, balancing supportive, challenging and developmental aspects (see Chapter 12).

The trainer also needs to utilize and balance the seven supervisory modes (see

Chapter 9), showing how to move the focus from the world of the client, to the coach's interventions, to the coaching relationship, to the coach's own process, as well as utilizing their own process and live relationship with the coach and the other trainees.

As soon as the trainees are ready to start practice with clients rather than their fellow trainees, then, we contend, they need to receive supervision. This could be in one-to-one or in a group setting and it should be provided by an experienced supervisor. The pros and cons of one-to-one versus group supervision are explored in Chapter 10.

In the early part of a trainee's practice the supervision needs to have a good balance of *qualitative, developmental* and *resourcing* aspects, and should be seen as an important forum for learning by both supervisor and supervisee.

A psychoanalyst once said that 'the problem with self-analysis was the counter-transference'. By this he meant that developing our self is fraught with many dangers, because of the illusions, delusions and collusions we have in dealing with ourselves. For this reason we believe that supervision should be a core feature of continuing professional development throughout the lifetime of one's professional practice. The nature of the supervision will need to change to adapt to the changing development needs of the supervisee. We believe that early on in one's career supervision should be provided by an experienced practitioner and trained supervisor. Later in one's career supervision might be on a peer basis, but this requires a level of maturity and rigour of process that is not usually found in the early stages of practitioner development.

A developmental model for supervision

Hogan (1964) wrote one of the early seminal works in this field, when he researched the area of training psychologists as psychotherapists. Many writers have followed since then, most notably Worthington (1987) and Stoltenberg and Delworth (1987). Hawkins and Shohet (2006) integrated the various concepts used in the literature and presented a combined developmental model of a supervisee's development, using four major stages, and here we present a modified version of their summary.

Level I: self-centred
The first stage is characterized by the trainee's dependence on the supervisor. Supervisees can be anxious, insecure about their role and their own ability to fulfil it. They may lack insight, but often they are highly motivated. A study by Hale and Stoltenberg (quoted in Stoltenberg and Delworth 1987) suggests that the two main causes of anxiety of new trainees are firstly, 'evaluation apprehension' and secondly 'objective self-awareness'. Objective self-awareness is a term borrowed from social psychology and is used to suggest that 'the process of being videotaped, audiotaped, or otherwise made to focus on oneself ... can elicit negative evaluations of one's performance and concomitant feelings of anxiety' (Stoltenberg and Delworth 1987: 61).

New trainees have not had the experience to develop grounded criteria on which to assess their performance and consequently can feel very dependent on their supervisor's assessment of their work. This apprehension may be linked to the supervisor having some formal assessment role in their training or in their work evaluation. Anxiety will also be present on a more day-to-day basis, showing in concern about how the supervisor is viewing their work, and how they compare to other supervisees that their supervisor sees.

We have found this concern to be particularly present when we tape sessions, or where trainees are asked to bring 'verbatims' or process accounts of sessions. However, supervision generally must help the supervisees to reflect back on themselves, and for the new trainee this is inevitably anxiety-provoking.

Level I workers tend 'to focus on specific aspects of the client's history, current situation, or personality assessment data to the exclusion of other relevant information. Grand conclusions may be based on rather discrete pieces of information' (Stoltenberg and Delworth 1987: 56).

It is difficult for coaches, mentors and consultants at this stage of development to have an overview of the whole development process as they have usually only worked with clients in the early stages of coaching or mentoring. This may make them impatient or fearful that the process will never move on from a current stuck place.

In order to cope with the normal anxiety of level I trainees, the supervisor needs to provide a clearly structured environment, which includes positive feedback and encouragement to the supervisees to step back from premature judgement of both the client and themselves and attend instead to what actually took place. Balancing support and uncertainty is the major challenge facing supervisors of beginning practitioners (Stoltenberg and Delworth 1987: 64).

Level II: client-centred

Here the supervisees have overcome their initial anxieties and begin to fluctuate between dependence and autonomy – and between overconfidence and being overwhelmed.

Hawkins (1980) described how this stage manifests itself in residential workers in therapeutic communities. In this paper, entitled 'Between Scylla and Charybdis', he shows how the trainee has to be supported by tutors and supervisors to steer a safe course between 'submergence and over-identification' with clients – representing the Charybdis on the one side – and 'flight into over-professionalism' – the Scylla – on the other side.

In their work with clients the level II trainee begins to be less simplistic and single focused both about the development process of the client and their own training: 'The trainee begins to realize, on an emotional level, that becoming a *(coach, mentor or consultant)* is a long and arduous process. The trainee discovers that skills and interventions effective in some situations are less than effective at other times' (Stoltenberg and Delworth 1987: 71, emphasis added).

Loss of the early confidence and simplicity of approach may lead some trainees to be angry with their supervisor, whom they see as responsible for their disillusionment. The supervisor is then seen as 'an incompetent or inadequate figure, who has failed to come through when he or she was so badly needed'

(Loganbill *et al.* 1982: 19). Some writers have likened this stage of development to that of adolescence in normal human development, with level I being similar to childhood, level III being early adulthood and level IV being full maturity.

Certainly level II can feel to the supervisor like parenting an adolescent. There is testing out of one's authority, a fluctuation in moods and a need to provide space for the trainees to learn from mistakes and also to offer a degree of holding and containment. In this stage the trainees can also become more reactive to their clients, who, like the supervisor, may also be felt as the cause of their own turbulence.

The supervisor of level II trainees needs to be less structured and didactic than with level I trainees, but a good deal of emotional support is necessary as the trainees may oscillate between excitement and depressive feelings of not being able to cope, or perhaps even of being in the wrong job.

Level III: process-centred

'The Level III trainee shows increased professional self-confidence, with only conditional dependency on the supervisor. He or she has greater insight and shows more stable motivation. Supervision becomes more collegial, with sharing and exemplification augmented by professional and personal confrontation' (Stoltenberg and Delworth 1987: 20).

The level III trainee is also more able to adjust their approach to clients to meet the individual and specific needs of that client at that particular time. They are also more able to see the client in a wider context and have developed what we call 'helicopter skills'. These are the skills of being fully present with the client in the session, but being able simultaneously to have an overview that encompasses the present content and process, in the context of the:

- total process of the client relationship;
- client's personal history and life patterns;
- client's external life circumstances;
- client's life stage, social context and ethnic background.

It is now less apparent what theoretical orientation the trainee has been schooled in, as they have by this stage incorporated the training into their own personality, rather than using it as a piece of learnt methodology.

Level IV: Process-in-context-centred

This stage is referred to as 'level III integrated' by Stoltenberg and Delworth. By this time the practitioner has reached 'master' level 'characterized by personal autonomy, insightful awareness, personal security, stable motivation and an awareness of the need to confront his or her own personal and professional problems' (Stoltenberg and Delworth 1987: 20).

Often by this stage supervisees have also become supervisors themselves and this can greatly consolidate and deepen their learning. Stoltenberg and Delworth quote a colleague: 'When I'm supervising, I'm forced to be articulate and clear about connections across domains and that makes it easier for me to integrate' (1987: 102).

We often find that we say things to our supervisees that we need to learn. It is as if our mouth is more closely linked to our subconscious knowing than is our mental apparatus! Certainly the stage of level IV is not about acquiring more knowledge, but allowing this to be deepened and integrated until it becomes wisdom; for as another Sufi teacher put it: 'Knowledge without wisdom is like an unlit candle'.

It is possible to compare the developmental stages of supervisees' development to other developmental approaches. We have already mentioned the analogy to the stages of human growth and development. We can also posit an analogy to the stages of development within the medieval craft guilds. Here the trainee started as a *novice*, then became a *journeyman*, then an *independent craftsman*, and finally a *master craftsman*. The model also has parallels in the stages of group development. Schutz (1973) describes how groups begin with the predominant concerns focusing on issues of *inclusion vs. exclusion:* can I fit in and belong here? Once this has been resolved the group will normally move on to issues of *authority* – challenging the leader, dealing with competitiveness etc. Only then will the group move on to look at issues of *affection* and *intimacy* – how to get close to the others and what is the appropriate degree of closeness. This progression of themes seems to be paralleled in the supervision-developmental approach, particularly where supervision is part of a training which is being carried out with other trainees.

Finally the four stages can be characterized by where the centre of focus and concern of the supervisee is located (see Table 7.3).

Table 7.3 Supervisee developmental stages

Level	Focus	Core concern
Level I	Self-centred	'Can I make it in this work?'
Level II	Client-centred	'Can I help this client make it?'
Level III	Process-centred	'How are we relating together?'
Level IV	Process-in-context-centred	'How do processes interconnect?'

Reviewing the developmental approach

The developmental model is a useful tool in helping supervisors to more accurately assess the needs of their supervisees, and to realize that part of the task of supervision is to help in the development of the supervisees, both within stages and between stages of development. The model also stresses that as the supervisees develop so must the nature of the supervision.

However, there are also some limits to the model's usefulness, which must be borne in mind. First, there is a danger of using the model too rigidly as a blueprint for prescribing how every supervisee at each stage should be treated, without enough reference to the particular needs of the individual, the style of the supervisor and the uniqueness of the supervisor-supervisee relationship.

Second, as Hess (1987) points out, supervisors also pass through developmental stages and we must therefore look at the interaction between both parties' developmental stages. This challenge is taken up in part by Stoltenberg and Delworth (1987: 152–67). They suggest a parallel model for supervisors' development as follows:

- *Level 1*. Anxious to do the 'right' thing and to be effective. Overly mechanistic. Attempting to play an expert role.

- *Level 2*. Sees that the process of supervision is more complex and multi-dimensional – a tendency to go on one's own as a supervisor, rather than get support for one's supervision practice.

- *Level 3*. Displays a consistent motivation to the supervisory role and is interested in constantly improving his or her performance. Able to make an honest self-appraisal (see Chapter 11).

- *Level 4*. Can modify their style to work appropriately with supervisees from any level of development, from different disciplines, different orientations and across cultural differences (see Chapter 14). Such supervisors are able to supervise supervision practice and may also teach or tutor supervision training (Stoltenberg and Delworth call this level 3 integrated).

An individual should not embark on giving supervision until they have reached level III or IV in their own practice. They then have to cope with being an advanced practitioner and an early stage supervisor. Stoltenberg and Delworth (1987) suggest that supervisors who have only reached their own developmental levels I and II can only successfully work with practitioners who are at level I in their development. They also need good supervision on their supervision practice.

To reinforce our earlier point, this model should not be applied too rigidly, but it can be a useful map for matching the right supervisee to the right supervisor, or to explore difficulties in the supervision relationship.

Finally, we would do well to remember that we can become egotistic, and over-inflated, in thinking that we are responsible for another person's development. Here is a story that makes this point beautifully. 'A man once saw a butterfly struggling to emerge from its cocoon, too slowly for his taste, so he began to blow on it gently. The warmth of his breath speeded up the process all right. But what emerged was not a butterfly but a creature with mangled wings' (Hawkins and Shohet 2006).

Despite these reservations, we would particularly recommend some acquaintance with this model to all supervisors who work in the context of a training course, be it for coaches, mentors, consultants or supervisors, in order that they may plan what kind of supervision is most appropriate for trainees in different stages of the course.

Conclusion

To understand the role and functions of supervision it is first important to understand the nature and process of professional development in its wider context. In this chapter we have argued that development is most effective when it is built on core principles of adult learning and unlearning that link the development to the current learning needs of the professional, utilizing what they already know and cycling between action, reflection, new thinking and planning.

In this chapter we also argue that 'learning is for life' and we provide an understanding of how both development and supervision need to change throughout one's professional career, from basic training to being an advanced expert practitioner in one's field. When we stop developing ourselves, we stop being effective at developing others; and when we are most alive to our own learning is often when we are of most value to others.

8

Supervision: why, what and how?

Introduction

At the core of continuing professional development is continual personal development, where our own development is weaved through every aspect of our practice, where every client is a teacher, every piece of feedback an opportunity for new learning, and we have practices that support the balanced cycle of action, reflection, new understanding and new practice. We believe that having supervision is a fundamental aspect of continuing personal and professional development for coaches, mentors and consultants, providing a protected and disciplined space in which the coach can reflect on particular client situations and relationships, the reactivity and patterns they invoke for them and by transforming these live in supervision, can profoundly benefit the client.

For some time there has been a debate in most of the coaching and mentoring organizations about the place and importance of supervision. Some have argued for it being essential to all quality practice, while others have seen it as only necessary for those in training or on special occasions. Also, for some time many of the leading writers in the USA and Europe in the field of coaching and mentoring have argued for some form of ongoing supervision or coaching for the coach/mentor.

Mary Beth O'Neill (2000: 207–8) does not use the term 'supervision', but talks of the importance of coaching for the coach. She writes:

> Everyone needs help to stay on track in the powerful interactional fields of organizations ... One of the best ways that coaches can stay effective in their role is to receive coaching themselves ... I used to think that my need for a coach would diminish once I had worked with numerous clients and had many years under my belt. Twenty years, and over a hundred clients later, my effectiveness has dramatically increased, but my desire to use a coach myself has remained high. I no longer see using a coach as a sign of incompetence but a smart investment.

For too long the themes of continuing professional development and in particular the supervision of coaches and mentors have been neglected. James Flaherty (1999: 147), writing in the USA about the area of coaches' continuing development, says: 'I haven't found this aspect of coaching in any other text on the topic, but self-development seems to be a self-evident component of coaching ... psychiatrists, physicians, teachers and lawyers all confer with peers and mentors in difficult cases. Coaches are, it seems to me, no exception to this practice'. Myles Downey (2003: 210), writing in the UK, in his very readable book on *Effective Coaching* says: 'Very few coaches have any supervision, but it is a vital ingredient in effective coaching'.

Supervision is one of the main integrating processes for ongoing personal and professional development of coaches, mentors and organizational consultants. At the 2005 European Mentoring and Coaching Council conference in Zurich, we took a straw poll of the 120 people attending our presentation. Well over 80 per cent thought that supervision was important for all coaches and mentors. However, only two-thirds said they were currently receiving supervision and only half of those said they were receiving supervision that was of a quality that constantly transformed their work with clients. Supervision is widely advocated, but poorly practised.

So what lies behind this lack of effective supervision? In talking to a wide range of coaches and mentors we have been offered a number of different explanations:

- lack of clarity about what supervision involves;
- lack of quality trained supervisors;
- lack of commitment to personal development as it makes us vulnerable;
- lack of discipline among coaches;
- addiction to be in the role of the person enabling others, rather than receiving.

Probably, all of these have some degree of truth and a full answer needs to include these and other factors. In the absence of a body of good theories, trainings and practitioners, many coaches have turned to counsellors, psychologists and psychotherapists for supervision or supervisory models. There is much we can learn from these and others people professions who have been practising quality supervision for longer than coaching. Yet there are also dangers that we outline below.

Becoming a supervisor

Being asked to be a supervisor can be both exhilarating and daunting. Without training or support the task can be overwhelming. It is not simply the same as coaching another coach.

This chapter and the others in this section will provide you with some core frameworks for carrying out supervision, but also for reviewing and evaluating your supervisory work and for receiving quality feedback on your sessions. We believe the first requirement for being a good supervisor is receiving good-quality supervision yourself, and hopefully these chapters will help you evaluate the supervision you are receiving as well as that which you give.

Why be a supervisor?

There are many reasons why you might, in the future, become or might have already become a supervisor. For some it is the natural progression that comes with promotion. Some coaches or consultants discover that they have become, over time, one of the most senior practitioners in their area, and supervisees start coming to them. For some the role of supervisor does fit more easily than for others. They find themselves at home in a role that requires both personal development and educational skills.

Some people are able to arrange their work so that they can mix some direct work with clients, with being a supervisor of others. We would recommend that wherever possible those who supervise or teach should still be practising whatever they teach or supervise. It is all too easy to get out of touch with the realities of being at the 'coal face' and to wonder why your supervisees are making such heavy weather of what seems perfectly straightforward from your perspective as supervisor. The mix of work can have advantages in both directions. Many new supervisors in several professions have remarked to us how having to supervise others helped them revitalize their own work with clients and started them thinking afresh about their own practice.

Many people become and stay supervisors through being attracted to the challenge and scope of the role. Here is an account from a colleague that is quoted in Hawkins and Shohet (2006):

> I feel most challenged and excited in supervision by the tension between the loving relationship and holding my own authority. Supervision is the place in my work where I can be at my most free ranging – playful, free to think aloud, able to comment on the process, challenge, take a journey into the unknown. Then there is the opposite side when I really have to hold the boundaries, own my own authority and risk the good relationship for the sake of the truth. Each time this has happened, I have found it risky, self-challenging, lonely for a

while, but also very mind-clearing and transformational and ultimately very strengthening to both ourselves and the relationship.

Being a supervisor provides an opportunity to develop one's educative skills in helping other practitioners to learn and develop within their work. As a new supervisor you are impelled to stop, reflect upon and articulate the ways you have worked as a practitioner, many of which you may have begun to take for granted. The challenge is then to use your own experience to help supervisees develop their own style of working and their own solutions to difficult work situations.

Another reason for becoming a supervisor, which is often denied, is a motivation to become 'one up' on your colleagues. Many of us will remember the joy when we entered our second year at a school – we were no longer the youngest or most gullible, there were now others we could tell 'what is what' to. New supervisors can be eager to mask their own anxieties by using their supervisees to bolster up their own pseudo-role of expert – the one who has all the answers.

Finally, another hidden motive in giving supervision can be when people who do not know how to get decent supervision for themselves can compensate by giving to others the sort of supervision they need and want for themselves, in the vain hope that this will magically lead to someone offering it to them!

Getting started

The first prerequisite for being a good supervisor is being able to actively arrange good supervision for yourself. A useful question to ask yourself is: 'Am I currently receiving adequate supervision, both for the work I am doing and for being a supervisor?'

Before you give your first supervision sessions, we think it is useful for you to sit down and reflect on your own overt and covert motives that you bring to supervision. This is not in order to suppress the more shameful motives but to find some appropriate way to meet the needs the motives represent.

It would also be worthwhile to sit down and write out examples of positive and negative supervision experiences you yourself have received. What are your positive role models and what sort of supervisory experiences would you want to avoid repeating for your own supervisees?

Your expectations may well set the tone for what happens in the supervision sessions you give. If you go into supervision expecting the sessions to be full of conflict or to be problematic they may well end up that way. If you go in expecting them to be interesting, engaging and cooperative, it is likely you will produce the necessary climate for that to happen.

Qualities needed to be a good supervisor

In later chapters we will describe the core competencies, capabilities and capacities that pertain to all coaches, mentors, consultants and supervisors. Here we wish only to draw out some of the particular qualities that pertain particularly to supervisors. Gilbert and Evans (2000) provide a very useful list of supervisor qualities based partly on the work of Leddick and Dye (1987) and further developed by Hawkins and Shohet (2006):

1   *Flexibility* in moving between theoretical concepts and use of a wide variety of interventions and methods.
2   *A multi-perspective view*: being able to see the same situation from a variety of angles.
3   *A working map* of the discipline in which they supervise.
4   *The ability to work transculturally* (see Chapter 15).
5   *The capacity to manage and contain anxiety*, their own and that of the supervisee.
6   *Openness to learning* from supervisees and from new situations that emerge.
7   *Sensitivity to the wider contextual issues* that impact on both the client work and supervisory process.
8   *Schooled in anti-oppressive practice* and can handle power appropriately.
9   *Humour, humility and patience.*

You will notice that most of these qualities and skills are ones you will already have or have developed in order to be a competent practitioner as a coach, mentor or consultant. Good coaching skills are a prerequisite for being a competent supervisor.

Brigid Proctor (1988a) makes this point well when she says:

> The task of the supervisor is to help him (the supervisee) feel received, valued, understood on the assumption that only then will he feel safe enough and open enough to review and challenge himself, as well as to value himself and his own abilities. Without this atmosphere, too, he is unlikely to be open to critical feed-back or to pay good attention to managerial instructions. It will also be the case that a worker often comes to supervision stressed, anxious, angry, afraid. It is our assumption that only if he feels safe enough to talk about these uncomfortable feelings, and fully acknowledge then for himself will he be 'cleared' to re-evaluate his practice.

As a supervisor you may recognize how relevant to this new task is the wealth of experience you have had as a practitioner. Some new supervisors need to be helped to adapt these useful skills to the new context; others hold onto their coaching skills too tenaciously and, as mentioned earlier, turn their supervisees into quasi-clients.

To start supervising, you will first find it important to understand the boundaries of supervision and be able to make clear, and mutually negotiated, contracts. Second, you need to develop your framework for supervising, which is appropriate to the setting in which you work. This framework needs to be clear enough to be explainable to your supervisees, but also flexible enough to be adapted to meet the changing needs of different supervisees, at different levels and with a variety of situations.

The most difficult new skill that supervision requires is what we call the 'helicopter ability'. This is the ability to switch focus between the following areas:

- the client that the supervisees are describing;
- the supervisees and their process;
- your own process and the here and now relationship with the supervisees;
- the client within their wider context and to help the supervisees do likewise;
- the wider context of the organization and inter-organizational issues.

This skill cannot be learnt before you start and indeed takes many years to develop. What is important is to know of the existence of all the possible levels and perspectives and then gradually to expand your focus within the sessions (see Chapter 9). However, do not try and get all the possible perspectives into every session, or your supervisees will get indigestion.

What is supervision?

Our definition of supervision is: 'The process by which a coach/mentor/consultant with the help of a supervisor, who is not working directly with the client, can attend to understanding better both the client system and themselves as part of the client-coach/mentor system, and transform their work'.

This has similarities and differences with other definitions that have recently been produced in the field, such as: 'Supervision sessions are a place for the coach to reflect on the work they are undertaking, with another more experienced coach. It has the dual purpose of supporting the continued learning and development of the coach, as well as giving a degree of protection to the person being coached' (Peter Bluckert, personal communication).

Or 'Coaching supervision is a formal process of professional support, which ensures continuing development of the coach and effectiveness of his/her coaching practice through interactive reflection, interpretative evaluation and the sharing of expertise' (Bachkirova et al. 2005).

Our own definition emphasizes both the multiple functions of supervision, as well as stressing the transformational aspects of the work (see Chapter 2). It also draws upon the earlier work we have done in supervision in the other helping professions (Hawkins and Shohet 2006). Supervision has been developed for much longer in the fields of psychology, psychotherapy, social work and counselling than in the fields of coaching, mentoring and consultancy, so it is from these fields that many of the definitions are drawn; although it is important that they are reforged in the context of business and organizational worlds.

Hess (1980), a psychologist, defines supervision as: 'A quintessential interpersonal interaction with the general goal that one person, the supervisor, meets with another, the supervisee, in an effort to make the latter more effective in helping people'. This is similar to the other most commonly-used definitions of supervision by Loganbill et al. (1982): 'An intensive, interpersonally focused, one-to-one relationship in which one person is designated to facilitate the development of competence in the other person'. The British Association of Counselling state that: 'The primary purpose of supervision is to protect the best interests of the client'.

But this is only the beginning of the story, because the task of supervision is not only to develop the skills, understanding and ability of the supervisee. Depending on the setting, it may have other functions. Combining the multiple functions is at the heart of good practice.

Similarities and differences in counselling and psychotherapy supervision

Whether we call the process supervision, or coaching on one's coaching, the need to have another attend to one's practice is increasingly being recognized as essential. The practice of supervision is quite new in the field of coaching and mentoring and so practitioners have often fallen back on using the models and approaches developed in the field of counselling supervision, or indeed going to counselling or psychotherapy supervisors for their supervision. It is important to remember that supervision in counselling and psychotherapy was only developed in the 1980s and when we and others in this field were developing our theories and methods we drew upon the fields of counselling psychology and social work, which had developed their approaches in the 1970s (see Hawkins and Shohet 2006).

There is much each of the helping professions can learn from the others, but it is also important to recognize the difference between the fundamental work of each professional group, and hence the dangers of over-applying the theories and models of one group to the work of another. One of the dangers of a coach going for supervision with a counsellor, or counselling psychologist, is that the supervisor's professional focus will naturally tend towards understanding the psychology of the client. Depending on their orientation, the supervisor might also focus on the relationship of coach and coachee and may have a tendency to focus more on pathology than on health! The biggest danger is when a fundamental orientation that is more interested in individuals than organizations tips over into an unrecognized tendency to see individuals as victims of 'bad' or 'unfeeling' organizations. At worst, we have worked with coaches who have slid into a classic drama triangle of 'organization as persecutor; coachee as victim and coach as rescuer' (Hawkins and Shohet 1989).

Supervisor roles

As a supervisor you have to encompass many functions in your role:

- a coach giving support;
- an educator helping your supervisees learn and develop;
- a manager with responsibilities;
- a manager or consultant with responsibilities to the organization paying for the supervision.

Several writers have looked at the complexity of roles that this provides for the supervisor (Bernard 1979; Hess 1980; Hawkins 1982; Holloway 1984, 1995; Ellis and Dell 1986; Carroll 1996; Hawkins and Shohet 2006). Among the sub-roles most often noted are:

- teacher;
- monitor evaluator;
- counsellor;
- coach;
- colleague;
- boss;
- expert technician;
- manager of administrative relationships.

Archetypes of helping relationships

In our training course on supervision we involve all the trainee supervisors in looking at the variety of helping relationships that they have experienced in their lives and the expectations and transactions that these roles involve. We ask them to brainstorm types of people they have gone to for help in their lives, what needs they take to these people and what they expect to receive. We end up with a list that typically looks like Table 8.1.

Table 8.1 Helping roles

Helping role	What you take to them	What you expect to receive
Doctor	Symptoms	Diagnosis, cure
Priest	Sins, confessions	Penitence, forgiveness
Teacher	Ignorance, questions	Knowledge, answers
Solicitor	Injustice	Advocacy
Judge	Crimes	Retribution
Coach	Poor performance	Improved performance
Friend	Yourself	Acceptance, listening ear
Mother	Hurts	Comfort
Car mechanic	Mechanical failure	Technical correction and servicing

When the roles are not clearly contracted for and defined in supervision, and to a lesser extent even when they are, supervisors and supervisees will fall back on other patterns of relating, which may be one of the typical transactions mentioned above. It is possible to have *crossed* or *collusive* or named transactions.

A collusive transaction happens when you go to your supervisor expecting a reassuring mum and your supervisor obligingly plays out that role by constantly telling you that everything is fine. Such a collusive transaction may feel good to both parties at the time, but would be unproductive as it would be feeding the neurotic needs of both parties rather than the needs of the supervision.

If, on the other hand, you went expecting a reassuring mum and your supervisor played judge, you would have a crossed transaction. In the latter case you would probably feel misunderstood and put down and that your supervisor was very unsupportive.

A named transaction is when one or other of the parties names the patterns and the games that are being played, so they become a choice rather than a compulsive process.

The supervisor has to be able to combine the roles of educator, supporter and at times manager, in an appropriate blend. As Hawthorne (1975) notes: 'It requires effort and experience to integrate these into a comfortable and effective identity'.

Taking appropriate authority and power

Much of the conflict around the role of the supervisor emerges from the difficulty that many supervisors have in finding an appropriate way of taking authority and handling the power inherent in the role. Lillian Hawthorne (1975) has written about this difficult and yet crucial task:

> Many supervisors, especially new ones, have difficulty adjusting to their new authority. The balance which they have worked out for their personal lives between dominance and submission is upset by the new responsibility. The supervisory relationship is complex, intense and intimate ... Sometimes the effort [to take on authority] is hampered by the supervisor's unfamiliarity with the requirements of his role, by difficulties stemming from personal experiences with authority, or by discomfort in the one-to-one relationship.

Hawthorne goes on to describe the sort of games supervisors play, either to abdicate power or to manipulate it. These draw on the work of Eric Berne and other writers in transactional analysis approaches to counselling and psychotherapy. Abdication games include:

- *'They won't let me':* I would like to agree to what you are asking, but senior management won't let me.
- *'Poor me':* 'I'm sorry about having to cancel our weekly conferences, but you have no idea how busy I am with these monthly lists for the director.'
- *'I'm really a nice guy':* Look at how helpful and pleasant I am being to you.
- *'One good question deserves another':* How would you answer that question?

Manipulation of power games include:

- *'Remember who is boss.'* Artificially asserting the power of one's role.

- *'I'll tell on you.'* Threatening to pass on information about the supervisee to more senior management.
- *'Father or mother knows best.'* Acting in a parental or patronizing manner.
- *'I am only trying to help you.'* Defending against criticism from the supervisee by pleading altruism.
- *'If you knew Dostoievsky like I know Dostoievsky.'* Showing off your knowledge to make the supervisee feel inferior.

In Chapter 15, on transcultural supervision, we explore the interplay between personal power, cultural power and role power. With the role of supervisor comes the responsibility to be aware of your own power in each of these three areas and to learn ways of utilizing this power in ways that are appropriate, well intentioned, anti-oppressive and sensitive to the particular background of the supervisee.

The functions of supervision

Kadushin (1976), writing about social work supervision, describes three main functions or roles, which he terms as *educative, supportive* and *managerial*. Proctor (1988b) makes a similar distinction in describing the main processes in the supervision of counselling, for which she uses the terms *formative, restorative* and *normative*.

Having worked with these two models for many years we have found both to be rather coloured by their own professional orientation, Kadushin's in social work and Proctor's in counselling. So we have developed our own model that defines the three main functions as *developmental, resourcing* and *qualitative*. Also Kadushin focuses on the role of the supervisor, Proctor on the supervisee benefit and our new distinctions on the process and relationship that both supervisor and supervisee are engaged in. We show the three together in Table 8.2.

Table 8.2 The functions of supervision

Hawkins	Proctor	Kadushin
Developmental	Formative	Educational
Resourcing	Restorative	Supportive
Qualitative	Normative	Managerial

The *developmental* function is about developing the skills, understanding and capacities of the supervisees. This is done through the reflection on and exploration of the supervisees' work with their clients. In this exploration, they may be helped by the supervisor to:

- understand the client better;
- become more aware of their own reactions and responses to the client;

- understand the dynamics of how they and their client were interacting;
- look at how they intervened and the consequences of their interventions;
- explore other ways of working with this and other similar client situations.

Supervision may also have a mentoring aspect where the supervisee takes time to consider their ongoing learning and development and how this fits in with their career aspirations.

The *resourcing* function is a way of responding to how any workers who are engaged in the intensity of work with clients are necessarily allowing themselves to be affected by the emotions of the client and how they need time to become aware of how this has affected them and to deal with any reactions. This is essential if practitioners are not to become reactive to emotions. These emotions may have been produced through empathy with the client or restimulated by the client, or be a reaction to the client. Not attending to these emotions soon leads to less than effective practitioners, who become either over-identified with their clients or defended against being further affected by them.

The *qualitative* function provides quality control in work with people. It is not only lack of training or experience that necessitates the need in us, as professionals, to have someone look with us at our work, but our inevitable human failings, blind spots, areas of vulnerability from our own wounds and our own prejudices. In many settings the supervisor may carry some responsibility for the work with the clients and how the supervisee is working with them. Supervisors may carry the responsibility to ensure that the standards of the agency or organizations in which the work is being done are upheld. Nearly all supervisors, even when they are not line managers, have some responsibility to ensure that the work of their supervisee is appropriate and falls within defined ethical standards (see Chapter 14).

In our work training supervisors, we have elaborated the supervisory functions by listing what we see as the primary foci of coaching, mentoring and organizational consultancy supervision, and relating these to the three categories (see Table 8.3).

Table 8.3   Primary foci of supervision

Main categories of focus	Function category
• To provide a regular space for the supervisees to reflect upon the *content and process* of their work	Developmental
• To develop understanding and skills within the work	Developmental
• To receive information and another perspective concerning one's work	Developmental/resourcing
• To receive both content and process feedback	Developmental/resourcing
• To be validated and supported both as a person and as a professional	Resourcing

• To ensure that as a person and as a professional one is not left unnecessarily carrying difficulties, problems and projections alone	Resourcing
• To have space to explore and express personal distress, restimulation, unaware evocation of behaviour patterns that may be brought up by the work	Qualitative/resourcing
• To plan and utilize their *personal and professional resources* better	Qualitative/resourcing
• To be proactive rather than reactive	Qualitative/resourcing
• To ensure quality of work	Qualitative

Thus supervision has developmental, resourcing and qualitative components, although in different settings some aspects will be more prominent than others and also the differing aspects are not totally separate but are combined in much of the supervisory focus. We have described elsewhere (Hawkins 1982) our own model that illustrates how these three areas are both distinct but also greatly overlap. A good deal of supervision takes place in the areas where developmental, resourcing and qualitative elements all intermingle.

The stages in the supervision process

The earliest model we developed for supervision in the 1980s was our five-stage coaching model CLEAR (see Chapter 2) to the stages of supervision.

In this model the supervisor starts by *contracting* with the supervisee on both the boundaries and focus of the work. Then the supervisor *listens* to the issues that the coach wishes to bring, listening not only to the content, but also to the feelings and the ways of framing the story that the coach is using. Before moving on, it is important that the supervisor lets the coach know that they have not only heard the story, but have got what it feels like to be in their situation. Only then is it useful to move on to the next stage to *explore* with the coach what is happening in the dynamics of both the coaching relationship and also in the live supervisory relationship, before facilitating the coach to explore new *action*. Finally *review* the process and what has been agreed about next steps. Much of the work of these stages is similar to that carried out in the coaching process but there are significant differences in the process of contracting.

Contracting for supervision

All forms of supervision relationship need to begin with a clear contract, which is created and formed by both parties, and also reflects the expectations of the organizations and professions involved.

Principal areas to explore

We propose that in contracting for supervision there are five key areas that should be covered:

1   Practicalities.
2   Boundaries.
3   Working alliance.
4   The session format.
5   The organizational and professional context.

Practicalities

In forming the contract it is necessary to be clear about the practical arrangements such as the times, frequency, place, what might be allowed to interrupt or postpone the session, and clarification of any payment that is involved etc.

Boundaries

A boundary that often worries both coachees and new coaches is that between supervision and counselling or therapy. The basic boundary in this area is that supervision should always start from exploring issues from work and should end with looking at where the coachee goes next with the work that has been explored. Personal material should only come into the session if it is directly affecting, or being affected by, the work discussed; or if it is affecting the coaching or supervision relationships. If such an exploration uncovers more material than can be appropriately dealt with in the supervision, the supervisor may suggest that the supervisee might want to get counselling or other forms of support in exploring these personal issues.

A supervision contract should also include clear boundaries concerning confidentiality. Confidentiality is an old chestnut, which brings concern to many new coaches and new supervisors. So many supervisors fall into the trap of saying or implying to the supervisee that everything that is shared in the supervision is confidential, only to find that some unexpected situation arises where they find it is necessary to share material from the supervision beyond the boundaries of the session. Thus, in contracting the appropriate confidentiality boundary for any form of supervision, it is inappropriate either to say everything is confidential that is shared here, or to say nothing here is confidential. The supervisor should rather be clear about what sort of information they might need to take over the boundary of the relationship; in what circumstances; how they would do this; and to whom they would take the information. Clearly every possible situation cannot be anticipated, but such a general exploration can diminish the possibility of what may be experienced as sudden betrayal.

We also give our supervisees the undertaking that we will treat everything they share with us in a professional manner and not gossip about their situation.

Working alliance

Forming the working alliance starts from sharing of mutual expectations. What sort of style of supervision the supervisee most wants, and on which of the possible foci do they wish the supervision to concentrate. The supervisor also needs to state clearly what their preferred mode of supervision is, and any expectations they have of the supervisee. We find it useful at the contracting phase to not only share conscious expectations but also hopes and fears. It can be useful to complete sentences such as: 'My image of successful supervision is ...'; 'What I fear happening in supervision is ...'.

A good working alliance is not built on a list of agreements or rules, but on growing trust, respect and goodwill between both parties. The contract provides a holding frame in which the relationship can develop, and any lapses in fulfilling the contract need to be seen as opportunities for reflection, learning and relationship-building, not judgement and defence.

The session format

As well as sharing hopes, fears and expectations, it is useful to ground the discussions in an exploration of what a typical session format might be like. Will all the time be spent on one situation? Do they expect the supervisee to bring written-up notes?

The organizational and professional context

In most supervision situations there are other critical stakeholders in the supervision contract besides the direct parties. There are the expectations of the organization, or organizations, in which the work is being carried out. The organization may have its own explicit supervision policy where the organizational expectations of supervision are clarified. Where a clear policy does not exist, it is still essential that the implicit expectations of the organizations are discussed. This could include articulating the degree of responsibility the organization might expect the supervisor to take, in ensuring good-quality work and what report they require on the supervision. Likewise it is important to clarify the professional and ethical codes of conduct to which both supervisor and supervisee may subscribe to.

Most professional associations have codes of conduct and statements of ethics, which stipulate the boundaries of appropriate behaviour between a worker and a client and also provide the right of appeal for the client against any possible inappropriate behaviour by the worker. Many professions are not as clear about their code of practice for supervision. We do not want to prescribe what we think are appropriate ethical standards for supervision, because this must invariably vary from one setting to another. However, we do consider it imperative that all new supervisors check whether there are ethics statements covering supervision within their profession and/or organization. If no such statement exists, we suggest that you review the ethical standards for work with clients and become clear within yourself which of them you feel apply to the supervision context. It is important that all supervisors are clear about the ethical boundaries of their supervision practice and are able to articulate these to their supervisees (see Chapter 14).

We will explore the skills of contracting more fully in Chapter 12.

Conclusion

To be a supervisor is both a complex and enriching task. It is deceptively similar to, and uses the same sort of skills as, one's coaching, mentoring and consulting work with clients, but the supervisor must be clear about how it is different in content, focus and boundaries. Furthermore, the work of the supervisor entails a more complex ethical sensitivity.

Our hope is that this chapter and the one preceding it will have provided readers with the tools to choose and/or clarify:

- the supervision framework they wish to use;
- how it is part of the bigger picture of professional development;
- how they will amend their basic framework depending on the work, the needs and developmental stage of the supervisees;
- how to use the CLEAR model for the stages of the supervision process;
- how they will balance the competing demands of the qualitative, developmental and resourcing functions of supervision;
- what sort of supervision contract they will negotiate, and what issues it will include.

However, the map is not the territory. Before setting off on an expedition into new terrain, you need to ensure that the map is as good as you can get, but once you have embarked on the journey you do not want to spend the whole time buried in your map. You only need the map to send you in the right direction, or to redirect you when you get lost and also to make periodic checks that you are all going in the right direction.

Finally, it is important that the map you develop is accessible to and understandable by your supervisees. Supervision is a joint journey and works best where there is a shared model and framework. Supervision is also a place where both parties are constantly learning and to stay a good supervisor is to return regularly to question, not only the work of the supervisees, but also what you yourself do as supervisor and how you do it. In the next chapter we will provide a more detailed map of the supervision process and the wide range of possible places a supervisor can focus and intervene.

9

The seven-eyed process model of supervision

Introduction

The double-matrix or 'seven-eyed supervisor model'

Integrating the processes

Linking the model to a developmental perspective

Conclusion

Introduction

Having presented, in the previous chapter, some of the maps and models of supervision that are currently available, we now turn to our own model of the supervision process. Our 'double-matrix' model, which we first presented in 1985 (Hawkins 1985), differs significantly from other ways of looking at supervision. In this model we change focus away from the context and the wider organizational issues to look more closely at the process of the supervisory relationship. This model has since been referred to as the 'seven-eyed model of supervision' (Inskipp and Proctor 1995), a name we have since adopted.

The model was originally developed for those who supervise counsellors or psychotherapists, but over the last 20 years we have found it a useful model for all those supervising right across the range of people professions – from teachers to executive coaches, from general practitioners to management consultants. We have now developed the model and changed some of the terminology to make it more readily available to supervising coaches, mentors and organizational consultants.

The double-matrix or 'seven-eyed supervisor model'

Our interest in the complexities of the supervision process began when we were trying to understand the significant differences in the way each member of our own peer group supervised – and the different styles of supervision that we had encountered elsewhere. These differences could not be explained by our developmental stage as a supervisor, our primary tasks or our intervention styles. From further exploration came the realization that the differences were connected to the constant choices about where to focus that we make as supervisors.

At any time in supervision there are many levels operating. At a minimum all supervision situations involve at least four elements:

- a supervisor;
- a supervisee;
- a client;
- a work context.

Of these four, normally only the supervisor and the supervisee are directly present in the supervision session, except in live supervision. However, the client and the context of the work can be equally alive in this interaction, both in what the supervisee talks about, as well as the ways in which he or she unconsciously reproduces issues from coaching in the supervision.

Thus the supervision process involves two interlocking systems or matrices:

- the client–supervisee matrix;
- the supervisee–supervisor matrix.

The task of the supervisory matrix is to pay attention to the supervisee/client matrix, and it is in how this attention is given that supervisory styles differ.

Our model divides supervision styles into two main categories:

- supervision that pays attention directly to the supervisee/client matrix, by reflecting on the reports, written notes or tape recordings of the client sessions;
- supervision that pays attention to the supervisee/client matrix through how that system is reflected in the here-and-now experiences of the supervision process.

Each of these two major styles of managing the supervision process can be further subdivided into three categories, depending on the emphasis accorded the specific focus of attention. This gives us six modes of supervision, plus a seventh mode that focuses on the wider context in which supervision and the client work happens (see Figure 9.1).

Before we go into detail as to the way in which a supervisor would focus on each of the seven modes (the type of questions to ask, the focus and concerns expressed in them) we need to mention that this model frames a view of the supervision task that involves 'helicoptering' in and out of focus in all these areas. We found over the years that the sequence in which these modes might be accessed does not obviously correspond to the number sequence. Because we all naturally focus on a few of these modes, the seven-eyed model is essential in keeping us aware of the other views and possibilities for exploring the situation in the round.

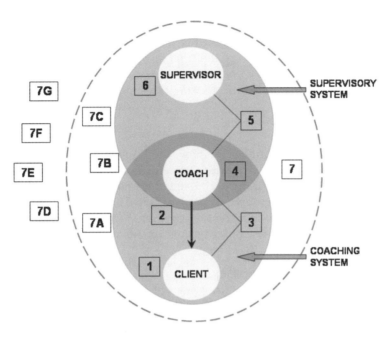

Figure 9.1   Seven modes of supervision

Let us first take a quick overview of all seven modes to sharpen our perception of the ground a supervisor needs to hold in awareness.

Focus on the client and what and how they present

In this first mode, attention is concentrated on the actual phenomena of the client session: how the clients presented themselves, what they chose to share, which area of their life they wanted to explore, and how this session's content might relate to content from previous sessions. The aim and goal of this mode of supervision is to help the supervisee pay attention to details about the client and their life, and the specific ways in which they are enacted in the coaching session.

Exploration of the strategies and interventions used by the supervisee

The focus here is on the choices of intervention made by the supervisee; not only what interventions were used but also when and why they were used. Alternative strategies and interventions might then be developed and their consequences anticipated. The main goal of this form of supervision would be to increase the supervisee's choices and skills in intervention.

Exploration of the relationship between the client and the supervisee

Here the supervisor will pay particular attention to what is happening consciously and unconsciously in the relationship between the supervisee and their client. This will include: how the session started and finished; what happened around the edges of the sessions; metaphors and images that emerged; and changes in voice and posture of both parties. The main goal of this form of supervision will be to help the supervisee step out of their own perspective and develop a greater insight and understanding of the dynamics of the working relationship with a particular client.

Focus on the supervisee

Here the supervisor concentrates on how the supervisee is consciously and unconsciously affected by the work with their clients and where they appear to be affected but unaware of that influence. It includes focusing on the supervisee's development and how they resource themselves (see Chapter 8). The main goal of this mode of supervision is to increase the supervisee's capacity for engaging with their clients and to use their responses to their clients more effectively.

Focus on the supervisory relationship

Here the supervisor focuses on the relationship between supervisor and supervisee as it is enacted in the supervision session. This is essential in two ways. Firstly, we need to ensure that there is regular attention given to the quality of the working alliance between the two parties. Secondly, we need to be alert to the ways in which the relationship between client and supervisee might get played out in supervision – the phenomenon of 'parallel process'.

Let us give an example of 'parallel process' here. Regularly in our coaching, mentoring or consultancy work, where we find ourselves temporarily embroiled in the dynamics of the client relationship we 'dance their dance', which means we get affected by and respond like the rest of the system – and are not necessarily aware of how or why that is happening. When we are not fully aware of what is taking place, we often unknowingly replicate the dance in supervision. It is the role of the supervisor to recognize the moment when the relationship in the room changes from the usual dynamics. For instance if the supervisee, John, started to explore his work with Jane, the chief executive of a major professional service firm, and in discussion becomes more tentative than usual, but still talks as though he is confident and in control, we might explore whether this pattern is in fact a parallel process with the work being done with his client or whether there is something else going on in the here and now solely concerned with the present moment. The beauty and goal of this mode is to enable the supervisee to surface coach/client dynamics of which they were previously unaware.

The supervisor focusing on their own process

Here the supervisor primarily pays attention to their own current experience in the supervision session: what feelings, thoughts and images are emerging for them in working with this supervisee and in response to the material that is shared about the work. The supervisor uses their own internal responses to provide another source of information about what might be happening in the supervisory, or in the client, relationship. The material and dynamics which the supervisee was not aware of in the client session may emerge in the thoughts, feelings and images experienced by the supervisor.

Focus on the wider contexts in which the work happens

Although the six foci are comprehensive in so far as they include all the processes within both the client and supervisory matrices, the supervisory and client relationships also exist within a wider context, which impinge upon and colour the present processes. The supervisor cannot afford to act as if the client-supervisee-supervisor threesome exists on an island without a defining context. There are professional codes and ethics, organizational requirements and constrictions, relationships with other involved organizations as well as social, cultural, political and economic worlds of influence. All of these need to be attended to and taken into consideration. We will develop what this seventh mode of exploration would look like later in the chapter.

It would be very unusual to find a supervisor who remained entirely in one of these seven modes of supervision and we would hold that good supervision must inevitably involve a movement between modes. However, distinguishing between the modes in their pure form is very fruitful. It allows supervisors to clarify their own style, its strengths and weaknesses – and which possible modes of supervision they might be avoiding out of habit or lack of familiarity and practice.

Not only does our model provide a way of increasing the options for the supervisor, it can also be used by the supervisee as a map within which to negotiate changes in supervision style and is a suitable tool in a regular two-way review and appraisal of the supervision.

The model is also beneficial in training supervisors to work with various elements of the supervision process. By learning the refinements of each focus separately, they can develop their own style and method of putting the different processes together. We liken this to musicians continuing to play scales each day to be able to perform concert pieces. Like them, when faced with a complex situation, going back to first principles, such as scales, often provides a way through the complexity of the piece in hand.

We will now look at each of the processes in more detail.

Mode 1

'It is the task of the supervisor to enable the supervisee to become more aware of what actually takes place in the session' (Shainberg 1983). A supervisor focusing upon what actually happened in the client session may sound deceptively easy, but there is one particularly difficult capacity that needs to come into play. To offer supervision in a way that allows the full richness of these observations to be understood and reflected upon requires me not to rush to solutions. In order not to rush to solutions, I have to feel comfortable with 'not knowing' – not knowing both what the significance of the data will be and not knowing what to do with them. Wilfred Bion (1973) in his writing on group process, constantly entreats us to stay empty and unknowing, uncluttered by premature judgement, theory and interpretation. He makes the rather startling comment that in every supervision session 'there ought to be two rather frightened people'. What he is driving at is that certainty, or the too quick imposition of 'understanding' and 'answers', is a way of managing our anxiety and is neither in service of the supervisee or the project. Being 'naked before the data' is scary – but allows for a rich vein of information to be accessed by which we can learn how to take the next steps. We know we are able to remain 'naked before the data' when the supervisee is able to describe what is going on in accurate, concrete and complete detail.

So often the first task in a supervisory exploration is to ask the supervisee to be specific in describing their clients: how they came to be having sessions; their physical appearance; how they move and hold themselves; how they breathe, speak, look, gesture etc.; their language, metaphors and images and the story of their life as they told it. It is almost impossible to do quality supervision on a particular client until the client has – metaphorically speaking – 'fully entered the room'.

The task requires the clear focus of a portrait painter or Zen archer, and the supervisor's job is to help the supervisee stay with this difficult task. In order to create this clear focus, we have to disrupt, in ourselves and our supervisee, the slide into interpretation and generating premature solutions. When the supervisee makes assumptions such as 'she was sad . . .' or 'he was angry about . . .', we need to ask them to return to what they actually saw or what the client specifically said, rather than let them develop these interpretations. Not only are we on the lookout for the slide away from the raw data, but also for the supervisee's internal 'editor' which, behind the scenes deletes certain data from our consideration. If a supervisee holds a belief that the expression of emotions is not significant, but actions are what really matter, they would tend not to report the physical expressions that accompanied significant activity because that material would not, from the supervisee's point of view, be worth mentioning. The supervisor therefore needs to be alert to what is not being said, or what is being edited out of the frame – as well as keeping the focus on what actually happens.

Of course, there is a place for theorizing, and using theory to understand what is happening in work with clients, but it must always come after direct encounter with the client, without editing our experience. Between the stage of concentrating on the direct observation and the content of what the client said, and turning to theoretical consideration, there are several further steps that need to be taken:

- an exploration of the connections between the content of one part of the session with material from elsewhere in the session;
- listening for the connecting pattern that is contained within each of the parts;
- the tentative linking of material from one session to material and sequences from previous sessions – supervisees who are new to the work often treat each session as if it was an isolated event rather than part of an ongoing process;
- an exploration of the links between the content of sessions and the life of the client, both outside and prior to these sessions – in this we can look at the

content in the supervisee/client session as a microcosm of the macrocosm of the client's life and relationships as a whole.

We have found two techniques particularly useful when exploring mode 1. One is to attend to the opening moments of the session, even before you think the session has started; to see how the client has first presented and revealed themselves, before the conversation got fully underway. Another useful approach is the occasional use of video or audio recordings of coaching sessions. Here one can move between the phenomena of the material and the feelings of the coach (Kagan 1980).

Mode 2

In this mode the supervisor focuses on what interventions the supervisee made in their work with the client, how and why they made them and interventions they would have preferred: 'I ask them what interventions they have made; what reasons they had for making them; where their interventions were leading them; how they made their interventions and when, and then I ask what they want to do with this client now?' (Davies 1987).

We always bear in mind Abraham Maslow's aphorism: 'If the only tool you have is a hammer, you will tend to treat everything as if it is a nail' – and remind ourselves that it is important to make sure your supervisees not only have a wide range of interventions in their tool box, but also that they use the tools appropriately and do not blame their chisels for being terrible screwdrivers!

We found that when supervisees express undue concern about what intervention to use, that this can be an indicator that they may be on the brink of getting stuck in dualistic thinking. We recognize this from statements which we term 'either-or-isms', such as:

- I either have to confront his arrogant behaviour or put up with it.
- I didn't know whether to wait a bit longer, or interrupt his silence.
- I don't know whether to continue working with her.

As you can see these statements do not always contain the words 'either-or', but they are always based on a supervisee seeing only two opposing options. The job of the supervisor is to avoid the trap of helping the supervisee evaluate which choice to make, to point out instead that they have reduced numerous possibilities to only two. Once the supervisee realizes that they are operating under a restrictive assumption, the supervisor can help them generate new options for intervening.

Generating new options can be undertaken by using a simple brainstorming approach. The basic rules of brainstorming are:

- say whatever comes into your head;
- get the ideas out, don't evaluate or judge them;

- use the other person's ideas as springboards;
- include the wildest options you can invent.

Brainstorming is helped by setting a high target for the number of options, as it is only when we have exhausted all the obvious rational choices that the creative mind starts to get going. 'Think of ten different ways you could help your client over his fear of confronting his boss!' Often it is the craziest idea that contains the kernel of a creative way forward. In group supervision it might be '20 ways of dealing with a supervisee's impasse'. Group supervision can use this mode very creatively. The group of supervisees will create a greater variety of styles in the room and can avoid the potential dualism inherent in one-to-one sessions, where there is only the supervisor's or the supervisee's approach.

In group supervision there is also a greater range of possibilities for active role-playing. Different group members can choose a variety of possible approaches they would like to try out from the list of brainstormed possibilities. Then, with supervisees playing the client, several different possible strategies can be tried and evaluated. If the supervisee in a one-to-one session is stuck with how to find creative alternatives to help their client then the supervisor can suggest proactive ways of exploring and seeing the issue. They could use the Gestalt technique of using an empty chair to represent the client and even role reverse as coach and client to gain further insight into the dynamics of the situation.

Many supervisors, when focusing in mode 2, offer their own intervention. There are dangers in doing this. It is easy as supervisor to want to show off your intervention skills without fully acknowledging how much easier it is to be skilful in the relative ease of the supervisory setting than when face-to-face with a client. The other danger is that the suggestions of the supervisor will be swallowed whole by the supervisee rather than critically evaluated in order to develop their own improved interventions.

Mode 3

In this mode the focus is neither on the client, nor the supervisee, nor their interventions, but on the system that the two create together. In mode 3, the supervisor focuses upon the relationship or 'chemistry' between the supervisee and the coachee, that is both what they are aware of and also what remains 'behind the curtain', but still influences interactions between them. To start with, the supervisor might ask one or more of the following:

- How and why did this client choose you?
- What did you first notice about the nature of your contact with this client?
- Tell me the story of the history of your relationship.

These interventions are clearly requesting something that is different from a case history and are intended to help the practitioner stand outside the client relationship in which they might be enmeshed or submerged and start to see its pattern and dynamic.

Other techniques and questions that encourage this distancing and detachment are:

- Find an image or metaphor to represent the relationship.
- Imagine what sort of relationship you would have if you and the client met in other circumstances or if you were both cast away on a desert island.
- Become a fly on the wall in your last session; what do you notice about the relationship?

These are all techniques to help the supervisee see the relationship as a whole, rather than just their own perspective from within the relationship. The supervisor can be listening to the relationship even when the supervisee is not referring to it. In this way the supervisor acts like a couple counsellor, in so far as they must hold the interests of both parties in balance, and simultaneously attend to the space, and relationship, between them.

The supervisor listens to the relationship in a variety of different ways. All approaches involve listening with the 'third ear' to the images, metaphors and 'Freudian slips' that collect around the supervisee's description of this particular client. Through this form of listening the supervisor is trying to discover the picture that the supervisee holds outside or beyond what they are able to articulate to the supervisor.

The supervisor is also interested in the way the client experiences the supervisee. By this we mean not only here-and-now feelings, but also feelings or attitudes that the client may have transferred from an earlier relationship or situation. For example, the coachee may have had real problems earlier in life with those people who represented authority for them. The rather combative current relationship may simply have been transferred unknowingly by the client, because the coach in some ways puts them in mind of being lectured at by teachers. In mode 4 we will move on to look at how the supervisee might be doing something similar, transferring attitudes and feelings from their previous relationships into the coaching relationship. It is necessary to move between these two modes and consider where if at all such views are being enacted between them. However, for the time being, we will separate the focus and look only at the client's situation.

Many of the questions used above which focus attention on images and metaphors will give important clues to what may be happening below the radar. If, for instance, the supervisee said that the relationship was like that of two sparring partners in a boxing ring, the quality would be very different from that of a supervisee who answered that their relationship reflected a 'little boy lost and in need of protection'.

Our concern about these phenomena is not one of prurient interest, but we are trying to understand what, if anything, might be getting in the way of a healthy open meeting between coach and coachee.

Mode 4

The focus here is on the coach beginning to look at themselves, both at what is being re-stimulated in them by the coachee's material and also how they operate as an instrument that registers what is happening beneath the surface of the coaching relationship.

In the world of psychotherapy this is called 'countertransference'. What all forms of 'countertransference' have in common is that they involve some form of predominantly unaware reaction to the client by the supervisee. It is important for the supervisor and supervisee to explore all forms of countertransference in order to create greater space to *respond appropriately* rather than merely *react* to the client. It is commonly recognized in supervision when the supervisee remarks, 'John seems to continually press my buttons. I find it really difficult not to get cross with him.' Understanding what the buttons are, and how they are being pressed, allows the supervisee to understand and unhook themselves from the dynamic and be more available for the client.

In mode 4 the supervisor helps the supervisee to work through any re-stimulation of their own feelings that have been triggered by the work with this client. Having identified the source(s) of reactivity, the supervisor can help explore how the supervisee's own feelings may in fact be useable data. They may assist in understanding what the coachee and their system are experiencing but unable to articulate directly. The supervisee also explores how their own blocks may be preventing them from facilitating the coachee and their system to change.

Those supervisors who have had previous therapy training may feel they want to offer more in-depth help around this mode. Others will provide adequate support to a supervisee by exploring the buttons that are being pressed and the sequence of behaviours that generated the complicated dynamic.

A series of questions can be asked of the supervisee to elicit this level of material:

- *Step 1:* ask the supervisee to share their immediate response to the question: 'Who does this client remind you of?' Keep repeating that until an association is made.

- *Step 2:* then ask the supervisee 'What needs to be said to the person they remind you of?'

- *Step 3:* following on from this, the supervisee is asked to describe all the ways their client is different from this person.

- *Step 4:* to finish the exploration the supervisee needs to be asked, 'What do you want to say to your client now?'

Also when looking at the supervisee's spontaneous responses, it is important to include an exploration of what Frank Kevlin (1987) calls 'the ideological editor'. This is the way the supervisee views the client through the lens of their own belief and value system. Obstacles to accurate perception include conscious prejudice, racism, sexism and other assumptions that colour the way we mis-see, mis-hear or mis-relate to the client.

One way of eliciting this ideological editor is through awareness of the supervisee's use of comparatives or associations. If a supervisee says about a client: 'She is a very obliging client' the supervisor can enter the exploratory process by asking: 'How is she obliging?' 'She is very obliging compared to whom?' 'Tell me how you think clients should oblige you?' Thus the supervisor is seeking to discover the assumptions about how clients 'should' be, that are hidden in this comparative term 'very obliging'.

Mode 4 also includes attending to the general well-being (resourcing aspect) and development (developmental aspect) of the supervisee's needs. Unless time is given to these aspects, the danger is that the supervision will become overly reactive to the impact of the latest difficult client, rather than proactively helping to build the capacity of the supervisee over time.

It is also essential to remember that the only part of the system that you can help to shift is the part that is present with you in the room.

Mode 5

In the previous modes the supervisor has been focusing outside themselves. In mode 1 they were concentrating on the client situation. Increasingly in modes 2 to 4 they have been focusing on the supervisee, encouraging the supervisee to look less for answers out in the client and to pay more attention to what is happening inside themselves. So far the supervisor has not started to look inside themselves for clues as to what is happening. In the final two modes the supervisor practises what they preach, and attends to how the work with the clients enter and change the supervisory relationship. In mode 6 we explore how these dynamics affect the supervisor. Without the use of modes 5 and 6, supervisors would lack congruence between what they were asking the supervisee to do and what they were modelling.

Harold Searles (1955), an American neo-Freudian, has contributed a great deal to the understanding of this supervision mode in his discovery and exploration of the paralleling phenomenon:

> My experience in hearing numerous therapists present cases before groups has caused me to become slow in forming an unfavourable opinion of any therapist on the basis of his presentation of a case. With convincing frequency, I have seen that a therapist who during occasional presentations appears to be lamentably anxious, compulsive, confused in his thinking, actually is a basically capable colleague who, as it were, is trying unconsciously by his demeanour during the presentation, to show us a major problem area in the therapy with his patient. The problem area is one which he cannot perceive objectively and describe to us effectively in words; rather, he is unconsciously identifying with it and is in effect trying to describe it by the way of his behaviour during the presentation.

The principle of 'parallel process' – describing how the pattern of the relationship in one area is enacted in another, with no conscious awareness of what is going on – allows us access to aspects of the supervisee/coachee relationship not otherwise available to us. This dynamic serves two purposes for the supervisee. One is that it is a form of discharge – 'I will do to you what has been done to me and you see how you like it!' The second purpose it serves is that it is an unconscious attempt at solving the problem through re-enacting it within the here-and-now relationship in supervision. The job of the supervisor is to notice and tentatively name the process and thereby make it available to conscious exploration and learning. If it remains out of awareness, the supervisor is likely to be submerged in the enactment of the process and enter the dance as a player – not an aware enquirer.

The important skill involved in working with paralleling is to be able to notice one's reactions and feed them back to the supervisee in a non-judgemental way, for example, 'I am feeling judged and as though I have to come up with the right answer right now. I wonder if that is how you feel with your coachee?' The process is quite difficult to work with as we are working with the paradox of the supervisee both wanting to deskill the supervisor as they felt deskilled by the client – and at the same time, work through and understand the difficult process in which they are ensnared.

Research on this process suggests that it is a component of any linked spheres of activity, such as coaching and supervision. Doehrman (1976) discovered that paralleling can go in both directions. Not only can unaware activity from the coaching session get mirrored in the supervision process, but also any unaware activity in the supervisory relationship can get played out in the coaching process.

In mode 5 we also attend to the quality of the live relationship between the supervisor and supervisee. It is important not to treat all difficulties in a supervision relationship as originating from client dynamics. Difficulties are not always due to parallel processes, and they may also emerge from the following:

- a lack of clear contracting around aspects of the supervision process;
- interpersonal issues between supervisor and supervisee;
- cultural, gender or other conflicts.

Irving Yalom (2002) writes about the importance of always attending to what is happening in the 'here and now' of all professional relationships. He says the here and now refers to the immediate, to what is happening *here* (in this office, in this relationship, in the *in-betweenness* – the space between me and you) and *now*, in this immediate hour. In his reasoning the rationale for using the here and now rests upon a couple of basic assumptions:

1   The importance of interpersonal relationships.
2   The idea of social microcosm.

So Yalom (2002: 68), in his first session, models how to comment on his relationship with the client with such interventions as:

- 'Let's take a minute to look at how you and I are doing today.'

- 'Any feeling about how we are working or relating?'
- 'Before we stop, shall we take a look at how we have worked together today?'

These interventions seem as relevant to the supervisory relationship as to the relationship with clients. Yalom's observations are helpful with regard to the 'in the room' focus we have encouraged in this book:

> There are few human situations in which we are permitted, let alone encouraged, to comment upon the behaviour of the other. It feels liberating, even exhilarating – that is precisely why the encounter-group experience was so compelling. But it also feels risky, since we are not accustomed to giving and receiving feedback.
>
> (2002: 68)

Orlans and Edwards (2001: 46) pick up on this theme: 'To truly collaborate on a joint learning venture could be experienced as risky for participants – at the very least it is likely to be filled with uncertainty for both supervisor and supervisee. It requires that the habitual maps which the person's present have so far evolved are laid open for perusal ...'.

The supervisory relationship can therefore also be a lively forum for modelling new ways of relating.

Mode 6

In mode 5 we explored how the relationship between the supervisee and their client can invade and be mirrored in the supervisory relationship. In mode 6 we focus on how that relationship can access the internal experience of the supervisor and how to use what arises from that process.

Often as supervisors we find that abrupt changes 'come over us'. We might suddenly feel very tired, but become very alert again when the supervisee moves on to discuss another client. Images, rationally unrelated to the material, may spontaneously erupt in our consciousness. We may find ourselves sexually excited by our image of the client or shuddering incomprehensibly with fear.

Over the years we have begun to trust these interruptions as being important messages about what is happening both here and now in the room and also out there in the work with the client. In order to trust these eruptions, supervisors must know themselves fairly well. I must know when I am normally tired, bored, fidgety, fearful, sexually aroused, tense in my stomach etc. in order to ascertain that this eruption is not entirely my own inner process bubbling away, but is an import from somewhere else.

In this process, material from the supervisee is being received by some kind of receptor in the supervisor, and the supervisor is tentatively bringing this material into awareness for the supervisee to explore.

The supervisor needs to be clear about their feelings towards a supervisee: 'What are my basic feelings towards this supervisee?' 'Do I generally feel threatened, challenged, critical, bored etc.?' Unless supervisors are relatively clear about their basic feelings towards their supervisees, they cannot notice how these feelings are changed by the import of unaware material from the supervisee and their clients.

In order to use this mode, supervisors not only have to be aware of their own inner life and its normal patterns of reaction, but must also be able to attend to their own shifts in sensation and peripheral half-thoughts and fantasies, while still attending to the content and process of the session. This may sound a difficult task, but it is also a key skill in being effective in coaching, mentoring and consultancy and it is therefore important that supervisors can model its use to those that they supervise.

Supervisors might use their awareness of their own changing sensations and feelings by making statements like:

- 'While you have been describing your work with X, I have been getting more and more impatient. Having examined this impatience it does not seem to be to do with you, or something I am bringing into the session from outside, so I wonder if I am picking up your impatience with your client?'
- 'I notice that I keep getting images of wolves with their teeth bared, as you describe your relationship with this client. Does that image resonate with your feelings about the relationship?'
- 'I am getting very sleepy as you "go on" about this client. Often when that happens to me it seems to indicate that some feeling is being shut off either to do with the client or right here in the supervision. What might you be holding back from saying?'

Mode 7

Here the supervisor moves the focus from the specific client relationships that foreground in the session to the embracing, contextual field, in which both the client work and the supervision work takes place.

This context surrounds all aspects of the supervisory process. The siren call for coaches, mentors, consultants and supervisors is to become endlessly fascinated by the detail of situations they and their clients are engaged in. It is often quite a shock to the system for us to look beyond the work with our client and their organization. By doing that, we start to see what is happening beyond that session and at the influences that the larger dynamics and events have upon the internal workings of the client organization, and their impact on what initially appeared to be an individual client issue only.

Hawkins and Shohet (2006) divided mode 7 into different categories (7.1, 7.2, 7.3, 7.4, 7.5, 7.6, 7.7) linked to each of the original six modes. Thus 7.1 is the external world of the client, 7.4 the external world of the coach and 7.5 the organizational context of the supervisory relationship etc.). Although this is important, we have also found that in the world of organizational consultancy, coaching and mentoring it is important to help supervisors bring a multi-layered business and systemic perspective to their supervisory work and have therefore developed a different way of viewing mode 7, which we will now present.

We think that supervisors will need to use mode 7 in a different way than, for example, psychotherapy supervisors. Coaches, mentors and consultants are not just involved with individual clients, but may also be involved with teams, departments or whole organizations. Wherever we are working, on the spectrum of individual to whole system, the common thread is that our clients are linked to organizations and subject to the whim of markets, governments and environmental challenges that affect our ability to do our jobs. When supervising coaches, mentors or consultants we have found that the most helpful way of gaining perspective on the situation is to 'helicopter up' from the picture of the physical environment in which they are actually working, through the levels of interest and influence on the organization in which they work, to the broader influences of government and the global environment. For instance, one can tell as much about the organizational context from the sort of office and support a senior executive is given as we can about the executive's agenda from their physical demeanour when we first meet them.

The issue, therefore, in using mode 7 for supervising executive coaches and others, is to see the interconnecting rings of influence (see Figure 9.2) which can affect the situation in which the supervisee and the coachee have to work. For example, if you are coaching the chief executive in a well-run manufacturing business making tracking equipment for lorries, who is finding it hard to take business decisions, one first needs to check out whether he has temporarily lost his nerve, has always had a problem with decision-taking, or whether this is a new phenomenon. If it is a new phenomenon then it may be that the market or the global situation is placing the CEO in a double-bind without him being entirely clear about it.

It is possible that:

- the shareholders are demanding growth, and
- the senior staff are coming up with new investment opportunities, while
- in the background the lowering of labour costs in other parts of the globe,
- combined with some recent prototype technology advances, which
- could render the current tracking equipment obsolete,
- are creating a background, but palpable, uncertainty. This may be
- further heightened by potential shifts in the way EU and US governments plan to tax transport, in order to further a green agenda.

It is therefore entirely understandable that the CEO feels unable to take a decision at this point in time. If we concentrated just on his personal issues and see his failure to make decisions as his personal problem, we may not give him the space to understand from where the uncertainty comes and upon what he needs to focus.

Mode 7.1

In working with either group supervision or in a one-to-one setting, one way of using this mode is to do it almost as a guided journey. The supervisor should start with helping the supervisee evoke the physical space in which the coachee works. If they don't know this, then ask them to focus instead on some details about the client organization's physical office space that would be indicative of the way the organization treats its staff. Often there are misalignments between rhetoric and reality. The engineering company that states boldly on all its documents 'Our staff are our greatest asset', while the toilet areas are unhygienic, poorly lit and bleak, highlights such a gap. If that gap is there, it may explain some of the 'issues' currently being seen as residing in the coachee. If a coach has absolutely no idea about the physical environment in which their coachee works, it at least raises the issue as to why that is.

Mode 7.2

The next stage in the helicopter journey to gain the full overview of the organizational influences, is to ask about typical behaviours that mark out life for senior people like the coachee in this organization. *'What are the ways things are done around there?'* This gives supervisee and supervisor clarity about whether what they are seeing is influenced by the culture of the place or more potently by the specific actions of the coachee. *'What have you learned from the stories told by the coachee about the values and assumptions operating in this organization?'*

Mode 7.3

Briefly summarizing the picture that has built up from these two initial views, the next level is to look at who the critical stakeholders are for the success of the overall company, and the coachee's particular area of responsibility. First one asks 'Who are the key internal stakeholders that will be interested in the success of the coachee's business role and the overall success of the organization?' We then go outside to other stakeholders who have an interest, such as shareholders, sister organizations, concerned partner organizations, as well as direct competitors. Here we are trying to get the supervisee to understand not only what is actually happening and sharpen their awareness of contextual issues, but also recognize where there may be critical gaps in the story. In this mode we are looking for the pressures that may well be subterranean, but can strongly influence how people experience their work environment in this particular organization at this time.

Mode 7.4

The next mode is taking a further step out, beyond the immediate focus on the organization and looking at the broad issues in the sector. In mode 7.3 we might look at the stakeholder assumptions, aspirations, anxieties and concerns that might influence – let's say – British Gas. In mode 7.4 we would be looking at the concerns, developments and challenges of the energy sector as a whole. This includes the regulatory environment in which it has to operate. We would be seeing whether it was a truly global market or whether there were different pressures depending on whether you looked at the energy sector from the UK, EU, first world or global perspective. This shows the business pressures from within the sector.

Mode 7.5

The energy sector, for example, sits in a broader economic context, which influences the energy sector's current profitability, its future growth prospects and its ability to invest. At any one period in time some areas of the world have a booming economy, while others go into temporary meltdown – as witnessed when the 'Dragon' economies hit turbulent waters around the Millennium. The interconnectedness of these events can play into perceived complications at the local level. As supervisor or coach, we may be tempted to interpret a presented problem as related to local difficulties: as personal to the individual, or the organization. In reality they may be connected to a macroeconomic trend that they simply have to ride out.

Mode 7.6

You will now rightly be seeing mode 7 as a nest of Russian dolls, rather than as a linear enquiry into the context in which the coachee's business exists. Having looked at the influences of the economic environment on the energy sector, and the influences of the broader energy sector on the energy company, we need to go broader again. We have to take into account the UK and European political, social, technological, legal and environmental issues (PESTLE) that shape up in the background and create challenges for the staff of the organization. For an energy company, for example, the political environment might become hostile if there are vote-winning possibilities in supporting the uptake of one type of fuel over another. We have seen with global energy companies, for instance, that they had to be highly aware of the political, technological and environmental issues that can negatively impact both an individual company site or their operation in a particular country. The push to develop technologies that get around the need for expensive fuel regularly challenges these organizations and could have huge potential impact on their future viability. Once again in discussing this mode with a supervisee it is as likely as not that they have no knowledge of this context. This could well mean that the coachee has not got adequate sight of it either. Highlighting this lack of awareness extends an encouragement for checking such issues out for the future.

Mode 7.7

The final view in this mode is the global view. This may seem to be too high-flown, if one is talking about the work of an executive in a small town in the Midlands, UK. However, even small organizations do things that affect or are affected by the global environment. This is particularly true for environmental issues, but may also be true in terms of other global issues, such as trade laws, resource shortages or wars.

As we said at various points during our exposition of mode 7, it is perfectly possible that the supervisee does not know anything about some of the mode 7 elements. But enquiry gives the supervisee some questions to take back to their coachee. This may at least allow them to see a different perspective on the issues they are working with.

We still believe that it is important not to subsume mode 7 into the other six modes, for this would lose the constant challenge that nearly all of us need

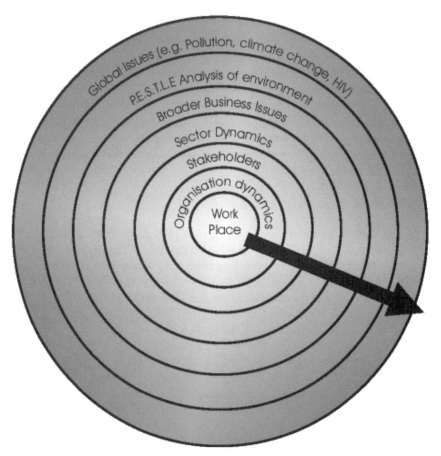

Figure 9.2 Mode 7 'the integrated systems overview'

regularly to move our attention from what is naturally in our field of vision to the wider domain in which we are operating.

Integrating the processes

It is our view that good supervision of in-depth work with clients must involve all seven modes, although not necessarily in every session. Therefore, part of the training with this model is to help supervisors discover the processes they more commonly use and those with which they are less familiar. We have found that some supervisors become habituated to using just one or two modes.

Having learnt to use each of the main processes skilfully, the trainee supervisor needs help in moving effectively and appropriately from one process to another (see Figure 9.3). To do this, it is important to develop the supervisory skills of appropriateness and timing. The supervisor needs to be aware of how different modes are more appropriate for different supervisees, and for the same supervisees – at different times. The most common pattern for using different modes in a

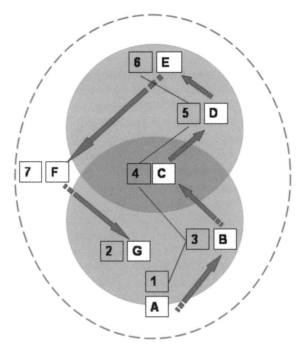

Figure 9.3   A pattern of use for the different modes during a session

supervision session is to begin with mode 1, discovering what happened in the session; for this to naturally lead on to modes 3 and 4, what happened in the relationship and how this affected the coach; and if and when this enters the supervision relationship to switch the focus to modes 5 and 6. At any of these stages one might move from the specific mode to the appropriate sub-mode of 7, so as to reflect on what is colouring the situation in the wider field. At the end of the exploration of a particular client, the supervisor might then focus back on mode 2 to explore what new interventions the supervisee might utilize at their next session with this client.

Linking the model to a developmental perspective

It is helpful for the supervisor to be aware of the developmental stage and readiness of the individual supervisee to receive different levels of supervision and to pay attention to their own potential pitfalls, which the hierarchical position can give rise to.

As a general rule new supervisees need to start with most of the supervision focusing on the content of the work with the client and the detail of what happened in the session. At first supervisees are often highly anxious about their own performance and require support in attending to what actually took place. They also need assistance in seeing the detail of specific sessions within a larger context and the supervisor will choose to operate mainly in modes 1 and 7; how material from one session links to the development over time; how it relates to the coachee's organization and their business activity. In supporting supervisees to develop this overview, it is very important not to lose sight of the uniqueness of the supervisee's relationship with their client. The supervisor must not give the impression that what is new, personal and often exciting for the supervisee could easily be put into a recognizable category.

As supervisees develop their ability to attend to what *is*, rather than getting away from their primary knowledge by premature theorizing and over-concern with their own performance, it is possible to spend more time profitably on mode 2, considering their interventions. Here the danger is that the supervisor falls into the habit of telling the supervisees how they could have intervened better. We have found ourselves uttering statements such as, 'What I would have said to this client would have been . . .' or 'I would have just kept quiet at that point in the session'. Having said such a line, of course we should kick ourselves for failing to practise what we preach and wish we had kept quiet at this point in the supervision session!

As the supervisees become more sophisticated, modes 3, 4, 5 and 6 become more central to the supervision. With a competent and experienced practitioner, it is possible to rely on their having attended to the conscious material and having carried out their own balanced and critical evaluation of their sessions. In such a case the supervisor needs to listen more to what is not being talked about by either the supervisee or the coachee, whose situation is under consideration. This necessitates focusing on what might be arising from the parallel process and other unaware dynamics, which can be played out within the supervision relationship.

Conclusion

In this chapter we have explored in detail the 'seven-eyed supervisor model' that we first developed in 1985. We have continued to teach and develop this model ever since and have found that it still provides a framework for new levels of depth and ways of creatively intervening in a supervision session. For us the power of the model shows in our ongoing learning process – and we gain new insights from working with it even after 20 years. It has proved useful beyond our original horizon of expectation. It has been used in a great variety of cultures and in different 'people' professions, from youth work to palliative care, from management development to executive coaching, and from education to organizational consultancy.

We have also found that this model holds good for adherents of many different theoretical approaches and orientations. It has been successfully used by coaches from humanistic, cognitive, behavioural, solutions focused and psychodynamic orientations, and those who are performance centred, development centred and transformational.

We have become increasingly convinced that to carry out effective supervision of any client work it is necessary for the supervisor to be able to use all seven modes of supervision, and hope to have encouraged you to have a go at using our map for your supervision activity.

10

Group and peer group supervision

Introduction

The emphasis so far has been mainly on individual supervision, because we see it as the best context in which to address many of the key issues and processes within supervision, before approaching the same issues in the more complex setting of a group. However, many of the topics covered thus far, such as contracting, modes of supervision, supervision roles and process also apply to supervision in groups.

In this chapter we will first explore the advantages and disadvantages of supervision, before going on to look at the practical skills of setting up and managing supervision groups. We then explore the particular issues involved in peer supervision, before explaining team supervision in the next chapter.

Group supervision

Advantages

There are several reasons why you might choose to supervise in a group rather than individually. The first of these reasons is related to economies of time, money or expertise. Clearly, if there is a shortage of people who can supervise or their time is very limited, supervisors can probably see more supervisees by conducting supervision groups. However, ideally, group supervision should come from a positive choice rather than a compromise forced upon the group and supervisor.

The second advantage is that, unlike a one-to-one supervision, the group provides a supportive atmosphere of peers in which new staff or trainees can share anxieties and realize that others are facing similar issues.

The third advantage is that group supervision gains from the supervisees' receiving reflections, feedback, sharing and inputs from their colleagues as well as the group supervisor. They also become aware of other people's styles of coaching first-hand. There is also the potential for this setting to be less dominated by the supervisor, making it less likely that they get embroiled in the concurrent dangers of over-influence and dependency. A group can, when working well, challenge collusion between the supervisor and the supervisees.

The final advantage of group supervision is that it enables a group client context to be reflected in the supervision. Thus, if the supervisees practise group coaching or team coaching, learning can be maximized through the supervision taking place in a group with other group leaders. This provides opportunities to learn from how the supervisor runs the group and also how the dynamics of the presented groups are mirrored in the supervision group itself (see section on 'paralleling' in Chapter 9).

Disadvantages

There are also some disadvantages to supervising in groups. Group supervision is less likely to mirror the dynamic of individual coaching as clearly as would individual supervision. Also, as soon as you work in a group, you have to contend with internal group dynamics. These can be a benefit if they are made conscious within the group and used as an adjunct to the supervisees increasing their self-awareness through experiencing their part in the group process. However, the group process can also be destructive and undermining of the supervisory process if, for example, there is a competitive spirit in the group. The dynamics of the supervisory group can also become a preoccupation. We have both been in supervision groups that have gradually become centrally concerned with their own dynamics almost to the exclusion of any interest in their clients.

The final disadvantage is that there is obviously less time for each person to receive supervision. The individual might therefore only get a turn every three meetings and if these are held fortnightly this could, in effect, mean supervision directly for oneself only every six weeks.

Selection of group members

This is a very important part of future group life for both members and leaders. Clarity of purpose and needs should be very carefully considered by all concerned, as should range of experience and skills. In terms of size, a supervision group needs to be three people at the very minimum, and no more than seven, otherwise members will have to fight to get enough time and attention.

Group members also need to have sufficiently similar types of clients they work with; their general theoretical outlook, and their level of accomplishment need to fit. However, in a group that is too similar in these three areas, the learning and challenge is limited and there is a danger of promoting 'consensus collusion' (Heron 1975).

Contracting

Once the group has been selected, the group supervisor needs to have the skills to manage the contracting. It is good to ensure clarity of purpose since there is often a hidden agenda of getting a bit of personal coaching on the side, for example, and the group needs to be clear about its policy on this, checking to see that expectations are realistic. The time factor and the number of clients that can be supervised also need acknowledging.

Some useful questions for the supervisor to bear in mind are:

- What should the goals of this supervision group be?
- What roles should the group supervisor adopt to permit the realization of these goals?
- What balance between didactic material, case conceptualization and interpersonal process is most productive for the learning of the participants?
- What kind of evaluation and feedback processes suit this group's purpose?

Some of the issues around this are similar to the contracting issues mentioned in Chapter 8, but the issues around confidentiality are more complex. We have found it necessary in some groups to have a ground rule that, if you think you know the client being presented, you declare this and, if necessary, leave the room for the duration of that particular presentation.

Setting the climate

The next task is to set a safe climate for the supervisees to open up their work to others, a process that is always beset with some fear and anxiety:

- 'Will I be found out?'
- 'Will everyone else find flaws that I am unaware of, not only in my work but who I am as a person?'
- 'Will they think why the hell does he think he can be a coach, mentor or consultant with those attitudes or hang-ups?'

The climate must be one that encourages a sharing of vulnerabilities and anxieties without group members being put down or turned into 'the group patient'. It is an easy escape route for group members to avoid their own insecurities by finding a 'group patient', which allows everybody else the chance to return to the much safer role of helper!

Simple ground rules help to avoid destructive group processes, such as ensuring that all statements are owned and group members speak from their own experience. Avoid good advice, 'If I were you, I would ...', and preaching, 'Coaches ought to be non-directive', etc. As described above, another useful ground rule is to ensure that feedback from group members is owned, balanced and specific. It is also important that the group supervisor ensures there is a roughly equal amount of sharing between all group members, both in terms of quantity and level of self-disclosure.

Self-disclosure can feel safer if group leaders also are open about their own insecurities, anxieties and times when they do not know, rather than always having to be the one with the answers (see Jourard 1971).

Acknowledging the group dynamic

It is essential the group leader ensures group dynamics do not proceed unacknowledged and finds ways of bringing the dynamics into awareness so that they can be attended to and learnt from, without taking over as the major focus of the group. Awareness of the here-and-now dynamics is an essential part of the learning process, but the distinction between a supervision group and a 'personal development' group must be maintained.

Group stages

To successfully run group supervision over time, it is necessary to understand the basic stages that groups go through and how to facilitate the group development in the various stages.

Margaret Rioch has written extensively on the interface between supervision and group dynamics, within the therapeutic setting. In her *Dialogues for Therapists* (Rioch *et al.* 1976) she charts a complete series of group supervisions (which she terms seminars) with therapists in training. After each seminar she comments on the group dynamics and concludes that 'It is also clear that the group interaction was an important part of the process, sometimes furthering, sometimes interfering with the learning'.

Most of the theories, and our own experience, would suggest that groups have to start by dealing with their own boundaries, membership and the group rules and expectations. Schutz (1973) calls this 'inclusion'; Tuckman (1965) 'the stages of Forming and Norming'. This is the contracting stage in group supervision, where issues of confidentiality, commitment to the group, how time will be allocated and what will be focused on and what will be excluded, need to be decided and clarified.

Following this period of clarifying the basic structure of the supervision group, there is often a period of testing out power and authority within the group. This can take the form of rivalrous competitiveness:

- Who does the best work?
- Who most cares about their clients?
- Who has the most difficult cases?
- Who makes the most penetrating insightful comments?

Or it may take the form of testing out the authority of the supervisor by challenging their approach, trying to show that one can supervise other group members better than they can, or inappropriately applying their recommendations to show that they do not work. This is called the stage of 'fight/flight' by Bion (1961), 'authority' by Schutz (1973) and 'storming' by Tuckman (1965).

It is only when these stages have been successfully handled that the group can settle to its most productive work, with a climate of respect for each individual and without either dependency or rivalry in its relationship to the supervisor.

Structuring the group

For the group supervisor there are a number of choices in how to structure the group session. Which one they choose will depend on the type and size of group as well as their own style and inclination.

One of us starts group supervision sessions with a round of each group member stating what issues they want to bring to the group. This is followed by negotiating the competing requests to decide on the order and how much time each person should have.

A variant that can be used with this approach is to follow the round by an exploration of whose issue most represents the current 'core concern' of the group. This can be done by asking group members to identify which issue, other than their own, they would learn most from exploring. This currently 'most interesting' issue takes precedence and moves to the centre of the work. This ensures that the person who is at the centre of the work is not just working for themselves, but has the energy and interest of the group.

Other colleagues divide the group time equally between all those present so that everybody knows they will get some attention in each group. This becomes impractical if the group is too large and/or the time too short.

The group may arrange a schedule where each group member knows in advance that they will be the one presenting on a particular day. This makes it possible for some outline notes on the coaching session to be circulated in advance. This moves proceedings more into a group case study with a greater emphasis on learning from an overview, rather than focusing on current concerns and difficulties. This structure may entail group members having separate supervision for their more immediate supervisory needs.

Another option is to 'trust the process' and to wait to see what emerges and where the interest of the group moves. You can also start by checking out what has happened to issues that were explored at the previous meeting.

Supervision style

Group members, unless they are very experienced, will mostly take their lead from the group supervisor and make interventions with a similar style and focus to that of the leader. It is thus very important that supervisors be aware of how they are modelling ways of responding to material that is presented. The supervisor needs to model or explain that there is a range of ways of listening and responding to what is shared, to encourage a multi-layered approach (see Chapter 9).

In Figure 10.1 we show four quadrants, each representing a different style of group supervision. In quadrant A, the supervision group is more directively led by the group supervisor and has a strong focus on the group process. In quadrant B, the supervisor is still taking the central lead, but the focus is more on the content of the cases brought. In quadrant C, the group moves over to take more leadership responsibility, but with a focus on the cases brought. In quadrant D, the group take responsibility for focusing on their own process.

Each quadrant has its own shadow side, if the supervision group gets stuck in just one style. Quadrant A groups can turn into a personal development group, attending to the personal needs of the members, but neglecting the client issues. Quadrant B groups can become a forum for the group supervisor to show off their expertise and create dependency in the group members. Supervision, which becomes stuck in quadrant C, can become competitive peer advice-giving, with group members trying to out do each other with, 'If I were you' solutions. Quadrant D supervision groups can become over-collusive peer support groups and, like groups in A, inward-looking and failing to attend to the task.

Good group supervision needs to be able to move flexibly through all these areas, depending on the needs of the group and the stage of group development. Most commonly a supervision group will begin in quadrant A in its forming and contracting phase, move into quadrant B, as it begins to settle to its task, and then gradually incorporate quadrants C and D, as the group becomes more mature and

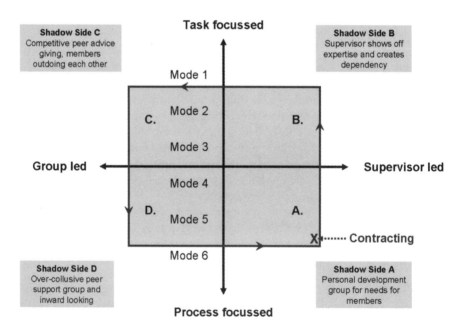

Figure 10.1 Models of group supervision styles

self-responsible. However, good supervision groups, once well-established, will cycle through all four quadrants, and avoid getting stuck in the shadow side of one.

This model can also be linked to our model of seven-eyed supervision (see Chapter 9). Each focus can be placed on the vertical axis, as in Figure 10.1.

Group supervisors need to be able to manage a number of simultaneous processes, because supervision in a group is contained within a number of rings of context (see Figure 10.2 and also Inskipp and Proctor 1995: 86 who offer a similar model).

The central skills of facilitating reflective supervision (A) are similar to working one-to-one. However, to use the richness of the group to the full, the group supervisor must facilitate the responses of the group members (B) and link these back to the case. The third contextual ring refers to managing the group dynamics (C), and attending to the developmental stage and developmental needs of the group process. The outer ring is concerned with ensuring that the supervision happens within an appropriate contract and boundaries (D). The group contract, as discussed above, is something that is not a one-off event, but a process that must be regularly revisited. The contract may also involve more than the group members and supervisor. It may be happening in the context of an organization, or members may be sponsored by a number of different organizations. The boundaries and relationship with these organizations becomes an important context that the supervisor must attend to for the supervision to feel appropriately contained.

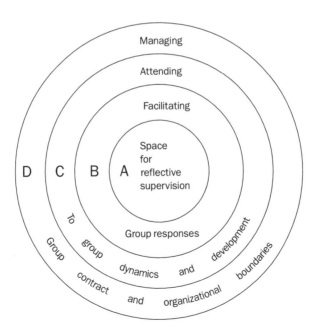

Figure 10.2 The concentric rings of the group supervision process

Group supervision techniques

Techniques for group supervision work best when the members of the group can usefully contribute and are actively engaged. Having so many resources and perspectives is one of the significant advantages of groups as described above.

A very simple technique to use is to let the person presenting a client talk for a set time (e.g. five minutes maximum). Each person in the group is then allowed to ask one question and the presenter is asked which question engages them most and that line of enquiry is then pursued.

A more complex version of this procedure is to ask each member of the group to be aware of what is happening to them, when someone is presenting a client. We explain that it is impossible to get it wrong. They need to register whether they are having a feeling of, say, hunger or a feeling of restlessness. Any experience is valid. Physical sensations, like pains, can yield very important information. If they are bored or unaccountably feeling sad or angry or switching off, that is useful too. We ask for thoughts, images, feelings, body sensations or fantasies. Framing it in this way does a variety of things. It gives everyone an opportunity to contribute. It allows for different modalities of experiencing. It does not put one response as being better than another. It gives permission for 'off the wall' responses, which, by definition, cannot be wrong – they are just experiences, and reflecting on them encourages members to start trusting their intuition.

By asking them to be aware of what they are experiencing when a case is presented, we are offering an opportunity to catch the parallel process (see Chapter 9, mode 5). In a group there are bound to be a range of different responses, and the job of the supervisor is to help the person presenting to see if any of them are useful. We give an example of this below.

A vital aspect of this process is to make sure that all responses are fed back to the group leader and not the presenter. The presenter just listens and should not feel either overwhelmed or having to show a positive response to please the person who has fed back.

In a group it is possible to re-enact the client session with a fellow group member playing the client. This can be developed through the use of sculpting and role-reversal techniques. Below are three re-enactments, the first described by Gaie Houston (1985) (see also Hawkins 1988a).

It is important that this supervision technique is given plenty of time and there is a chance for each 'coach' to receive feedback, first from the role-played client, in terms of what was helpful and what was unhelpful or difficult, and then from the group, who must likewise give feedback, which is owned, balanced and specific. It is too easy to give clever advice and damning criticism from the audience; it is quite another matter to do what you advise on stage (see Argyris 1982).

A third technique that is appropriate for groups is an enacted role set. A supervisee presents a client and the rest of the group are enrolled as different parts of the client's network. For example, someone could be enrolled as the supervisee's boss who is putting pressure on the supervisee to sort out this difficult client. This is affecting the quality of her work, as she feels distracted by this additional agenda and cannot be fully present to the client. Someone else can play the boss's boss and explore the pressure he or she is putting on the boss. Someone can play the client's difficult customer with whom they are trying to improve their relationship. The point is that these (and many more) factors are all present in the one-to-one coaching, but are often not recognized explicitly. The supervisee sees the problem as only to do with the client and does not take into account the system to which the client belongs. What then happens is that there is a short role-play of a session and the rest of the enrolled members listen in role as if they were a fly on the wall. They then feed back their responses in role and the supervisee is often astonished to find out that what they say corresponds to the positions the people take in real life. The problem can then be related to the total context, not just the interpersonal or intrapersonal one.

One of the techniques we have used to great effect is 'tag supervision'. We use it in conjunction with the seven modes. How it works is that someone elects to be supervisee and we place an empty chair opposite them. We then assign modes to each of the other members of the group. It works especially well in training groups where there is the possibility of more than one person playing each mode. The supervisee starts with a sentence such as I'd like to bring my client X, who finds giving challenging feedback to staff unbearably stressful. The facilitator shouts out a number, like four, and the person who has been assigned mode 4 comes and sits in the empty chair and makes an intervention like, 'Does this person remind you of anyone?' or 'What do you experience when you are with this person?' or any other mode 4 intervention. The rules are that a person can clap themselves out, anyone from the group can clap themselves in, or the supervisor can clap and suggest a mode. After initial hesitation, people want to rush in and try an intervention.

Tag supervision has proved useful in many ways. It gives an opportunity to practise the modes and watch others using them. It also gives an opportunity to see how they fit together.

As well as presenting actual cases, we sometimes try a variation, which involves asking people what is the worst situation they could face or have faced as a supervisor. We ask them to come up with an opening sentence. A very common one is, 'I don't think this is working. I want to change supervisor'. Another one every supervisor fears is, 'I have to tell you I am having a relationship with my client'.

A final technique is when someone has presented to ask them to sit outside the group and listen while the group discusses what they have presented as if behind their back. We give ourselves permission to say whatever comes to mind and bounce ideas off each other. The supervisee can then take or leave what is being said.

Example of group supervision

In 2003 the School of Coaching pioneered training in coaching supervision for their faculty. The Bath Consultancy Group provided the programme. Subsequently, the School introduced a quarterly group coaching supervision with John Bristow, one of the principal trainers from the Bath Consultancy Group.

The three-hour session follows a specific format. A short check-in enables the group to reconnect. This allows time for questions to emerge and to co-create the focus of the day. Then all participants are asked for cases on which they would like supervision. Through discussion, one person volunteers to be the supervisee, another offers to be supervisor while the others observe the process as 'shadow supervisors'. Since the faculty has been trained in our seven-eyed model, they work primarily in this mode. After about 15–20 minutes, the supervisor, facilitator or an observer suggests a 'time-out' of the supervision dialogue. During this 5–10-minute period of 'time-out', the observers have a conversation with the supervisor about the session progress, the supervisor's interventions, the observer's perceptions, hypothesis and recommendations. Normally, the 'supervisee' listens in on this discussion but does not directly engage. The purpose of this 'time-out' is to equip the supervisor with insights and new choices for the remaining part of the session. Often this discussion will encourage the supervisor to be aware of what is happening for themselves in mode 6. Questions will often get the supervisor to attend to impact on the 'here and now' in the relationship between the supervisor and coach. The facilitator and observers encourage the supervisor to be aware of their own internal processes, feelings, thoughts and fantasies that are evoked when listening to the client system. The observers will also often identify parallel process that the supervisor and coach may be mirroring regarding the coach, coachee and the organizational system. The 'time-out' can also be used to identify mode 7 aspects of the wider system and the stakeholders of the situation being discussed.

When the supervisor is ready, the supervision dialogue continues. Occasionally, if another participant has a specific line of enquiry that the group wants to explore, the supervisor role may be swapped.

At the end of the supervision session, feedback is given to the supervisor on what they did well and what they could do differently. Typically, the supervisor has the first go at self-assessment, followed by the supervisee and finally any observer who wants to give feedback. There may be a short discussion on any aspect of supervision that has emerged in the session.

This process enables all participants to learn from both the supervisor and coach perspective.

Following a short break, the group divides into trios or a combination of trios and pairs/quads depending on numbers. The small group configuration changes from one quarterly meeting to the next. This enables each participant to be supervised and observe every other member over time.

The format is similar to the above process with one person as supervisor, one as supervisee and one or two as observers or shadow supervisors. There are usually less 'time-outs'. There may be time for more than one session in the small groups. In this case, the roles will rotate around so there is a new supervisor, supervisee and shadow supervisor(s).

Benefits of supervision

Since the School of Coaching supervision group has been running for an extended period of time, there are a number of benefits that the individuals, the team and organization are experiencing:

- Since it is one of the few regular meetings of the faculty, it is an important opportunity to reconnect with colleagues. It is valued as an opportunity to learn together. It also has the side benefit of creating a window into the way a particular individual works with clients. Mike Munro Turner describes this as 'endlessly intriguing and revelatory' (personal communication 2006).

- From a personal point of view, Turner acknowledges that whenever one works with a client it is inevitable that the coach will get entwined in some of the system dynamics. It is critical to give up an element of one's detached, independent perspective in the process of getting alongside the client. Supervision provides the opportunity to 'go up a couple of steps' and get disentangled in order to look on the client-system-coach dynamic afresh. 'Supervision consistently helps me to have greater "choicefulness" in how I work with a client'. This in turn enables the client to have more choice in how they respond in their situation.

- The School of Coaching does not have any formal process to evaluate the impact or return on investment of the coaching supervision. Turner says 'I know in my gut that this is important, we don't have to have data to support this decision'.

Peer supervision

This section is derived from Hawkins and Shohet (2006) with their useful guidelines, which can be applied to coaches, mentors and consultants who are setting up peer supervision groups.

Many professionals on our courses complain that they cannot get good supervision as their immediate line senior has neither the time nor the ability to supervise them. We are often surprised that they have not even considered the possibility of setting up peer supervision for themselves.

We offer an illustration on how to cope with such a predicament. The example is taken from the therapeutic world again because there simply aren't many examples currently within the world of coaching, mentoring and supervision. The pattern of the example though is completely transferable. Peter Hawkins ran a therapeutic community and his immediate line manager was the assistant director of a large mental health charity, who had no direct experience of either therapeutic communities or supervision. This experience is similar to many of the situations we find with senior practitioners in various professions who are nominally supervised by senior managers with little or no practical experience of their area of activity.

In response to this situation Peter started a series of peer supervisions. One was with the Association of Therapeutic Communities, where he set up a peer supervision group for senior staff within and across therapeutic communities. He was surprised to find that many other senior practitioners in voluntary organizations, social services departments and the NHS shared the same shortage and need for supervision. This proved a rich and rewarding group with the opportunity to focus on whole community problems and dynamics. This group went on existing well after Peter and the other original members had left.

When practising in psychotherapy, one of us had his own peer supervision setting for his psychotherapy work, which was a peer triad with a consultant psychiatrist/psychotherapist and a clinical psychologist/psychotherapist. At each meeting one of the three members took his turn at being supervisor. The other two got 40 minutes' supervision each. At the end of each person's supervision the supervisees shared with the supervisor what he found helpful and difficult and then the supervisor shared his own reflections of the session. This was followed by the third member, who has been observing, giving feedback, both positive and negative, to the supervisor. This suited the needs of those in the triad who received not only supervision on their psychotherapy but reflections and learning on how they supervised. We have used this model recently to set up a similar process for supervision of our own coaching work and supervision of our supervision.

This piece of autobiography illustrates how peer supervision can be either individually reciprocal or based upon a group of workers with similar needs, approach and level of expertise. It also illustrates how it is possible to look for peer supervisors not only within your immediate workplace but also in similar workplaces within your own organization or with workers from different organizations. We have been involved in helping a number of staff set up their own peer supervision systems. These include trainees on our coaching supervision training, senior HR leaders and organizational consultants.

Peer supervision clearly has many advantages, but there are also many pitfalls and traps. In the absence of a group leader, there is a greater need for a firm and clear structure and it requires greater commitment from the group members.

Gaie Houston (1985) has written about some of the 'traps' or 'games' that we have known peer groups to fall into (see also Berne 1970).

1   *'Measuring cocks'*. Houston describes a group where the various members used phrases about their groups such as: 'Mine are so cooperative . . .' 'Mine say I have helped them a lot', 'It was such a powerful experience'. She goes on to write: 'An American consultant I know calls this activity measuring cocks. All the statements in it add up to "Mine's Better Than Yours". Everyone feels tense, knowing that if one person wins and has the biggest or best, everyone else has lost' (Houston 1985).

2   *Ain't it awful?* In this game, the peer group sits around, reinforcing each other's sense of powerlessness. One variant of the game is to spend the time sharing how you must be mad to work for this company or organization. Another variant is for coaches or mentors to spend their time showing how difficult, devious or disruptive their clients are, because they resist our best endeavours at every attempt. This can spill over into another game called 'get the client'.

3   *'We are all so wonderful'*. Peer group members can avoid having their anxieties about being criticized, or found out, by heaping fulsome praise on other peer members as an unacknowledged payment for returning the favour. This becomes a covert form of protection racket and in the long term ensures that the group is too fearful to let new members join or old members leave as this

might threaten the unearthing of what is buried. John Heron (1975) refers to this as 'consensus collusion'.

4 *'Who is the best supervisor?'* This is a straightforward, but often undisclosed or unacknowledged, competition to fill the void left by not having a group supervisor. It can emerge through group members straining to make the cleverest or most helpful comments, or through distracting peripheral arguments on the efficacy of this or that approach. Peer groups often have no mechanism for dealing with their group dynamics and unfortunately group members who point out the processes that are going on may get caught up in the competition to be the 'supervisor'.

5 *'Hunt the patient'.* Groups, like families, can identify one member to be the patient and the focus for the inadequate or difficult feelings to which the others do not wish to own. Having an identified patient also allows the other group members to retreat into the safe and known role of helper. While the other members 'help' this member explore their fears, they also protect themselves from facing similar fears within themselves.

These games are not the sole prerogative of peer groups, but there is more risk of peer groups falling into some of them, as there is no outside facilitator who will watch the process.

How to form a peer supervision group

It is clear from these reflections that peer supervision has many pitfalls, but if properly organized it also has many advantages. In workshops we have run we are often asked for advice in starting and running peer groups and we generally give the following recommendations:

- Try to form a group that has shared values but a range of approaches. It is important that you can talk together within a reasonably shared language and belief system but, if you all have the same training and style of working, the group can become rather collusive and lack a broader perspective.

- The group needs to be no larger than seven people. It must also ensure that it has enough time to meet the needs of all its members. It is no good having a peer supervision group of seven people, all of whom have a large number of clients for whom they want supervision, unless the group meets regularly for at least two or three hours at a time.

- Be clear about commitment. It is not helpful for the group members to commit themselves because they think they ought to, and then fail to meet their commitment. Members must be encouraged to share their resistance to meeting for supervision and, if possible, to share how they might avoid or otherwise sabotage the supervision group. For example, one member may warn the group that they are likely to get too busy with more pressing engagements, while another member may say that their pattern is to get bad headaches.

- Make a clear contract. You need to be specific about frequency of meeting and place of meetings, time boundaries, confidentiality, how time will be allocated and how the process is to be managed. You might need to be clear how you will handle one group member knowing the clients that other members bring for supervision; will the person leave the group while that client is being discussed or will the coach be expected to get supervision on that person elsewhere?

- Clarify the range of expectations. Some members may expect a greater focus on their personal process than others are comfortable with. Some members may expect all their client work to be covered by the group, while others may also have individual supervision elsewhere. Some members may expect a greater amount of advice on what to do next, while others may expect to use role-play or other experiential techniques. Try to discover if there are any hidden group agendas. We came across one peer group that consisted of two separate sub-groups that were working out their relationships.

- Be clear about role expectations. Who is going to maintain the time boundaries or deal with any interruptions? Who is going to organize the rooms? Is there going to be one person each time who carries the main responsibility for facilitating or will this emerge out of the group process?

- Build some time into each meeting (it need only be five or ten minutes) to give feedback on how the supervision process has been for each person. This can include appreciations and any resentments.

- Plan to have a review session every three months when all the members receive feedback on their role in the group, the dynamics of the group are looked at and the contract is renegotiated. Many of the exercises and approaches that we described in this chapter can be adopted by a peer group in its own review.

Organizing a peer supervision meeting

Many of the suggestions made above, about structuring group supervision, also apply to peer group supervision:

- Set ground rules like: members are expected to give direct, balanced and owned feedback; avoid patronizing advice; time is equally shared.

- Either start each session by discovering who has what needs or have a set rotational system for allocating time.

- Encourage all the members to be clear about what they need from the group in relation to what they are sharing – do they need just to be listened to; given feedback; facilitated in exploring their countertransference; or helped in exploring where to go next, choosing between various options, etc.? It is often useful if you do not know what the person wants to ask – 'What has led you to bring this particular issue today?' or 'What is it you need in relation to this client?'

- Decide about informal time. Often, if you have no social or informal time scheduled, the need to catch up with each other's news, to gossip and to make personal contact can interrupt the other tasks of the group. Some peer groups schedule a short social time at the beginning and/or end of the supervision group.

Team supervision

It is important to recognize that team supervision is different from group supervision. It involves working with a group that has not come together just for the purposes of joint supervision, but has a more or less involved work life outside the group. Thus, although many of the approaches to group supervision that we have outlined already are relevant, there are other factors that have to be managed.

There is a difference between teams that share work with the same clients, such as an account team of organizational consultants, who are working with a shared client organization, or a community of internal coaches within the same organization and a team who, although they work with similar approaches and in the same geographical area, have separate clients, like a coaching organization. A simple way of classifying the nature of teams is to use a sports analogy. In football teams all members play the same game, although with different special roles, at the same time, and are highly interdependent. In tennis teams, the team members play the same game, but do so either individually or in pairs. In athletics, team members take part in very different sports, at different times, but occasionally work together (relays), train together, combine their scores and support each other's morale.

When conducting team supervision there are still issues about group selection. Firstly, it is necessary to decide where the boundary of the team is drawn. Do you include clerical staff or trainees? If it is an interprofessional team, issues of inclusion and exclusion are even more highly charged.

Secondly, good team supervision should alert the team to the potential danger of filling vacancies with 'more people like us'. There is a need for teams to have some degree of homogeneity, but teams also need a balance in personality types, age, gender and skills. Belbin (1981) has carried out a classic study of what range of roles a team needs in order to be effective.

The concept of team supervision involves supervision of all the team members and also supervision of the team itself, as a discrete entity. We consider the team as an entity to be more than the sum of its parts and to have a personality and intrapsychic life of its own. This is termed by some writers as the team culture or the team dynamic. We say more about this in the chapters on team and organizational coaching (Chapters 4 and 5). It is important to note that team supervision is different from other forms of supervision, in that it inevitably involves some form of team coaching or team development.

Conclusion

Group supervision clearly has many advantages over individual supervision in the range of possible learning opportunities and different perspectives that it can provide. It also has many potential pitfalls. Those leading supervision groups need to be aware of, and work with, the group dynamic and this necessitates that they have some training in group leadership and dynamics. Peer groups also need to have a system for attending to their own process so that it supports the task of supervision in a healthy way, rather than diverting or sabotaging it.

The mode of supervision used in a group should reflect what is being supervised, so some form of group supervision is ideally suited for those being supervised on their group or team coaching. Group supervision is also useful in expanding the range of perspectives that one draws upon in reflecting on one's individual work, but we would recommend that, in the case of in-depth individual coaching or mentoring, group supervision should be an adjunct to, rather than a replacement for, individual supervision. The exception to this is that peer or group supervision can be quite adequate for senior practitioners who have developed not only their own individual competence but also an integrated form of self-supervision.

11

Shadow consultancy of consultant teams

Introduction

Shadow consultancy

Conclusion

Introduction

In the last chapter we looked at supervision carried out in groups and also the supervision of teams. One of the places where team supervision is most common is in providing shadow consultancy to a team of organizational consultants working on the same client account.

Shadow consultancy

The term 'shadow consultancy' was first defined by Marjan Schroder in 1974: 'The term "shadow consultant" denotes a consultant who, at the request of a colleague and by means of a series of mutual discussions in which he uses a socio-scientific approach, helps evaluate and, if necessary, change the diagnosis, tactics, or role adopted in a certain assignment'. This original definition of shadow consultancy was very helpful in opening up this field and beginning the exploration of modes of coaching and supervision for consultants. Since the 1970s shadow consultancy has been developed in several places, most notably by Bill Critchley and David Casey (1993) at Ashridge Management College, Roger Harrison in the USA (1995) and Peter Hawkins and colleagues at the Bath Consultancy Group, where it has been a core feature of our practice since 1986.

At the Bath Consultancy Group we discovered that the Schroder definition was too limited, with its emphasis on trying to evaluate the problem presented and arriving at a better approach. Our experience suggested that the most effective coaching of a consultant came from the shadow consultant focusing less on the problem presented and more on attending to the consultant as part of the system with which they were trying to work. The part of the system that shadow consultancy can most affect is the part that is actually in the room, namely the consultants. The shadow consultant then helps the consultants explore what they need to shift in themselves, in order to shift their relationship with the client system, so that the client system itself shifts.

As part of this, the shadow consultant can also provide the space for the consultants to reflect in tranquillity on the large amount of data they have absorbed from the client system but which may be outside their direct awareness or even buried in their unconscious. Often what the client cannot tell you directly they make you *feel* – and the job of the shadow consultant is to process and verbalize the unprocessed dynamics of the client system.

More recently we have started to call this deeper form of shadow consultancy 'systemic shadow consultancy' to distinguish it from the more problem-solving approaches, and have defined it as:

> The process by which a consultant (or team of consultants) with the help of an experienced shadow consultant, who is not working directly with the client, attends to understanding better the client system and themselves as part of the client/consultant system. Systemic shadow consultancy focuses on the interconnections between what the consultant(s) need to shift in themselves; their relationship with the client system; and in the client system – in order to be more successful. Attention also is paid to what is happening in the parallel process in the shadow consultancy system.

To develop this model we turned to other parallel fields such as anthropology, psychotherapy or family therapy (Hawkins and Miller 1994). Family therapy, particularly in the last 20 years, has grappled with the difficulties of changing ingrained habituated family patterns. It was discovered that the individual therapist soon gets caught in the web of family dynamics and becomes another symptom of family pathology. Even co-therapists can quickly replicate the family system by enacting family conflicts in their polarized perceptions of what is happening. This has led to family therapy approaches that are systemic and rely on having one therapist relating closely to the family, while one or more other therapists watch the process from behind a one-way mirror, often in telephone contact with the therapist in the room to intervene with questions and reframings at appropriate times. Another image for this process is the diver immersed in the ocean, surveying the buried material, while linked by radio to their support people in the boat on the surface.

The approach we developed has been to use the seven-eyed model (see Chapter 9) for attending to:

- the dynamics of the client organization (mode 1);
- the interventions and the projects carried out by the consultancy team (mode 2);
- what is happening dynamically in the relationship(s) between the consultancy team and their client (mode 3);
- how the consultancy team is operating and its team dynamics (mode 4);

- what happens live in the systemic shadow consultancy session between the team and the shadow consultants and how this might parallel the relationship dynamics in or with the client (mode 5);
- what emerges in and between the shadow consultants that might illuminate the work (mode 6);
- attending to the wider system dynamics and how these are affecting the work (mode 7).

Not only have we been using this approach with our consultancy work, but we have also worked with a wide range of consultancy organizations and professional services firms, both introducing and training shadow consultants, as well as providing shadow consultancy to some of their key client account teams.

Shadow consultancy of an account team

We were approached by one of the major global consultancies asking for help in developing their approach to global transformation and fast-track change. We began to explore with them their current and recent large-scale change programmes with client companies. We looked at what had most limited the scale and speed of the transformation. Repeatedly we found that one of the major limiting factors was the consultancy team process and how the team started to replicate the cultural blocks and dynamics of the client system.

We became convinced that the consultancy would never do really effective corporate transformation without building regular systemic shadow consultancy into the consultancy team. Since then we have undertaken a number of team shadow consultancy processes for this firm and this has confirmed our belief. We worked with one team of 25 consultants who were undertaking a major business process engineering and cost cutting exercise with a major client organization. The scoping and design work had gone really well, but as they had worked with the separate sub-businesses, the work had become more and more stressful.

The team leaders were angry with those out in the sub-businesses for not providing accurate and timely data on progress so they could keep the corporate centre informed. The team members were furious with the leaders, and felt they did not support them. They thought that their team leader was only interested in keeping those at head office happy, so they got a good client appraisal.

The first day of getting the whole team together enacted the conflict. The partner in charge sent a message to say he would not arrive till lunchtime, as he had to meet the project director at the corporate head office. Heated phrases were expressed like: 'He does not care about us, or about helping us get the job done, just about how it looks to those at the top.'

When the partner arrived at the team event, he became aware of the anger and low morale. He tried to provide leadership and lift morale by telling the team how positively the project was being viewed by those at the top. However, this only further incensed many of the team members, who were convinced that he and the organization top team were only concerned with appearances and not real change.

As we applied systemic shadow consultancy to unravel the process it became more and more clear that the team was enacting the parallel process to the client system. In the client's organization, the typical pattern was for change to be launched from the corporate centre, with a lot of good analysis and design, but running into problems at the implementation stage in the separate businesses. The businesses did not trust the corporate centre and did not own the problem that the change was introduced to address. They saw the change processes emerging from the centre as demands not support, and would resist them, by not supplying data, or responding to requests, and in extremes falsifying the data on progress that they sent back. This would cause the corporate centre to push harder and authoritatively demand more.

The same process was now happening in the consultancy team. The team needed to become aware of its own parallel process, in a non-blaming but interested way, in order to then attend to the systemic pattern in their client system. When change hits against such ingrained resistance, pushing harder just makes the difficulty worse.

To carry out systemic shadow consultancy in a large assignment team requires at least two experienced systemic shadow consultants, who are not only trained in the model, but also understand and can facilitate team dynamics.

Developing the account team

The systemic shadow consultant may also develop an ongoing relationship with the account team where they act as team coach, not just on the team functioning (see Chapter 4), but also on the development of the relationship with the client system. From this experience of combining the role of account team coach and systemic shadow consultant with a number of global account teams in major professional services firms, we developed a model of 'account transformation' (Bath Consultancy Group 1999).

The account transformation model shown in Figure 11.1 identifies four potential types of relationship roles with clients.

- *Solution supplier* is the area where current needs, known to the client, are delivered by you as the supplier. Here the work is often won through competitive tender and tightly specified by the purchasing department.

- *Strategic adviser* is the section where future needs, known to the client, are anticipated and where you add value to the client's forward strategy through adding your own expert knowledge about the sector trends.

- *Integrated trust* is the area where current patterns, processes, culture and needs, hidden from the client's view (blind spots) are revealed compassionately and appreciatively – so that the client experiences you as adding value in areas they could not originally have foreseen.

- *Performance partner* is the section where there is joint investment and shared risk between client and consultant, focused on addressing future needs that cannot be predicted with certainty.

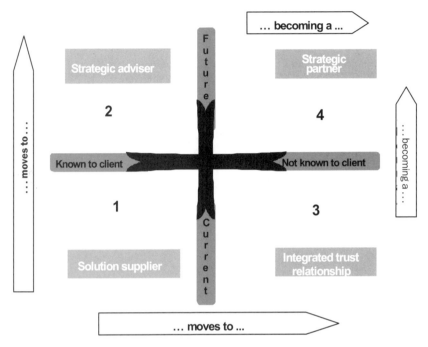

Figure 11.1 Account transformation model: new roles

Each relationship role requires a different language and mode of engagement from the consultants.

As a *solution provider*, your language is most often couched in terms of the client bringing problems and the consultants bringing a solution. The language is one of technical expertise and the mode of discourse often at Torbert's level (see Chapter 3) and the interventions 'prescriptive and informative' (see Heron model, Chapters 7 and 12).

As *strategic adviser* your language is more focused on challenges and opportunities, and is future-orientated. The discourse is more at the Torbert levels of 'achiever' and 'strategist' (Chapter 3), the interventions more catalytic. There is greater mutuality of dialogue.

As '*trusted adviser*', your language shifts to focusing more on patterns, processes and culture. Instead of concentrating on the immediate problem, attention shifts to the systemic patterns and dynamics of which this problem is just one symptom. The discourse is more at the Torbert stages of 'individualist and strategist' (Chapter 3) and interventions use more of both confrontative and supportive styles (Chapters 7 and 12).

As *performance partner* all the above languages may be in play, and the language of joint endeavour and creating win-win relationships is essential (see Figure 11.2).

Each relationship role also requires the consultancy team to bring different values and expertise. As solution provider, the consultant brings their technical

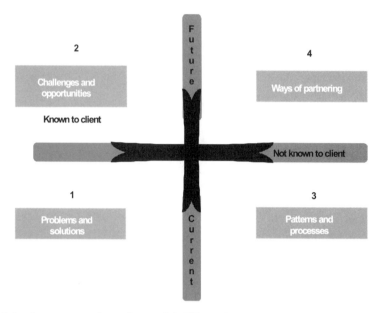

Figure 11.2   Account transformation model: different languages

expertise – for example, to restructure, cut costs, provide leadership development or coaching. As strategic adviser, they bring their understanding of the business and the business context, not only as it currently exists, but as it is developing into the future. As trusted adviser, one is bringing company or organizational insight, gleaned from having worked with the organization at different levels and in different ways. In Chapter 5, we talked about how the last one to know about the sea is the fish, and that organizational culture is what you stop noticing when you have worked there for over three months. Well, the trusted adviser can bring insights about the culture as it manifests when you try and change anything in the organization. So instead of just helping it carry out a successful change project, the consultancy can increase the organization's change capability for future change projects, through better understanding of what blocks and what enables change in their particular culture. As performance partner, the value you bring includes a joint commitment to a shared endeavour with your client/partner organization. This role needs to encompass the value brought from all the previous three roles, but also skill and capacity in partnering and ways to create win-win relationships (see Figure 11.3).

Conclusion

For a large consultancy team or a professional services account team to be adding real value to their client, they need to ensure that the value they bring is more than the sum of the various assignments they have with that organization. Whether they be accounts, legal advisers, corporate financiers or systems consultants, the account team needs to develop from delivering a series of technically efficient

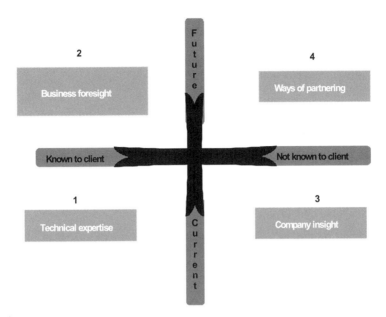

Figure 11.3 Account transformation mode: points of view

projects to their client – to being able to also bring both business foresight and company insight. The business foresight comes from their experience of working across a range of companies or organizations in the same sector or field, from which they can glean the collective trends. The company insight comes from being a regular visitor from outside the company culture and engaging with the company through various different parts of the system.

Often account teams lack both the discipline and the skills to generate this collective knowledge and deliver the value they could bring to their client, which would differentiate them from other professional service providers. Often we have found that account team meetings simply exchange information and check on the progress of each assignment. The shadow consultant or team coach's role is to provide both processes and facilitation to explore the trends in the wider sector and also the cultural patterns and processes of the company with whom they are working. The account team coach then helps them travel the journey from being one of many suppliers the client uses for professional services – through the stages of becoming a strategic and trusted adviser – to being a long-term performance partner, who is key to the client company moving forward.

SECTION 3
The skills and capacities for coaches, mentors, consultants and supervisors

Introduction to Section 3

In the first section of this book, we explored the different aspects and levels of the core craft that link coaching, mentoring and consultancy, all of which enable real-time learning in people at work. In the second section we outlined the process of developing and supervising the practitioners of these crafts. In this final section we will begin by laying out the core skills, which we believe are essential for coaching, mentoring, organizational consulting and also for supervising. For those who supervise coaches, mentors and consultant the skill set is very similar to the skill set for those practising the crafts that are being supervised. What is different is the context, the focus and the levels of complexity inherent in the two practices. When asked how coaching and supervising differ, our answer is that coaching is for the development of the coachee and the organization they work for. Supervision is for the development of the supervisee, the organization they work for, and, importantly, the clients they work with.

In all these roles, development of another in the service of a broader group, beyond the immediate client, is essential. In all these roles we emphasize the transformational change process that we first outlined in Chapter 1: namely that transformational change always starts with the parts of the system that are present in the room and require a felt-shift, for transformational change to begin in that person. This transformational shift needs to be more than intellectual insight and commitment to change, but involves a shift in our body, emotions, ways of relating, actions and the choices we make. Thus it needs to involve development in all seven of the domains in human functioning as we will outline below.

Aspects of the craft: the territories of development

To be effective in enabling the real-time learning and development of another person requires a lifelong commitment to the developing of oneself. Not only does this mean acquiring knowledge and skills, but more broadly, developing the whole of one's being. In Chapter 7, we argued that personal development was at the heart of professional development, and here we posit that at the heart of personal development is developing all of one's capacities in a balanced way.

In collaboration with our colleague, Chris Smith, we produced a model of the key territories of development for leaders that we believe applies equally well to coaches, mentors, consultants and their supervisors, and builds on the important work done by Gardner (1999), Senge (1990a), Wheatley (1994) and others (see Figure 2).

For many years there was an emphasis on developing one's intellectual intelligence (IQ), and for the last 20 years there has been a great deal written about the equal importance of emotional intelligence (EQ). The Smith and Smith model is proposing that there are six key intelligences and that we need to develop our capacity in all six dimensions as well as develop the presence of the seventh, our core self, which connects and integrates the other six dimensions, as well as bringing a meta-awareness that can be conscious of each aspect of ourselves as it is in play. The core self is both at the heart of each one of us, and also transcends us.

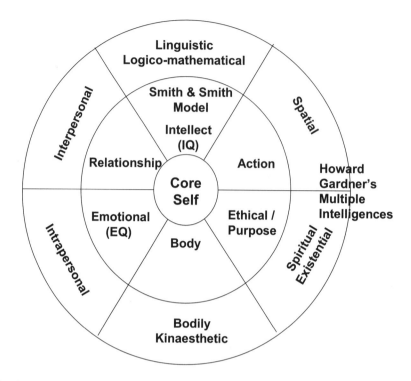

Figure 2   Seven territories of development
Source: Smith and Smith (2005)

It is at the connecting heart of all the other domains and also like a rim that runs round the circumference, where the domains engage with the world. The notion of multiple intelligences has been around for some time. Howard Gardner of Harvard University has identified ten of them.[1] Without getting into a debate about 'exactly how many?' we think the important thing to note here, is the fact that there is strong evidence for a number of intelligences, other than the linguistic and logical-mathematical ones that we normally highly prize and measure. In Figure 12.1 we lay Gardner's intelligences upon the map of the intelligences of the seven territories, to see how they play out.

Scoping the seven territories

We will briefly build some detail around each of the seven territories, so that the reader will get more of a sense of the ground that they cover and the challenges we face in developing them both singly and together.

---

[1] The ten intelligences are: linguistic, musical, logico-mathematical, spatial, bodily/kinaesthetic, naturalist, spiritual, existential and two types of personal intelligence (interpersonal and intrapersonal).

- *Intellectual:* this is the capacity to think, to make sense and understand; to analyse and problem solve but also to reflect, see patterns and make connections; to communicate; and also the practical knowledge of how to do things.

- *Relationship:* this is the ability to create meaningful and effective relationships, with a wide variety of people fairly quickly, in a way that helps them open up new depths and potential from within themselves and to new worlds and possibilities. Later in this section we provide a model that we use to help people explore their relationship engagement capacity and ways of developing it.

- *Action:* this area requires three Cs – capability to know where and when and how to apply one's competencies; courage to be decisive and to act fearlessly; and commitment of the will to ensure that the intent gets translated into completed action.

- *Emotional:* EQ has a number of key elements such as self-awareness; sensitivity to and perceptiveness of others; the ability to emotionally respond rather than react; and the ability to offer a range of emotional expressiveness.

- *Ethical:* here the key elements include: integrity – congruence between all aspects of myself; authenticity – doing what you say and following through; making clear moral choices; and acting in good faith, which involves knowing clearly what your work is in service of.

- *Body:* Our body is the vehicle through which we relate, act, sense and express our emotions, reflect and make sense. When we are stressed or tired not only does our physical capacity shrink, but also the other capacities are affected. When we are energized but relaxed, alert yet receptive, still yet flowing, we can listen more fully not only to others but to ourselves and have the vitality to choose which of our other capacities to use appropriately for the context. To achieve this state more often in our work requires lifelong attention and development.

- *Core self:* this element of the model is less a territory and more a space, like the hole at the centre of a wheel. The space makes the rest of the wheel function at its best. As we have said already, this space is both the container for the constituent parts of ourselves, but it holds that part of us that is essential, the part that gives us the ongoing sense of ourselves, despite the other six territories changing and developing over time. Depending on the reader's own belief system, this aspect, that we have termed the core self, could be termed the soul, the higher self, or our essence, among other things. When we think about developing our practice, we need to bear in mind which parts of this territory we avoid, which we give cursory acknowledgement to, and which we use regularly. In this section we distinguish between the skills (see Chapter 12) and the core capacities that need to be developed (Chapters 13, 14 and 15). They need be rooted in all seven territories of development and not just absorbed intellectually, but engaged with and embodied. Later in this section we will look at the core skills we will be outlining for supervisor development and locating them on this model. If readers feel that there are particular parts of the territory that have been, up to now, under explored, this will help them become more specific about how to develop them.

Competencies, capabilities and capacities

As discussed in Chapter 7 on development, we have been influenced by Broussine and others in distinguishing between the three Cs: *competencies, capabilities and capacities*.

- *Competencies* we see as the ability to utilize a skill or use a tool.
- *Capability* is the ability to use the tool or skill, at the right time, in the right way and in the right place.
- *Capacity* is a human quality, rather than a skill and more to do with how you are, rather than what you do.

Capabilities, like competencies, can be learnt and developed, and are the focus of Chapter 12. They are about know-how. However, the difference between the two is seen in the way the learning is generated. Competencies can be learned in the classroom, but capabilities can only be learned live and on the job. The skills and techniques we introduce in Chapter 12 are linked to the CLEAR coaching process, which we first outlined in Chapter 2 in relation to individuals and then developed further in Chapter 4 regarding coaching teams, and in Chapter 7 with supervising others. We provide a tool kit of approaches for each stage of the CLEAR coaching and supervision process (see Figure 7.1 on p. 124). The danger is that one can acquire a very large tool kit of skills, without developing the capability of knowing when to use each skill and in what way. The next chapter will therefore discuss the competencies to practise coaching, mentoring, organizational consultancy and supervision. Supervision has a vital role to play in helping the supervisee turn their competencies into capabilities, and to ensure that the capabilities are held within an ever-increasing capacity to work with others with fearless compassion.

Capacities relate to one's being, rather than one's doing. They are human qualities that can be nurtured and refined. Capacities can also be thought of in their root meaning of the space you have within you for containing complexity. We have all met people who seem to have little internal space from which to relate to you – and others who carry a seemingly infinite internal spaciousness, which tells you that they are fully present with whatever you feel you need to share or do. In Chapter 13 we refer to this as the relationship engagement capacity, which is one of eight core capacities we describe. The full list is:

1   Appropriate leadership.
2   Authority, presence and impact.
3   Relationship engagement capacity.

4   Encourages, motivates and carries appropriate optimism and develops self-supervision skills in supervisee.

5   Awareness of and ways of managing one's deference threshold.

6   Working across difference, transculturally sensitive to individual differences.

7   Ethical maturity.

8   A sense of humour and humility.

Capacities 6 and 7 are both given their own chapters (14 and 15) because of their complexity.

Capacities are not things to be acquired or places to arrive at. Each capacity takes our whole life to develop and development is not a uni-directional process. Without attention to our practice and supervision, each of these capacities can atrophy within us, and our effectiveness decline. Development and learning is for life, not just for school. The joy is that there is always more to be learnt.

At the end of the main body of Chapter 12, we will come back to the seven territories model again and incorporate the key development skills onto it, so that readers will see the specific ways the skills link with the development opportunities of the model.

12

Core skills and capabilities

Introduction

Many of the key skills necessary to be an effective supervisor are also key to being an effective coach, mentor and consultant. When training coaches, mentors and consultants in supervision, we find it very helpful for the participants to return to many of the skills they have learnt in their core training and to relearn these in the new context of supervision. Many participants have reported how their supervision training has radically improved their core practice.

While many of the skills may be the same, the context in which they are used is fundamentally different. As a coach you are listening intently to the client, in the interests of assisting them in hearing themselves and widening the options of their development. As a supervisor you are listening to the coach and indirectly the coach's client and their joint relationship, to enable all three to progress (see Chapter 9).

The other key difference is that, as a supervisor, part of your function is to assist the skill development of the supervisee. This is a central aspect of the developmental function of supervision. The most potent means of carrying out this developmental function is not by teaching but by how you role-model the core skills in your work and relationship with the supervisee.

Self, and other, assessment for supervisors

We have developed a self, peer, supervisor and supervisee assessment questionnaire for supervisors, which we encourage supervisors to use to assess themselves and to give to their supervisor, supervisees and peer trainees to get feedback and compare the different perspectives. You can view, and download the assessment form by going to www.bathconsultancygroup.com. You may find it useful to score yourself before going on to read about the different skills below and then rescore yourself once you have read more.

This self-assessment questionnaire affords you the opportunity of getting 360-degree feedback from supervisees, peers, tutor and supervisor. Each person is asked to rate each area of skill on a 1 to 5 scale. To create some common understanding of how to use this rating scale we offer the following descriptions:

1 Professional learning need – don't know how to do this.
2 Personal learning need – know how to but unable to make it happen.
3 Sporadically competent – occasionally do it fine.
4 Consistently competent – this has become part of my natural way of doing things.
5 Mastery – can role-model this and can teach it to others.

We suggest people use an appropriately wide range of scoring. We ask them not to reduce everything to a median score. After scoring themselves, they send copies of this self-assessment questionnaire to two supervisees, two peer group trainees, and their supervisor. They then arrange feedback from each person who fills in one of these forms. The objective is not so much to arrive at a score, but to start a series of 360-degree conversations that will hopefully stimulate further learning and new areas of focus for the development of their practice.

In Chapter 13, we will explore eight key capacities for all those enabling the learning of others, where as in this chapter we will look at the core competencies. The key skills or competencies for coaches, mentors, consultants and supervisors can be usefully classified by relating them to the CLEAR model. As we said in Chapter 8, it can also be used as a model for supervision.

CLEAR 1: contracting phase skills

Forming the contract

All forms of supervisory relationship need to begin with a clear contract, which is created and formed by both parties, and also reflects the expectations of the organizations and professions involved. Page and Wosket (1994) propose that a contract should attend to the following:

- ground rules;
- boundaries;

- accountability;
- expectations;
- relationship.

Carroll (1996) elaborates four principal areas that need to be explored:

- practicalities;
- working alliance;
- presenting in supervision;
- evaluation.

We have discussed in some depth the whole issue of how to contract between supervisor and supervisee in Chapter 8. We will simply remind the reader here about the five key areas that should be covered:

1 Practicalities.
2 Boundaries.
3 Working alliance.
4 The session format.
5 The organizational and professional context.

A number of authors, including Page and Woskett (1994), Brown and Bourne (1996), Carroll (1996), Hewson (in Holloway and Carroll 1999) have detailed sections on the process of contracting, if readers want to make a special study of this area of supervision practice.

Negotiating the contract

Inskipp and Proctor (1995) have provided a very helpful checklist for areas to be covered in an initial exploratory contracting meeting by a counselling supervisor. We have slightly amended this to be appropriate for coaches, mentors, consultants and supervisors (see Table 12.1).

All forms of supervisory relationship, like coaching and mentoring, need to begin with a clear contract which is created and formed by both parties, and also reflects the expectations of the organizations and professions involved.

CLEAR 2: listening phase skills

Four levels of listening

'Listening is as powerful an act as speaking, reading as writing, asking as answering, and there are no true speakers who are not also listeners, writers who are not also readers, answerers who are not also askers' (Grudin 1996: 211).

Table 12.1 The exploratory contracting interview

Negotiate	The working alliance	Information to supervisee about me
Time, length, when, frequency, where? Cost: how much? Method of payment, who pays, when, invoice/cheque/ cash? Missed sessions payment, holidays, notice	Beginning to set up a trusting relationship to produce a working alliance by communicating: empathy, respect, genuineness	Theoretical background and training experience as a professional Supervisory experience etc. Present work Support for supervision Membership of professional associations
Discuss and negotiate	*Basic relationship skills*	*Information wanted from the supervisee*
Recording (client, supervision, agreement) Boundaries Reviews Evaluation/assessment Code of ethics	For relationship building, exploring and negotiating Paraphrasing, reflecting, summarizing, focusing, questioning, self-disclosure, immediacy and purpose, stating and preference stating	Experience, qualifications Theoretical models Professional organization, code of ethics Freelance/organization/ agency Where working Number of clients, and other counselling work Any agency requirements Professional needs and development In counselling or therapy
Final decision	**Can we still work together?**	

Listening to somebody is, at one level, a simple everyday task, but it is also a deep and subtle skill. It is a skill that few of us are taught to do well, and which very few of us ever practise. Most of us have had the occasional experience of being so well listened to that we come away refreshed and more clear about our own thoughts and feelings. However, this contrasts with many experiences of talking to people and knowing that they may be hearing your words and understanding them, but that they are not understanding you, or really getting what it is you want to convey.

In marriages or long-term partnerships, we often hear the complaint, 'You are not listening to me!' The accused party will frequently respond defensively with: 'Yes, I am!' – and even repeat the words they heard said. The complainant may then respond with: 'You may have heard the words, but you were not listening to me!'

Listening happens at many levels. To clarify what these levels are, we have developed a model that articulates four levels of listening. It distinguishes between the listening levels by the effect the listening has on the person being listened to, as well as the activity of the listener that produces this effect (see Table 12.2). A complex skill set goes with each of these four levels.

Table 12.2   Levels of listening

Level	Activity of listener	Outcome registered in the person being listened to
1: Attending	Eye contact and posture demonstrate interest in the other.	'This person wants to listen to me.'
2: Accurate listening	Above, plus accurately paraphrasing what the other is saying.	'This person hears and understands what I am talking about.'
3: Empathic listening	Both the above, plus matching their non-verbal cues, sensory frame and metaphors; feeling into their situation.	'This person feels what it is like to be in my position, they get my reality.'
4: Generative empathic listening	All the above, plus using one's own intuition and 'felt sense' to connect more fully what one has heard, in the way one plays it back.	'This person helps me to hear myself more fully than I can by myself.'

Level 1: attending skill set

Attending well to another person requires giving them full and undivided attention. This involves providing a time and space undisturbed by outer distractions, such as the telephone ringing or other interruptions. It also requires being free of internal distractions of one's other thoughts, concerns or feelings, so one has the space to be receptive. To do this involves the practice of emptying oneself. This may be at the simple level of listing all the things you need to do or are worried about, so that you don't feel the need to think about them during the conversation. By putting the list away in a drawer – to return to later – you relax your anxieties about forgetting important tasks, and become available to the other person more fully. It can also involve preparing oneself with a few moments of silent meditation or stilling oneself, by sitting quietly with one's eyes closed and focusing on one's breathing and just noticing thoughts and feelings that come up and allowing them to float away.

Undisturbed space is a prerequisite, but not sufficient. The listener needs to be giving the right non-verbal signals that they are not only attending to the other, but are interested in what they are saying. This also involves the skills of non-verbally matching the other person (see the section below on matching and mismatching).

Level 2: accurate listening skill set

Having given full attention, one can then proceed to the second level of accurate listening to the content of what the other person is telling you. This involves two types of activity:

- Reflecting the content: when you feed back to the speaker the content of what you have heard them say. 'I hear you saying that you have tried to get a clear decision on this one, but have never managed it.'
- Paraphrasing when you feed back to the speaker the gist of the content of what they are saying. For example: 'If I've heard you right, the essence of what you are saying is ...'

Accurate listening is enhanced by the ability to match the language of the other person, both in terms of the sensory modes they use and also in terms of their use of metaphors, as we describe in the 'matching and mismatching' section.

Level 3: empathic listening skill set

This involves listening not only to the words being spoken, but also to the feelings being conveyed. If we think of the words as the melody line of a piece of music, then the feelings are carried in the harmonies that are conveyed through the body language, and the music of the voice – its pitch, volume, rhythm, timbre etc. Empathic listening entails acknowledging the emotions of the other person by giving feedback to the speaker about the feelings they are expressing – either verbally or non-verbally through the way they are speaking, for example, 'It sounds to me as though you are feeling really frustrated with this lack of agreement'. Such feedback is most effective when it is said in an emotionally expressive way that matches the feeling of the speaker. We will elucidate how this can be developed in the section on 'expanding your range of emotional expression'.

Level 4: generative empathic listening skill set
The skill of this level is for the listener to be able to play back the thoughts and feelings that are on the periphery of the speakers awareness. It requires a way of expressing what you sense 'at the edges' of what is said and probably have only half understood. It is therefore important that the tone of how it is fed back is tentative and allows the speaker to correct or develop what you have heard between the lines.

Matching skills to build rapport

In today's world it is important to be able to quickly achieve rapport with a wide range of individuals, from different cultures and different professional backgrounds. It is also important to be able to effectively shift the agenda, mindsets and emotions either in a relationship or in a meeting. Research indicates that most individuals can relate well to between 10–30 per cent of other people they work with. With good training and development it is possible for most people to double their starting percentage. The key skills that must be developed are those of matching and mismatching.

Matching
Research shows that the ability to build rapport quickly is dependent on how well one can match the person or people to whom one is relating. Matching takes place on many different levels, which include:

- *Language* – the ability to listen accurately to the other person and demonstrate understanding by paraphrasing their issues and concerns in language similar to that which they have used.

- *Sensory modes* – it has been shown that better rapport is achieved if you use the same sensory modality as the other person, e.g. they may use a visual language talking about wanting to 'look at an issue that appears to be coming down the road' at them; if their dominant mode was auditory they might say, 'I want you to hear how loudly the alarm bells are ringing'; while a kinaesthetic (feeling/sensation focused) person might say, 'I have got this real fear in my gut about what is going to hit us'.

- *Metaphors* – the ability to use similar metaphors to the other person means they are more likely to feel understood (e.g. mechanical metaphors, sailing metaphors, sporting metaphors or family metaphors etc.).

- *Body posture* – concerns the importance of matching the formality and informality, appropriate distance, level and uprightness etc.

- *Gestures and level of animation* – e.g. arms folded across the chest, fist clenched, face flushed.

- *Voice level* – volume, rhythm, pitch, tone, tempo and timbre of the voice.
- *Emotional tone* – the ability to reflect the emotional tone or undertone of the other person (see 'Expanding the range of one's emotional expression' on p. 221).

It is important not to try and mimic or copy the other person, but to do enough matching in the above areas to provide the other person with a sense that they are being empathetically listened to and that you know, understand and appreciate their world. It is also important to find a way of matching the other, while staying authentic to your own way of being.

Mismatching
Mismatching is the ability to shift the way of thinking or relating in the room, through shifting one's own mode of being. Mismatching can be achieved through any of the modalities listed in the section on matching. Therefore the art of mismatching is to be able to imagine the emotional and energy shift that is required in either the situation being explored or the person or team you are engaging with – and then to create that shift first in your own way of being, expressing and relating. For instance, if you believe that the other person needs to be more passionate and more challenging in their attempts to get other people on board with the change process, then it is not effective to just discuss this in a reflective tone, which is low energy. Instead the challenge and the passion must be embodied by the intervener, and bodily modelled. Words alone do not create a shift.

Asking good-quality questions

Another skill most people think they already have, but most of us have poorly developed, is the ability to ask good-quality questions and to utilize a wide range of questioning approaches. To be an effective questioner you need a whole tool kit of questions, otherwise you will treat everything as if it was data.

There are five main types of question:

1 *Closed* questions – those seeking data ('How many apples do you have?').
2 *Open* questions – those seeking information ('Why did you plant apple trees?').
3 *Leading* questions – those that seek information and indirectly suggest how they want the question answered ('Why do you like apples best?').
4 *Inquiry* questions – those inviting active enquiry ('What are the criteria for judging the best apple?').
5 *Mutative* questions – those that not only invite active enquiry but also create an emotional shift in the person being asked ('What would it take for you to begin to like apples?').

CLEAR 3: exploration phase skills

Expanding the range of one's contributions

Often in meetings – or other forms of conversation – dialogue degenerates into debate or discussion through a form of interchange that relies too much on individuals advocating proposals or solutions – and others proposing alternative solutions. Bill Torbert, in his research on effective leadership and leadership development (Fisher and Torbert 1995), has developed a model that shows that effective leaders use a balance of four 'types of speech' – *framing, advocating, illustrating* and *enquiring*.

Framing

This refers to explicitly stating the purpose for the present occasion, the dilemma you are trying to resolve and the assumptions you think are shared or not shared – but need to be tested, out loud, for clarity. This is the element of speaking most often missing from conversations and meetings. The leader or initiator assumes the others know and share the overall objective. Explicit framing (or reframing, if the conversation appears off-track) is useful precisely because the assumption of a shared frame is frequently untrue. When people have to guess at the frame, they often guess wrongly and impute negative, manipulative motives ('What's he getting at?').

Instead of starting with the first item of the meeting, the leader can provide and test an explicit frame, for example:

> 'We're about halfway through to our final deadline and we've gathered a lot of information and shared different approaches, but we haven't yet made a single decision. To me, the most important thing we can do today is agree on something, make at least one decision we can feel good about. I think XYZ is our best chance, so I want to start with that. Do you agree with this assessment, or do you think something else is more important?'

Advocating

This refers to asserting an option, perception, feeling or proposal for action explicitly in relatively abstract terms (e.g. 'We've got to get shipments out faster'). Some people speak almost entirely in terms of advocacy, others rarely advocate at all. Either extreme – only advocating or never advocating – is likely to be relatively ineffective. For example, 'Do you have an extra pen?' is not an explicit advocacy, but an enquiry. The person you are asking may truthfully say, 'No' and turn away. On the other hand, if you say 'I need a pen (*advocacy*). Do you have an extra one (*enquiry*)?' the other is more likely to say something like, 'No, but there's a whole box in the office drawer.'

The most difficult type of advocacy to make effectively is – for most people – an advocacy about how we feel, especially how we feel about what is occurring at this moment. This is difficult partly because we are often only partially aware of how we feel; also, we are reluctant to become vulnerable. For both these reasons, feelings usually enter conversations only when they have become so strong that they burst in, and then they are likely to be offered in a way that *harshly evaluates* others ('Damn it, will you loud-mouths shut up!'). This way of advocating is usually ineffective because it invites defensiveness. By contrast, a *personally owned request* is more likely to invite honest sharing by others ('I'm feeling frustrated and shut out by the machine-gun pace of this conversation and it would help me if we could all slow this down and listen more carefully').

Illustrating

This involves telling a concrete story that puts meat on the bones of the advocacy and thereby orients and motivates others more clearly (e.g. 'We've got to get shipments out faster (*advocacy*). Jake Tarn, our biggest client, has got a rush order of his own, and he needs our parts before the end of the week' (*illustration*). The illustration suggests an entirely different mission and strategy than might have been inferred from the advocacy alone. The advocacy alone may be taken as a criticism of the subordinate or another department and may unleash a year-long system-wide change, when the real target was intended to be much more specific and near-term.

You may be convinced that your advocacy contains one and only one implication for action, and that your subordinate or peer is at fault for misunderstanding. But in this case, it is *your* conviction that is a colossal metaphysical mistake. Implications are by their very nature *inexhaustible*. There is *never* one and only one implication. That is why it is so important to be explicit about each of the four types of speech and to interweave them sequentially.

Enquiring

This, obviously, involves questioning others in order to learn something from them. In principle, it is the simplest thing in the world; in practice, it is one of the most difficult things in the world to do effectively. Why? One reason is that we often enquire rhetorically, as we just did. We don't give the other the opportunity to respond; or we suggest by our tone that we don't really want an answer, at least, not a *true* answer. 'How are you?' we say dozens of times each day, not really wanting to know. 'You agree, don't you?' we say, making it clear what answer we want.

A second reason why it is difficult to enquire effectively is that an enquiry is much less likely to be effective if it is not preceded by framing, advocacy and illustration. Naked enquiry often causes the other to wonder what frame, advocacy and illustration are implied and to respond carefully and defensively (e.g. 'How much inventory do we have on hand?'; 'Hmm, he's trying to build a case for reducing our manpower').

Exercise

- *Step 1* – recall a recent situation where you were coaching, consulting or supervising and you were less effective than you would like to have been.
- *Step 2* – write out on a blank piece of paper a verbatim account of five minutes of the most critical part of the meeting. Leave a two-inch column on the right-

hand side of the paper clear so that you can add what thoughts and feelings were going on in parallel inside you.

- *Step 3* – using the Bill Torbert's 'four types of speech', mark each of your interventions either F, A, Il or En depending on which type of speech they were.

- *Step 4* – consider which alternative form of speech you might have beneficially used. Write out the sentence you would like to have delivered.

- *Step 5* – seek out feedback and coaching on your dominant and under used types of speech and explore how you might achieve a greater balance.

Signalling intent: simple ways of framing one's contribution

Many miscommunications that interrupt the flow of dialogue happen because one party has misunderstood the intent behind the contribution of the other party. Sometimes person A intends to offer a comment that builds on what person B had previously said, but person B, instead of feeling validated, hears this as a rebuttal of their suggestion and becomes defensive. Also many contributions fail to add to the flow of the dialogue, as those listening are unclear how it links to previous comments and what form of contribution it is.

Dialogue can be greatly enhanced by individuals becoming more skilled at framing their contribution as they begin to speak. Three simple guidelines are helpful:

- be clear about your intent;

- frame your intent at the very beginning of your contribution;

- signal, verbally and non-verbally, an openness to others to build on your contribution as you end.

Bill Torbert's framework for leadership interventions can provide a good model for thinking about the different ways of flagging the intent of one's contribution. If we take his four intervention styles of advocacy, illustrating, reframing and enquiry, each of these can be used either to come alongside and support a previous contribution, or to offer a different perspective in a non-combative way, or to create a link between two previous contributions. Here are examples of ways of signalling intent in each of the 12 categories (see Table 12.3).

A: coming alongside
- A1 'I would like to build on what Jane has said ...' – supportive advocacy.

- A2 'I would like to give an example of what Jane has said ...' – supportive illustrating.

- A3 'Another way of understanding what Jane has said would be to ...' – supportive reframing.

- A4 'How might you develop that idea Jane?' – supportive enquiry.

Table 12.3 The four intervention styles

	Coming alongside	Non-combative contradicting	Linking and integrating
Advocacy	A1	B1	C1
Illustrating	A2	B2	C2
Reframing	A3	B3	C3
Enquiry	A4	B4	C4

B: non-combative contradiction

- B1 'I would like to offer another view alongside Jane's' – advocating difference.

- B2 'Let me offer a story which I think runs contrary to Jane's idea, but someone might be able to connect them for us' – illustrating from difference.

- B3 'I would like to introduce another way of looking at the situation to put alongside Jane's perspective' – reframing from difference.

- B4 'How might your idea work in situation X?' – enquiring from scepticism.

C: integrating and linking comments

- C1 'Can I offer a way we can connect these two different proposals and see if it meets both needs?' – advocating a link.

- C2 'Let me tell you about a time when I saw these two needs being connected …' – illustrative linking.

- C3 'A framework that might connect these two different viewpoints is …' – linking reframing.

- C4 'Is there a way we can connect Jane's proposal with Ian's?' – linking enquiry.

Intervention styles – John Heron

The other major area of skill learning that needs to be included in any basic supervision training is to review the practitioner facilitation skills of the course members and help them adapt and develop them in an appropriate way for supervision. One useful tool in doing this is the Heron model of six categories of intervention, which we have mentioned at other points through the book already, because we believe it is a central skill in creating transformational change. Heron (1975) developed a way of dividing all possible interventions in any facilitating or enabling process into six categories. They apply equally to one-to-one and group situations. Although they may not be exhaustive, they help us to become aware of the different interventions we use, those we are comfortable with and those we avoid. We can, with practice, begin to widen our choices.

The emphasis in our definitions is on the intended effect of the intervention on the client. There is no implication that any one category is more or less significant and important than any other. The six categories are:

- *Prescriptive* – give advice, be directive, e.g. 'You need to write a report on that'. 'You need to challenge your coachee'.
- *Informative* – be didactic, instruct, inform, e.g. 'You will find similar reports in the filing cabinet in the office'. 'This is a useful book on coaching'.
- *Confrontative* – be challenging, give direct feedback, e.g. 'I notice when you talk about this particular client you always smile'.
- *Cathartic* – release tension, abreaction, e.g. 'What is it you really want to say to your client?'
- *Catalytic* – be reflective, encourage self-directed problem solving, e.g. 'Can you say some more about that?' 'How can you do that?'
- *Supportive* – be approving, confirming, validating, e.g. 'That must feel really difficult.'

The six types of intervention are only of any real value if they are rooted in care and concern for the client or supervisee. They are valueless when used 'degenerately' or 'perversely'. Heron defines 'degenerate interventions' as those which happen when the practitioner is using them in an unskilled, compulsive or unsolicited way. They are usually rooted in lack of awareness, whereas a 'perverted intervention' is one that is deliberately malicious.

We have used this model widely in helping supervisors look at their style of intervening. We ask them to appraise themselves in terms of which category they most dominantly use and which they feel least comfortable using. We then have all trainee supervisors carrying out individual supervisions with a fellow trainee, while a third trainee records the pattern of interventions they use.

This opens up the possibility of the trainees deciding to develop one of their less used intervention skills. Also for many new supervisors it provides an opportunity to consider how their intervention style needs to be different as a supervisor than as a practitioner. A non-directive coach may find that their previous training and experience have led them dominantly to use catalytic interventions and that as a supervisor they have to incorporate more informative and confrontative interventions.

We have also found that some workers completely switch styles and abandon many of their very useful coaching skills when they move into a managerial or supervisory role. These workers need help in revaluing their own practitioner skills, albeit within a new context and role.

This model can also be used by trainee supervisors in mapping their own supervision style. Some trainees have recorded their supervision sessions and then scored each of the interventions that they have used. Others have used the model for both the supervisee and themselves to reflect back on the session and in particular the supervisor's interventions; then to explore how each party would like the emphasis in intervention style to change.

Expanding the range of one's emotional expression

Some brilliant musicians find certain musical pieces that they cannot play well, not because of their technical competence, but because it demands that they to access an emotional rhythm that is outside their normal repertoire. Likewise actors can struggle with certain theatrical roles, and senior executives can find they are unable to move certain recurring situations, such as conflict, in their team or organization – and more insight and explanation do not help.

When watching a foreign film, opera or play, it is often possible to be very moved by the emotions of the performance despite not understanding the dialogue. The emotions are carried in the rhythms, not just of the music, but of the performer's voice, posture and gestures.

Emotional rhythms are similar across different cultures and seem to be universally recognizable. They were researched by Manfred Clynes (1977), who called them 'sentic states'. He discovered seven basic rhythms, which are universal, namely: anger, hatred, grief, love, sensuality, joy and awe. Since his initial academic research, others have developed and taken his work forward including Richard Borofsky in the USA and Malcolm Parlett in the UK who introduced the system to the Bath Consultancy Group. These authors developed the ideas into ways of working with performers, executives, consultants and psychotherapists, to help them extend their emotional range of expression.

The seven sentic states

All seven emotional rhythms have a positive and negative side. The fully mature person can express all seven states clearly and appropriately. It is important before we look at these seven states that we mention a word of caution about the terms used. Terms like 'anger' and 'hatred' should be treated like unrecognizable technical terms and not invested with all the emotional resonance that such words may have for you. In our experience treating them as ciphers helps us understand what Clynes is saying, and stops us fighting the process.

In Figure 12.1 we show how the seven sentic states link to different parts of the body and to different energy chakras in the famous Hindu system of the human body and its energy distribution.

Anger – the first of the fundamental rhythms is located at the base of the spine. Anger should not be confused with aggression, for clear anger sets boundaries in time and space and gives clear instructions. It does not attack the other person. Without the rhythm of anger, as it is understood here, it is very hard to attract the attention of a class, workshop or large group of people to start an event, or bring a large discussion to a close. The rhythm of anger is essential in assertiveness training in order to say 'no' or set a clear boundary. In music it can be heard in the opening of Beethoven's fifth symphony or at the start of Bernstein's *West Side Story*.

Hatred – is located in the gut, and is the energetic rhythm used to end things and to creatively destroy. Hatred is used to tear things up, break off dead wood, end a relationship. Without hatred we become constipated; have lofts and cellars full of things we never use but cannot throw away; and can never end projects or

Seven rhythms of emotional expression

Awe

Joy

Sensuality

Love

Grief

Hatred

Anger

Figure 12.1   Seven rhythms of emotional expression

relationships. Hatred helps us finish off, break out and break through our business blocks, as well as confront stuck situations that are being denied. The rhythm can be heard in Wagner's *Das Rheingold* in Alberich's arias and in Mime's aria in *Siegfried*, and also in Verdi's *Othello*.

Grief – deep grief originates in the lower chest and diaphragm. It is the rhythm of mourning and sadness from gentle sobbing to the wailing that can be heard in Middle Eastern funerals. It is also the rhythm of letting go, of surrender and forgiveness. Without this rhythm it is impossible to fully empathize with another's pain or grief. It can be heard in the slow movement of Mahler's fifth symphony or the hymn 'Abide with Me'.

Love – this rhythm originates from the heart. It is the rhythm used to welcome and include people, to express acceptance of others and a concern and caring for them. This rhythm can be heard in Brahm's *Lullaby*, which beautifully helps children go to sleep, or the Countess's song at the end of Mozart's *Marriage of Figaro*.

Sensuality is often expressed through the mouth and hands, this rhythm is the expression of sensual pleasure and excitement. It can be seen in the savouring of delicious food or enjoying another's company. It is used by leaders to excite interest in a description of what their vision would look like, sound like or feel like and by trainers to engage their audience energetically. Without the energy of sensuality our relationships can become dry and sterile. In music the rhythm can be heard in Bizet's *Carmen* and Ravel's *Bolero* as well as a lot of great jazz saxophone music.

Joy is a rhythm that goes right through the body but is most expressed through the eyes. Through joy we celebrate and affirm the positive. It can be seen in sport as players do a 'high five' slapping of hands or the crowd jump in the air. In music it can be heard in Beethoven's *Ode to Joy* in his ninth symphony; in Handel's 'Unto us a Child is Born', in the *Messiah*; and in Copeland's *Appalachian Spring* in the tune used for the modern hymn 'Lord of the Dance'.

Awe – when we see a beautiful sunset, or a spectacular view that takes our breath away, we express awe. The same rhythm is used to celebrate and affirm how impressively another person or group has performed. 'Wow that was fantastic!', we might say. It is the rhythm of being taken beyond ourselves, which can be heard in the last movement of Mahler's second symphony or Richard Strauss' *Four Last Songs*.

Other emotional states

Of course, we encounter other emotional states apart from these seven, such as jealousy, pride, shame, revenge, anxiety, fear etc. However, most of these are conflations of one or more sentic state packaged up with a variety of other beliefs and judgements rather than new states in their own right.

An apparent exception is fear. Like the earlier seven sentic states it is located in a part of the body – the stomach. Typically it is like a pit or chasm opening up. When felt more lightly, it is like butterflies in the tummy; here the feeling borders alongside anxiety and excitement. The rhythm of fear can be heard in the jagged cascades of the strings in the soundtrack of Hitchcock's film *Psycho*.

Like anger, fear is a product of an ancient biological 'fight or flight' mechanism associated with adrenalin secretion and an increased pulse rate. But, unlike anger, instead of producing an increased blood flow to the face and upper torso, it drains it away downwardly and internally.

And this is the difference between fear and the sentic states. With the seven sentic states a person's energy is already moving outwards into interpersonal space. In the case of fear, however, energy is moving inwards. With fear, active listening and acknowledgement are also important for helping people to become unfrozen and, in the process this can sometimes give vital data about the issue the person is struggling with. But it is only when the person's energy begins to flow outward again that they become effective players in the interpersonal space of organizational life.

Emotional expression and EQ

Daniel Goleman (1996) and others have written extensively about the need for successful executives and other professionals to combine a sharp intelligence (IQ) with a well-balanced emotional intelligence (EQ). He breaks EQ down into 25 key competencies such as: 'influence', 'building bonds', 'understanding others' etc. These are very important skills, which require the individual to inwardly access the appropriate emotional energy and find the right rhythm with which to express the appropriate competency.

Each of us tends to develop one or two dominant modes of expression and have other rhythms where, because of our culture, personality or personal history, we find it harder to be fully expressive. Our applied research leads us to believe that personalities do not change easily or quickly, if at all, but within our personalities we can begin to:

- expand our range of emotional expression;
- use each emotional rhythm more cleanly and clearly;
- increase our awareness of the non-verbal emotional expression of others.

To do this we need honest feedback from others, frameworks for understanding the range of choice, practice of new modes of expression and coaching.

Creating 'shift in the room'

We frequently talk about the coach or supervisor's ability to create 'shift in the room'. For us it is a key skill that underpins all our work. Initially some people find it hard to understand what we are referring to. The idea is so important to us though, that we have set aside a separate section at the end of the chapter to give the topic an extended airing. At this point in the chapter though, we wish to lightly touch on all the core skills so that they can be seen 'in the round'. Therefore 'shift in the room' needs to be mentioned.

Our experience shows that if someone responds to an intervention we make, by behaving physically in exactly the same way they did previously, but becomes intellectually excited, we know that we have not created a 'shift in the room'. 'Intellectual excitement', 'insight' and 'realization' modify the mental and emotional landscape, but only within the familiar range of behaviours a person already embodies. Transformational coaching or supervision is looking to expand the range of ways we can embody ourselves, and a measure of our success in engaging with this is the somatic recognition by the coachee or supervisee at key moments in the work, of the transformational shift that is being made. When we have created joint, and integrated, impact at physical, psychological and emotional levels with our intervention, then we have the beginning conditions of transformational change. At the end of this chapter we explore what these things mean and how a practitioner can develop these competencies, capabilities and capacities.

CLEAR 4: action phase skills

Specific planning

Rudyard Kipling wrote a doggerel poem about the key skills of being a journalist in which he said:

> I keep six honest serving-men
> (They taught me all I knew);
> Their names are What and Why and When
> And How and Where and Who.
>
> (Kipling, *The Elephant's Child* 1902)

At the stage of action, in either coaching or supervision, all of these very useful soldiers come into play except for 'why?' 'Why' questions can at times be useful in the exploration stage, but when we move into action the useful questions are:

- 'So *what* are you going to do?'
- '*How* are you going to engage them?'
- '*Exactly what* are you going to say?'
- '*When* and *where* are you going to do it?'

The action stage is about moving to specific commitments. In the supervisory process model this type of question has its place when we move very much into mode 2, focusing on the practitioner's interventions.

Fast-forward rehearsal

As we discussed in the section on systemic transformational coaching (see Chapter 2), to move from talking about what action the supervisee is going to take, to a point when the supervisee has made a transformational commitment, it is often very useful to have a fast-forward rehearsal. Here the supervisor may invite the supervisee into direct expression: 'Imagine I am the client that you said you are going to challenge in this new way next Tuesday afternoon in their office. Try out the first few lines now.' After such a rehearsal it is important that the supervisor provides immediate feedback, which follows the principles of effective feedback (see below). This might take the form of:

- 'What you did that was very effective from my perspective was ...'
- 'What really engaged me and was convincing to me in the role of your client was ...'
- 'I felt I was drifting away from you at one point. What could have been more effective was if you looked at me and used more emotional expression in your voice.'

Following the feedback the supervisee might be invited to try a second rehearsal and receive new feedback.

CLEAR 5: review phase skills

Giving and receiving feedback

The process of telling another person how they are experienced is known as feedback. Giving and receiving feedback is fraught with difficulty and anxiety because negative feedback re-stimulates memories of being rebuked as a child, while positive feedback goes against the injunction not to have 'a big head'. Most people only give or experience feedback when something is amiss. The feelings surrounding feedback therefore often lead to it being given badly, so that fears of it are most likely reinforced. Here are a few simple rules for giving and receiving feedback that help it to be a useful transaction, which can lead to change.

Giving feedback

In offering clear feedback, unaffected by other agendas, we are offering a rare gift to people. So much of our day-to-day feedback is clouded with trying to get others to do what we want. This is not the case here. Therefore we have to be able to listen and observe 'cleanly' and then feed back what we have actually experienced, in the service of the other person's development. It is important that we also recognize that all feedback says as much about the person giving it as it does about the person it is given to. A mnemonic that serves as a reminder of how to give good feedback is CORBS: Clear, Owned, Regular, Balanced and Specific.

- *Clear:* try to be clear about what the feedback is. Being vague will increase the anxiety in the receiver and will not be understood. Your appearance of uncertainty will transfer to the other person and make them uncertain in turn about what you are saying.

- *Owned:* the feedback you give is your own perception and not an ultimate truth. It therefore says as much about you as it does about the person you are giving it to. It helps the receiver if this is stated or implied in the feedback, e.g. 'I find you . . .' rather than 'You are . . .'.

- *Regular:* if the feedback is given regularly, it is more likely to be useful. If this does not happen, there is a danger that grievances are saved and then delivered in one large package. Try to give the feedback as close to the event as possible and early enough for the person to do something about it, i.e. do not wait until someone is leaving to tell them how they could have done the job better!

- *Balanced:* it is good to balance negative and positive feedback. If you find that the feedback you give to an individual is always either positive or negative, this probably means that your view is distorted in some way. This does not necessarily mean that every piece of negative feedback must always be accompanied by something positive, but rather that a balance should be maintained. On the other hand, if you have six negative things you want to say and can only think of one positive, restrict the number of negative comments in any one session, otherwise the person you are giving feedback to will not be able to hear and understand them all at once.

- *Specific:* generalized feedback is hard to learn from. Phrases like 'You are irritating' can only lead to hurt and anger. 'It irritates me when you forget to record the telephone messages' gives the receiver some information, which they can choose to use or ignore. This form of expression also entails that the feedback giver must consider that the source of their irritation lies with themselves.

Receiving feedback

It is not necessary to be completely passive in the process of receiving feedback. It is possible to share the responsibility that the feedback you receive is well given. What is done with the feedback is entirely up to the receiver.

● If the feedback is not given in the way suggested above, you can ask for it to be more clear, balanced, owned, regular and/or specific.

● Listen to the feedback all the way through without judging it. Jumping to a defensive response can mean that the feedback is actually misunderstood.

● Try not to explain why you did something, or explain away positive feedback. Try to hear the feedback as that person's experience of you. Often it is enough to simply hear the feedback and say 'Thank you'.

● Ask for feedback you have not been given, but would like to hear.

Feed forward

It is common to give feedback on what the other person has done and how it affected you. It is even more beneficial if this can be combined with a feed forward, where you tell the other what you would like to encourage them to do differently on the next occasion they engage with a similar event or task. Like feedback, this should be delivered in a way that is clear, owned, regular, balanced and specific.

Summary

In this chapter we have set out the skills that we believe need to be developed by coaches, mentors, organizational consultants especially when they begin to practise as a supervisor of other people's practice. We have tried to help the supervisor see where in their supervision practice they might need to check out and develop these new skills. At the beginning of Section 3 we explored the seven territories model and initially laid on top of this the Gardner multiple intelligences to show that the idea of multiple intelligences was an important developmental frame. We then built from this the fact that our intelligences do not come to us ready-honed. Some things we have immediate ability to use and perform well, other intelligences can take a great deal of blood, sweat and tears to bring to a passable state. A star mathematician may start a long way back in terms of their kinaesthetic awareness and ability to speedily absorb instructions about body movement, while having no difficulty responding to advanced calculus equations.

In using the CLEAR model to map where the various skills would fit into supervision practice we talked about relating them also to the seven territories model so that when supervisors were looking at their own development they had some indication of the sort of skills that could be enhanced (see Figure 12.2).

In the next chapter, we will look at the aspect of capacity development, to take this conversation about the importance of the seven territories to a deeper level. But before we move off onto a new topic we need to return to a more detailed exposition of creating 'shift in the room'.

Figure 12.2   Seven territories of development with core skills overlaid

Extended discussion section

Creating shift in the room

We frequently talk about the coach or supervisor's ability to create 'shift in the room'. For those unfamiliar with the term, it sounds like just another piece of professional jargon – one that has all the attributes of 'apple pie' and 'motherhood' but no immediate clarity as to what it is or how one can learn to create it.

When teaching this concept, some course participants, who are finding it hard to move from a more 'expert' style of coaching to the transformational coaching we advocate, have experienced us as browbeating a coachee into identifying a 'felt shift', when we have noticed it occurring. Initially, they are not sure what they are looking for and don't see anything that gives flesh to this idea. They do not yet have a concept, or an experience, of patterns being cut through by an intervention that creates palpable impact. At that moment of impact, the coachee experiences an emotional realization of the complex shape of their situation in a new and helpfully fresh way. From such an experience of visceral comprehension, a different way of being, doing or seeing things, more or less intuitively, arises. Since the process that generates the shift is to a large extent non-rational rather than intellectual, it can be difficult to value, or cognitively grasp, at first.

When we begin training coaches as supervisors, we start with the following key premises:

- coaching/supervision is 'transformational' in intent;
- working in the moment gets people to be, and do, differently;
- we aim to get people to feel the necessary change, not just think about it;
- it requires 'fearless compassion' on the part of the supervisor.

One of the central elements in our coaching dialogue is how we use the feedback we are receiving. This tells us whether a 'shift in the room' has been created.

What does 'shift in the room' look like?

The first issue to tackle is 'What does it look like?' or 'How would we recognize it when it occurs?' Our long experience of working with this phenomenon shows that it is easily observable, once people understand what they are looking for. Apart from anything else it is something that will be felt physically by the coachee. The phenomena we typically observe when 'shift in the room' is achieved are:

- *Physical movement:* at the moment of shift, people are physically moved by the experience. I saw it most clearly when someone was asked, 'so why have you never done that then?' He had been operating from a belief system that assumed that others had the responsibility for change and not him. This question happened to be the remark that cut through his current limiting assumption. The person, who was sitting forward in his chair, leaned right back onto the back legs of the chair, put his hands behind his head and waited there a few seconds – as though fully absorbing the impact of the question – and then slowly moved forward again to say, 'You know, I had never thought of it like that – you're right – it is my job to make it happen, isn't it?' This person showed a typical physical reaction to a transformational challenge that had truly connected. It is registered in the body, where we can observe it. Sometimes the shift is quite small, e.g. a slight flushing of the cheeks, or massive, e.g. the person rocks right back on their chair, but the impact is registered somatically and, therefore, observably.
- *A sharp intake of breath:* the body protects itself automatically from both physical and psychological external impact in similar ways. If one has been winded – either physically or psychologically – the body's automatic response is to hold its breath, followed by a sharp intake of breath.
- *A change in mood:* someone had been uncharacteristically closed and low in mood, when they were challenged that 'you seem to be carrying the load for everyone else ...'. This intervention triggered tears and a release of emotion

that 'cleared the air' and helped the person to work through why they had become so stuck with their issue.

- *A change in the quality of the relationship:* having been quite guarded and on edge with the supervisor, the supervisee relaxes and becomes much more engaged, open and warm, after some transformative work helped to break through to a different 'reality', a significantly different perception about what is happening.

Why do we need a felt shift?

'Intellectual excitement', 'insight' and 'realization' modify the mental and emotional landscape, but only within the familiar range of behaviours a person already embodies. Transformational coaching or supervision is looking to expand the range of ways we can embody ourselves, and a measure of our success in engaging with this is the somatic recognition of such movement by the coachee or supervisee at key moments in the work. When we have created joint impact at physical, psychological and emotional levels with our intervention, then we have the beginning conditions of transformational change. For people who have not had much experience working in this way, the thought of trying to create impact at the physical, psychological and emotional levels may seem very difficult, if not impossible!

From one point of view they are right. The truth is that if we were to sit down to manufacture an intervention that will achieve all these goals, we are very unlikely to create such a complex change. We would be working from faulty assumptions that envisage:

- the coach/supervisor as the 'expert', who is using all their expertise to 'fix' the coachee's issues;
- that the answers are, or should be, inside the supervisor's head;
- that the coachee has, or is, the 'problem to be fixed'.

However, we believe that both the problem and its solution are maintained in the space between people. By being fully 'present' in that space, we believe we will be presented with new possibilities for change. If you are not working to impose a solution, you have to work with and evaluate what is emerging between you. Each of you is giving the other feedback on what is working and what is not. Some of it is conscious and can be verbalized and some of it can be picked up from non-verbal clues. The phenomenon of 'shift in the room' is part of that feedback between the people concerned, signalling that a specific sort of impact has been created. If we critically edit our responses to the other person, by evaluating whether the remarks will achieve the goals we have set, before we say them, that process would effectively remove us from being in the moment and would rule out the possibility of the situation itself suggesting its own solutions.

The situation suggesting its solution? This may seem 'New Age', and far removed from professional consultancy. However, those who have experienced working closely with individuals or groups, whether as therapists or coaches, know that if you can locate yourself 'in the moment', ideas, thoughts and questions arise from the situation, the quality of the dialogue and the shared commitment of seeking new solutions for pressing dilemmas. Sometimes the ideas appear bizarre, inappropriate or plain crazy from a logical point of view. They are not manufactured, but pop up into the mind wholly formed. We know that the more we trust these 'pop-ups', the more we can create 'shift in the room'. These thoughts or feelings often contain solutions to loosening the Gordian knot in front of us. Clearly, not every idea is a winner. Having a sense of what it looks like, when an intervention promises transformational impact, allows us to understand and develop potentially useful avenues of dialogue together.

This style of coaching/supervising appears highly risky from the 'expert' point of view, since we are committing ourselves to a situation where:

- we don't have control, because
- we don't have the answers, and
- we don't know where the conversation will take us.

However, when the transformational coaching process is allowed to unfold, it cuts through quickly and deftly to the core issue, and creates strong impact that engages busy people in learning, which reshapes the way they conduct themselves in the world. 'Shift in the room' is a key concept for transformational coaches, because it provides the systemic feedback that shows what to build upon and what to leave alone.

What are the triggers that indicate a need for shift?

So far we have talked quite generally about how we put ourselves in a position to create 'shift in the room'. It may seem from what we said that all we need to do is put ourselves 'in the zone' and it is all done for us. This is not the case though. What we find instead is that by sharpening our awareness of what arises in the space between us and our coachee, we can accelerate the process of change. We have learned over time how focusing on this has improved how we, and others, do this work. There are four particular signs that require extra vigilance on our part, when working with a client. They provide us with signals that indicate how things may be stuck and what might free them up. We become very alert when:

- *Conversations end up in polarities* – 'either-or' discussions that seem to pose as opposites (e.g. 'My coachee either has to sort things out with his boss or get another job'; 'I don't know whether to do more coaching or more consultancy?').
- *On checking, we find a 'reality gap'* – between the client's current discourse and their aspirations (e.g. the coachee talks about creating shift in the room and yet is saying 'but I can't upset the client because it could endanger the larger contract!').

- *We notice that the supervisee keeps backing off too quickly* from robustly challenging their client (e.g. 'So why don't you tell your boss that his behaviour is inappropriate?'; 'I did but he didn't listen!'; 'Oh, so what else do you think you could try?'). We need to model how a coach holds his or her coachee's 'attention to the source of the fire' and not allow them to become diverted from difficult conversations (e.g. 'You keep saying you'll do it, but I don't get any sense that you have the energy or enthusiasm to really do it with impact!').

- *We see the conversation and/or the behaviours going round the same loops* again and again. The content can be physical, psychological and/or emotional, but it is the pattern that counts. The repetitive loop is what needs to be interrupted, in order to generate an impact for change.

How do we create impact?

The four common clues that pointed out 'stuckness' in the coaching or supervision session help us see the need for change. How do we achieve it though? Let us now consider how we might understand the systemic patterns behind it and how we might move the situation on.

Ending up in polarities

Gregory Bateson defined the idea of the 'double bind' as 'a situation in which no matter what a person does, he or she can't win' (Bateson 1973). In a situation where polarities have been constructed in such a way as to make sure, whatever we try, we can't win, then as coaches and supervisors we need to first understand the systemic pattern that drives it, and then how we might help to 'unlock' it. In his groundbreaking work on schizophrenia, Bateson set out the systemic conditions that create the underlying communications impasse, which he posits drives vulnerable people into 'mad' behaviour. The patterns of relationship and communication that he and his colleagues laid out had the following elements:

- it had to be played in the space between two or more people and create an intense relationship between them;
- it had to be a repeated pattern of interactions;
- there had to be a primary negative injunction such as: 'Don't do that or I will punish you';
- a secondary injunction that conflicts with the first at a more abstract level such as: 'Don't act on my negative injunctions', which would be implied by body language/tone of voice rather than words, so the person might laugh as they were saying it;
- and a tertiary injunction that stopped the players from escaping the relationship/situation.

Bateson rejected the notion of 'binder' and 'victim' (i.e. the issues residing in the individual); rather he saw the process 'in terms of people caught up in an ongoing system, which produces conflicting definitions of the relationship and consequent subjective distress' (Bateson 1985: 201–27). This pattern was referred to in the technical literature as the 'paradoxical double bind' theory. In the coaching situation, if we see the coachee creating a limiting polarity in the room (e.g. 'the client needs to change, but he won't'), we look for the conflicting 'injunctions' that are in play. We sense double bind because the coachee draws us into enacting the polarity in the space between us. The more we try and shift them the more they need to confirm that they are right and we are wrong. So they present us with the paradox that they will change as long as we agree to their view of the situation, which is that change is impossible! The Milan Group, a family therapy school researching and working at its peak in the 1970s and 1980s, took Bateson's ideas further. They experimented with ways of effectively challenging the frozen ways of thinking that mark dysfunctional families. They used the contradictory nature of the client's communication as the means for creating change. One of their famously effective interventions they called 'prescribing the problem'. Let us illustrate by an example what such a prescription could look like:

Coach: I agree with you – you should under no circumstances try to create shift in the room with this person!

Client: Why do you say that? I thought you were saying I should?

Coach: Well you have helped me understand how dangerous it would be for you if you did.

Client: I don't understand ...

Coach: You have helped me see that it would not be safe trying to create shift with this client – since deep down you don't really believe they need to change and therefore avoiding creating that shift is absolutely the right strategy for you.

What is going on here? Some people initially criticize this approach as ethically unsound. It may appear that we are saying things we don't really believe, or are 'playing' with the client, and therefore the approach must be suspect. This sort of 'moral' stance takes as one of its assumptions that communication is essentially 'neutral' – that it does 'exactly what it says on the tin', to borrow an advertising slogan. However we do not subscribe to the notion that any of us can communicate in a way that is totally free from agenda or bias. It is not possible to communicate without personal 'spin', either in what we choose to say and not say, how we say it or when we choose to intervene. We are meaning- and context-creating beings.

Our understanding of 'polarity' conversations is that they indicate that the conversation being had is not the one that needs to be had. The polarity dance takes over as a way of making sure that the situation stabilizes in its instability rather than resolving it. Polarity conversations are there to confirm and justify the presenting stuckness. Any discussion between coach and coachee is, in the mind of the coachee, therefore simply a process for reinforcing the rightness of the coachee's view and not a neutral attempt at generating new ways of moving on.

From a transformational coaching point of view, the issue is that the coachee/

supervisee has shut down all their options in this area and the situation, understandably, is not, of itself, going to loosen and resolve. It has become a struggle about 'rightness' and not a journey towards a new solution. So the transformational coach/supervisor is faced with a challenge that if they push back, the struggle will continue, probably without resolution, and if they don't raise it, the client will also stay the same or take the dilemma elsewhere to play it out. Neither of these positions does more than allow the pattern to continue. In this situation one has to engage with, but not directly oppose, the client's position in order to stand a chance of creating change and shift. This stance engages by 'agreeing with' the position of the coachee/supervisee. But just agreeing does not create shift, it simply reinforces the frozen assumption that no change is possible. Therefore, the 'agreement' needs to be bound up in an injunction of 'no change'. It is framed as an order, 'You must continue to do . . .', as a direct challenge to the supervisee's expectation that they will be pushed to change. Their response to challenge is to reject it – but you have just told them to do what they have been doing. This creates a dilemma. If they 'agree' with you and carry on not going for shift the supervisor will have 'won', which is not tolerable. So they may need to create a shift after all, which is what will allow the situation a greater chance of resolution. As coach/supervisor, we can live with being in the wrong, when the supervisee does what they were told not to do – create shift. And we can also keep our options open for the future if we are proved to be right, if the supervisee does not create the shift.

Our experience of this is that reframing any aspect of the presenting situation can free the supervisee to respond differently. By the coachee rejecting this initial injunction of 'no change', they need to show that their initial position was not anchored as deeply as they initially believed, and this then allows further movement to a new resolution. This type of paradoxical intervention can be spectacularly impactful at times and when it works, quickly transforms very stuck situations. It is of vital relevance here that in 'prescribing more of the same', or when using any other reframing/paradoxical intervention device, all the interventions must be generated from genuinely possible angles of viewing the current problem. It is clearly conceivable that some work situations are very difficult to shift indeed, and that courage may truly falter. The coach must be able to deliver such an intervention with complete authenticity. The ability to deliver the convincing intervention arises from the coach's own ability to see each situation from many different angles and therefore truly 'see' alternatives.

Gap between aspiration and reality. When we perceive a gap opening up between a client's rhetoric and the reality we see in the room, we should explore whether there is a blockage of some sort stopping the reality from matching the rhetoric. One of the most useful ways of doing this is to keep in mind Heron's six intervention styles (Heron 1975). When asking the question 'What is the blockage that needs shifting in me so I can help to shift the supervisee, in order to shift the client issue?' we consider six areas of potential blockage and the appropriate Heron intervention (see Figure 12.3). By working through in our minds the areas of potential blockage, we begin to get an intuitive 'fix' on what type of blockage we are presented with. The intervention styles then give us a clue as to how we might

Diagnosis	Intervention Style	
• Lack of Confidence • Locked 'in the Box' • Feelings Getting in the Way	(Supportive) (Catalytic) (Cathartic)	Facilitative

| • Needing a New Awareness
• Don't Have Necessary Info
• Can't Choose Direction | (Confronting)
(Informative)
(Prescriptive) | Authoritative |

Figure 12.3 Potential blockage and interventions

address the blockage. So for example if we felt the blockage in the coachee/supervisee was emotional (e.g. we experienced our client as highly anxious about doing something because of previous negative life events), then using a cathartic intervention seems a good starting point.

Strong repetitive behaviour loops. When we are faced with repetitive behaviour loops from those we are either coaching or supervising we can use any technique described above, or we can try other techniques, which have been generated by systems therapists from the late 1960s onwards, for example, therapists such as Milton Erikson, Virginia Satir and Salvador Minuchin evolved strongly individual ways of creating the possibility of change for clients. They analysed ways in which they could interrupt behaviours that were ingrained and difficult to shift. The habitual nature of the behaviour implies that it happens outside awareness. A behaviour that cannot be recognized for what it is has become an automatic response, which responds to the trigger repetitively and outside conscious recognition. The conscious mind no longer needs to be involved, the response just gets implemented in 'appropriate' circumstances as a default mechanism. One way forward is to bring the automatic/autonomic response back into awareness and an example will help to clarify this intervention. The example we used earlier in the chapter of a clear and irritating 'tic' that is undermining the authority, presence and impact of a coachee or supervisee, is Alan's use of the phrase 'If you know what I mean?' He kept adding this phrase to the end of any statement he made. This habit had the effect of making him sound unsure and weak. Alan did not realize that he was using this 'bid for agreement' once in every five words. In order to get this very undermining 'tic' to recede, the first step was to make the pattern conscious. Words or phrases that people use to distraction – common examples are inserting or adding 'like'; 'you know'; 'right?' into our speaking patterns – once brought to the surface can quite quickly be deleted from the vocabulary. These verbal tics can be found in all of us, but if you have, or are in close proximity to, teenagers, you can sometimes observe this phenomenon in its full glory!

However, more complex emotional reaction patterns or somatic habitual responses do not reverberate inside the head with the same intensity as verbal tics do. Verbal tics are therefore more easily brought to attention in the first place. The same theory can be applied in these more deeply-rooted responses, but we need to use different techniques. The issue is the same – we need to get the person to become aware of what it is that is happening in this behaviour loop, but ways of doing this are worth listing in some detail. The important points for a coachee or supervisee are to:

- *Increase/decrease the rate at which the problem behaviours get enacted.* We may ask the client to slow the behaviour or its description right down, thereby interrupting the automatic nature of the response. By getting more and more detail of the finer aspects of the behaviour we make it available to awareness, and the slowing down can also help with making the next technique more efficacious.

- *Increase/decrease the intensity with which the behaviour is experienced.* If someone is playing down the importance of bullying in the organization, for example, we could turn up the heat by saying, 'How can you play down something as serious as that? I know someone who had a nervous breakdown because of being bullied. The bully always tries to play down what they do so that they can continue to do it. It is physical and emotional abuse.' The reason this situation is not 'seen' for what it is, and tackled, is because the emotional temperature in which it is held by staff is 'ambient' (i.e. just normal – it doesn't register as hot or cold). To make it noticeable, we have to make it appreciably hotter or cooler than the coachee's current ambient emotional temperature. This example shows how we may escalate pressure by telling parallel stories. We can reinforce this by reframing bullying as abuse, and/or using the next technique, which deserves special mention.

- *Change the meaning of what they see happening.* This involves the whole concept of 'reframing'. This technique is so central in our work that we will explore its power and uses next.

- *Change the point of view from which the person is viewing their predicament.* We may suggest a potentially liberating change of perspective by asking, 'What do you think X would have been thinking at this point?' or 'It is clear that the organization was feeling under pressure, but what would the customer's view have been?' The ability to create a change of view is particularly helpful when unconscious assumptions are driving unhelpful behaviour loops.

It will be clear from these four ways of intervening that they are not separate and isolated techniques but rather aspects of the process of raising unaware behaviour to the level of consciousness in order to make it available for change. These interventions will, in all probability, be used together or in parallel to greater effect.

Reframing – creating a shift in perspective

We sometimes think that we are being funny when we make personal remarks about someone else. And even if the other person doesn't laugh, we assume it is their lack of humour, rather than that the remark was hurtful. For us to stop making personal remarks about others, we would have to see the activity from a different point of view. We would have to recognize that such actions are a form of bullying or teasing that will be hurtful to most people. If we make that shift in our thinking, and how we understand our behaviour in its systemic effect, then it is unlikely we will do it again, unless it gets triggered unknowingly.

The whole area of changing the meaning we give to things we do or experiences we have was helpfully explored in depth by Bandler and Grinder (1982: 1). They followed and developed the work of Milton Erickson and Gregory Bateson. The concept of 'reframing' was formulated as a highly effective tool in transformational work.

It reminds us of a story about Nasrudin, who was a farmer in a poor country village. He was considered very well-to-do, because he owned a horse, which he used for ploughing and for transportation. One day the horse ran away. All his neighbours exclaimed how terrible it was, but Nasrudin simply said 'Maybe'. A few days later the horse returned and brought two wild horses with it. The neighbours all rejoiced at his good fortune, but Nasrudin said 'Maybe'. The next day Nasrudin's son tried to ride one of the wild horses; the horse threw him and he broke his leg. The neighbours all offered their sympathy for his misfortune, but Nasrudin again said 'Maybe'. The next week conscription officers arrived in the village to take young men for the army. They rejected Nasrudin's son because of his broken leg. When the neighbours told him how lucky he was, he simply replied 'Maybe ...'

The meaning that we ascribe to events depends upon the frame in which we perceive them. When we change the frame, we change the meaning. Having wild horses is a good thing, until it is seen in the light of the son's broken leg. The broken leg seems bad in the context of peaceful village life but in the context of conscription and war it suddenly becomes good. Reframing is concerned with changing the frame in which a person perceives events in order to change their meaning. When the meaning changes, the person's responses and behaviours also change.

In this extended discussion of some of the practice issues involved in creating shift in the room, we have tried to outline not only what might be done, but also refer back to the people and theories that lie at the foundations of this type of practice. It is clear that to develop a lot of these techniques requires us to become more mature. To become more mature we need to develop the seven territories inside ourselves in an overall balanced way. When we take a relational view of things there is a wisdom in the relationship that is significantly brighter than any of the participants. Developing ways of letting ourselves trust this dimension will in our experience deepen our craft in impactful and important ways.

13

The key qualities and capacities

Introduction

The core capacities

Conclusion

Introduction

In this chapter, we are focusing on the capacities needed to work in the areas of coaching, mentoring, organizational consultancy and supervision. Capacities are the human qualities that can be developed and refined in the development journey. These are mapped in the seven territory model set out in Chapter 12 (see Figure 2 in the Introduction to Section 3).

The core capacities

Some of the core capacities we consider essential for being an effective coach, mentor, consultant and supervisor fit neatly into one of the territories outlined in Figure 2 on page 204, such as practising ethical maturity, but others such as 'authority, presence and impact' span across a number of territories, involving action, relationship, intellectual knowledge, emotional intelligence and ethical choice. These capacities are:

1 Appropriate leadership.
2 Authority, presence and impact.
3 Relationship engagement capacity.
4 Ability to encourage, motivate and carry appropriate optimism and develop self-supervision skills in supervisee.
5 Holding one's ability to impact.
6 Working across difference, transculturally sensitive to individual differences.

7   Ethical maturity.

8   Sense of humour and humility.

Taking appropriate leadership

Developing leadership in others is a central task for coaches, mentors and organizational consultants. It is one of the most discussed subjects in our field, but very little has been written about the leadership capacity, which needs to be developed in a coach, mentor or consultant.

When one of the UK bodies for coaching was launched, a great deal of concern was expressed about the danger of coaches lacking sufficient psychological training or capability. We think that there is an equal danger of future coaches lacking organizational experience. Many people go into coaching through the counsellor/psychotherapist/psychologist route and have never undertaken leadership roles within organizations. This group tries to enable others to increase their capability in leading, but have never stood in a position of organizational responsibility and leadership.

The challenge for coaches, whose professional roots are in counselling, is not to slip into a belief system which can be summarized as 'individual good – organization bad' – and who could therefore get caught in unconsciously trying to support the individual against the organization, which is seen as the persecutor. This can develop into a classic form of Karpman's drama triangle (Karpman 1968), which illustrates the interconnecting dynamics of 'persecutor', 'victim' and 'rescuer' (see Figure 13.1). We believe that some direct experience of taking leadership in an organization is a core aspect of developing a coach, mentor or consultant who is intending to work with organizational leaders. This direct experience can increase the coach's empathic understanding of the leader and the pressures they experience. The experience helps to avoid the splitting dynamic inherent in the drama triangle. Many people in the helping professions are focused on supporting individuals. Organizational leaders though experience first hand the challenge of balancing multiple complex needs: the needs of different individuals, the needs of different stakeholder groups and the needs of the collective organization.

However, leadership is not just a role we inhabit – it is also an attitude to life and its challenges. Leadership begins when we stop blaming others and making

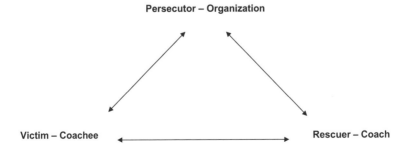

Figure 13.1   Individual vs organization. Karpman's drama triangle

excuses when things go wrong. Leadership begins when we start to explore 'How can I best make a difference?'

Even more importantly we believe that all three types of professional have to develop their leadership capacity in their own roles. Some people have argued with us that it is wrong for coaches to take leadership, for that could mean the coach becomes inappropriately directive. We argue that there is an essential and appropriate form of leadership which needs to be developed by the coach or organizational consultant if they are to balance support and challenge with the interests of the multiple clients they need to hold in mind. The coach or consultant has to be able to challenge executives and, at times, represent the needs of the wider system. On many occasions we have been asked: 'When do you know it is appropriate to challenge your client?' and 'What moral authority do you have to challenge your client?' To both of these questions we answer from a systemic perspective: 'When we genuinely feel that the client is not in alignment with themselves or with the larger system of which they are part and we sense we are representing the needs of the larger system.'

The larger system might be:

- their own long-term needs rather than the situation to which they are immediately reacting;
- the team they are part of;
- the needs of the whole organization;
- the needs of the stakeholder system;
- the needs of the sector or profession and its purpose.

The follow-up question is then: 'Why are the needs of the organization more important than their immediate needs?'

Our belief is that only by acting in alignment with the systems you are part of, are you truly serving your own long-term needs. The environmental law that a species that destroys its habitat sooner or later destroys its own chances for life, can be seen as a metaphor for what happens at other systemic interfaces. Only by serving the wider system are we truly serving our own long-term needs.

As coaches, mentors, consultants or supervisors we need to be able to speak our truth, to name what we see, hear, feel and understand – and to do so with *fearless compassion*. This courage to take leadership within the relationship needs to be balanced by an appropriate humility and openness. It is important to avoid knowing better or knowing first, to speak one's truth but always with an element of uncertainty, recognizing that we never have the complete picture or a full understanding, and neither does the client. Through dialogue we can with the help of the disciplines of our craft develop a fuller picture and understanding than both perspectives put together.

Authority, presence and impact

Learning to assume appropriate authority, while being sensitive to the various aspects of power operating in the coaching and supervision relationship is an important and challenging task. As Kadushin (1976) writes: 'The supervisor must accept, without defensiveness or apology, the authority and related power inherent in his position. Use of authority may sometimes be unavoidable. The supervisor can increase its effectiveness if he feels, and can communicate, a conviction in his behaviour'.

We divide personal power and influence into three main aspects (see Figure 13.2):

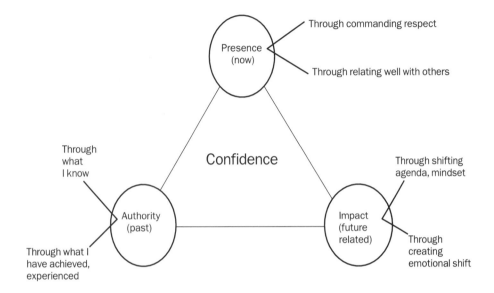

Figure 13.2 Authority, presence and impact

Authority

Authority is about our credibility. It can derive from what, or who, you know or what you have done in the past. Your achievements and experience may be embodied in titles, qualifications or role. They may also be embedded in your curriculum vitae, references, how you are introduced or how you refer to knowledge and experience. To carry true authority in your being is embodied in how you enter a room, how you greet another, and also in how you hold your experience open as a resource for others, while not imposing it on those who do not ask. To fully take authority, I need to take my rightful space without embarrassment, to stand my ground, on my ground and be well grounded physically, intellectually and ethically.

Exercising and referencing one's authority can open doors and achieve initial attention. However, it doesn't, by itself, create lasting relationships or effect change. Over-exercising or over-referring to one's authority invariably creates a negative effect with other people wondering why you are trying so hard to promote yourself or resenting what they consider to be showing off. We have noticed that different sectors think about authority in different ways. There is also a gender difference often in how it is expressed.

Presence

Presence involves creating relationship and community. is the ability to be fully present with a quality of immediacy and to develop relationship and rapport quickly and with very different types of people. In some sectors presence is measured by ability to command attention and respect in a wide range of situations in others it is less individualist and more collegial.

To have strong presence requires a meta-awareness, which embraces and comprehends what is happening on all levels for both oneself and others. This includes among others the levels of thoughts, feelings, actions and intuitions: 'Unless we develop in our presence we are not wholly here. We exist in our thoughts, in our desires, but not in our Being. And therefore we can not fully relate because we are not fully here. Without presence our dialogue is primarily mental or emotional' (Helminski 1999). With presence we demonstrate poise, grace and provide a spaciousness for others to connect with us. It also involves 'becoming open to what is seeking to emerge and discovering our genuine source of commitment' (Senge *et al.* 2005).

Impact

'Impact' is the Yang, or outgoing energy, to the Yin, or attracting energy of 'presence'. It is concerned with making a shift live in the room, which will create a shift in commitment and enable actions to go forward. People with high levels of impact can shift the direction of a meeting, conversation or event. They have the ability to intervene in a way that shifts or reframes the way issues under discussion are being perceived and addressed. The other aspect of impact is the ability to shift the emotional climate of a meeting, relationship or conversation by the skilful introduction of a different emotional energy, such as the introduction of humour, assertive and focused challenge or by changing levels in the discourse and giving expression to collectively felt but unnamed feelings.

Impact opens doors and windows to new possibilities and connects to depths not previously realized. It brings into the room candour and directness that takes the focus to the core of the matter and creates the alignment behind realizing and enacting new possibilities.

Relationship engagement capacity

At the core of all the people professions is the capacity to relate to others. Often our clients or supervisees will be people coming from very different backgrounds to ourselves and experiencing the world very differently. In Chapter 14, we write about how to work with difference in supervision, but this applies equally to our work with coachees, mentees, teams and organizations. These clients become our teachers in finding new ways to expand our capacity to relate and engage. Our partners, children and friends often become our teachers in new ways of relating, especially when we experience them as difficult! In our work with teachers, a new model was shaped to help them explore their educative capacity. We developed this framework into a more generally applicable model of 'relationship engagement capacity' (see Figure 13.3).

In the western sector of Figure 13.3 the ability to achieve rapport not only with people like ourselves, but across a wide breadth of differences, is located. In the eastern sector, we find the ability to stay very engaged with another, without becoming reactive, when the relationship is full of difficult emotions (e.g. you may be attacked, or re-stimulated by your clients' distress or anxiety). This sector closely links with the concept of the good-enough supervisor and the good-enough worker, who can hear the communication of their client without becoming reactive to the client or feeling bad about themselves (Hawkins and Shohet 2006). The southern domain contains the ability to gauge the level of depth of engagement. You may ask yourself questions here like: 'Do you just address the content of the problem, or comment directly on their behaviour in the here and now?' 'Do you also connect with their mindsets or frames of reference, their feelings, their values and their sense of purpose?' The final dimension, in the north, represents the ability to open new windows and doors for other people, to connect with new worlds and possibilities.

The figure provides a map on which the individual can plot their own capacity using a 1 to 10 scale (numbering from the centre to the outside) on each dimension. The area covered by joining the four plotted scores provides a self-evaluation of one's own current capacity. If you shade in the area inside the lines, the shape of the area will also tell you something about your engagement style.

Those who have shaded mostly in the north-west quadrant tend to towards the style of 'the motivational speaker', the 'evangelist' and 'entertainer'. Those who have shaded mostly in the south-west are more the 'facilitator' with the ability to

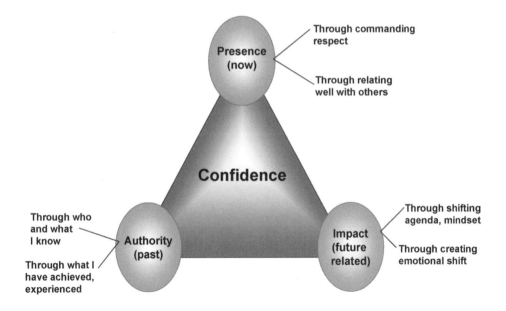

Figure 13.3 The four dimensions of relationship capacity

create deep connections between those who are present in the room. Those in the south-east will be predominantly 'counsellors' and 'supervisors' who can attend well to the inner life of those they teach. Those in the north-east are more the 'coach', engaging with the client at the edge of what they do not know (see Figure 13.4).

Those whose shape is drawn out along the horizontal dimension tend more towards a supportive and enabling style, while those who have a shape drawn out along the vertical dimension tend more to a challenging and impacting style.

We have also found it useful to plot three different facets of one's own capacity:

- my capacity when I am at my worst;
- my capacity when I am functioning at my best;
- what I believe my potential capacity could be.

This can then provide the springboard for other types of enquiry:

- What conditions and stressors in myself, my personal life, the consultancy, the organization and the profession push or shrink my capacity to this lower level?
- What conditions and enablers in myself, my personal life, the consulting space, the organization and the profession support my capacity to flourish at this higher level?
- What development in myself, my personal life, the consulting room, the

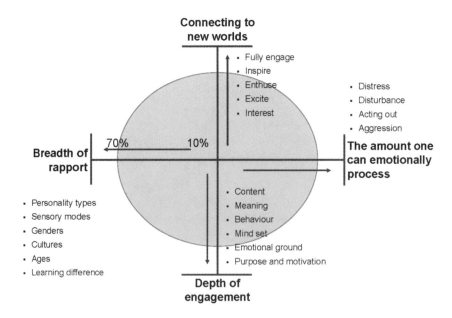

Figure 13.4   Engagement capacity types

organization and the profession would grow my capacity towards my full potential?

- What capacities do I exhibit outside work that I leave at the door when going into work?

Ability to encourage and motivate

All supervisors need to remain aware that there is always a danger as we develop our leadership capacity that it becomes too dominant in the relationship and creates feelings of either inadequacy or dependency in the supervisee. We always need to reflect on issues around dominance – but also consider how we can open doors for those we work with to unfold their own leadership capacity. The skills for strengthening our leadership capacities need to be balanced by the capacity to enable other people to find their own strengths and leadership – and develop their 'internal supervisor'. A good leader creates leaders, or to put it another way, a good leader liberates dormant leadership in others.

In the previous chapter we provided a number of tools and methods which enable and draw out the strengths and capacities of the other, both live in the room and when they are engaging with their world of work outside the room. Our central learning from years of supervision is that as supervisees we were enabled to develop our internal supervisor, who in the heat of engagement with others can provide an internal space for reflection, awareness and insight. This internal voice or space has been the critical factor in supporting ourselves, when we have encountered the consultant's equivalent of the 'moment of truth'. These are those moments when you feel you have been put on the spot and what you do next will make or break the relationship; when you might be caught between a fight and a flight response – wanting to argue back and defend against the attack, or disappear through the nearest hole in the floor! Hard work in supervision helped us to gain access to a 'fearlessly compassionate internal supervisor'. This capacity is developed by consistently turning inward and moving away from being reactive. It moves us towards a new understanding, and then requires us to respond with fearless compassion.

One of our colleagues, Danny Chesterman, recounts one of these moments in his dealings with a local authority chief executive:

> I was discussing the issues arising from a leadership programme and was suddenly aware that the chief executive was scrutinizing me with an intensity that was making me feel threatened and vulnerable. For a second, I wondered if the chief executive wanted me to feel 'small' so that he could reassert his authority. Then my internal supervisor asked me to pause and think (but quickly!!) what another framing of his intention might be. I felt compassion re-emerging and managed to remember that this chief executive had a great gift in analysing things in his determination to get the root causes of things. I looked him in the eye and said 'Sometimes your absolute commitment to discover the root of the problem creates an intensity in your eyes that I could find quite intimidating. I wonder if this is what others feel? I wonder how you might be able to bring your undoubted powers of enquiry to bear in a way that creates confidence in others?'
>
> (Personal communication 2006)

Holding one's power

This may sound like a rather aggressive and domineering capacity – exerting power over others. What we are talking about here is not domination but holding our ability to be potent, to create impact in the world even when under pressure. In our experience, it is quite common for certain situations, or types of people, to trigger what we have termed 'the deference threshold'. For some of us, this could be triggered by people we see as in 'high authority', for others it may be settings of extreme formality. The deference threshold is where we hand over our ability to create transformational impact for any one of a multitude of reasons.

The capacity we are looking to develop is one in which we strengthen our ability as a transformational coach, mentor, consultant or supervisor. Knowing what triggers our deference is a good starting point on the journey to always being ready to engage with someone else from our own depth and strength. It is by being knocked from our centre that we lose that capacity, and by maintaining our centredness that we can offer it to others.

Working across difference

Working across difference has become increasingly important in recent years. We feel that although it fits into this chapter, it is such an important topic that it deserves a chapter of its own. We therefore look at this capacity in more depth in Chapter 15.

Ethical maturity

We address the complex issues contained under this heading in Chapter 14.

Humour and humility

While trying to develop all the competencies, capabilities and capacities mentioned in this and the previous chapter, there is a great danger of taking oneself far too seriously. The ability to laugh at oneself is, we believe, a prerequisite for thriving in any of the roles of coach, mentor or consultant, and even more important for the supervisor. We have to be able to sometimes laugh at ourselves and with our clients, at the absurdity of what we humans get up to.

Humour is a great teacher. It can sometimes delicately embrace a paradox, or help liberate us from our fixed ways of seeing the world. Hawkins (2005) celebrates the uses of the wise fool Nasrudin's humorous stories in leadership development:

> Humour is used to shock us into seeing situations and ideas that we have become very familiar with, from a different perspective. Nasrudin invites us to embrace paradox and to realize that causality is not a linear process, but emerges from underlying interconnected patterns. Within the Sufi tradition the stories should work at least at three levels:
> - the creative jump of humour
> - the psychological shift in one's mind-set, and

- the spiritual dimension of releasing us temporarily from our personal fixity of being.

A good Nasrudin story always has an after-taste or a good kickback. The story slips into the house by its engaging good humour, but once inside it can start to re-arrange the furniture and knock new windows through the walls. This can be very releasing if you recognize the prison in which you often live, but very disconcerting if you have grown attached and comfortable in your institutionalized home.

Laughter has been shown to have beneficial effects on the human body and human health, releasing endorphins and vitalizing our systems. It can also create more space in our minds, change the way we make connections and be a way of making contact across difference. In the *Wise Fool's Guide to Leadership* (2005) Peter Hawkins has used humour to provide an 'unlearning' curriculum for leaders, which is equally applicable to coaches, mentors, consultants and supervisors.

Humility is strengthened by being able to laugh at oneself, but it is also fundamentally about avoiding the trap of omnipotence. This requires the recognition that ultimately it is not us as coaches and consultants who help others to develop and change; we are only the stewards, who maintain the enabling space in which learning, change and transformation can happen. We clear the space for grace and learning to emerge and polish the mirror so that reflection can be more accurate.

Yet humility comes with its own capacity for ironical reversal. This is shown wonderfully in an old Jewish joke, which captures the paradox of humility.

One day a rabbi has an ecstatic vision and rushes up before the ark in his synagogue and prostrates himself, saying: 'Lord, Lord, in Thine eyes I am nothing.' The cantor (singer) of the synagogue, not wishing to be outdone, also rushes up to the altar and prostrates himself saying: 'Lord, Lord, in Thine eyes I am nothing.' The shamash (caretaker) sees the other two and decides to do the same. He rushes up and prostrates himself with the same words: 'Lord, Lord, in Thine eyes I am nothing.' Whereupon the rabbi turns to the cantor and says: 'Look who thinks he's nothing.'

(Hawkins and Shohet 2006)

Conclusion

We do not believe that these eight capacities are in any way exhaustive. However, we have found in our work that they represent the core dimensions that we utilize, when we practise enabling others to learn.

Given that a core purpose of coaching, mentoring, organizational consultancy and supervision is to develop the human capacities of our clients, it is essential that we have a clear understanding and recognition of each of these capacities both in ourselves and in others. However, there is always further to go! Sooner or later life will provide us with a challenge that demonstrates the limits of one or more of our capacities, and the opportunity to develop further.

14
Ethical capacity

Introduction

A professional is one who professes, one who can go and stand in the market square and publicly declare what they believe and stand for. To practise ethically is to attest to the standards you wish to be judged by and to provide a mechanism whereby you can be held accountable for living up to those standards. Ethical practice in coaching, mentoring and consultancy is to be able to balance the appropriate needs of multiple clients, with due regard and fairness to all parties and the delicate threads and web of relationships between them.

Too often ethics have been reduced to rules and laws that those who belong to a professional association must abide by. Ethics then become like the dogmas of an ossified religion, rather than embodying aspiration and vision and providing a vibrant call to higher forms of craft and practice.

In this chapter we will not only look at how one evaluates the rightness of choices a supervisor may need to make while working with a supervisee, but also how to help a supervisee engage with ethical dilemmas in a constructive and impactful way.

Whom does the work serve?

If we apply one of Stephen Covey's habits of highly effective people – 'start with the end in mind' (Covey 1989) – to the activity of coaching, mentoring and consultancy, we open an interesting and complex debate.

'Starting with the end in mind' means that we take some responsibility for the direction and end goal of our coaching activity. To polarize the choices: we could be coaching someone to work for the betterment of their colleagues, the community and the wider society or we could be helping someone gain maximum personal profit from the situation, at the expense of those around them and the eventual ruin of future generations. Our view is that we have some responsibilities, not just for the process of coaching and supervision, but also the outcome and end point.

Taking a systemic view of the world, which we do, the particular end purpose of the individual cannot be assessed without assessing its overall impact on the wider system. Everything is connected. Recent advances in the understanding of genetic codes and how they operate reinforces this view. It is now clear that in many areas events at key times in one individual's life will switch on or off particular genetic switches, which are then locked in to the genetic (DNA) code and passed on to future generations. The effect of personal abuse (over-drinking, smoking etc.) or trauma (post-traumatic stress disorder etc.) can predispose succeeding generations to the consequences of these events, without the future victim having any knowledge of, or immediate connection with, the original person to whom that event happened. It starts at a biological level and underscores the fact that individual activity, both positive and negative, affects others in real and concrete ways and has a 'half life' considerably longer than we previously gave it credit for.

How would we go about answering the question 'What is our effort building?', when applied to our coaching or supervision activity? This question immediately pulls us into a potentially complex discussion about ethics, values and purpose. Pragmatically however, we need to accept that completely falling in with the other person's agenda and goal is a moral choice, as much as challenging this agenda would be. This question, and its possible answers are also linked inextricably with the issue of taking 'leadership' as a coach, mentor, consultant or supervisor. Some would advocate that this group of professionals needs to adopt a neutral moral stance and not overly influence the client. We do not believe that it is possible to take a neutral stance. Any stance, whether it is to refrain from action or to act, embodies a moral stance. We know that there is much in the belief that for 'bad things to happen, good people have only to refrain from action'. How we decide what is 'good' or 'bad' is part of the challenge of being a moral person.

Systemic transformational coaching and supervision will create an impact in terms of how someone goes about the day-to-day pursuit of their business. It will align this operational concern with building the overall effectiveness of their endeavour – the strategy. Now however we are adding in a third level of influence and enquiry – robust debate with the client about the purpose of their endeavour and its appropriate alignment with the effectiveness and efficiency of their activity.

The responsibility we bear in this area is starkly and almost apocalyptically set out by Matthew Fox in his book *The Reinvention of Work* (1995). He writes, 'by our work we either assist one another in our journey through the dark night of the soul ... or we help put people and creation itself into a pit of darkness from which it may never recover' (p. 50).

Our understanding of ethics

We would follow writers like Michael Carroll (1996) and Tim Bond (1993) in believing that ethical practice is not merely a matter of signing up to an ethical code and obeying all its clauses, but of constantly refining one's ethical behaviour to achieve ethical maturity. We define ethical maturity as: 'the increasing capacity to embrace ethical complexity and deal with appropriate respect and fairness to all parties involved in a situation'.

The core of all ethical systems throughout history has been the golden rule that appears and reappears in all the world's major religions. *Do unto others what you would like them to do unto you.* This simple but profound rule can inform our ethical practice, but it cannot resolve some of the ethical dilemmas that practitioners in our field will sooner or later encounter. Also, as a consequence of believing that in some way other people are like you, one can be led into discounting the different ways in which people prefer to be treated because of their cultural norms and traditions. Thus this golden rule has to be balanced by a transcultural sensitivity (see Chapter 15).

This complexity is partly attributable to the power dynamics in any professional relationship, which bring with them the potential for abusing that power. Having more than one stakeholder to serve in nearly all coaching, mentoring, consultancy and supervisory situations frequently creates apparently contradictory loyalties and sometimes there will be a conflict of interest between the various stakeholders. Let us offer some examples:

- A coach/manager wants to respect his coachee's need to have more delegated responsibility, so they can develop new skills, but also has increased pressure to deliver the team's demanding targets, which means relying on skilled team members who can deliver faster and with less risk.

- Very often personal and organizational agendas will be imperfectly aligned and the external coach may find themselves in effect helping the coachee leave the organization, while at the same time advocating to the organization greater investment in coaching.

- The coaching client wants a confidential space to explore their vulnerability and difficulties, and simultaneously the employing organization wanting the internal or external coach to comment on the suitability of the coachee for current or future positions.

- The organization wants to respect the confidentiality of the setting but also wants to show evidence of outcomes and value for money in this particular investment.

- A consultancy team is required to offer team coaching to all the regional and international teams in a company, in a way that is both highly tailored for the local context and delivered to a consistent standard across all parts of the organization.

We believe it is essential to all coaching, mentoring, consultancy and supervisory training that time is spent helping trainees define their own ethical standards and increase their capacity for handling ethical dilemmas. We have chosen to attend to this developmental need towards the end of the supervisor training process, because by then there is normally a good range of practice experience in the group and thus the potential to learn from each other's ethical challenges. Ethical difficulties that are encountered early on in training, we believe, should be taken to individual supervision and worked through in that context.

One trap that people often fall into is to formulate the rules exclusively in negative terms as restricting or prohibiting various activities – the 'thou shalt not' syndrome. One problem with such a one-sided approach is that people then tend to frame the whole area of ethics as about things that potentially get in the way of what they might otherwise want to do. This sets up a conflict between ethics and desire which either diminishes the energy of engagement or tends to make people behave unethically.

We would therefore advise participants to find a good balance between 'enabling' rules (or ethical principles) and 'conforming' rules in doing the work. 'Enabling' rules are ones which give me permission to do what I might not otherwise have the courage or authority to do. Examples of 'enabling' rules might include such things as 'making sure that I/my client get a good work/life balance'; 'having permission to attend to the needs of the wider system' etc.

Generating one's own rules and guidelines

To assist you in generating your own ethical rules and guidelines we will give an extended example of the process we use with coaches, mentors consultants and supervisors on our advanced training course in supervision. The intention of this process is for all the trainees to generate ethical rules, principles and guidelines, which can become a framework they take back into their everyday workplace to support them expanding their ethical capacity live in their practice.

In this process we go through four stages:

1   Asking all trainees to write down the ethical rules they think are important for practice and then share these back into the whole group.
2   To share with the group the most difficult ethical dilemmas they have come across in their professional experience.
3   To explore which of the rules they had previously written down would help them better cope with these ethical dilemmas.
4   To generate ethical principles that would better enable them to manage the ethically complex situations they had generated.

Before reading further you may well like to undertake those four steps for yourself.

On our course the most frequent ideas that came up as rules for coaches were:

- The relationship between coach and coachee should not be manipulated for the personal gain of the coach (financially, sexually, to gain preferment etc.). Appropriate personal and professional boundaries need to be maintained. This falls into the area made explicit by professional institutes in their codes of ethics.
- The coach should follow the client's agenda (both explicit and tacit).
- There should be explicit and agreed confidentiality guidelines, and a list of possibilities under what conditions confidentiality cannot be maintained (e.g. if there is abuse or illegal activity).
- A coach should get permission from the coachee to take their material to supervision.
- The coachee should be responsible for their choices and feel that they have their autonomy – the coach should avoid encouraging dependency.
- Coaches should be aware of the power balance between themselves and their client.
- The coach should be willing to recontract when the context or needs of the coachee change.
- A coach needs to get the coachee's agreement for any explicit references required about the coachee.
- A coach should take on the key element of the Hippocratic oath – 'do no harm!'
- Always work within your competency and capacity.
- A coach has to take action on illegality.
- Avoid as far as possible becoming entangled in collusive splitting.

For supervisors the range of issues they raised were much 'thinner':

- Don't steal your client's clients.
- Seek permission of clients to use the shared experience as an example in other work situations and for alternative purposes.
- Take appropriate action on illegality.

We find that very soon after such a brainstorming process, debates arise when some group members invariably find situations in which the other member's rules would not work – 'But what if ...?' 'What would you do when ...?' It soon becomes clear to trainees that hard and fast rules will not ensure that they can steer through the choppy ethical waters of practice.

We then go on to write down and share one important ethical dilemma that they perceive from their supervisor activity. The dilemmas that most often emerge are:

- A supervisee reporting that their coaching client had shared information about activity that was likely to be damaging to the organization, but had got the coach to promise they would not share this information with anyone else.
- The supervisor has information from another coach they supervise in the same organization that directly contradicts what they are being told by their supervisee.
- The supervisor is concerned about the mental stability of the client being presented, but the coach keeps reassuring them that they can handle the client. The supervisor has grave misgivings about this.
- The supervisor suspects that the coach is having a sexual affair with the coachee, but this is not declared openly, only inferred.
- The supervisor thinks that the coach is acting beyond their level of competence and is in danger of damaging their own reputation and that of coaching in the organization.
- The supervisor receives feedback from the organization that the coach has a reputation for being rather bullying in their approach.

In collectively exploring how one might handle such dilemmas, it becomes clear that 'conforming' rules (which imply acting within) are less useful than 'enabling' rules, or ethical principles (which imply acting from), which one needs to develop the capacity to apply in ever more complex situations.

Principles of ethical coaching

One aspect of the ethical context of appropriate coaching and supervision would be to articulate the principles of how you choose and shape that relationship to provide the best service to both the individual and their organization.

Here is an example of the ethical principles that emerged from one of the advanced supervision courses:

- Assume that we are working with reasonably functioning, adult, healthy individuals.
- If your potential client does not score positively on these dimensions they may need deeper and more intensive therapeutic help to create the needed shift.
- It is important to name the moral dilemma that one perceives in the room.
- The coach has to act in integrity to self, other and the organization.
- The coach should encourage direct communication.
- If you are coaching two or more parties in the same organization, you need to be aware that you are also implicitly coaching the relationship between them (see Chapter 7).

We strongly believe that every practitioner needs to develop their own ethical principles, which both speak of what they will avoid doing, but also of what they will aspire to and what will guide their professional journey. In our own work we are inspired by the following ethical aspirations:

- do unto others what you would like them to do unto you;
- act in the spirit of compassion.

Compassion involves moving beyond judging everything from one's own perspective, to attempting to see the world from the perspective of the other, and to feel and think with them; to enter different worlds with openness and active curiosity and an imaginative engagement, rather than being an interpersonal tourist.

In our supervision work we hold to seven basic principles:

1   Balancing appropriate responsibility for the work of the supervisee with respect for their autonomy.

2   Showing due concern for the well-being and protection of the client with respect for their autonomy.

3   Acting within the limits of one's own competence and knowing when to seek further help.

4   Fidelity – being faithful to explicit and implicit promises made.

5   Showing commitment to anti-oppressive practice (see Chapter 15).

6   Being open to challenge and feedback combined with an active commitment to one's own ongoing learning.

7   First and foremost, 'do no harm'.

Bramley (1996) has two very readable and useful chapters on ethics, which make very relevant links between ethical maturity and the ethical importance of respecting cultural difference (see Chapter 15). Just to link back to our eighth capacity (Chapter 13) – to always come into the work equipped with the tool of humour we quote Bramley's last injunction: 'Do for heaven's sake laugh!'

The legal constraints on supervisors to disclose

The legal context differs according to the country where the supervisor or practitioner is working. Mostly, legal contexts are obvious, but they mark out the importance of clarifying the need for an agreed contract with your client before they disclose, rather than trying to renegotiate after you have been given evidence you are obliged to disclose.

The main legal boundaries currently in the UK concern:

- *Child abuse:* one has a legal responsibility if one becomes aware through one's work of child abuse taking place to notify the local child protection team.

- *Terrorism and money laundering:* recent counter-terrorism legislation in the

UK is beginning to make it incumbent on professionals to report any knowledge they have of planned terrorist activity or money laundering.

- *Data protection:* clients should have knowledge of and access to any data you keep about them electronically. Their details should not be transferred to a third party without their written permission.

- *Person who is a danger to themselves or others:* – there is not a legal obligation to take action, but at an inquest you can be held to account for how you responded to a client who was acting in a way that could make you presume to think they were a danger to themselves or others.

Fortunately such situations are very rare in the fields of coaching, mentoring and consultancy, but they do happen. The first response should always be to challenge the client to take responsibility and seek further help and support. However, if the client is in denial or for other reasons unable or unwilling to address the issue, then the professional needs to inform them that they will be taking action and how they will be doing this.

Applying ethical principles

Michael Carroll (1996) articulates how acting ethically is full of complexity and ambiguity. He provides a very useful four-stage process for ethical decision-making:

1 *Creating ethical sensitivity* involves becoming aware of the implications of behaviour for others and having insight into the possibility of ethical demands within interpersonal situations.
2 *Formulating a moral course of action* represents how the interplay between the facts of the situation, professional ethical rules and our ethical principles may jell into a moral course of action.
3 *Implementing an ethical decision* refers to the need to follow through and implement the ethical decisions made while coping with the resistances both inside and outside, such as politics, self-interest, protection of a colleague, fear of making a mistake.
4 *Living with the ambiguities of an ethical decision* indicates that coping with doubt and uncertainty is a vital capability for containing a moral dilemma.

To become capable of managing all four stages well, it is important not only to encourage all practitioners to develop their own ethical rules and principles, and explore with peers common ethical dilemmas, but also to practise working directly with ethical challenges.

In our supervision training courses we use an exercise that builds on the 'practicum' method we described in Chapter 7, to provide the opportunity for trainee supervisors to apply their ethical principles with real issues brought by their colleagues (see Figure 14.1).

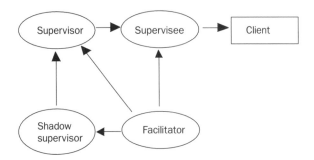

Figure 14.1   Training supervisors to help with ethical issues: the practicum method

- The 'supervisee' brings a 'live' and current case in which they are struggling with an ethical issue (e.g. 'who is my client in this situation?').

- The supervisor before working with the supervisee clarifies what their 'learning edge' is currently. This allows them to get the most learning they can out of the interaction.

- The supervisor or the shadow supervisor can call time-outs in order for the supervisor to get quick coaching on how to create the necessary shift in ethical maturity live in the room.

Conclusion

In Appendices I–IV at the end of this book, we include the ethical and practice guidelines from four major professional associations. We believe that every coach, mentor, consultant and supervisor needs to have spent time clarifying their own ethical principles, whether or not they are registered with a professional association, which has developed collective ethical standards. All practitioners need to have spent time exploring the range of ethical dilemmas that may occur in their work or have occurred in the work of their colleagues, and practised working with these ethical issues.

Just as with other core capacities that we have discussed in this book, the ethical capacity is one that we continue to develop and expand throughout our lifetime, and is part of our personal and professional development. Ethical development most commonly goes through many stages. In childhood we learn the ethical mores of our family and society, both by direct teaching and by the unwritten rules of our culture. In adolescence, we often test out the limits of what is acceptable and rebel against what we have received, as a prelude to finding our own beliefs and ethical stance. Further stages of ethical development proceed through encountering and finding ways of responding to greater and greater ethical complexity. As we discussed at length in Chapter 3, the expansion of our capacity to embrace ethical maturity is at the heart of our professional and leadership development.

In our work with clients, both individual leaders, teams and organizations, we are frequently called upon to help with their moral dilemmas. Our ability to respond to this need is very dependent on how well we have developed our own ethical capacity.

15

Working with difference: transcultural capacity

'Bon Appetit'

Nasrudin soon became rich on his earnings as a renowned management consultant and, like many rich fools, decided to go on a cruise. The first night of the voyage he was given a table with a Frenchman. At the beginning of the meal the Frenchman greeted him with 'Bon appetit'. Nasrudin thought that the Frenchman was politely introducing himself, so he responded by saying 'Mulla Nasrudin'. They had a pleasant meal.

However, the next morning breakfast started with the same ritual, the Frenchman saying 'Bon appetit' and Nasrudin who now thought the Frenchman must be a little deaf said even more loudly, 'MULLA NASRUDIN'.

At lunch the same thing happened and by now Nasrudin was getting a little irritated with what he thought must be a very dim-witted Frenchman. Luckily that day he got talking to a fellow passenger who spoke French and was an intercultural consultant and coach. He was able to enlighten Nasrudin and tell him that 'Bon appetit' was a polite French greeting, that meant 'have a nice meal'.

'Ah! Thank you,' said the enlightened and relieved Nasrudin. All afternoon he practised, walking up and down the deck of the boat. That evening he very proudly sat down at dinner, smiled and said to his new French friend, 'Bon appetit'.

'Mulla Nasrudin', the Frenchman replied.

(Hawkins 2005: 70)

Introduction

In 1998 Gregerson *et al.* carried out a survey of Fortune 500 Companies in the USA and discovered that:

- 85 per cent do not think they have adequate number of global leaders;
- 67 per cent think their existing leaders need additional skills and knowledge in working globally.

To coach, mentor or consult to senior executives in large corporations requires that all such professionals are well skilled in working transculturally. Even companies that do not work internationally, or those working in the public or voluntary sectors in one region, need to be able to work with the increasing multicultural group of staff and be able to help their clients be more effective with working with diversity.

Various studies including the one by Gregerson *et al.* have identified the qualities needed to be an effective global leader and we would propose that the same qualities are necessary for any coach, mentor, consultant or supervisor who wants to be effective at working internationally, or across difference (see Table 15.1).

Table 15.1 Effective global leaders and global consultants

Identity	*Conceptual ability*	*Interpersonal relations*
• Personal self-concept • Authenticity • Adaptive to others • Sees self/own culture in context • Guided by principles • Open to differences	• Global socioeconomic perspective • Contextual thinking	• Interprets behaviour carefully • Matches style to context • Makes self understood • Respects people equally • Open to influence

Cultural literacy

In this chapter we will focus on the sensitivity and awareness needed to work with different minority groups. We will show how this sensitivity and awareness applies as much, if not more, to our own culture and cultural assumptions as it does to those of others. Minority groups are often discriminated against because of some aspect of their difference to the majority. We will in particular concentrate on the area of culture as it has implications not only for 'race' and ethnicity, but also for class and other groupings, which develop their own 'sub' culture.

Zulfi Hussein (Megginson and Clutterbuck 2005: 98) writes: 'In order to mentor a person from a different culture, the mentor needs to be able to determine how their own culture, and the culture of the mentee, will impact their communication'. She goes on to emphasize the importance of what she calls 'cultural literacy', which she defines as understanding the values, beliefs and symbols of the dominant culture, one's own culture, the mentee's culture and the culture of the organization in which the mentee works.

Although it is important to take steps to understand other cultures, we have also found our usual stance of openness to enquiry to be useful. This is partly because we generally believe that an open attitude to learning means that we ourselves keep alive and creative, rather than formulaic in the work, but also because if we are to really honour, rather than deny, cultural diversity, we need to find a way of dialoguing across difference. If we see our task as merely to understand the other's perspective, then no real meeting has happened. We are, ourselves, absent. In a supervisory relationship, this means not only a willingness to encourage and explore difference in the supervisee/client relationship, but also an openness to ourselves and our relationship with our supervisees.

Tyler *et al.* (1991, quoted in Holloway and Carroll 1999) identify three ways of responding to culture:

1 *The universalist* denies the importance of culture and puts difference down to individual characteristics. In coaching, a universalist will understand all difference in terms of individual needs and issues.

2 *The particularist* takes the polar opposite view, putting all difference down to culture.

3 *The transcendentalist* takes a view more similar to our own. Coleman (in Holloway and Carroll 1999) discusses this perspective as follows: 'both the client and [*the coach*] have vast cultural experiences that deeply influence their world views and behaviour'. He says that 'it is the individual, who has to make sense of and interpret those experiences. The transcendent or multicultural perspective suggests there are normative assumptions that can be made about individuals, based on cultural factors such as race, gender and class, but that it is just as important to understand how these normative assumptions become reality, through the idiosyncratic choices made by individual members of a group'.

Eleftheriadou (1994) makes a helpful distinction between 'cross-cultural' work and work that is 'transcultural'. In the former we use our own reference system to understand another person rather than going beyond our own world views. Transcultural work denotes the coach's need to work beyond their cultural differences and be able to operate within the frame of reference of other individuals and groupings.

The ability to work in this way is important: entering the terrain of the other is a key part of honouring the diversity that they bring with them. Being able to adapt to this new terrain is a significant skill to learn. At a deeper level, however, there is a more generative dimension, in which both parties move beyond honouring the difference that each brings and mutually create an additionally shared language and set of frameworks for their enquiry. An open attitude to enquiry enhances the ability to work transculturally from a transcendentalist perspective. This enquiry optimally takes place within a dialogue in which both parties participate in the learning.

One particularly complex area is the way issues of power and authority are present for all those concerned. The supervisory relationship is already complicated in this way, because of the authority vested in the role of the supervisor. In working with difference, power dynamics are compounded because of the inequality of power between majority and minority groups. We will look at how power invested in different roles, cultures and individual personalities comes together to make a complex situation, which is nevertheless better explored than ignored or denied. We will see how supervision can play its part in ensuring that differences are understood and responded to appropriately. We will explore the importance of:

- taking culture and other areas of difference into account when supervising;
- cultural factors that need to be worked with;
- power dynamics and difference;
- how difference affects the seven modes of supervision (Chapter 9);
- best practice in supervision, which is sensitive to difference.

But first we will explore what we mean by 'culture'.

Understanding culture

'To integrate culture into coaching, what is needed first is a language to talk about culture' (Rosinski 2003: 49). We understand 'cultural differences' as referring to the different explicit and implicit assumptions and values that influence the behaviour and social artefacts of different groups (Herskowitz 1948). Rosinski provides a simpler working definition for coaches: 'A group's culture is a set of unique characteristics that distinguish its members from another group' (2003: 20). An understanding of culture in relation to our clients must also include an understanding of our own cultural assumptions and beliefs.

Culture is not just something within us, which we *have*, but rather resides in the milieu in which we live. Culture affects primarily not *what* but *how* we think, although what we think may alter as a result of our cultural assumptions. It exists in the spaces between us, just as an organism is grown in a 'culture' in a laboratory. One of us (Hawkins 1995, 1997) has developed a model of five levels of culture, each level being fundamentally influenced by the levels beneath it:

1 *Artefacts*: rituals, symbols, art, buildings, policies etc.
2 *Behaviour*: the patterns of relating and behaving; the cultural norms.
3 *Mindsets*: the ways of seeing the world and framing experience.
4 *Emotional ground*: the patterns of feeling that shape making of meaning.
5 *Motivational roots*: the fundamental aspirations that drive choices.

This model has already been explored more fully in Chapter 5.

We all belong to multiple groups, and therefore have some experience of living in different cultures. Some writers fall into the trap of focusing on culture as if it is only a national phenomenon (Japanese, British, French, American etc.), while others recognize the multi-layedness of our cultural membership.

Rosinski (2003: 21) lists different categories of culture membership:

- *Geography and nationality*: region, religion, ethnicity.
- *Discipline*: profession, education.
- *Organizations*: industry, corporation, union, function.
- *Social life*: family friends, social class, clubs.
- *Gender and sexual orientation*.

Cultural orientations

National and ethnic groups, and different sub-groups, based on gender, class, sexual orientation, profession, religious affiliation etc. have different cultural norms, in behaviour, mindsets, emotional ground and motivational roots, that distinguish them from other groups. To try and learn the cultural orientations of the myriad of different cultures would be an impossible task. What we can do is become sensitized to the different dimensions of cultural orientations. Rosinski (2003: 51–2) provides a useful 'cultural orientation framework' that has seven dimensions:

1 Sense of power and responsibility.
2 Time management approaches.
3 Identity and purpose.
4 Organizational arrangements.
5 Territory – both physical and psychological.
6 Communication patterns.
7 Modes of thinking.

Other variables, which have been identified by a variety of writers (e.g. Kluckhohn and Strodtbeck 1961; Sue and Sue 1990) include:

- equality versus hierarchy;
- self-disclosure;
- outer-directed versus inner-directed;
- cause and effect orientation;
- achievement orientation;
- universalist to particularist;
- adaptive versus protectionist;
- time as sequence versus time as synchronization.

Ryde (1997) has written about two dimensions very pertinent to coaching across cultures. These are:

- a continuum between the valuing of the experience of individuals and the valuing of the group;
- a continuum between emotional expressiveness and emotional restraint.

To explore the ways these dimensions interact, they may be arranged as shown in Figure 15.1.

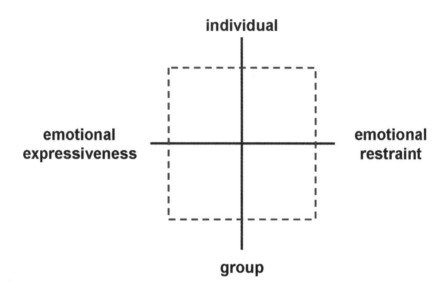

Figure 15.1   The dimensions of cultural norms

We may then place a particular culture on the diagram at a position that demonstrates the culture's position in regard to these polarities. For example, the dominant British and most north European cultures can be plotted in the individual/emotional restraint box. While the diagram does not cover all possible cultural differences, it does help us to orientate ourselves more easily to two important variables and therefore to think in a more culturally sensitive way. A similar mapping process can be used for other cultural dimensions.

Transcultural capacity

The more we can understand the ways in which the world looks different, through different cultural lenses, the more able we are to work well across cultures. Van Weerdenburg and Brinkmann (van Weerdenburg 1996; Brinkmann and van Weerdenburg 1999) have created and researched a developmental model of intercultural sensitivity based on the work of Dr Milton Bennett (1993), which maps the stages individuals go through as they become more transculturally effective. These are:

- *Denial:* where one sees one's own culture as the only real one.
- *Defence:* against cultural difference, where one sees one's own culture as the only good one.
- *Minimization:* in which elements of one's own cultural world view are experienced as universal.
- *Acceptance:* in which there is a recognition that one's own culture is just one of a number of equally complex world views.
- *Cognitive adaptation:* where one can look at the world 'through different eyes'.
- *Behavioural adaptation:* where the individual can adapt their behaviour to different cultural situations and relationships.

The first three stages of this development they term 'ethnocentric' and the later three stages 'ethnorelative' (see Figure 15.2). We would contend that the first two stages represent culturally insensitive work, the second two the beginnings of cross-cultural practice but only the last two stages equate with transcultural supervision. These stages provide a parallel developmental path to the general stages of supervisor development outlined in Chapter 7.

David Thomas (1998) carried out research into mentoring relationships that went across racial boundaries. He found some mentoring pairings discussed the racial differences very directly and saw them as a strength of the relationship (ethnorelative). Other pairings ignored, denied or mentioned the differences only very superficially (ethnocentric). One of his interesting findings was that this co-related with the age difference between the mentor and mentee. The former group were mainly close in age, while the latter group had a much greater age disparity.

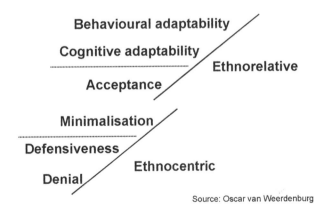

Source: Oscar van Weerdenburg

Figure 15.2 Transcultural capacity: from ethnocentric to ethnorelative

Awareness of culture and other differences in supervision

Several writers on supervision (Brown and Bourne 1996; Carroll and Holloway 1999; Gilbert and Evans 2000; Hawkins and Shohet 2006) have pointed out that the supervision situation creates a more complicated set of relationships than relating one-to-one. In supervision there are at least three relationships: client-supervisee, supervisee-supervisor and client-supervisor. (There are more than three in group supervision and if there is a supervisor of a supervisor.) This is complicated further in a situation of cultural difference. Any one of the three may be culturally different and, indeed, all three may be culturally different to each other. In the situation where the client comes from a different cultural background, it is particularly important that the supervisee and supervisor do not collude to misunderstand factors which are based in culture rather than personal psychology, as we will see below.

Where there are smaller ethnic groups within a dominant culture, it is not uncommon for the second generation of these groups to experience problems in trying to exist in two cultures at once.

Perceived cultural differences are often focused on physical characteristics, the colour of the skin, the shape of the nose etc. The dominant group can often be ruthless in denigrating and marginalizing those with real or perceived differences. Rather than face this vicious prejudice, people will go to a great deal of trouble to disguise the difference or deny its effect.

Other marginalizing differences may not be immediately obvious to the eye, but can cause as much alienation through the cultural rejection of people with these differences. A person's sexual orientation is one of the less visible differences. While moves are being made to ban discrimination on this and other grounds, prejudice remains and is likely to be found, consciously or unconsciously, in the supervisor and supervisee.

Power and difference

Society may be greatly enriched by the multitude of differences brought by populations of different cultures living side by side. However, the majority culture tends to be more powerful in the community and this imbalance of power is inevitably played out in professional relationships, including the relationship between supervisee and supervisor and between supervisee and client. As we saw above, Brown and Bourne (1996) have pointed to the different combinations of relationships present in supervision and they also explore in some depth the different power relationships. They point out (p. 39) all the different possible combinations that can arise when someone from a minority group is in each of the possible roles and the complex power dynamics that result. They particularly emphasize race and gender, although other factors such as sexual orientation, disability and class also have inbuilt power imbalance.

Inskipp and Proctor (1995) have also pointed to the dynamics in therapy relationships between black and white in a series of eight triangles showing all the possible combinations of supervisor, client and counsellor with each being black or white. Each triangle has its own dynamic, which is influenced by the different power dynamics inherent in the roles and the ethnic grouping. We believe that this work is directly relevant to the role of coach, mentor, organizational consultant or supervisor.

To draw this out further, we consider there to be another triangle: one that demonstrates the complex power dynamics inevitably present in cross-cultural supervision. At each corner we can have different types of power: role power, cultural power and personal power (see Figure 15.3).

Role Power

Cultural Power   **Personal Power**

Figure 15.3   The role triangle

- *Role power* points to the power inherent in the role of supervisor, which will vary depending on the organizational setting in which supervision is taking place. This includes what has been termed: *legitimate* power, invested in the role; *coercive and reward* power, meaning respectively power to require the supervisee to do something and power to offer or withhold rewards; and *resources* power, which is the power a supervisor may have to offer or withhold resources (French and Raven 1959).
- *Cultural power* derives from the dominant social and ethnic group. In Northern Europe or the USA this would be someone who was born within the white, western majority group. This power is emphasized if that person is male, middle class, heterosexual and able-bodied.
- *Personal power* points to the particular power of the individual, which may be over and above that given to the person through role or culture. It derives both from the authority of their expertise, as well as from the presence and impact of their personality. It also comprises what French and Raven term *referent* power, that derives from the supervisee wishing to identify with or be like their supervisor.

When all three different sources of power are brought together in the same person the effect may be quite overwhelming. The dominant cultural and/or personal power does not necessarily lie with the supervisor. When they do, the power dynamics may be simpler, but could well be insensitively misused, or even overlooked, as they are taken for granted. When cultural and/or personal power is not with the supervisor, there may be conflict in establishing authority or a need to compensate by over-emphasizing it. Whatever the case, power relationships in the supervision are better explored than ignored.

While it is spurious for power, and therefore authority, to be automatically invested in those from a cultural majority, it may be appropriate for a supervisor to carry greater authority through their role. Another example from the world of therapy supervision highlights issues that can possibly occur in supervision of coaches or mentors. One well-intentioned, white supervisor felt nervous, but excited, about having her first black supervisee. The supervisee was a counselling student who had been taken on to a counselling course in spite of the fact that she did not have the initial experience of counselling normally expected of students starting the course. This 'positive discrimination' had been one clear factor that had led the supervisee to struggle to be able to understand and use basic counselling techniques and theories.

The supervisor, not wanting to appear racist, was very tentative in confronting the supervisee on her tendency to advise clients rather than listen to them. In fact the supervisor's worst fears were realized when the supervisee complained to her tutor that her supervisor was racist. This led to a further backing off from confrontation.

In order to understand this complex situation it is helpful to bear in mind Karpman's drama triangle (Karpman 1968), which illustrates the interconnecting dynamics of the persecutor, victim and rescuer. This dynamic was further explored in our paper 'Anti-discrimination and oppression in supervision' (CSTD 1999). This dynamic is characterized by the way in which these roles, having been established, tend to revolve between the players (see also Chapter 11). Here the supervisor appears to be the persecutor, the supervisee the victim and possibly the tutor the rescuer. In this example, the roles changed with the accusation of racism, so that the supervisor apparently took the victim role.

In fact the 'role power' dynamic was with the supervisor. Had she been more experienced and confident, she may have been able to work with the supervisee more effectively in the first place to explore the situation in all its complexity: the way the power dynamics of the supervisee/supervisor relationship are compounded by the cultural context of a difference in 'race'; the cultural context in which a student is taken on to a course without the usual preparatory experience; an exploration of the difference experienced by clients in being listened to rather than given advice; and any cultural meanings given to 'being listened to' and 'being given advice' in the different cultures of supervisee and supervisor.

By appropriately keeping her authority and not being afraid to open up the complexity of the issues knotted up in this situation, the supervisee (and supervisor) would have received a rich learning experience, which any student might rightly expect where appropriate authority is taken.

If the supervisor had hounded this supervisee out of the course it would have been a clear abuse of power. As it was, the misuse of power was much more subtle: appropriate authority was not taken and the supervisee's difficulties with her course were compounded. One might go so far as to say that the supervisor exhibited, if not racism, then clear cultural prejudice in her assumption that these issues cannot be tackled openly and honestly.

Learning to take appropriate authority, while being sensitive to the various aspects of power operating in the coaching and supervision relationships is an important and challenging task.

Anti-oppressive practice

To effectively work transculturally, it is essential to operate in a framework of anti-oppressive practice, which goes beyond merely avoiding discriminatory behaviour. Brown and Bourne (1996) discuss this issue at length, building on the work of Julia Philipson (1992: 13):

> Oppression is a complex term which relates to structural differences in power, as well as the personal experiences of oppressing and being oppressed. It relates to race, gender, sexual orientation, age, and disability as separate domains and as overlapping experiences.
>
> (Philipson 1992: 13)

> Philipson suggests that, whereas anti-discriminatory practice relies on a model of challenging unfairness, and is essentially 'reformist in orientation', 'anti-oppressive practice works to a model of empowerment and liberation and requires a fundamental rethinking of values, institutions and relationships'.
>
> (Brown and Bourne 1996)

To be anti-oppressive not only entails attending to the experiences of oppression in both the supervisees and the clients, but also to becoming aware of our own cultural biases and becoming more adaptive to difference.

So while the need to avoid oppressive behaviour is obviously important, to leave matters there might give the impression that supervising and coaching across cultural difference is just an additional burden that must be carried before the real work can begin. The implication then might be that it is slower, less productive and less efficient than working exclusively within one's own culture. But there are also great riches to be gained from working across cultural diversity; indeed by having at one's disposal a whole multiplicity of reference frames, one is able to expand the range of options and find solutions that would otherwise be inaccessible.

Training in transcultural supervision

We usually begin a workshop in this area by asking people to share something about their cultural background. This can be done by asking them to share the history of their names. We have developed a pair exercise to deepen an enquiring attitude to transcultural issues in a relationship:

1   Person A says to person B 'What I would like you to know about my cultural background is . . .'

2   Person B says 'What I heard was ...'

2a Person A clarifies.

3   Person B says 'How I would supervise you differently on the basis of what I have heard is ...'

4   Person A gives feedback on what they would find helpful of the suggestions made by B.

5   Steps 1–4 are carried out with A and B reversing roles.

6   Having explored their differences A and B share ways in which they may be unknowingly similar.

This can be followed by using the practicum group method (see Chapter 7) and having the supervisee supervised on a client situation that involves working across difference and asking the others in the group, who are shadow supervisors, to monitor different aspects of the transcultural dynamics:

1   What cultural assumptions may be in operation, in the behaviour and mindsets of the client and their organization?

2   What cultural assumptions may be in operation, in the behaviour of the supervisee?

3   What cultural assumptions may be in operation, in the behaviour and mindsets of the supervisor?

4   How might they need to change their mindsets and behaviour to work with a greater transcultural capacity?

5   How might we coach the supervisor to create a shift in the whole transcultural field?

This can be followed by a time-out, to coach the supervisor, or a fast-forward rehearsal of different ways of the coach intervening in the transcultural dimensions of the client session.

Conclusion

This chapter concludes the eight key capacities that we believe are essential for coaches, mentors, organizational consultants and supervisors. Each one encompasses a lifetime's developmental journey. They are not skills we can eventually master, but capacities we constantly need to enhance. Without our constant attention, the capacities we developed do not remain constant, but begin to immediately erode, as we become stale and complacent in our practice.

Supervision provides a setting where the coach, mentor or consultant can notice and reflect their various capacities as they play out in their practice with clients, as well as live in supervision. The supervisor, in their developmental function, needs to monitor and help the supervisee cultivate these capacities, and to do this it is essential that the supervisor keeps these capacities flourishing within themselves.

16

Conclusion: polishing the professional mirror

At the heart of all our endeavours is the intent to help individuals, teams, organizations, and even wider systems, fulfil their potential and make a greater contribution to the world they inhabit. In today's complex and interconnected world (where the libraries of the world and networks of relationships are available to us with a click on our laptop, where we live longer and can travel further) more and more is potentially achievable. We are richer than ever before in material and knowledge resources, but our human capacity struggles to keep pace with all that is possible. Expanding our human capacity, to keep pace, needs skilled help from others, who in their turn need to be supported and supervised by experienced practitioners in their own field.

For coaching to be of value, it must ultimately be in service not of the needy, driven part of me that is forever hungry, but rather the part that is still and calm, and has a sense of deeper meaning. Coaching is there to enable people to be the best they can be, and contribute positively in the world.

Necessity has often been called the mother of invention, but it is also the father of our maturity, teaching us to do not what we whim, but what is required. The voice of strategic necessity asks us: 'What is it that you can uniquely do that the world of tomorrow needs?' Necessity's more immediate voice asks us: 'What is necessary right now and what does that require from you?' This voice might also be the voice of our inner supervisor, who sits next to us as we coach, mentor or consult. The inner supervisor helps us to discover how we can get out of the way, so we can be of service, to assist what is necessary both for the individual (or individuals) we are with right now, and for their work in the wider world.

We are not just in service of any work in the wider world, but rather, of work that creates value. To create value, the artisan takes the wool, spins, dyes it with many colours, then weaves a carpet that not only has utility but also sustainability and beauty. They have not only added colour to the wool, but value to the basic material they started with.

To create value the coach engages the manager or coachee, listens to their challenge and looks for the hidden potential in the manager that is needed to meet this challenge. The coach explores how this hidden potential can be released and how together they can create new connections between the coachee's intellect, emotions, skills, capacities and the challenge waiting to be addressed. The value created is not just in the challenge now managed, the problem resolved, but also in the potential realized, the skills increased and the capacity enhanced in the coachee. It is also in the new connections made, through the new work of the coachee in the wider organization, and through further possibilities released by these new connections for this organisation.

To get there, we need to adopt a vitally important practice that we have discussed at various points in the book. Others frame it differently but, we believe, with the same intent. For example, Mary Beth O'Neill (2000: 13) stresses what for her are the two most important qualities of a coach, 'backbone' and 'heart': 'Backbone is about saying what your position is, whether it is popular or not. Heart is staying in relationship and reaching out even when that relationship is in conflict'.

In our work developing coaches, mentors and consultants we have developed a very similar core principle, which we term *fearless compassion* – the fearlessness of the backbone that can stay apart, speak the truth as you see it and challenge the other, with the compassion of the heart that can emotionally and mentally experience the world of the other and lovingly support them. This phrase is deliberately paradoxical, combining the capacity to relate with warmth and empathy to another with the ability to stand apart and hold a place of external witness. Without fearlessness, our compassion becomes collusive sympathy and without compassion our fearlessness becomes confrontational and judgemental challenge that will almost certainly lead to defensiveness in the other.

The development path common to all four professions has at its core the personal discipline of developing one's own humanity and supporting others in their journey. Our ability to relate at a deep level with others is the basis of transformational work. As we have shown in this book, there are many skills and techniques we can learn. There is a great deal of useful knowledge about individual, team and organizational psychology, and much we can know about the various sectors and organizations we work with, but none of this knowledge by itself will get our development to the place where we are profound and effective transformational coaches, mentors, consultants or supervisors.

Throughout this book we have stressed the benefits we see systemic transformational coaching having for our clients, in whatever role we work with them. At the end of this journey with you, our reader, we also want to stress the benefits that we believe you will gain for yourself in this process. At the core of continuing professional development is continual personal development, where our own development is weaved through every aspect of our practice, where we try to make every client a teacher, every piece of feedback an opportunity for new learning, and we have practices that support the balanced cycle of action, reflection, new understanding and new practice.

In this book we have shown why we believe that having supervision is a fundamental aspect of continuing personal development for coaches, mentors, organizational consultants and supervisors, providing a protected and disciplined space in which we can reflect on particular client situations and relationships, the reactivity and patterns they invoke in us and by transforming these live, in supervision, profoundly benefit our clients.

Mary Beth O'Neill does not use the term 'supervision', but does talk of the importance of coaching for the coach. She writes:

> Everyone needs help to stay on track in the powerful interactional fields of organizations ... One of the best ways that coaches can stay effective in their role is to receive coaching themselves ... I used to think that my need for a coach would diminish once I had worked with numerous clients and had many years under my belt. Twenty years and over a hundred clients later, my effectiveness has dramatically increased, but my desire to use a coach myself has remained high. I no longer see using a coach as a sign of incompetence but a smart investment.
>
> (O'Neill 2000: 207–8)

For too long the themes of continuing development and supervision of coaches and consultants have been neglected. James Flaherty, about the area of the coach's continuing development, says: 'I haven't found this aspect of coaching in any other text on the topic, but self-development seems to be a self-evident component of coaching ... Psychiatrists, physicians, teachers and lawyers all confer with peers and mentors in difficult cases. Coaches are, it seems to me, no exception to this practice' (Flaherty 1999: 147). Myles Downey, from the School of Coaching in the UK, says, in his very readable book *Effective Coaching*: 'Very few coaches have any supervision but it is a vital ingredient in effective coaching' (Downey 2003: 210).

It is time that coaches, mentors and consultants walked their talk and put their own continuing development at the heart of their professional life. Our wish and hope is that this book has provided a foundational text to support all these practitioners to begin to think about their development and know how to set about arranging the help and support they need from peers, supervisors and trainers.

As we have said elsewhere, the craft journey is not just a process of acquiring skills and capabilities, nor is it just about acquiring accreditations with which to adorn our curriculum vitaes. The process is also about learning more about ourselves, how we relate to others and what gets in the way of us relating fully. It is a process as much about unlearning as it is about learning, and similar to the learning path that has been written about in many of the world's spiritual traditions.

One of these traditions, sometimes known as Sufism, describes this learning path as a lifetime's work of 'polishing the mirror'. Here is how one modern Sufi teacher describes it:

> As we become empty [of our everyday concerns and obsessions] we are able to show up to life. To show up is to be present without our predetermined ideas and judgments. This is both simple and rigorous. We do this challenging work of 'cleaning our mirror' not in a monastery or hidden in a cave but in [the hurly-burly of] everyday life ... There is no distant realm to be reached after

lifetimes of striving; no journey from here to there. What the Sufi seeks is only and always just here, just now … And yet, there is a road to be travelled.

(Amidon 2005)

The goal of our practice is to be totally present in each of our professional encounters. This requires that we polish our professional mirror, so that we can more fully 'show up'. It requires the same mixture of simplicity and rigorous discipline as has been described above. It doesn't just require personal discipline and practice though, it also needs the active involvement of other skilled colleagues. These colleagues need to be willing to meet us with fearless compassion: professional friends who are prepared to challenge us as loving enemies; and experienced practitioners who are willing to value our uniqueness and contribution, and call us to be more than we are currently being.

By polishing the professional mirror we are developing our craft as a 'real-time learning enabler', so we can more fully reflect the qualities needed by our clients and the wider world. However, to allow our professional mirror to be polished, we have to be open to the smoothing and the scouring of feedback, the learning from failure as well as success, and to go beyond the acquisition of knowledge and skills to unlearn and become empty.

In our world of equality and democracy, there is a tradition that still lingers in certain professional worlds that requires one to address the professional by the quality or value it is their job to exemplify. Thus a judge is called 'your honour'; an archbishop 'your grace'; a head of a craft guild or a mayor 'your Worship' (originally 'your worthship'); a king, 'your majesty' etc. By using this form of address, we are traditionally both honouring that quality within the person carrying the role and also evoking that quality from them. This is not a quality they own like a possession, but a quality they profess, embody and reflect in their work and those that engage them in their professional capacity.

This set us thinking. We began to wonder what term we would use to address a master practitioner in the field of enabling, work-based learning and development. What are the core qualities that you would like to reflect in your work and have reflected in how you are addressed? We came up with a number of possibilities:

- 'your courage';
- 'your candour';
- 'your enabling presence';
- 'your fearless compassion'.

This exercise while at one level being a bit of fun, does get us to think through the highest ideal we seek in our practice, one that we feel would raise our game and challenge us to our best. We invite you to have some serious fun and choose your own! In doing so you are choosing the quality you wish to invoke in your work as a coach, mentor, consultant or supervisor: the quality that you wish to reflect in your work with others and for which you will undertake the work of polishing your professional mirror.

Appendix I: APECS ethical guidelines

Introduction

The Association for Professional Executive Coaching and Supervision (APECS) is the top-level professional body for the provision of executive coaching and for the supervision of executive coaches. The ethical guidelines contained in this document are indicators of that professionalism and the high standards seen as essential to the various relationships involved in executive coaching and supervision. We want the safest and most effective conditions for clients (those being coached), the clearest and most transparent understanding with host companies who commission executive coaching and/or supervision and the highest professional standards for our coaches and supervisors.

Nature of the guidelines

These guidelines set out the principles, standards and sometimes procedures that guide our work. Members of APECS accept these as part of their contract with APECS and would be expected to tell APECS if there was any part or parts of the guidelines with which they could not agree and which they could not practice. Failure to abide by these standards by any member of APECS may be reported to APECS for investigation under its complaints procedure. These procedures will be set out in a further document entitled 'APECS Complaints Procedure'.

Communication of this code of ethics and conduct

Whatever the contracting arrangements are with a coaching client (individual) or his/her sponsoring organization, it must be brought formally to the attention of the individual client and the sponsoring organization that these ethical guidelines and the APECS complaints procedure exist and where to obtain copies if required.

Definitions

For the purposes of this code: 'coach' refers to the person who carries out professional executive coaching of the 'client', the individual receiving coaching. 'Sponsoring organization' or 'sponsor' refers to the company, institution or body which is funding the coaching. Professional executive coaching or 'coaching' refers to a one-to-one developmental relationship with clearly focused aims related to the clients' effectiveness in a particular role in the sponsoring organization. 'Supervision' or 'supervisor' refers to the relationship between the coach and a qualified person who is not in any managerial relationship with the coach.

Guidelines

In general, executive coaches and supervisors of executive coaches will behave in ways which demonstrate:

- Respect for individuals and organizations (rights and dignity).
- Awareness and sensitivity to difference (race, culture, gender, disability etc.).
- Their concern for fairness and justice at all levels of their work.
- Openness to new knowledge, competencies and attitudes that further the quality of their work.
- The importance of context in their work.
- Commitment to establishing high-quality and high-level healthy relationships with individuals and organizations.
- Ensuring insights into the impact of their behaviour on others.
- They engage with provisions that develop and enhance autonomy in individuals and organizations.

APECS executive coaches and supervisors will hold firmly to the foundation principles underpinning ethical thinking and behaviour:

- Autonomy – to help individuals and companies make their own decisions and move towards increasing self-authority.
- Fidelity – to be faithful to contracts, relationships and promises made.
- Beneficence – to do what benefits the well-being of all.
- Non-maleficence – to avoid whatever might harm others.
- Justice – to maintain fairness.
- Caring for self – to look after oneself physically, emotionally, mentally and motivationally so that clients and organizations receive the best service possible.

These guidelines (values) will influence decisions made by executive coaches and supervisors in areas such as:

1   Qualifications.
2   Ongoing professional development.
3   Setting up and engaging in executive coaching relationships.
4   Boundary management.
5   Requirements for supervision.
6   Other requirements.

1 Qualifications

The coach will:

- Be properly qualified to carry out the work (see APECS accreditation criteria guidelines).
- Ensure that the requirements of the coaching contract are within their professional ability to deliver or make clear to the client and the sponsor where the shortfall may be.
- Continue to learn and grow in their professional knowledge and expertise.
- Invest in personal development work to enhance their self-awareness and emotional balance.
- Work with an approved supervisor (see APECS accreditation criteria guidelines) to ensure client safety, review their client case work and monitor their own well-being and effectiveness.

2 Ongoing professional development

Executive coaches and supervisors with APECS will be committed to their own learning and development and take steps to ensure that they are up to date with current thinking and knowledge. They will review the steps they take to ensure this in professional supervision and they and their supervisor will agree an annual development plan that will be part of their supervisor report.

3 Setting up and engaging in executive coaching or supervision relationships

The coach or supervisor will:

- Take proper steps to ensure a sound understanding of the nature of the sponsor's and client's expectations of coaching.
- Where there appear to be inappropriate expectations of understandings of the nature of coaching, explain its limitations and uses appropriately and simply.

- Explain this code of ethics and conduct to the sponsor and the client including the confidentiality requirements and the rare exceptions to it.
- Establish a clear contract with the sponsor and the client which covers:
  - The process of coaching/supervision
  - The aims of the specific coaching engagement/under supervision
  - The duration, hours provision and periodicity of the engagement
  - Specifically who will be involved in the process and at which stages
  - The matters of confidentiality and boundary management (see below)
  - Fee and cancellation arrangements
- The coach/supervisor will not in any way use his/her position of influence to take advantage of the client and will always act in the client's and sponsor's best interests.

4 Boundary management

The coach and supervisor will:

- Maintain proper confidentiality of personal information gained within the coaching/supervision context.
- Maintain confidentiality of the names and roles of those who are or have been coached/supervised.
- Maintain commercial confidentiality regarding any aspects of the sponsoring organization's business and plans.
- Only disclose information from the coaching/supervision context to the sponsor with the specific permission of the client and then only if there are special reasons why this is in the best interests of the client.
- Be prepared to disclose to the sponsor or the competent authorities any matter which indicates an illegal or illicit action by the client or where there is a significant risk to another person or body should this not be disclosed. In such rarer circumstances the client should be given the first opportunity to disclose unless the timing indicates that urgent action is needed by the coach/supervisor.

5 Requirements for supervision

Each executive coach will choose a form of supervision and a supervisor that best fits their learning needs. In ongoing and regular supervision they will discuss confidentially their thoughts, feeling and reactions to their work at all levels: clients, relationships, interventions, contracts, impasses, joys, upsets etc. Supervision will be a forum for reflection on coaching work where supervisees will take responsibility for their own learning. Supervisors will provide APECS with a short annual report on supervisees assuring APECS that they are working ethically and to an acceptable standard.

6 Other requirements

- The coach and supervisor will ensure the safekeeping of all related records and data connected with the coaching contract and its delivery.
- The coach and supervisor will have professional liability insurance of at least £1million.
- Where necessary the coach and supervisor will have proper public liability and employers' liability insurance cover.
- The coach and supervisor will always observe and comply with any UK or EU requirements or those governing the geographic area in which they work.

Breaches of the code

APECS coaching and supervisory members will endeavour to behave in a way which models exemplary professionalism and which will reflect well on the coaching profession. Should a situation arise where it appears that a coach or a supervisor has behaved in a way which is in breach of these ethical guidelines and if the matter can not be resolved by them or is of high importance then APECS can be approached to invoke its complaints procedures by contacting the association: info@apecs.org.

Appendix II: EMCC guidelines on supervision

Introduction

The European Mentoring and Coaching Council (EMCC) has been established to promote best practice and ensure that the highest possible standards are maintained in the coach/mentoring relationship, whatever form that might take, so that the coach/mentoring environment provides the greatest opportunity for learning and development.

Purpose

This ethical code sets out what the clients and sponsors can expect from the coach/mentor in either a coach/mentoring, training or supervisory relationship and should form the starting point for any contract agreed. All members of the EMCC accept the principles and aims of the EMCC. We recognize that members may not always maintain these ethical principles. The EMCC have therefore agreed a process by which breaches of the code by a member can be reported and investigated. This is referred to later in this document. A copy of this ethical code should be given by all EMCC members to their clients at the contracting phase.

Terminology

The term 'coach/mentoring' is used to describe all types of coaching or mentoring that may be taking place, both in the work environment and outside. The EMCC recognize that there will be many types of coach/mentoring taking place and these will need to be defined when more detailed standards are produced.

The term 'client' denotes anyone using the services of a coach/mentor. We believe the term 'client' is interchangeable with any other term that the parties to the coach/mentoring relationship might be more comfortable with, such as 'colleague', 'learner', 'partner', 'coachee' or 'mentee'.

It is recognized that there are circumstances where the coach/mentor may have two 'clients', the individual being coached and the organization who may have commissioned the coach/mentoring. In this code we have used the term 'sponsor' to differentiate the latter. The terms 'supervision' and 'supervisor' describe the process by which the work of the coach/mentor is overseen and advice/guidance sought. The terminology is the same, but the process may differ in significant ways from that undertaken in other professions, such as psychotherapy and counselling.

The code

The coach/mentor must acknowledge the dignity of all humanity. They must conduct themselves in a way which respects diversity and promotes equal opportunities.

It is the primary responsibility of the coach/mentor to provide the best possible service to the client and to act in such a way as to cause no harm to any client or sponsor.

The coach/mentor is committed to functioning from a position of dignity, autonomy and personal responsibility.

The EMCC ethical code covers the following:

- Competence
- Context
- Boundary management
- Integrity
- Professionalism

Competence

The coach/mentor will:

a   Ensure that their level of experience and knowledge is sufficient to meet the needs of the client.

b   Ensure that their capability is sufficient to enable them to operate according to this code of ethics and any standards that may subsequently be produced.

c   Develop and then enhance their level of competence by participating in relevant training and appropriate continuing professional development activities.

d   Maintain a relationship with a suitably-qualified supervisor, who will regularly assess their competence and support their development. The supervisor will be bound by the requirements of confidentiality referred to in this code. What constitutes a 'suitably-qualified' supervisor is defined in the EMCC's standards document.

Context

The coach/mentor will:

a   Understand and ensure that the coach/mentoring relationship reflects the context within which the coach/mentoring is taking place.
b   Ensure that the expectations of the client and the sponsor are understood and that they themselves understand how those expectations are to be met.
c   Seek to create an environment in which client, coach/mentor and sponsor are focused on and have the opportunity for learning.

Boundary management

The coach/mentor will:

a   At all times operate within the limits of their own competence, recognize where that competence has the potential to be exceeded and where necessary refer the client either to a more experienced coach/mentor, or support the client in seeking the help of another professional, such as a counsellor, psychotherapist or business/financial adviser.
b   Be aware of the potential for conflicts of interest of either a commercial or emotional nature to arise through the coach/mentoring relationship and deal with them quickly and effectively to ensure there is no detriment to the client or sponsor.

Integrity

The coach/mentor will:

a   Maintain throughout the level of confidentiality which is appropriate and is agreed at the start of the relationship.
b   Disclose information only where explicitly agreed with the client and sponsor (where one exists), unless the coach/mentor believes that there is convincing evidence of serious danger to the client or others if the information is withheld.
c   Act within applicable law and not encourage, assist or collude with others engaged in conduct which is dishonest, unlawful, unprofessional or discriminatory.

Professionalism

The coach/mentor will:

a   Respond to the client's learning and development needs as defined by the agenda brought to the coach/mentoring relationship.
b   Not exploit the client in any manner, including, but not limited to, financial,

sexual or those matters within the professional relationship. The coach/mentor will ensure that the duration of the coach/mentoring contract is only as long as is necessary for the client/sponsor.

c   Understand that professional responsibilities continue beyond the termination of any coach/mentoring relationship. These include the following:

- Maintenance of agreed confidentiality of all information relating to clients and sponsors
- Avoidance of any exploitation of the former relationship
- Provision of any follow-up which has been agreed to
- Safe and secure maintenance of all related records and data

d   Demonstrate respect for the variety of different approaches to coaching and mentoring and other individuals in the profession.

e   Never represent the work and views of others as their own.

f   Ensure that any claim of professional competence, qualifications or accreditation is clearly and accurately explained to potential clients and that no false or misleading claims are made or implied in any published material.

Breaches of the code

EMCC members must at all times represent coaching and mentoring in a way which reflects positively on the profession.

Where a client or sponsor believes that a member of the EMCC has acted in a way which is in breach of this ethical code, they should first raise the matter and seek resolution with the member concerned. Either party can ask the EMCC to assist in the process of achieving resolution.

If the client or sponsor remains unsatisfied they are entitled to make a formal complaint. Complaints will be dealt with according to the EMCC's 'Complaints and disciplinary procedure'. EMCC members will provide a copy of this document upon request. A copy can be obtained by writing to:

European Mentoring & Coaching Council,
Sherwood House, 7 Oxhey Road,
Watford, Hertfordshire, WD19 4QF
or e-mail: info@emccouncil.org

In the event that a complaint should be made against an EMCC member, that member must cooperate in resolving such a complaint.

EMCC members will confront a colleague when they have reasonable cause to believe they are acting in an unethical manner and, failing resolution, will report that colleague to the EMCC.

Appendix III: AC code of ethics and good practice

The Association for Coaching (AC) is committed to maintaining good practice. This code of ethics and good practice sets out the essential elements of sound ethical practice. For the purposes of this code, the person receiving coaching is called the client.

All clients should expect a high standard of practice from their coach. To ensure that this is achieved coaches commit to operate in accordance with the Association's code of ethics and good practice for ethical, competent and effective practice.

1 Coaches are required to recognize both personal and professional limitations:

Personal – with respect to maintaining their own good health and fitness to practice. Should this not be the case, coaches are required to withdraw from their practice until such time as they are in good health and fit to resume. Clients should be offered appropriate, alternative support during any such period.

Professional – with respect to whether their experience is appropriate to meet the client's requirements. When this is not the case, clients should be referred to other appropriate services, e.g. more experienced coaches, counsellors, psychotherapists or other specialist services. In particular, coaches are required to be sensitive to the possibility that some clients will require more psychological support than is normally available within the coaching remit. In these cases, referral should be made to an appropriate source of care, e.g. the client's GP, a counsellor or psychotherapist, psychological support services and/or agencies.

2 Coaches are responsible for ensuring that clients are fully informed of the coaching contract, terms and conditions, prior to or at the initial session. These matters include confidentiality, sessional costs and frequency of sessions. All claims made by the coach should be honest, accurate and consistent with maintaining the coaching profession's good standing.

3 Coaches are required to be frank and willing to respond to their client's requests for information about the methods, techniques and ways in which the coaching

process will be conducted. This should be done both prior to contract agreement and during the full term of the contract.

4 Coaches must be sensitive to issues of culture, religion, gender and race.

5 Coaches must respect the client's right to terminate coaching at any point during the coaching process.

6 Coaches are required to maintain appropriate records of their work with clients, ensuring that any such records are accurate and that reasonable security precautions are taken to protect against third party disclosure. Attention must be given to the coachee's rights under any current legislation, e.g. data protection act.

7 Coaches are required to monitor the quality of their work and to seek feedback wherever possible from clients and other professionals as appropriate.

8 Coaches are expected to have regular consultative support for their work.

9 A coach should aim to undertake a minimum of 30 hours of continuing professional development in the theory and practice of coaching on an annual basis.

10 Coaches are required to keep themselves informed of any statutory or legal requirements that may affect their work.

11 Coaches are required to have current professional liability insurance.

12 Coaches are required to consider the impact of any dual relationships they may hold with regards to their clients and/or any sponsoring organizations.

13 Coaches must act in a manner that does not bring the profession of coaching into disrepute.

Appendix IV: International Coach Federation code of ethics

The following is used by permission of the International Coach Federation (ICF). All rights reserved.

ICF definition of mentor coaching (coaching supervision)

'The ICF currently only defines mentor coaching (coaching supervision) in our requirements for individual credentials: for purposes of credentialing, mentor coaching means an applicant being coached on their coaching skills rather than coaching on practice building, life balance, or other topics unrelated to the development of an applicant's coaching skill.'

Part one: the ICF philosophy of coaching

The ICF adheres to a form of coaching that honors the client as the expert in his/her life and work and believes that every client is creative, resourceful, and whole. Standing on this foundation, the coach's responsibility is to:

- Discover, clarify, and align with what the client wants to achieve
- Encourage client self-discovery
- Elicit client-generated solutions and strategies
- Hold the client responsible and accountable

Part two: the ICF definition of coaching

Professional coaching is an ongoing professional relationship that helps people produce extraordinary results in their lives, careers, businesses or organizations. Through the process of coaching, clients deepen their learning, improve their performance and enhance their quality of life.

In each meeting, the client chooses the focus of conversation, while the coach listens and contributes observations and questions. This interaction creates clarity and moves the client into action. Coaching accelerates the client's progress by providing greater focus and awareness of choice. Coaching concentrates on where clients are now and what they are willing to do to get where they want to be in the future. ICF member coaches and ICF credentialed coaches recognize that results are a matter of the client's intentions, choices and actions, supported by the coach's efforts and application of the coaching process.

Part three: the ICF standards of ethical conduct

Professional conduct at large

As a coach:

1 I will conduct myself in a manner that reflects positively upon the coaching profession and I will refrain from engaging in conduct or making statements that may negatively impact the public's understanding or acceptance of coaching as a profession.

2 I will not knowingly make any public statements that are untrue or misleading, or make false claims in any written documents relating to the coaching profession.

3 I will respect different approaches to coaching. I will honor the efforts and contributions of others and not misrepresent them as my own.

4 I will be aware of any issues that may potentially lead to the misuse of my influence by recognizing the nature of coaching and the way in which it may affect the lives of others.

5 I will at all times strive to recognize personal issues that may impair, conflict or interfere with my coaching performance or my professional relationships. Whenever the facts and circumstances necessitate, I will promptly seek professional assistance and determine the action to be taken, including whether it is appropriate to suspend or terminate my coaching relationship(s).

6 As a trainer or supervisor of current and potential coaches, I will conduct myself in accordance with the ICF code of ethics in all training and supervisory situations.

7 I will conduct and report research with competence, honesty and within recognized scientific standards. My research will be carried out with the necessary approval or consent from those involved, and with an approach that will reasonably protect participants from any potential harm. All research efforts will be performed in a manner that complies with the laws of the country in which the research is conducted.

8 I will accurately create, maintain, store and dispose of any records of work done in relation to the practice of coaching in a way that promotes confidentiality and complies with any applicable laws.

9   I will use ICF member contact information (email addresses, telephone numbers etc.) only in the manner and to the extent authorized by the ICF.

Professional conduct with clients

10 I will be responsible for setting clear, appropriate, and culturally sensitive boundaries that govern any physical contact that I may have with my clients.

11 I will not become sexually involved with any of my clients.

12 I will construct clear agreements with my clients, and will honour all agreements made in the context of professional coaching relationships.

13 I will ensure that, prior to or at the initial session, my coaching client understands the nature of coaching, the bounds of confidentiality, financial arrangements and other terms of the coaching agreement.

14 I will accurately identify my qualifications, expertise and experience as a coach.

15 I will not intentionally mislead or make false claims about what my client will receive from the coaching process or from me as their coach.

16 I will not give my clients or prospective clients information or advice I know or believe to be misleading.

17 I will not knowingly exploit any aspect of the coach-client relationship for my personal, professional or monetary advantage or benefit.

18 I will respect the client's right to terminate coaching at any point during the process. I will be alert to indications that the client is no longer benefiting from our coaching relationship.

19 If I believe the client would be better served by another coach, or by another resource, I will encourage the client to make a change.

20 I will suggest that my clients seek the services of other professionals when deemed appropriate or necessary.

21 I will take all reasonable steps to notify the appropriate authorities in the event a client discloses an intention to endanger self or others.

Confidentiality/privacy

22 I will respect the confidentiality of my client's information, except as otherwise authorized by my client, or as required by law.

23 I will obtain agreement from my clients before releasing their names as clients or references, or any other client identifying information.

24 I will obtain agreement from the person being coached before releasing information to another person compensating me.

Conflicts of interest

25 I will seek to avoid conflicts between my interests and the interests of my clients.

26 Whenever any actual conflict of interest or the potential for a conflict of interest arises, I will openly disclose it and fully discuss with my client how to deal with it in whatever way best serves my client.

27 I will disclose to my client all anticipated compensation from third parties that I may receive for referrals of that client.

28 I will only barter for services, goods or other non-monetary remuneration when it will not impair the coaching relationship.

Part four: the ICF pledge of ethics

As a professional coach, I acknowledge and agree to honour my ethical obligations to my coaching clients and colleagues and to the public at large. I pledge to comply with the ICF code of ethics, to treat people with dignity as independent and equal human beings, and to model these standards with those whom I coach. If I breach this pledge of ethics or any part of the ICF code of ethics, I agree that the ICF in its sole discretion may hold me accountable for so doing. I further agree that my accountability to the ICF for any breach may include loss of my ICF membership and/or my ICF credentials.

ICF professional coaching core competencies

The following 11 core coaching competencies were developed to support greater understanding about the skills and approaches used within today's coaching profession as defined by the ICF. They will also support you in calibrating the level of alignment between the coach-specific training expected and the training you have experienced. Finally, these competencies were used as the foundation for the ICF credentialing process examination.

The core competencies are grouped into four clusters according to those that fit together logically based on common ways of looking at the competencies in each group. The groupings and individual competencies are not weighted – they do not represent any kind of priority in that they are all core or critical for any competent coach to demonstrate.

A *SETTING THE FOUNDATION*

1 MEETING ETHICAL GUIDELINES AND PROFESSIONAL STAN-DARDS

2 ESTABLISHING THE COACHING AGREEMENT

B *CO-CREATING THE RELATIONSHIP*

3 ESTABLISHING TRUST AND INTIMACY WITH THE CLIENT

4 COACHING PRESENCE

C *COMMUNICATING EFFECTIVELY*

5 ACTIVE LISTENING

6 POWERFUL QUESTIONING

7 DIRECT COMMUNICATION

D *FACILITATING LEARNING AND RESULTS*

8 CREATING AWARENESS

9 DESIGNING ACTIONS

10 PLANNING AND GOAL SETTING

11 MANAGING PROGRESS AND ACCOUNTABILITY

NOTE: Each competency listed on the following pages has a definition and related behaviors. Behaviors are classified as either those that should always be present and visible in any coaching interaction (in regular font), or those that are called for in certain coaching situations and, therefore, not always visible in any one coaching interaction (in italics).

A SETTING THE FOUNDATION

1 **Meeting ethical guidelines and professional standards** – Understanding of coaching ethics and standards and ability to apply them appropriately in all coaching situations

a   Understands and exhibits in own behaviors the ICF standards of conduct (see list)

b   *Understands and follows all ICF ethical guidelines (see list)*

c   *Clearly communicates the distinctions between coaching, consulting, psychotherapy and other support professions*

d   *Refers client to another support professional as needed, knowing when this is needed and the available resources*

2 **Establishing the coaching agreement** – Ability to understand what is required in the specific coaching interaction and to come to agreement with the prospective and new client about the coaching process and relationship

a   *Understands and effectively discusses with the client the guidelines and specific parameters of the coaching relationship (e.g., logistics, fees, scheduling, inclusion of others if appropriate)*

b   *Reaches agreement about what is appropriate in the relationship and what is not, what is and is not being offered, and about the client's and coach's responsibilities* c   *Determines whether there is an effective match between his/her coaching method and the needs of the prospective client*

B CO-CREATING THE RELATIONSHIP

3 **Establishing trust and intimacy with the client** – Ability to create a safe, supportive environment that produces ongoing mutual respect and trust

a   Shows genuine concern for the client's welfare and future

b   Continuously demonstrates personal integrity, honesty and sincerity

c   Establishes clear agreements and keeps promises

d   Demonstrates respect for client's perceptions, learning style, personal being

e   Provides ongoing support for and champions new behaviors and actions, including those involving risk taking and fear of failure

f   *Asks permission to coach client in sensitive, new areas*

4 **Coaching presence** – Ability to be fully conscious and create spontaneous relationship with the client, employing a style that is open, flexible and confident

a   Is present and flexible during the coaching process, dancing in the moment

b   Accesses own intuition and trusts one's inner knowing – 'goes with the gut'

c   Is open to not knowing and takes risks

d   Sees many ways to work with the client, and chooses in the moment what is most effective

e   Uses humor effectively to create lightness and energy

f   *Confidently shifts perspectives and experiments with new possibilities for own action*

g   *Demonstrates confidence in working with strong emotions, and can self-manage and not be overpowered or enmeshed by client's emotions*

C COMMUNICATING EFFECTIVELY

5 **Active listening** – Ability to focus completely on what the client is saying and is not saying, to understand the meaning of what is said in the context of the client's desires, and to support client self-expression

a   Attends to the client and the client's agenda, and not to the coach's agenda for the client

b   Hears the client's concerns, goals, values and beliefs about what is and is not possible

c   Distinguishes between the words, the tone of voice, and the body language

d   Summarizes, paraphrases, reiterates, mirrors back what client has said to ensure clarity and understanding e   Encourages, accepts, explores and reinforces the client's expression of feelings, perceptions, concerns, beliefs, suggestions etc.

f   Integrates and builds on client's ideas and suggestions

g   *'Bottom-lines' or understands the essence of the client's communication and helps the client get there rather than engaging in long descriptive stories*

h   *Allows the client to vent or 'clear' the situation without judgement or attachment in order to move on to next steps*

6 **Powerful questioning** – Ability to ask questions that reveal the information needed for maximum benefit to the coaching relationship and the client

a   Asks questions that reflect active listening and an understanding of the client's perspective

b   Asks questions that evoke discovery, insight, commitment or action (e.g., those that challenge the client's assumptions)

c   Asks open-ended questions that create greater clarity, possibility or new learning

d   Asks questions that move the client towards what they desire, not questions that ask for the client to justify or look backwards

7 **Direct communication** – Ability to communicate effectively during coaching sessions, and to use language that has the greatest positive impact on the client

a   Is clear, articulate and direct in sharing and providing feedback

b   Reframes and articulates to help the client understand from another perspective what he/she wants or is uncertain about

c   Clearly states coaching objectives, meeting agenda, purpose of techniques or exercises

d   Uses language appropriate and respectful to the client (e.g., non-sexist, non-racist, non-technical, non-jargon)

e   *Uses metaphor and analogy to help to illustrate a point or paint a verbal picture*

D FACILITATING LEARNING AND RESULTS

8 **Creating awareness** – Ability to integrate and accurately evaluate multiple sources of information, and to make interpretations that help the client to gain awareness and thereby achieve agreed-upon results

a   Goes beyond what is said in assessing client's concerns, not getting hooked by the client's description

b   Invokes inquiry for greater understanding, awareness and clarity

c   Identifies for the client his/her underlying concerns, typical and fixed ways of perceiving himself/herself and the world, differences between the facts and the interpretation, disparities between thoughts, feelings and action d   Helps clients to discover for themselves the new thoughts, beliefs, perceptions, emotions, moods etc. that strengthen their ability to take action and achieve what is important to them

e   Communicates broader perspectives to clients and inspires commitment to shift their viewpoints and find new possibilities for action

f   Helps clients to see the different, interrelated factors that affect them and their behaviours (e.g., thoughts, emotions, body, background)

g   Expresses insights to clients in ways that are useful and meaningful for the client

h   *Identifies major strengths vs. major areas for learning and growth, and what is most important to address during coaching*

i   *Asks the client to distinguish between trivial and significant issues, situational vs. recurring behaviours, when detecting a separation between what is being stated and what is being done*

9 **Designing actions** – Ability to create with the client opportunities for ongoing learning, during coaching and in work/life situations, and for taking new actions that will most effectively lead to agreed-upon coaching results

a   Brainstorms and assists the client to define actions that will enable the client to demonstrate, practice and deepen new learning

b   Helps the client to focus on and systematically explore specific concerns and opportunities that are central to agreed-upon coaching goals

c   Engages the client to explore alternative ideas and solutions, to evaluate options, and to make related decisions

d   Promotes active experimentation and self-discovery, where the client applies what has been discussed and learned during sessions immediately afterwards in his/her work or life setting

e   Celebrates client successes and capabilities for future growth

f   *Challenges client's assumptions and perspectives to provoke new ideas and find new possibilities for action*

g   *Advocates or brings forward points of view that are aligned with client goals and, without attachment, engages the client to consider them*

h   *Helps the client 'do it now' during the coaching session, providing immediate support*

i   *Encourages stretches and challenges but also a comfortable pace of learning*

10 **Planning and goal setting** – Ability to develop and maintain an effective coaching plan with the client

a Consolidates collected information and establishes a coaching plan and development goals with the client that address concerns and major areas for learning and development

b Creates a plan with results that are attainable, measurable, specific and have target dates

c Makes plan adjustments as warranted by the coaching process and by changes in the situation

d *Helps the client identify and access different resources for learning (e.g., books, other professionals)*

e *Identifies and targets early successes that are important to the client*

11 **Managing progress and accountability** – Ability to hold attention on what is important for the client, and to leave responsibility with the client to take action

a Clearly requests of the client actions that will move the client toward their stated goals

b Demonstrates follow through by asking the client about those actions that the client committed to during the previous session(s)

c Acknowledges the client for what they have done, not done, learned or become aware of since the previous coaching session(s)

d Effectively prepares, organizes and reviews with client information obtained during sessions

e *Keeps the client on track between sessions by holding attention on the coaching plan and outcomes, agreed-upon courses of action, and topics for future session(s)*

f *Focuses on the coaching plan but is also open to adjusting behaviors and actions based on the coaching process and shifts in direction during sessions*

g *Is able to move back and forth between the big picture of where the client is heading, setting a context for what is being discussed and where the client wishes to go*

h *Promotes client's self-discipline and holds the client accountable for what they say they are going to do, for the results of an intended action, or for a specific plan with related time frames*

i *Develops the client's ability to make decisions, address key concerns, and develops himself/herself (to get feedback, to determine priorities and set the pace of learning, to reflect on and learn from experiences)*

j *Positively confronts the client with the fact that he/she did not take agreed-upon actions*

Appendix V: the deference threshold

Joe, an experienced coach and supervisor, brought the following experiences to his monthly supervision. 'I was recently asked to go and meet the CEO of a highly successful global investment company. She had a reputation for being extremely tough and hard-nosed and made it clear that I was only one of three or four people she was interviewing as a potential coach. As soon as I walked into her office, on the top floor of a plush City of London office block, I felt 'off-balance'. She waved me over to a seat and looked quizzically at me. I felt under immediate pressure. I felt that I had to respond to her quizzical-ness, even though that was not where I would have wanted to begin. I began burbling about what I did, and felt almost in my 'panic zone'. All my experience and skill – I have worked very successfully with some extremely tough and senior executives in the past – deserted me, I felt. I couldn't wait to finish the meeting and I had no real conviction that I would get the coaching contract!'

So what was it that reduced Joe, an experienced and skilled coach, to a highly ineffective version of himself, and created a self-fulfilling prophecy of failure to engage? Our contention is that Joe had unwarily crossed his own 'deference threshold'.

In our working life as coaches and supervisors, we will all have come across moments where it feels that the client or the situation have rendered us considerably less effective than we normally are. We could just be having an 'off day'; we might simply dislike the person or group that we are with; we may be presented with a situation we do not understand or do not appreciate. There are many potential causes.

We want to look at one of these potential causes, which we believe is an occasional but significant problem for all of us as coaches and supervisors and is not specifically related to the experience level of the supervisor or coach. We think it important to address it, because it impacts on our professional effectiveness. The consequence of such reactivity can sow unhelpful and potentially destructive seeds of professional self-doubt, and can drive various unhelpful and dysfunctional behaviours. The positive side of looking at this issue is that we can exercise control over it, allowing us to improve our supervision and coaching skills, and offer an important awareness to those we work with.

So what is a 'deference threshold'? We have noticed in our own practice and that of many others too, a variety of ways of explaining this phenomenon such as:

- losing the plot;
- behaving like a novice;
- being organized by the client;
- feeling on the back foot;
- feeling small;
- needing to get on the right side of . . .

Such feelings can creep into otherwise skilled practice. It is the unpredictability of their appearance, and our lack of awareness, until it's too late, that, in our opinion, marks the deference threshhold out from inexperience or just plain bad practice.

Not being aware of our own particular deference threshold means that we don't know whether our next client meeting is another prime candidate for tripping over the threshold. If we become aware of the triggers, we have the option of lightly avoiding it. As we can see from the list, it is not a precise feeling. It seems to have many faces, and effects, but, the more we look behind what is happening we will see that in each case the coach or supervisor hands over their authority, presence and impact to the other person. We defer to the other person. Each of us will probably have our specific and individualized point where this internal pressure to defer kicks in. In people who are relatively inexperienced, it can kick in quite often, and even with relatively junior clients. For others, like Joe, it may happen very occasionally with a particular type of high-flying executive.

The deference threshold is not just triggered by lack of experience, although it can be. For the inexperienced, the trigger is more often deference to other people's assumed experience and authority, and they down-rate the value of their own experience in comparison to the other person's. However, experience *per se* does not protect you, as Joe found out. Even the most experienced coaches and supervisors can trigger this reaction in themselves. However, the coach's personal temperament means that it may be harder to pick up in some than others. For example, those with a strong sense of self-worth, or maybe a strong 'ego', will seem to trigger their deference threshold less frequently, or perhaps less obviously, than those who might allow for the possibility of self-doubt. This can set a real challenge for a supervisor, in that the phenomenon may be reported as 'some muppet of a chief executive who was hopeless and I just walked away, because I couldn't work with someone like that'. On the surface, not maybe an area to stop and dwell on, and gently prod, since the energy coming from the other person is to 'move on' and 'get to something worth talking about'! It is interesting here to observe how this can also be seen to trigger the drama triangle we discussed earlier (Chapter 13). It either catapults us into victim or persecutor, but then engages others in the other roles, as discussed above.

We will look more closely at the triggers themselves, and how we might help someone explore the thresholds that engage them later on, but in outlining the overall shape of the phenomenon, we can see that, for all of us, there is a point where our professional skills and confidence get sidelined by a disempowering story in our heads. Such a story can have a variety of themes, but what they all have in common is that they put us into the role of the outsider, who does not have a legitimate reason for being there.

What can we do about it in our own practice, and how can we help others address these issues in their own professional life? First we have to understand the mechanism that can trigger this type of event. It may be easier to take an example from another sphere entirely in order to see its sequence more clearly. If you look at the performance of elite sports teams, in any area of sport, you can see that, however talented the players and however good the tactics and the training, a team can play 'like a drain' on occasions. The important point here is that the players and the coaches cannot easily predict the temporary 'blips' in performance. Any supporter of such team sports will have their own list of supremely frustrating, 'inexplicable' moments, when their team 'gave it away', 'lost the plot' or 'performed like amateurs'. Interestingly for our discussion on supervision, the triggers in these cases are not caused by incipient self-doubt, although that could be a feature for some players.

What is the natural 'state' of play for an elite sportsperson? When a sportsperson is playing at their best, they are often described as 'in the zone'. Many of you will be familiar with the concept of 'flow' – 'being in the zone', –the state in which the sportsperson has a heightened state of awareness of what is going on around them. This is characterized by such phenomena as:

- an ability to see the patterns in what is happening in front of me;
- time appearing to slow down to give me much more response time;
- seeing where things are going and being ahead of the 'action';
- being in a 'tranquil' place, aloof from the consequences of the activity;
- responding in ways that you could not possibly have thought to do but which 'fit' the need.

We suggest that the underlying pattern that links all these experiences is that individuals, or indeed team units, have maintained emotional disengagement with what is going on around them. This may seem a strange thing to say. Surely passion to succeed, aggression, drive are the very qualities that create winning play? These emotions, or our perceived lack of them on the pitch, are certainly what the media concentrate upon. They are also what we concentrate upon in bar-room philosophizing and terrace coaching. Our contention in this book directly challenges this 'wisdom'. We would say that these very emotions, which the less sophisticated professional coaches use to try to energize their teams for success, actually drive the unpredictability of their team's performance. Why? Because there is a direct link between emotional entanglement in a situation and a person's inability to be in the flow state. There is a further link between emotional entanglement in a situation and increasingly poor fine motor skill. The fact that you are emotional, for example angry, physically 'tightens' your muscles. Your muscles tightening will mean that you cannot perform fine motor skills with the same dexterity as when you are emotionally relaxed. Your sudden below-par performance increases other emotions such as anxiety and doubt, which reinforce your emotional entanglement in the game, and sets up the possibility of a downward spiral of performance in a game. Emotions are a two-edged sword. Anger, for example, may be motivational in that it creates and underpins commitment to the team, but it can also impair performance of physical tasks.

We also see the activity of supervision or coaching, at its best, mirroring the flow state, since in it we experience all the qualities that we mentioned above in regard to the experience of elite sportspeople. We also see that the trigger for a supervisor or coach tripping over the deference threshold is linked to an unaware emotional reaction to the situation we are in. Thinking back to Joe's experience with the chief executive of the City investment company, we can posit that there was some emotional hook that got sprung before or immediately on entry into the office that focused Joe on his feelings of deference – rather than simply being aware of what he was 'picking up' as the meeting moved forward. The consequence of having his own feelings centre-stage was that it triggered the unaware behaviours that he had constructed from childhood, when he was frightened and felt out of control. These behaviours, at root, are quite basic and unsophisticated. They are variations of the 'fight or flight' response. We do however find ways of dressing these responses up as we become socially more adept.

As a supervisor we may get a report of the 'flight' phenomenon, as we did with Joe's report of his initial interview. Joe's reaction was to back off, want the interview to be over, feel he was not going to get the contract, and that he didn't want it anyway. The supervisor might instead have got the 'fight' response, where Joe, if he had brought the situation at all, would have dismissed the event as a waste of time, the executive as arrogant and not workable with, and that he had better things to do with his time. This reaction is much easier to miss.

If these emotional responses are so deep, how can we address them in ourselves or help others to become aware of theirs? Well, the good news is that awareness is the key to making the shift. The bad news is that we have to be aware to do it! Awareness of what though? One of the skills that we see as important, for the supervisor particularly, is the ability, live in a session, to be able to monitor when and how they have become emotionally engaged by the discussion in the room. Once they can register what they think or feel 'in the moment' they then need to have strategies for getting themselves disentangled, while in the room, and use the event for the benefit of the session and the supervisee. We have mentioned elsewhere that most of us start with a natural talent for either being able to 'dance' with ease in another's dance, or of being detached enough to be able to see the patterns and process in what is going on around us.

Our view is that both these skills have to be held in tension. We need both these skills developed to be able to coach or supervise well. The trick we have to learn is to be able to 'get sucked in' to our client's world, in its emotional technicolour as well as its logical detail. This alone will give us compassion for our client, but it does not offer a perspective from which to develop the fearlessness we need, to help support real change. If we sit with our client and hold a clear overview of what is and is not happening for them in their world, we have lots of observations about what is going on, but no contract which allows us to use that emotional information for personal change. Unlike the elite sportsperson, the trick for the supervisor is to be able to move in and out of the emotional engagement with the client. They have to feel what it is like for them, they have to 'really get it' – in order to create the emotional link that allows challenge to be taken as helpful and supportive, and not just well intentioned criticism.

The deference threshold can be seen to be a crucially important disruption to this process, because it unknowingly trips us into emotional engagement, but in such a way as to make it very hard to use the experience for the benefit of the client. Therefore the flight or fight response 'locks' us into either unaware emotional connection that unhooks us from our expertise or into antipathy for the client with the consequence that we don't engage at all. That way we sever any useful connection with the client and may need to rebuild trust for further work to be possible.

Let us look at some of the ways in which we experience this phenomenon of deference. By looking at the way we reinforce these 'thresholds', or tripwires for the unwary, and by adding to the list over time, we build our explicit awareness of how we inhabit this particular area of our emotional landscape, and are therefore more likely to recognize the territory when we stray into it. So what are some of the features of this deference landscape?

The disempowering story

One common way in which we notice that we have entered this territory is that it triggers or creates a disempowering story of some kind. These stories are most obvious for those who have a natural 'flight' response to such situations. The flight stories can be as straightforward as 'Oh no, I find it really hard to work with powerful women executives' or 'It always goes pear shaped when I work with large groups!' Such a story gets born out of a need to limit the effect of a bad experience. Rather than suddenly feeling totally incompetent across the whole range of our activity, we choose to isolate this 'disaster' into a particular part of our experience. We therefore find an explanation as to why it 'only' happens here. The unfortunate and unintended consequence of this is that it reinforces this incompetence, and is likely to trigger it again at other times. It is useful for coaches and supervisors, who are likely to react in this way to such events, to set down our disempowering stories, and then look at how they have arisen and how we can rewrite them in a more constructive way. Constructiveness here is more about creating a story for ourselves which allows the flexibility to change and do things differently, rather than explain or cover our lack of performance in the situation we have described.

For those of us who find 'fight' more likely in 'deference' situations, such disempowering stories would look more like 'I can't stand pushy chief executives!' or 'The media sector doesn't interest me!' Even though these stories look different to the flight ones, their function is the same. They diminish the effect of a bad experience. However, the common link between all such stories is that we create limiting assumptions for ourselves. We do not want to go too deeply into how we can work with limiting assumptions here, since it is dealt with very effectively in other literature, particularly NLP (neuro-linguistic programming) ideas of shaping assumptions to deliver the goals you intend. Suffice it to say that in order to allow our practice as either coach or supervisor to go to a higher level, helping to transform such limiting assumptions is a fruitful area of self-development.

'Retreating to nice'

'Retreating to nice' is another strategy that allows the other person to take our voice and our effectiveness from us. The voice that gets taken away is the one that speaks with fearless compassion in any situation. 'Nice' triggers all sorts of old patterns, mainly from our childhood, about the social rules for being liked, praised and included. They are triggered by uncertainty and the worry that we won't be acceptable. Clearly, for the successful coach or supervisor we are not implying that this is a general state of anxiety – or we would *never* be able to offer that fearless compassion to clients. We are raising it here because we know that there are moments when these old patterns can be triggered by our deference, even in the most experienced practitioner.

The felt experience of this 'story' – i.e. the wish to be liked and accepted – is that we are uncertain of our acceptability in a particular situation, which may be triggered by either the individual we are with, the level they operate at, the demeanour they express, or the area in which they work. So we may find it 'easy' to embody our skills when talking to chief executives of global companies but find that our deference gets triggered talking to the prime minister of the country. This form of trigger means that we go not into self-doubt, and incompetence, but into trying to win them over as people. We need, in this context, to feel sufficiently accepted to do our work. The deeper need to feel accepted, though, hits all the school playground 'traumas' of being the last one to be selected for the team game, the one whom nobody wishes to pair up with, or the one who is seen as different. 'Needing to be accepted' can also play out in some situations as 'the need to be given permission' before we become fearless in our compassion. In either case, we become emotionally hooked by experiences in our past, and rather than ask what they are saying about the present moment, and the experience of the other person, we internalize this feeling as exclusively our own. In doing this we block off the possibility of being of help to the potential new client, and lock ourselves instead into our own personal, and in this case, incapacitating space.

The challenge of initial mismatch

At an initial meeting with a client have you ever been 'thrown' by their manner, the way they present themselves to you? If you are someone who values social awareness, a concern for the other person and the ability to be sociable, meeting a person who appears aggressive can be very disconcerting and throw us out of our professional power and skill and 'discombobulate' us into ineffectiveness. It is not just aggressiveness that can do this. We may find that, through our own previous experiences in life, aggression is something we deal very well with. If we have worked in various private sector environments, this may simply be what we have had to understand and find ways of coping with, to get to where we are now professionally. The 'aggressive' client may be more of a challenge for those of us who have arrived in coaching and supervision along the counselling route. We know from our own experience of working in this field that an aggressive mode of expression is not seen as a normal part of everyday behaviour. Aggression therefore is not the only emotion we might run up against that might knock us off our effectiveness perch. For some, 'vagueness' can be a trigger – because we get irritated by this perceived vagueness and tell ourselves they need to move on. For others it is 'sadness' or 'depression' which they are reactive to. Yet again, 'lack of confidence' or 'fear' may be the emotion-fuelled behaviour that throws us. What each of these triggers do is to engage our emotions, and create a story with us at the centre. This story makes us blind to what is happening in the room and what is happening for the new client, and dramatically reduces our professional effectiveness.

The parallel process challenge

Talking about 'parallel process' and the deference threshold, we want to underline again that these kinds of experiences do not telegraph themselves beforehand. Our experience is that we suddenly find ourselves 'up to our necks'. It is as though we have flown in to a 'deference triangle', which professionally can have the same untimely results as a flight through the 'Bermuda Triangle'. In order to make it less likely that these deference reactions disempower us, we need to understand the complex mechanisms at work in situations when the parallel process raises its head.

    To do our work as coaches and supervisors well, we need to have some natural ability to 'read' what is going on in other people. We intuitively pick up the feelings and questions 'in the room'. Honed by our training and practice we learn to trust these feelings as relevant to the work we are doing with individuals or teams. We have labelled this skill as 'mode 5' in the supervision model set out in Chapter 9.

    Let us try to lay bare the sequence that gets triggered by our 'deference'. The most significant thing we experience is that we feel, and therefore interpret, the situation in an intensely personal way. This intensity creates a power that stops our ability to see its cause located anywhere but in ourselves. We are therefore blinded to the possibility that this may be an example of mode 5 in action in the room. By framing this experience as something 'true' about us, rather than as possibly an action replay from another situation, which provides information for the coaching process, we immediately block our ability to use our skills to help the other person.

    It seems easy enough, if unpredictable, to get into these deference states, but how can we work towards not being caught by them in the future? As we have already described, our first reaction, when we experience these strong emotions, is to 'suck the problem into ourselves'. In order to create a path out, as a coach, we need to become aware of the personal 'emotional hooks' that make this feeling credible to us. As supervisors, we need not only to know our own patterns, but also how to recognize different patterns of deference ownership in others. Having recognized these intense moments as 'deference', we have to understand that slipping into this morass serves neither us nor our clients. That is not too difficult to grasp intellectually, but learning to leave this maze may require a guiding thread and emotional understanding of how we maintain this threshold.

The issue is not to take the intense emotional experience personally, and this is much easier said than done! One of the reasons for this difficulty is that it feeds the 'I am not worthy' syndrome, which a lot of us suffer from at some level, however deeply buried. 'I am not worthy' is probably one of the deepest doubts we harbour and which, because of its vicinity to shame, we feel unable to share with others. (Therapists recognize this phenomenon as 'countertransference'. In making the switch from therapy to coaching and supervision, there is often very little support to identify and work with it. For those who have had no such background training it may not figure at all.) Once we can see that it is something 'in the room' that we insist in taking as purely personal, then we have the possibility of using it for the client's good, rather than wallowing in our own angst.

Why does the feeling seem so intensely personal? It goes back to the fact that, for many good coaches and supervisors, part of their core skill is the intuitive ability to read non-verbal 'stuff' in the room. They have developed and used that skill as their experience increases. It is our Trojan horse for getting beyond our own and our clients' defences. Because of our professional sophistication, we have worked through the more obvious triggers that might hook us, for example 'competitiveness', sexual attraction or gender stereotypes. For this trigger to do its work, there have to be areas of personal experience that have lain relatively dormant, and unexplored in conversation. In their very nature, they are probably our biggest fears about ourselves (e.g. 'deep down I am not worthy'; 'somebody will find me out'; 'I am unlovable' etc.). The hook is our fear. Because it is a fear about our core self, and concerns our fitness to be in the world, it draws any 'parallel process' that we have picked up and taken personal responsibility for – instead of recognizing that it is at best a co-created process. Our natural skill in picking up feelings becomes, in this moment, our professional undoing. Our very ability to pick up parallel process in a number of areas creates feelings which need to be properly located. Our personal doubts will 'suck this data in' and see it as solely about 'me'. This makes us blind to such questions as:

- Why am I feeling this now?
- What might it be echoing in the room?
- What relevance do these feelings of self-doubt have for the person sitting opposite?

And because it all feels so personal, we are not able to see our blindness at this moment, and do not see that the experience may be fuelled by parallel process.

The way forward

We are at the stage where we have recognized certain experiences as examples of us falling over our deference threshold. This allows us to see that this personally powerful feeling (such as self-doubt) which we are experiencing might also give us important information about what is happening for the client. When a client is unable to verbalize what is happening to them, they will often recreate the situation outside the superversion room, by treating the supervisor as they are treated. This experience may lie below the line of their awareness, and is therefore enacted rather than intellectualized.

At this point of recognition, and of potential action, we are faced with how we can best use our experience in the service of the client. At this moment we are often only in possession of half the story. Let us go back to the story of Joe's chief executive to illustrate this point. Joe felt strong self-doubt in her presence. To believe that there is only 'self-doubt' in the room would be to miss the point. The new client is getting us to experience two realities that almost seem contradictory. They inhabit the strong, in control, dynamic element of their reality and create the other experience that they need us to understand, the one that is most difficult and disabling, which is of self-doubt and powerlessness.

To intervene in this difficult situation, it is important not just to voice the 'bit' of the puzzle you are experiencing. It is most helpful to present the tension in the room, the dilemma that you see expressed in the situation. First off we need to ask ourselves 'what is the other half of the tension that I am experiencing in the room at the moment?' Then we have to frame the next intervention in the form of a dilemma: 'If I were in your shoes, I think one of the dilemmas I would face is how do I hold all my skills and experience as a media executive at the same time as my doubts about the new challenges facing us, which no one has experience of solving. Is that a tension for you at this time?'

If you are in a group situation when 'deference' hits, you will recognize it either by feeling discomfort with what is happening and the need to grab the situation and move it on, or of withdrawing and letting either the group or the other presenter get on with it. If the flight or fight response kicks in, it is helpful to articulate the dilemma, perhaps between competence and incompetence, which is being played out in the room. If we only acknowledge our part of the dilemma, we reinforce the tension in the situation, by leaving it on its own 'in the room'. It does not help to just take in the dilemma in the room. While it is still being enacted it cannot be usefully internalized. Eventually, holding the tension of this dilemma inside, containing it, is what allows us all to move forward. While we are acting it out as 'us' and 'them' we are blindly unaware and cannot do more than stay locked in an unproductive cycle of 'Yes, you are!' and 'No, I am not!' altercations. It is in helping others to be aware of, and locate, the tension inside themselves, where it belongs, that we can give our clients the means for creating necessary changes.

Resources

Here we offer a guide to other sources of information about coaching and mentoring that you may find useful in developing your skills and experience. As things are changing so rapidly, we offer basic details about the orientations and approach of each rather than evaluating them.

Professional organizations

The following are organizations that have a contribution to make to the field and may provide readers with membership benefits.

The Association for Coaching (www.associationforcoaching.com) sees itself as promoting excellence and ethics in coaching. It has both individual and provider organization members. It has a code of ethics and good practice and a complaints procedure, and offers qualified members a certificate.

The Association for Professional Executive Coaching & Supervision – APECS (www.apecs.org) is the top-level professional body for fully-qualified executive coaches and executive coaching supervisors.

Chartered Institute of Personnel and Development (www.cipd.co.uk) CIPD's commercial arm, CIPD Services, offers a (200 learning hours) largely e-delivered Certificate in Coaching and Mentoring (Vocational Qualification Level 3) which leads to Associate Membership of CIPD. It also organizes a one-day conference annually. The membership and education side of CIPD was in 2004 considering developing standards at masters level. Its Professional Knowledge Department produced, in June 2004, a *Guide to Coaching and Mentoring*.

The Coaching and Mentoring Network (www.coachingnetwork.org.uk) is a UK-focused web-based network offering subscribers free impartial information about referrals (it charges coaches to register) and resources. It offers software and internet development services, a coach matching service, and does not accredit its members.

The Coaching Psychology Forum (www.coachingpsychologyforum.org.uk) was founded in 2002 in response to concerns about untrained or poorly trained coaches and the need to promote improved standards of practice. In 2004 the CPF had 400 members and affiliate members from within the British Psychological Society, more than 75 per cent of whom were chartered members.

The European Mentoring and Coaching Council (www.emccouncil.org) arose out of the European Mentoring Centre that was founded in 1992. It exists to promote good practice in mentoring and coaching across Europe. By 2004 it had developed and applied a widely agreed code of ethics in coaching and mentoring, guidelines on supervision, a diversity policy and a complaints procedure. It was bringing to a conclusion a wide-ranging project to identify common competencies as a basis for agreeing a set of professional standards for both coaching and mentoring. It produced a similar set of standards for mentoring schemes. It has established an electronic professional and academic journal, *The International Journal for Mentoring and Coaching*, and holds a major conference each year. EMCC is growing fast and in 2004 had more than 250 individual members and more than 25 organizational members.

The Institute of Management Consultancy (www.imc.co.uk) is the professional body for management consultants. It sets, maintains and raises the standards of both professionalism and competence for the profession.

The International Coach Federation (www.coachfederation.org) describes itself as the professional association of personal and business coaches that seeks to preserve the integrity of coaching around the globe. It is a US-based individual membership international organization with more than 6000 members and 145 chapters in more than 30 countries. It has developed a code of ethics and of professional standards, offers a coach referral service and has a system for accrediting members. It holds an annual conference.

The Management Consultancies Association (www.mca.org.uk) was formed in 1956 to represent the consultancy industry to its clients, the media and government. Today the members represent around 65 per cent of the UK consulting sector.

The National Mentoring Network (www.nmn.org.uk) was founded in 1994 and mainly focuses on mentoring schemes in schools. It aims to promote the development of mentoring and quality standards; to offer advice and support to those developing mentoring programmes; and to exchange information on good practice. It has 1500 organization members and 400 individual mentor members. It has an annual conference, a library, regional networks and a scheme accreditation process leading to approved provider standard. NMN founded, in 1998, the UTK Mentoring Strategy Group to influence mentoring across the UK.

The Worshipful Company of Management Consultants (www.comc.org.uk)

Coaching mentoring training

The Academy of Executive Coaching (www.academyofexecutivecoaching.-com) offers a master coach development programme and an MSc degree accredited by Middlesex University. The programme has an interesting Gestalt therapy orientation.

i-coach Academy (www.i-coachacademy.com) Accredited by Middlesex University, i-coach Academy runs a postgraduate certificate and a professional masters degree (both part-time). The certificate year focuses on participants identifying their own model for coaching; the masters year produces critiques of these models using a multiplicity of frameworks. The related International Centre for the Study of Coaching (also accredited by Middlesex University) runs a professional doctoral programme in a number of centres throughout the world.

Oxford Brookes University (www.brookes.ac.uk) Embedded in the Education Faculty of the university, this was the first masters programme to be offered in the UK. Some participants of the OSCM (see below) courses move on to the Oxford Brookes course, carrying a modest credit of M-level points.

The School of Coaching (www.theschoolofcoaching.com) runs open programmes and programmes tailored to specific needs, either at their clients' or the school's premises, or in other suitable locations. The programmes combine skill-building workshops and one-to-one coaching support with extensive practice, observation and feedback.

Wolverhampton University (www.wlv.ac.uk) The newest programme that we have found on coaching in a UK university.

Consultancy training

Ashridge (www.ashridge.org.uk) The Masters in Organization Consulting is designed by consultants for consultants who, like managers, are expected to take their own development seriously.

Roffey Park (www.roffeypark.com) The Roffey Park Masters in People and Organizational Development is an innovative, two-year, part-time MSc programme that has been run by professional developers and for professional developers since 1991. The degree is designed to bring together theory, practice and experience.

Sheffield Hallam University (www.shu.ac.uk) Linked to a suite of programmes in change and consultancy, this programme has both the authors of this book involved in its delivery, so it would be invidious to comment further.

University of Surrey (www.surrey.ac.uk) The Masters Degree in Management Consultancy enables consultants or those who want to move into consultancy to develop advanced consulting skills, which are not present in other business management courses.

Supervision training

The Bath Consultancy Group (www.bathconsultancygroup.com) offers the Certificate in Supervision of Coaches, Mentors & Consultants. This training programme, run jointly by Centre for Supervision & Team Development (CSTD) and Bath Consultancy Group, is aimed at experienced coaches, mentors and consultants and is taught by experts in this field. It consists of two three-day courses, an initial foundation course that is followed by the advanced course and two additional modules from the CSTD.

Centre for Supervision & Team Development (CSTD) (www.cstd.co.uk) provides supervision training both as open and bespoke courses for organizations across the helping professions. These include social services departments, hospitals, drug and alcohol treatment centres, clinical psychology departments, clergy, Relate, counselling and psychotherapy organizations. They also offer a modular certificate course that can be taken over a flexible period of time chosen by participants at one of three locations. The course consists of four modules, supervision and tutorials.

Michael Carroll (www.mpcarroll.com) is an accredited executive coach and executive coach Supervisor with APECS. He coaches business owners, artisans and managers in the skills and techniques needed to grow their business.

Oxford School of Coaching and Mentoring (OSCM) (www.oscm.co.uk) offers a CIPD programme, as well as its own certificate which leads into the masters programme at Oxford Brookes University.

Feedback request

We would welcome any feedback on this book and any suggestions or contributions for further editions or future publications. These should be sent to:

Peter Hawkins and Nick Smith
Bath Consultancy Group
Edgar House
16–17 George St
Bath BA1 2EN

Tel: + 44 (0)1225 333737
Fax: + 44 (0)1225 333738
Email: peter.hawkins@bathconsultancygroup.com
        nick.smith@bathconsultancygroup.com

Bibliography

Abbotson, S. and Ellis, F. (2001) *Best Practice in Executive Learning*. Bath: BCG.

Ahmad, B. (1990) *Advanced Award for Supervisors: Implications for Black Supervisors*. London: CCETSW.

Albott, W. (1984) Supervisory characteristics and other sources of supervision variance, *The Clinical Supervisor*, 2(4): 27–41.

Aldridge, L. (1982) *Construction of a Scale for the Rating of Supervisors of Psychology*. Auburn University, USA.

American Association for Counseling and Development (1989) *Standards for Counseling Supervisors*. Pacifica, CA: AACD.

Amidon, E. (2006) www.sufiway.org.

Ancona, D., Bresman, H. and Kaeufer, K. (2002) The comparative advantage of x-teams, *MIT Sloane Management Review*, 43(3): 33–9.

Anderson, W. (1996) *The Face of Glory: Creativity, Consciousness and Civilisation*. London: Bloomsbury.

Argyris, C. (1982) *Reasoning, Learning and Action: Individual and Organizational*. San Francisco: Jossey-Bass.

Argyris, C. (1991) Teaching smart people how to learn, *Harvard Business Review*, 69(3): 99–109.

Argyris, C. and Schön, D. (1978) *Organizational Learning*. Reading, MA: Addison-Wesley.

Arundale, J. (1993) *Psychotherapy Supervision: Impact, Practice and Expectations*. London: University of London.

Association for Counselor Education and Supervision (1989) *Standards for Counseling Supervisors*. Alexandria, VA: ACES.

Association for Counselor Education and Supervision (1993) *Ethical Guidelines for Counseling Supervisors*. Alexandria, VA: ACES.

Attwood, G. E. and Stolorow, R. D. (1984) *Structures of Subjectivity*. New York: The Analytic Press.

Bachkirova, T., Stevens, P. and Willis, P. (2005) *Coaching Supervision*. Oxford: Oxford Brookes Coaching and Mentoring Society.

Badaines, J. (1985) Supervision: methods and issues, *Self and Society: Journal of Humanistic Psychology*, XIII(2): 77–81.

Bandler, R. and Grinder, J. (1975) *The Structure of Magic*. Utah: Science and Behavior Books.

Bandler, R. and Grinder, J. (1979) *Frogs Into Princes: Neuro Linguistic Programming*. Utah: Real People Press.

Bandler, R. and Grinder, J. (1981) *Trance-formations*. Utah: Real People Press.

Bandler, R. and Grinder, J. (1982) *Reframing: NLP and the Transformation of Meaning*. Utah: Real People Press.

Bartell, P. A. and Rubin, L.J. (1990) Dangerous liaisons: sexual intimacies in supervision, *Professional Psychology: Research and Practice*, 21(6): 442–50.

Bast, M. and Thomson, C. (2003) *Out of the Box: Coaching with the Enneagram*. Portland, OR: Stellar Attractions.

Bateson, G. (1973) *Steps to an Ecology of Mind*. New York: Bantam.

Bath Consultancy Group (1999) *Account Transformation*. Bath: BCG.

Beckhard, R. and Harris, R. (1977) *Organisational Transitions: Managing Complex Change*. Reading, MA: Addison-Wesley.

Belbin, M. (1981) *Management Teams: Why they Succeed or Fail*. London: Heinemann.

Bennett, M. J. (1993) Towards ethnorelatativism: a developmental model of intercultural sensitivity, in R. M. Paige (ed.) *Education for the Intercultural Experience*, 2nd edn. Yarmouth, ME: Intercultural Press.

Bennis, W. (1989) *On Becoming a Leader*. Reading, MA: Addison-Wesley.

Bennis, W. and Nanus, B. (1985) *Leaders: The Strategies for Taking Charge*. New York: Harper & Row.

Bernard, J.M. (1979) Supervisory training: a discrimination model, *Counselor Education and Supervision*, 19: 60–8.

Bernard, J.M. (1994a) Multicultural supervision: a reaction to Leong and Wagner, Cook, Priest and Fukuyama, *Counselor Education and Supervision*, 34: 159–71.

Bernard, J.M. (1994b) Ethical and legal dimensions of supervision, in L.D. Borders (ed.) *Supervision: Exploring the Effective Components*. Greensboro, NC: University of North Carolina.

Bernard, J.M. and Goodyear, R. (1992) *Fundamentals of Clinical Supervision*. Boston, MA: Allyn & Bacon.

Berne, E. (1970) *The Games People Play: The Psychology of Human Relationships*. Harmondsworth: Penguin.

Berne, E. (1975) *What Do You Say After You Say Hello?* London: Corgi/Transworld.

Bettelheim, B. (1991) *The Uses of Enchantment*. London: Penguin.

Binney, G., Wilke, G. and Williams, G. (2005) *Living Leadership: A Practical Guide for Ordinary Heroes*. London: Prentice Hall.

Bion, W.R. (1961) *Experiences in Groups*. London: Tavistock.

Bion, W.R. (1973) *Brazilian Lectures 1*. Rio de Janeiro: Imago Editora.

Birkinshaw, J. and Piramal, G. (eds) (2005) *Sumantra Ghoshal on Management: A Force for Good*. London: Prentice Hall.

Blake, R., Avis, W. and Mouton, J. (1966) *Corporate Darwinism*. Houston, TX: Gulf Publishing.

Bluckert, P. (2004) Improving professional practice – the role of supervision in coaching, www.pbcoaching.com.

Bohm, D. (1980) *Wholeness and the Implicate Order*. London: Routledge & Kegan Paul.

Bohm, D. (1987) *Unfolding Meaning*. London: Routledge & Kegan Paul.

Bohm, D. (1989) Meaning and information, in P. Pylkkanen (ed.) *The Search for Meaning*. Northamptonshire: Crucible/Thorsons.

Bohm, D. (1994) *Thought as System*. London: Routledge.

Bolton, C., Howlett, S., Lago, C. and Wright, J.K. (2004) *Writing Cures: An Introductory Handbook of Writing in Counselling and Psychotherapy*. Hove: Brunner-Routledge.

Bolton, G. (2001) *Reflective Practice: Writing and Professional Development*. London: Paul Chapman.

Bond, T. (1993) *Standards and Ethics for Counselling*. London: Sage.

Borders, L.D. (1994) *Supervision: Exploring the Effective Components*. Greensboro, NC: University of North Carolina.

Borders, L.D. and Leddick, G.R. (1987) *Handbook of Counseling Supervision*. Alexandria, VA: Association for Counselor Education and Supervision.

Boyatzis, R., Howard, A., Kapisara, B. and Taylor, S. (2004) Target practice, *People Management*, March: 26–32.

Boyd, J. (1978) *Counselor Supervision: Approaches, Preparation, Practices*. Muncie, IN: Accelerated Development.

Bramley, W. (1996) *The Supervisory Couple in Broad-Spectrum Psychotherapy*. London: Free Association Books.

Bridger, H. (1990) Courses and working conferences as transitional learning institutions, in F. Trist and H. Murray (eds) *The Social Engagement of Social Science, Vol.1: The Socio-Psychological Perspective*. London: Free Associations Books.

Brinkmann, U. and van Weerdenburg, O. (1999) The intercultural development inventory: a new tool for improving intercultural training? Paper presented at the Sietar Europe Conference, Trieste, Italy.

British Association for Counselling (1990) *Information Sheet No. 8: Supervision*. Rugby: BAC.

British Association for Counselling (1995) *Code of Ethics and Practice for Supervisors of Counsellors*. Rugby: BAC.

Brockbank, A. and McGill, I. (2006) *Facilitating Reflective Learning Through Mentoring & Coaching*. London: Kogan Page.

Broussine, M. (1998) *The Society of Local Authority Chief Executives and Senior Managers (SOLACE): A Scheme for Continuous Learning for SOLACE Members*. Bristol: University of the West of England.

Brown, A. (1984) *Consultation: An Aid to Effective Social Work*. London: Heinemann.

Brown, A. and Bourne, I. (1996) *The Social Work Supervisor*. Buckingham: Open University Press.

Bruch, B. and Ghoshal, S. (2002) Beware the busy manager, *Harvard Business Review*, 80(2): 62–9.

Bruner, J. (1990) *Acts of Meaning*. London: Harvard University Press.

Burke, W. (2002) *Organization Change: Theory and Practice*. London: Sage.

Burke, W.R., Goodyear, R.K. and Guzzard, C.R. (1998) Weakenings and repairs in supervisory alliances: multiple case study. *American Journal of Psychotherapy*, 52(4): 450–62.

Butler-Sloss, E. (1988) *Report of the Inquiry in Child Abuse in Cleveland 1987*. London: HMSO.

Butterworth, C. A. and Faugier, J. (eds) (1992) *Clinical Supervision and Mentorship in Nursing*. London: Chapman & Hall.

Buzan, T. (1995) *Use Your Head*. London: BBC Books.

Campbell, B. (1988) *Unofficial Secrets: Child Sexual Abuse. The Cleveland Case*. London: Virago.

Canfield, J., Hansen, M.V. and Hewitt, L. (2000) *The Power of Focus*. Deerfield Beach, Fl: Health Communications.

Capewell, E. (1996) Staff care, in B.T. Lindsay (ed.) *Working with Children in Grief and Loss*. London: Bailliere Tindall.

Capewell, E. (1997) *Handouts of Working with Trauma*. Newbury: Centre for Crisis Management and Education.

Caplan, G. (1970) *The Theory and Practice of Mental Health Consultation*. London: Tavistock.

Caplan, J. (2003) *Coaching for the Future: How Smart Companies Use Coaching and Mentoring*. London: CIPD.

Carifio, M. S. and Hess, A.K. (1987) Who is the ideal supervisor? *Profession Psychology: Research and Practice*, 18: 244–50.

Carroll, M. (1987) Privately circulated papers, Roehampton Institute, University of Surrey.

Carroll, M. (1994) Counselling supervision: international perspectives, in L.D. Borders (ed.) *Supervision: Exploring the Effective Components*. Greensboro, NC: University of North Carolina.

Carroll, M. (1995) The stresses of supervising counsellors, in W. Dryden (ed.) *The Stresses of Counselling in Action*. London: Sage.

Carroll, M. (1996) *Counselling Supervision: Theory, Skills and Practice*. London: Cassell.

Carroll, M. and Holloway, E. (1999a) *Counselling Supervision in Context*. London: Sage.

Carroll, M. and Holloway, E. (1999b) *Training Counselling Supervisors*. London: Sage.

Carroll, M. and Tholstrup, M. (eds) (2001) *Integrative Approaches to Supervision*. London: Jessica Kingsley.

Casement, P. (1985) *On Learning from the Patient*. London: Routledge.

Casey, D. (1985) When is a team not a team? *Personnel Management*, 9.

Casey, D. (1993) *Managing Learning in Organisations*. Buckingham: Open University Press.

Centre for Staff Team Development (1999) *Supervision Workbook*. Bath: Bath Consultancy Group.

Chen, E.C. and Bernstein, B.L. (2000) Relations of complementarity and supervisory issues to supervisory working alliance: a comparative analysis of two cases, *Journal of Counseling Psychology*, 47(4): 485–97.

Cherniss, C. (1980) *Staff Burnout: Job Stress in the Human Services*. Beverly Hills, CA: Sage.

Cherniss, C. and Egnatios, E. (1978) Clinical supervision in community mental health, *Social Work*, 23(2): 219–23.

CIPD (2004) *Reorganising for Success – A Survey of HR's Role in Change*. London: CIPD.

Clarkson, P. (1995) *Change in Organisations*. London: Whurr.

Claxton, G. (1984) *Live and Learn: An Introduction to the Psychology of Growth and Change in Everyday Life*. London: Harper & Row.

Clutterbuck, D. (1998) *Learning Alliances*. London: CIPD.

Clutterbuck, D. (2003) *The Making of a Mentor*. London: Gower.

Clutterbuck, D. (2004) *Everyone Needs a Mentor: Fostering Talent in your Organisation*. London: CIPD.

Clutterbuck, D. and Gover, S. (2004) *The Effective Coach Manual*. Burnham: Clutterbuck Associates.

Clutterbuck, D. and Hirst, S. (2002) *Talking Business*. Oxford: Butterworth-Heinemann.

Clutterbuck, D. and Megginson, D. (1997) *Mentoring in Action: A Practical Guide for Managers*. London: Kogan Page.

Clutterbuck, D. and Megginson, D. (1999) *Mentoring Executives and Directors*. Oxford: Butterworth-Heinemann.

Clutterbuck, D. and Megginson, D. (2004) All good things must come to an end: winding up and winding down a mentoring relationship, in D. Clutterbuck and G. Lane (eds) *The Situational Mentor*. Aldershot: Gower.

Clutterbuck, D. and Megginson, D. (2005) *Making Coaching Work: Creating a Coaching Culture*. London: CIPD.

Clutterbuck, D. and Ragins, B.R. (2002) *Mentoring and Diversity*. Oxford: Butterworth.

Clutterbuck, D. and Sweeney, J. (1998) Coaching and mentoring, in *Gower Handbook of Management*. Hampshire: Gower.

Clynes, M. (1977). *Sentics: The Touch of the Emotions*. Dorset: Prism Unity.

Coche, E. (1977) Training of group therapists, in F.W. Kaslow (ed.) *Supervision, Consultation and Staff Training in the Helping Professions*. San Francisco: Jossey-Bass.

Colley, H. (2003) *Mentoring for Social Inclusion: A Critical Approach to Nurturing Mentor Relationships*. London: RoutledgeFalmer.

Conn, J.D. (1993) Delicate liaisons: the impact of gender differences on the supervisory relationship within social services, *Journal of Social Work Practice*, 7(1): 41–53.

Connor, M. and Clawson, J. (eds) (2004) *Creating a Learning Culture: Strategy, Technology and Practice*. Boston, MA: Cambridge University Press.

Cook, D.A. (1994) Racial identity in supervision, *Counselor Education and Supervision*, 34, 132–41.

Cook, D. A. and Helms, J.E. (1988) Visible racial/ethnic group supervisees' satisfaction with cross-cultural supervision as predicted by relationship characteristics, *Journal of Counseling Psychology*, 35(3): 268–74.

Coulson-Thomas, C. (1993) *Creating Excellence in the Boardroom*. Maidenhead: McGraw-Hill.

Covey, S. (1989) *The Seven Habits of Highly Effective People*. London: Simon & Schuster.

Covey, S.R. (1990) *Principle-Centred Leadership*. New York: Simon & Schuster.

Covey, S.R. (2004) *The 8th Habit: From Effectiveness to Greatness*. London: Simon & Schuster.

Cranwell-Ward, J., Bossons, P. and Gover, S. (2004) *Mentoring: A Henley Review of Best Practice*. Basingstoke: Palgrave Macmillan.

Csikszentmihalyi, M. (1992) *Flow: The Psychology of Happiness*. London: Rider.

CSTD (1999) Anti-discrimination and oppression in supervision, www.cstd.co.uk.

Daniels, J.A. and Larson, L.M. (2001) The impact of performance feedback on counseling self-efficacy and counselor anxiety, *Counselor Education and Supervision*, 41(2): 120–31.

Darwin, J., Johnson, P. and McAuley, J. (2002) *Developing Strategies for Change*. Harlow: Prentice Hall.

Dass, R. and Gorman, P. (1985) *How Can I Help?* London: Rider.

De Bono, B. (1990) *Six Thinking Hats*. Harmondsworth: Penguin.

De Mello, A. (1985) *One Minute Wisdom*. Anand, India: Gujarat Sahitya Prakash.

Dearnley, B. (1985) A plain man's guide to supervision, *Journal of Social Work Practice*, 2(1): 52–65.

Disney, M. J. and Stephens, A.M. (1994) *Legal Issues in Clinical Supervision*. Alexandria, VA: American Counseling Association.

Doehrman, M. J. (1976) Parallel processes in supervision and psychotherapy, *Bulletin of the Menninger Clinic*, 40(1).

Donkin, R. (2004) *HR and Reorganisation – Managing the Challenge of Change*. London: CIPD.

Donnison, P. A. (2000) Images of outdoor management development. A synthesis of the literature and participants' experiences on outdoor courses. Unpublished dissertation, Lancaster University.

Downey, M. (2003) *Effective Coaching: Lessons from the Coaches' Couch*. New York: Texere/Thomson.

Doyle, B. and O'Neill, N.V. (2001) *Mentoring Entrepreneurs: Shared Wisdom from Experience*. Cork: Oak Tree Press.

Dryden, W. and Norcross, J.C. (1990) *Eclecticism and Integration in Counselling and Psychotherapy*. London: Gale Centre Publications.

Dryden, W. and Thorne, B. (eds) (1991) *Training and Supervision for Counselling in Action*. London: Sage.

Dyke, G. (2004) *Greg Dyke: Inside Story*. London: HarperCollins.

Eckstein, R. (1969) Concerning the teaching and learning of psychoanalysis, *Journal of the American Psychoanalytic Association*, 17(2): 312–32.

Eckstein, R. and Wallerstein, R.W. (1972) *The Teaching and Learning of Psychotherapy*. New York: International Universities Press.

Edelwich, J. and Brodsky, A. (1980) *Burn-Out*. New York: Human Sciences.

Eleftheriadou, Z. (1994) *Transcultural Counselling*. London: Central Book Publishing.

Ellis, M. V. and Dell, D.M. (1986) Dimensionality of supervisor roles: supervisors' perceptions of supervision, *Journal of Counseling Psychology*, 33(3): 282–91.

English, P. (2004) *Succeeding at Interviews Pocketbook*. Alresford: Management Pocketbooks.

Erikson, E. (1950) *Childhood and Society*. New York: Norton.

Ernst, S. and Goddison, L. (1981) *In Our Own Hands: A Book of Self-Help Therapy*. London: The Women's Press.

Farrelly, F. and Brandsma, J. (1974) *Provocative Therapy*. Cupertino, CA: Meta Publications.

Feltham, C. and Dryden, W. (1994) *Developing Counsellor Supervision*. London: Sage.

Fineman, S. (1985) *Social Work Stress and Intervention*. Aldershot: Gower.

Fink, S.L., Beak, J. and Taddeo, K. (1971) Organizational crisis and change, *Journal of Applied Behavioral Science*, 17(1): 15–37.

Fisher, D. and Torbert, W.R. (1995) *Personal and Organizational Transformations*. Maidenhead: McGraw-Hill.

Flaherty, J. (1999) *Coaching: Evoking Excellence in Others*. Woburn, MA: Butterworth-Heinemann.

Fleming, I. and Steen, L. (eds) (2004) *Supervision and Clinical Psychology: Theory, Practice and Perspectives*. Hove: Brunner-Routledge.

Fordham, F. (1991) *An Introduction to Jung's Psychology*. Harmondsworth: Penguin.

Fox, M. (1995) *The Reinvention of Work*. San Francisco: Harper.

Frankham, H. (1987) Aspects of supervision. Unpublished Dissertation, University of Surrey.

Freeman, E. (1985) The importance of feedback in clinical supervision: implications for direct practice, *The Clinical Supervisor*, 3(1): 5–26.

Freitas, G.J. (2002) The impact of psychotherapy supervision on client outcome: a critical examination of two decades of research, *Psychotherapy*, 39(4): 354–67.

French, J.R.P. and Raven, B. (1959) The bases of social power, in D. Cartwright (ed.) *Studies in Social Power*. Ann Arbor, MI: Institute for Social Research.

Freud, S. (1927) *The Future of an Illusion*. London: Hogarth Press.

Friedlander, M.L. and Ward, L.G. (1984) Development and validation of the supervisory styles inventory, *Journal of Counseling Psychology*, 31(4): 541–57.

Friedlander, M.L., Siegel, S. and Brenock, K. (1989) Parallel processes in counseling and supervision: a case study, *Journal of Counseling Psychology*, 36: 149–57.

Fukuyama, M.A. (1994) Critical incidents in multicultural counseling supervision: a phenomenological approach to supervision research, *Counselor Education and Supervision*, 34(2): 142–51.

Galassi, J. P. and Trent, P.J. (1987) A conceptual framework for evaluating supervision effectiveness, *Counselor Education and Supervision*, June: 260–9.

Gardner, H. (1999) *Intelligence Reframed: Multiple Intelligences for the 21st Century*. New York: Basic Books.

Gardner, L. H. (1980) Racial, ethnic and social class considerations in psychotherapy supervision, in A.K. Hess (ed.) *Psychotherapy Supervision: Theory, Research and Practice.* New York: Wiley.

Garratt, B. (1987) *The Learning Organisation.* London: Fontana/Collins.

Garratt, B. (1996) *The Fish Rots from the Head: The Crisis in our Boardrooms.* London: HarperCollins Business.

Garratt, B. (2003) *Thin on Top.* London: Nicholas Brealey.

Garvey, B. (1994) A Dose of mentoring. Paper presented at the 1st European Mentoring Conference, Sheffield.

Gaunt, R. and Kendal, R. (1985) *Action Learning: A Short Manual for Set Members.* London: Greater London Employer's Secretariat.

Geertz, C. (1973) *The Interpretation of Cultures.* New York: Basic Books.

Gendlin, E.T. (1981) *Focusing,* 2nd edn. New York: Everest House.

Gerstner, L. (2002) *Who Says Elephants Can't Dance? How I Turned Around IBM.* London: HarperCollins.

Ghoshal, S. and Moran, P. (2005) Towards a good theory of management, in J. Birkinshaw and G. Paramal (eds) *Sumantra Ghosal on Management: A Force for Good.* London: Prentice Hall.

Gilbert, M. and Evans, K. (2000) *Psychotherapy Supervision – An Integrative Relational Approach.* Maidenhead: Open University Press.

Gitterman, A. and Miller, I. (1977) Supervisors as educators, in F.W. Kaslow (ed.) *Supervision, Consultation and Staff Training in the Helping Professions.* San Francisco: Jossey-Bass.

Goleman, D. (1996) *Emotional Intelligence.* London: Bloomsbury.

Golembiewski, R.T. (1976) *Learning and Change in Groups.* London: Penguin.

Grant, A. (2000) Paper presented at the University of Sydney.

Grayling, A.C. (2004) *What is Good?* London: Orion.

Greene, J. and Grant, A. (2003) *Solution-focused Coaching: Managing People in a Complex World.* London: Momentum.

Gregerson, H., Morrison, A. and Black, J. (1998) Developing leaders for the global frontier, *Sloan Management Review,* 40(1): 21–33.

Grudin, R. (1996) *On Dialogue: An Essay in Free Thought.* Boston, MA: Houghton Mifflin.

Guggenbuhl-Craig, A. (1971) *Power in the Helping Professions,* Dallas, TX: Spring.

Hale, K.K. and Stoltenberg, C.D. (1988) The effects of self-awareness and evaluation apprehension on counselor trainee anxiety, *The Clinical Supervisor,* 6: 46–69.

Hall, D., Otazo, K. and Hollenbeck, G. (1999) Behind closed doors: what really happens in executive coaching, *Organizational Dynamics,* 27(3): 39–53.

Hall, L. M. and Duval, M. (2004) *Meta-Coaching: Volume 1: Coaching Change for Higher Levels of Success and Transformation.* Clifton, CO: Neuro-Semantics Publications.

Hamel, G. and Prahalad, C.K. (1996) *Competing for the Future.* Boston, MA: Harvard Business School Press.

Hammer, M. R. (1998) A measure of intercultural sensitivity: the intercultural development inventory, in S.M. Fowler and M.G. Mumford (eds) *The*

Intercultural Sourcebook: Cross-cultural Training Methods, vol. 2. Yarmouth, ME: The Intercultural Press.

Handy, C. (1976) *Understanding Organizations*. London: Penguin.

Hardingham, A. with Brearley, M., Moorhouse, A. and Venter, B. (2004) *The Coach's Coach: Personal Development for Personal Developers*. London: CIPD.

Harrison, R. (1995) *The Collected Papers of Roger Harrison*. London: McGraw-Hill.

Hawkins, P. (1979) Staff learning in therapeutic communities, in R. Hinshelwood and N. Manning (eds) *Therapeutic Communities, Reflections and Progress*. London: Routledge & Kegan Paul.

Hawkins, P. (1980) Between Scylla and Charybdis, in E. Jansen (ed.) *The Therapeutic Community Outside of the Hospital*. London: Croom Helm.

Hawkins, P. (1982) Mapping it out, *Community Care*, July: 17–19.

Hawkins, P. (1985) Humanistic psychotherapy supervision: a conceptual framework, *Self and Society: Journal of Humanistic Psychology*, 13(2): 69–79.

Hawkins, P. (1986) *Living the Learning*. Bath: University of Bath.

Hawkins, P. (1988a) A phenomenological psychodrama workshop, in P. Reason (ed.) *Human Inquiry in Action*. London: Sage.

Hawkins, P. (1988b) The social learning approach to day and residential centres, in A. Brown and R. Clough (eds) *Groups and Groupings: Life and Work in Day and Residential Settings*. London: Tavistock.

Hawkins, P. (1991) The spiritual dimension of the learning organisation, *Management Education and Development*, 22(3).

Hawkins, P. (1993) *Shadow Consultancy*. Bath: Bath Consultancy Group.

Hawkins, P. (1994a) The changing view of learning, in J. Burgoyne (ed.) *Towards the Learning Company*. London: McGraw-Hill.

Hawkins, P. (1994b) *Organizational Culture Manual*. Bath: Bath Consultancy Group.

Hawkins, P. (1994c) *Organizational Evolution and Revolution*. Bath: Bath Consultancy Group.

Hawkins, P. (1994d) Taking stock, facing the challenge, *Management Learning Journal*, 25(1).

Hawkins, P. (1995) Supervision, in M. Jacobs (ed.) *The Care Guide*. London: Mowbrays.

Hawkins, P. (1997) Organizational culture: sailing between evangelism and complexity, *Human Relations*, 50(4).

Hawkins, P. (1998) The Hawkins model of career stages. Presentation to PricewaterhouseCoopers conference, Bath.

Hawkins, P. (1999) Organizational unlearning. Learning Company conference, University of Warwick.

Hawkins, P. (2005) *The Wise Fool's Guide to Leadership*. Winchester: O Books.

Hawkins, P. (2006) in J. Passmore (ed.) *Excellence in Coaching*. London: Kogan Page

Hawkins, P. and Chesterman, D. (2004) *Developing Leadership Capacity in Local Government: The Contribution of SOLACE and its Scheme for Continuous Learning*. London: Solace.

Hawkins, P. & Chesterman, D. (2006) *Every Teaching Matters*. London: Teachers' Support Network

Hawkins, P. and Maclean, A. (1991) *Action Learning Guidebook*. Bath: Bath Consultancy Group.

Hawkins, P. and Miller, E. (1994) Psychotherapy in and with organizations, in M. Pokorny and P. Clarkson (eds) *Handbook of Psychotherapy*. London: Routledge & Kegan Paul.

Hawkins, P. and Schwenk, G. (2006) *Coaching Supervision*. London: C.I.P.D. Change Agenda.

Hawkins, P. and Shohet, R. (1989) *Supervision in the Helping Professions*. Buckingham: Open University Press.

Hawkins, P. and Shohet, R. (1991) Approaches to the supervision of counsellors, in W. Dryden (ed.) *Training and Supervision for Counselling in Action*. London: Sage.

Hawkins, P. and Shohet, R. (1993) A review of the addictive organisation by Schaef and Fassel, *Management Education and Development*, 24(2): 293–6.

Hawkins, P. and Shohet, R. (2006) *Supervision in the Helping Professions* 3rd edn. Maidenhead: Open University Press.

Hawthorne, L. (1975) Games supervisors play, *Social Work*, May: 179–83.

Hedberg, B. (1981) How organizations learn and unlearn, in P. Nystrom and W. Starbuck (eds) *Handbook of Organizationals design, Vol 1: Adapting Organizations to their Environments*. Oxford: Oxford University Press.

Helminski, K. (1999) *The Knowing Heart*. Boston, MA: Shambhala.

Herman, N. (1987) *Why Psychotherapy?* London: Free Association Books.

Heron, J. (1974) Reciprocal counselling. Unpublished Human Potential Research Project, University of Surrey.

Heron, J. (1975) *Six-Category Intervention Analysis*. Guildford: University of Surrey.

Herskowitz, M.J. (1948) *Man and His Works*. New York: Knopf.

Hess, A.K. (1980) *Psychotherapy Supervision: Theory, Research and Practice*. New York: Wiley.

Hess, A.K. (1987) Psychotherapy supervision: stages, Buber and a theory of relationship, *Professional Psychology: Research and Practice*, 18(3): 251–9.

Hickman, C. R. and Silva, M.A. (1985) *Creating Excellence*. London: Allen & Unwin.

Hillman, J. (1979) *Insearch: Psychology and Religion*. Dallas, TX: Spring.

Hinshelwood, R. and Manning, N. (1979) *Therapeutic Communities: Reflections and Progress*. London: Routledge & Kegan Paul.

Hirsh, S. A. and Kise, J.A.G. (2000) *Introduction to Type and Coaching*. Palo Alto, CA: Consulting Psychologists Press.

Hofstede, G. (1980) *Culture's Consequences: International Differences in Work-related Values*. Beverly Hills, CA: Sage.

Hogan, R.A. (1964) Issues and approaches in supervision, *Psychotherapy: Theory, Research and Practice*, 1: 139–41.

Holbeche, L. (2005) *The High Performance Organization*. Oxford: Elsevier Butterworth-Heinemann.

Holloway, E.L. (1984) Outcome evaluation in supervision research, *The Counseling Psychologist*, 12(4): 167–74.

Holloway, E.L. (1987) Developmental models of supervision: is it development? *Professional Psychology: Research and Practice*, 18(3): 209–16.

Holloway, E.L. (1995) *Clinical Supervision: A Systems Approach*. London: Sage.

Holloway, E.L. and Carroll, M. (eds) (1999) *Training Counselling Supervisors*. London: Sage.

Holloway, E.L. and Gonzalez-Doupe, P. (2002) The learning alliance of supervision research to practice, in G.S. Tyron (ed.) *Counseling Based on Process Research: Applying What We Know*. Boston, MA: Allyn & Bacon.

Holloway, E.L. and Johnston, R. (1985) Group supervision: widely practised but poorly understood, *Counselor Education and Supervision*, (24): 332–40.

Holloway, E.L. and Neufeldt, S.A. (1995) Supervision: its contributions to treatment efficacy, *Journal of Consulting and Clinical Psychology*, 63(2): 207–13.

Honey, P. and Mumford, A. (1992) *The Manual of Learning Styles*. London: Peter Honey Publications.

Houston, G. (1985) Group supervision of groupwork, *Self and Society: European Journal of Humanistic Psychology*, XIII(2): 64–6.

Houston, G. (1990) *Supervision and Counselling*. London: Rochester Foundation.

Hunt, J.M. and Weintraub, J.R. (2002) *The Coaching Manager: Developing Top Talent in Business*. Thousand Oaks, CA: Sage.

Hunt, P. (1966) Supervision, *Marriage Guidance*, spring: 15–22.

Illich, I. (1973) *Deschooling Society*. London: Penguin.

Inskipp, F. and Proctor, B. (1993) *The Art, Craft & Tasks of Counselling Supervision: Pt 1: Making the Most of Supervision*. Twickenham: Cascade Publications.

Inskipp, F. and Proctor, B. (1995) *The Art, Craft & Tasks of Counselling Supervision: Pt 2: Becoming a Supervisor*. Twickenham: Cascade Publications.

Jarvis, J. (2004) *Coaching and Buying Coaching Services*. London: CIPD.

Jones, M. (1982) *The Process of Change*. London: Routledge & Kegan Paul.

Jourard, S. (1971) *The Transparent Self*. New York: Van Nostrand.

Joy-Matthews, J., Megginson, D. and Surtees, M. (2004) *Human Resource Development*. London: Kogan Page.

Juch, B. (1983) *Personal Development*. Chichester: Wiley.

Kaberry, S.E. (1995) *Abuse in Supervision*. Birmingham: University of Birmingham.

Kadushin, A. (1968) Games people play in supervision, *Social Work*, 13.

Kadushin, A. (1976) *Supervision in Social Work*. New York: Columbia University Press.

Kadushin, A. (1977) *Consultation in Social Work*. New York: Columbia University Press.

Kagan, N. (1980) Influencing human interaction – eighteen years with IPR, in A.K. Hess (ed.) *Psychotherapy Supervision: Theory, Research and Practice*. New York: Wiley.

Kareem, J. and Littlewood, R. (1992) *Intercultural Therapy: Themes, Interpretations and Practice*. Oxford: Blackwell Science.

Karpman, S. (1968) Fairy tales and script drama analysis (selected articles), *Transactional Analysis Bulletin*, 7(26): 39–43.

Kaslow, F.W. (ed.) (1977) *Supervision, Consultation and Staff Training in the Helping Professions*. San Francisco: Jossey-Bass.

Katzenbach, J. and Smith, D. (1993) The discipline of teams, *Harvard Business Review*, March/April: 111–20.

Kaye, B. and Jordan-Evans, S. (1999) *Love 'Em or Lose 'Em: Getting Good People to Stay*. San Francisco: Berrett-Koehler Publishers.

Kelly, G.A. (1955) *The Psychology of Personal Constructs*, vols 1 & 2. New York: Norton.

Kevlin, F. (1987) Interview with Robin Shohet.

Kevlin, F. (1988) *Peervision. A Comparison of Hierarchial Supervision of Counsellors with Consultation amongst Peers*. London: University of Surrey.

Khan, H.I. (1972) *The Sufi Message*, vol. IV. London: Barrie Books.

Khan, M.A. (1991) Counselling psychology in a multicultural society, *Counselling Psychology Review*, 6(3): 11–13.

Kirkpatrick, D.L. (1967) Evaluation of training, in R.L. Craig and L.R. Bittel (eds) *Training and Development Handbook*. New York: McGraw-Hill.

Kluckhohn, F.R. and Strodtbeck, F.L. (1961) *Variations in Value Orientations*. New York: Row, Peterson & Co.

Kohlberg, L. (1981) *Philosophy of Moral Development: Moral Stages and the Idea of Justice*. New York: Harper & Row.

Kolb, D.A. (1984) *Experiential Learning*. Englewood Cliffs, NJ: Prentice Hall.

Kolb, D.A., Rubin, I.M. and McIntyre, J.M. (1971) *Organizational Psychology: an Experimental Approach*. New York: Prentice Hall.

Krause, I. (1998) *Therapy Across Culture*: Sage.

Krishnamurti, J. (1954) *The First and Last Freedom*. Bramdean: KFT Ltd.

Kubler-Ross, E. (1991) *On Death and Dying*. London: Macmillan.

Ladany, N. (2004) Psychotherapy supervision: what lies beneath, *Psychotherapy Research*, 14(1): 1–19.

Ladany, N., Ellis, M.V. and Friedlander, M.L. (1999) The supervisory working alliance, trainee self-efficacy and satisfaction, *Journal of Counseling and Development*, 77: 447–55.

Lago, C. and Thompson, J. (1996) *Race, Culture and Counselling*. Buckingham: Open University Press.

Lambert, M.J. and Arnold, R.C. (1987) Research and the supervisory process, *Profession Psychology: Research and Practice*, 18(3): 217–24.

Landsberg, M. (1996) *The Tao of Coaching*. London: HarperCollins.

Langs, R. (1978) *The Listening Process*. New York: Jason Aronson.

Langs, R. (1983) *The Supervisory Experience*. New York: Jason Aronson.

Langs, R. (1985) *Workbook for Psychotherapists*. Emerson, NJ: Newconcept Press.

Langs, R. (1994) *Doing Supervision and Being Supervised*. London: Karnac Books.

Lave, J. and Wenger, E. (1991) *Situated Learning: Legitimate Peripheral Participation*. Cambridge: Cambridge University Press.

Leddick, R. and Dye, H.A. (1987) Effective supervision as portrayed by trainee expectations and preferences, *Counselor Education and Supervision*, 27: 139–54.

Lee, G. (2003) *Leadership Coaching: From Personal Insight to Organisational Performance*. London: CIPD.

Leong, F. T. L. and Wagner, N.S. (1994) Cross-cultural counseling supervision: what do we know? What do we need to know? *Counselor Education and Supervision*, 34: 117–31.

Levinson, D.J., Darrow, C.N., Klein, E.B., Levinson, M.H. and McKee, B. (1978) *The Seasons of a Man's Life*. New York: Knopf.

Lewin, K. (1952) Defining the field at a given time, in D. Cartwright (ed.) *Field Theory in Social Sciences*. London: Tavistock.

Liddle, B.J. (1986) Resistance to supervision: a response to perceived threat, *Counselor Education and Supervision*, December: 117–27.

Lievegoed, B.C.J. (1973) *The Developing Organisations*. London: Tavistock.

Lincoln, S. (2006) In the blend, *Coaching at Work*, March/April.

Lindsay, G. and Clarkson, P. (1999) Ethical dilemmas of psychotherapists, *The Psychologist*, 12(4): 182–5.

Lipnack, J. and Stamps, J. (1996) *Virtual Teams: People Working Across Boundaries with Technology*. New York: Wiley.

Liss, J. (1985) Using mime and re-enactment to supervise body orientated therapy, *Self and Society: Journal of Humanistic Psychology*, XIII(2): 82–5.

Local Government Management Board/Institute of Local Government Studies (1991) *Quality and Equality: Service to the Whole Community*. Birmingham: University of Birmingham.

Loevinger, J. and Blasi, A. (1976) *Ego Development*. San Francisco: Jossey-Bass.

Loganbill, C., Hardy, E. and Delworth, U. (1982) Supervision, a conceptual model, *The Counseling Psychologist*, 10(1): 3–42.

Loizos, P. (2002) Misconceiving refugees, in R.K. Papadopoulos (ed.) *Therapeutic Care for Refugees: No Place Like Home*. London: Karnac.

Madden, C. and Mitchell, V. (1993) *Professional Standards and Competence – A Survey of Continuing Education for the Professions*. Bristol: University of Bristol.

Marken, M. and Payne, M. (eds) (nd) *Enabling and Ensuring: Supervision in Practice*. Leicester: National Youth Bureau and Council for Education and Training in Youth and Community Work.

Marshall, J. (1982) Job stressors: recent research in a variety of occupations. Paper presented at the 20th International Congress of Applied Psychology, Edinburgh.

Martin, I. (1996) *From Couch to Corporation: Becoming a Successful Corporate Therapist*. New York: Wiley.

Martin, I. (2001) *The President's Psychoanalyst*. New York: Painted Leaf Press.

Martin, J.S., Goodyear, R.K. and Newton, F.B. (1987) Clinical supervision: an intensive case study, *Professional Psychology: Research and Practice*, 18(3): 225–35.

Martindale, B., Morner, M., Rodriquez, M.E.C. and Vidit, J. (1997) *Supervision and its Vicissitudes*. London: Karnac.

Maslach, C. (1982) Understanding burnout: definitional issues in analysing a complex phenomenon, in W.S. Paine (ed.) *Job Stress and Burnout*. Beverley Hills, CA: Sage.

Maslow, A. (1954) *Motivation and Personality*. New York: Harper & Row.

Matthews, S. and Treacher, A. (2004) Therapy models and supervision in clinical psychology, in I. Fleming and L. Steen (eds) *Supervision and Clinical Psychology: Theory, Practice and Perspectives.* Hove: Brunner-Routledge.

Mattinson, J. (1975) *The Reflection Process in Casework Supervision.* London: Institute of Marital Studies.

McAdams, D.P. (1993) *The Stories We Live By.* New York: Guildford Press.

McBride, M. C. and Martin, G.E. (1986) Dual-focus supervision: a non-apprenticeship approach, *Counselor Education and Supervision,* 25(3): 175–82.

McDermott, I. and Jago, W. (2001) *The NLP Coach.* London: Piatkus.

McLean, A. (1986) *Access Organization Cultures.* Bath: University of Bath.

McLean, A. and Marshall, J. (1988) *Working with Cultures: A Workbook for People in Local Government.* Luton: Local Government Training Board.

McLeod, A. (2003) *Performance Coaching: The Handbook for Managers, HR Professionals and Coaches.* Bancyfelin, Carmarthen: Crown House.

Mearns, D. (1991) On being a supervisor, in W. Dryden and B. Thorne (eds) *Training and Supervision for Counselling in Action.* London: Sage.

Megginson, D. (1999) Creating intellectual properties: a sensemaking study. Unpublished doctorate, Lancaster University Management School.

Megginson, D. (2000a) Chamber music and coaching managers, *Industrial and Commercial Training,* 32(6): 219–24.

Megginson, D. (2000b) Current issues in mentoring, *Career Development International,* 5(4–5), 256–60.

Megginson, D. and Clutterbuck, D. (1995) *Mentoring in Action.* London: Kogan Page.

Megginson, D. and Clutterbuck, D. (2005) *Techniques for Coaching and Mentoring.* Oxford: Elsevier Butterworth-Heinemann.

Megginson, D. and Whitaker, V. (2003) *Continuous Professional Development.* London: CIPD.

Menzies, I.E.P. (1970) *The Functioning of Social Systems as a Defence Against Anxiety.* London: Tavistock Institute of Human Relations.

Mezirow, J. (1991) *Transformative Dimensions of Adult Learning.* Oxford: Jossey-Bass.

Miller, E. (1993) *From Dependency to Autonomy: Studies in Organization and Change.* London: Free Association Press.

Mintz, E. (1983) Gestalt approaches to supervision, *Gestalt Journal,* 6(1): 17–27.

Modood, T., Berthoud, R. *et al.* (1997) *Ethnic Minorities in Britain; Diversity and Disadvantage.* London: Policy Studies Institute.

Morgan, G. (1986) *Images of Organization.* London: Sage.

Morgan, G. (1993) *Imaginization.* Newbury Park, CA: Sage.

Morrison, T. (1993) *Staff Supervision in Social Care: An Action Learning Approach.* London: Longman.

Munson, C. E. (1987) Sex roles and power relationships in supervision, *Profession Psychology: Research and Practice,* 18(3): 236–43.

Murray, W. H. (2002) *The Evidence of Things not Seen: A Mountaineer's Tale.* London: Baton Wicks.

Nelson, M.L. and Holloway, E.L. (1990) Relation of gender to power and involvement in supervision, *Journal of Counseling Psychology,* 37: 473–81.

Nixon, B. (2000) *Global Forces: A Guide for Enlightened Leaders*. Chalford: Management Books.

O'Neill, M.B. (2000) *Executive Coaching with Backbone and Heart: A Systems Approach to Engaging Leaders with their Challenges*. San Francisco: Jossey-Bass.

Okri, B. (1997) *An African Elegy*. London: Vintage.

Orlans, V. and Edwards, D. (2001) A collaborative model of supervision, in M. Carroll and M. Tholstrup (eds) *Integrative Approaches to Supervision*. London: Jessica Kingsley.

Owen, H. (1998) *Open Space Technology: A User's Guide*. San Francisco: Berrett-Koehler Publishers.

Owen, H. (2000) *The Power of Spirit: How Organizations Transform*. San Francisco: Berrett-Koehler Publishers.

Page, S. (1999) *The Shadow and the Counsellor*. London: Routledge.

Page, S. and Wosket, V. (1994) *Supervising the Counsellor: A Cyclical Model*. London: Routledge.

Papadopoulos, R.K. (1997) *Multiple Voices: Narrative in Systemic Family Psychotherapy*. London: Duckworth.

Papadopoulos, R.K. (2002) Refugees, home and trauma, in R.K. Papadopoulos (ed.) *Therapeutic Care for Refugees: No Place Like Home*. London: Karnac.

Parker, M. (1990) *Supervision Constructs and Supervisory Style and Related to Theoretical Orientation*. Guildford: University of Surrey.

Parsloe, E. (1999) *The Manager as Coach and Mentor*. London: CIPD.

Patterson, K., Grenny, J., McMillan, R. and Switzler, A. (2002) *Crucial Conversations: Tools for Talking When Stakes are High*. New York: McGraw-Hill.

Patton, M. J. and Kivlighan, D.M. (1997) Relevance of the supervisory alliance to the counseling alliance and to treatment adherence in counselor training, *Journal of Counseling Psychology*, 44(1): 108–15.

Payne, C. and Scott, T. (1982) *Developing Supervision of Teams in Field and Residential Social Work* (no. 12). London: National Institute for Social Work.

Pederson, B.P. (1997) *Culture-Centred Counseling Interventions*. London: Sage.

Pederson, B.P. (ed.) (1985) *Handbook of Cross-Cultural Counseling and Therapy*. London: Praeger.

Pedler, M. (1996) *Action Learning for Managers*. London: Lemos & Crane.

Perls, F. (1971) *Gestalt Therapy Verbatim*. New York: Bantam.

Persaud, R. (2001) *Staying Sane: How to Make Your Mind Work for You*. London: Bantam.

Peters, T. (1987) *Thriving on Chaos*. New York: Knopf.

Peters, T.J. and Waterman, R.H. (1982) *In Search of Excellence*. New York: Harper & Row.

Peterson, F.K. (1991) *Race and Ethnicity*. New York: Haworth.

Pettigrew, A. and Massini, S. (2003) Innovative forms of organizing, in A. Pettigrew *et al.* (eds) *Innovative Forms of Organizing*. London: Sage Publications.

Pettigrew, A. *et al.* (eds) (2003) *Innovative Forms of Organizing: International Perspectives*. London: Sage.

Philipson, J. (1992) *Practising Equality: Women, Men and Social Work*. London: CCETSW.

Phillips, K. (nd) *Coaching in Organisations: Between the Lines*. Bath: Claremont.

Pines, A.M., Aronson, E. and Kafry, D. (1981) *Burnout: From Tedium to Growth*. New York: The Free Press.

Plant, R. (1987) *Managing Change and Making it Stick*. London: Fontana/Collins.

Ponterotto, J.G. and Zander, T.A. (1984) A multimodal approach to counselor supervision, *Counselor Education and Supervision*, 24: 40–50.

Pope, K.S. and Vasquez, M.J.T. (1991) *Ethics in Psychotherapy and Counseling: A Practical Guide for Psychologists*. San Francisco: Jossey-Bass.

Pritchard, J. (1995) *Good Practice in Supervision*. London: Jessica Kingsley.

Proctor, B. (1988a) *Supervision: A Working Alliance* (videotape training manual). St Leonards-on-sea: Alexia Publications.

Proctor, B. (1988b) Supervision: a co-operative exercise in accountability, in M. Marken and M. Payne (eds) *Enabling and Ensuring*. Leicester: National Youth Bureau and Council for Education and Training in Youth and Community Work.

Proctor, B. (1997) Contracting in supervision, in C. Sills (ed.) *Contracts in Counselling*. London: Sage.

Ramos-Sanchez, L., Esnil, E., Riggs, S., Goodwin, A., Touster, L.O., Wright, L.K., Ratanasiripong, P. and Rodolfa, E. (2002) Negative supervisory events: effects on supervision satisfaction and supervisory alliance, *Professional Psychology: Research and Practice*, 33(2): 197–202.

Rapkins, C. (1996) Best practice for continuing professional development: professional bodies facing the challenge, in I. Woodward (ed.) *Continuing Professional Development: Issues in Design and Delivery*. London: Cassell.

Reason, P. (1988) *Human Inquiry in Action*. London: Sage.

Reason, P. (1994) *Participation in Human Inquiry*. London: Sage.

Reason, P. and Bradbury, H. (2000) *Handbook of Action Research: Participative Inquiry and Practice*. London: Sage.

Reddin, W. (1985) *The Best of Bill Reddin*. London: Institute of Personnel Management.

Regen, F. (2005) *Faith Communities Toolkit*. London: Centre for Excellence in Leadership.

Revans, R. (1998) *The ABC of Action Learning*. London: Lemos & Crane.

Revans, R.W. (1982) *The Origins and Growth of Action Learning*. London: Chartwell-Bratt, Bromley & Lund.

Richards, M., Payne, C. and Sheppard, A. (1990) *Staff Supervision in Child Protection Work*. London: National Institute for Social Work.

Ridley, C. R. (1995) *Overcoming Unintentional Racism in Counseling and Therapy: A Practitioner's Guide to Intentional Intervention*. London: Sage.

Rioch, M. J., Coulter, W.R. and Weinberger, D.M. (1976) *Dialogues for Therapists*. San Francisco: Jossey-Bass.

Roberts, J. (2004) *The Modern Firm: Organizational Design for Performance and Growth*. Oxford: Oxford University Press.

Rogers, C.R. (1957) The necessary and sufficient conditions of therapeutic personality change, *Journal of Counseling Psychology*, 21: 95–103.

Rogers, J. (2004) *Coaching Skill: A Handbook*. Maidenhead: Open University Press.

Rooke, D. and Torbert, W. (2005) Seven transformations of leadership, *Harvard Business Review*, April: 67–76.

Rosinski, P. (2003) *Coaching Across Cultures: New Tools for Leveraging National, Corporate and Professional Differences*. London: Nicholas Brealey.

Rowan, J. (1983) *Reality Game: A Guide to Humanistic Counselling and Therapy*. London: Routledge & Kegan Paul.

Ryde, J. (1997) *A Step Towards Understanding Culture in Relation to Psychotherapy*. Bath: Centre for Psychotherapy and Counselling.

Ryde, J. (2004) *BCPC Refugee and Asylum Seeker's Project 2004 Snapshot Review*. Bath: Centre for Psychotherapy and Counselling.

Ryde, J. (2005) *White Racial Identity and Intersubjectivity in Psychotherapy*. Bath: University of Bath.

Saint-Onge, H. and Wallace, D. (2003) *Leveraging Communities of Practice for Strategic Advantage*. Oxford: Butterworth-Heinemann.

Sansbury, D.L. (1982) Developmental supervision from a skills perspective, *The Counseling Psychologist*, 10(1): 53–7.

Savickas, M. L., Marquart, C.D. and Supinski, C.R. (1986) Effective supervision in groups, *Counselor Education and Supervision*, 26(1): 17–25.

Schaef, A.W. (1992) *When Society Becomes an Addict*. Northamptonshire: Thorsons.

Schaef, A.W. and Fassel, D. (1990) *The Addictive Organization*. San Francisco: Harper & Row.

Schein, E.H. (1985) *Organizational Culture and Leadership*. San Fransisco: Jossey-Bass.

Schön, D. (1983) *The Reflective Practitioner*. New York: Basic Books.

Schroder, M. (1974) The shadow consultant, *The Journal of Applied Behavioral Science*, 10(4): 579–94.

Schutz, W.C. (1973) *Elements of Encounter*. Big Sur, CA: Joy Press.

Searles, H.F. (1955) The informational value of the supervisor's emotional experience, in *Collected Papers of Schizophrenia and Related Subjects*. London: Hogarth Press.

Searles, H.F. (1975) The patient as therapist to his analyst, in R. Langs (ed.) *Classics in Psychoanalytic Technique*. New York: Jason Aronson.

Senge, P. (1990a) *The Fifth Discipline: The Art and Practice of the Learning Organization*. New York: Doubleday.

Senge, P. (1990b) The leader's new work: building learning organizations, *Sloan Management Review*, 32(1): 7–23.

Senge, P., Kleiner, A., Ross, R., Roberts, C. and Smith, B. (1994) The Fifth Discipline Fieldbook: Strategies and Tools for Building a Learning Organization.

Senge, P., Kleiner, A., Roberts, C., Ross, R., Roth, G. and Smith, B. (1999) *The Dance of Change*. New York: Doubleday/Currency.

Senge, P., Jaworski, J., Scharmer, C. and Flowers, B. (2005) *Presence: Exploring Profound Change in People, Organizations and Society*. Cambridge, MA: Nicholas Brealey.

Shainberg, D. (1983) Teaching therapists to be with their clients, in J. Westwood (ed.) *Awakening the Heart*. CO: Shambhala.

Sharpe, M. (ed.) (1995) *The Third Eye: Supervision of Analytic Groups*. London: Routledge.

Shaw, P. (2002) *Changing Conversations in Organizations: A Complexity Approach to Change*. London: Routledge.

Shearer, A. (1983) Who saves the social workers? *Guardian*, 6 July.

Sherman, S. and Freas, A. (2004) The Wild West of executive coaching, *Harvard Business Review*, 82(11): 82–90.

Shipton, G. (1997) *Supervision of Psychotherapy and Counselling: Making a Place to Think*. Buckingham: Open University Press.

Shohet, R. (1985) *Dream Sharing*. Wellingborough: Turnstone Press.

Shulman, L. (1993) *Interactional Supervision*. Washington, DC: NASW Press.

Skovholt, T.M. and Ronnestad, M.H. (1995) *The Evolving Professional Self: Stages and Themes in Therapist and Counselor Development*. Chichester: Wiley.

Smith, C. and Smith, N. (2005) *Multiple Intelligences*. Bath: BCG.

Smith, D. (1985) The client as supervisor: the approach of Robert Langs, *Self and Society: European Journal of Humanistic Psychology*, XIII(2): 92–5.

Spice, C.G.J. and Spice, W.H. (1976) A triadic method of supervision in the training of counselors and counseling supervisors, *Counselor Education and Supervision*, 15: 251–8.

Srivastva, S. and Cooperrider, D.L. (eds) (1990) *Appreciative Management and Leadership: The Power of Positive Thought and Action in Organizations*. San Francisco: Jossey-Bass.

Starr, J. (2003) *The Coaching Manual*. London: Prentice Hall.

Stevens, A. (1991) *Disability Issues: Developing Anti-discriminatory Practice*. London: CCETSW.

Stolorow, R.D. and Attwood, G.E. (1992) *Contexts of Being*. New York: The Analytic Press.

Stoltenberg, C.S. and Delworth, U. (1987) *Supervising Counselors and Therapists: A Developmental Approach*. San Francisco: Jossey-Bass.

Subby, R. (1984) Inside the chemically dependent marriage: denial and manipulation, in *Co-dependence: An Emerging Issue*. Hollywood Beach, FL: Health Communications.

Sue, D.W. and Sue, D. (1990) *Counseling the Culturally Different: Theory and Practice*. New York: Wiley.

Surowiecki, J. (2005) *The Wisdom of Crowds: Why the Many are Smarter than the Few*. London: Abacus.

Suzuki, S. (1973) *Zen Mind, Beginner's Mind*. NY: Weatherhill.

Symington, N. (1986) *The Analytic Experience: Lectures from the Tavistock*. London: Free Association Books.

Teitelbaum, S. H. (1990) Supertransference: the role of the supervisor's blind spots, *Psychoanalytic Psychology*, 7(2): 243–58.

Thomas, A. (1998) Scientific and practical aspects of cross-cultural cooperation and management in the context of European integration, *Studia Psychologica*, 40: 69–77.

Thompson, J. (1991) *Issues of Race and Culture in Counselling Supervision Training Courses*. London: Polytechnic of East London.

Thompson, N. (1993) *Anti-Discriminatory Practice*. London: BASW/Macmillan.

Tichy, N. M. (1997) *The Leadership Engine: How Winning Companies Build Leaders at Every Level*. New York: HarperCollins.

Tomlinson, H. (1993) Developing professionals, *Education*, 182(13): 231.

Tonnesmann, M. (1979) The human encounter in the helping professions. Paper presented at the London Fourth Winnicott Conference, London, UK, March.

Torbert, W. *et al.* (2004) *Action Inquiry: The Secret of Timely and Transforming Leadership*. San Francisco: Berrett-Koehler.

Trist, E. and Murray, H. (eds) (1990) *The Social Engagement of Social Science, Vol 1: The Socio-Psychological Perspective*. London: Free Association Books.

Trivasse, M. (2003) Counselling through an interpreter, *Counselling and Psychotherapy Journal*, 14(4): 21–2.

Trompenaars, A. and Hampden-Turner, C. (eds) (1994) *Riding the Waves of Culture*. Burr Ridge, IL: Irwin.

Tuckman, B. (1965) Developmental sequence in small groups, *Psychological Bulletin*, 63(6): 384–99.

Tyler, F. B., Brome, D.R. and Williams, J.E. (1991) *Ethnic Validity, Ecology and Psychotherapy: A Psychosocial Competence Model*. New York: Plenum Press.

van Gennep, A. (1960) *The Rites of Passage*. Chicago: University of Chicago Press.

van Ooijen, E. (2003) *Clinical Supervision Made Easy: A Practical Guide for the Helping Professions – The 3-Step Method*. Oxford: Churchill Livingstone.

van Weerdenburg, O. (1996) Thinking values through and through, in B. Conraths (ed.) *Training the Fire Brigade: Preparing for the Unimaginable*. Brussels: efdm.

Vince, R. and Martin, L. (1993) Inside action learning: an exploration of the psychology and politics of the action learning model, *Management Education and Development*, 24(3): 205–15.

Watson, T. (1996) Motivation: that's Maslow, isn't it? *Management Learning Journal*, 27(4): 447–64.

Weick, K.E. (1995) *Sensemaking in Organizations*. London: Sage.

Weiler, N.W. and Schoonover, S.C. (2001) *Your Soul at Work*. Boston, MA: Paulist Press.

Wester, S. R., Vogel, D.L. and Archer, J.Jr. (2004) Male restricted emotionality and counseling supervision, *Journal of Counseling and Development*, 82(1): 91–8.

Wheatley, M. (1994) *Leadership and the New Science*. San Francisco: Berrett-Koehler Publishers.

Whitmore, J. (1992) *Coaching for Performance: A Practical Guide to Growing Your Own Skills*. London: Nicholas Brealey.

Whitmore, J. (1996) *Coaching for Performance – The New Edition of the Practical Guide*. London: Nicholas Brealey.

Whitmore, J. (1997) *Need, Greed or Freedom: Business Changes and Personal Choices*. London: Nicholas Brealey.

Whitmore, J. (2002) *Coaching for Performance: Growing People, Performance and Purpose*. London: Nicholas Brealey.

Whitworth, L., Kimsey-House, H. and Sandahl, P. (1998) *Co-Active Coaching*. Palo Alto, CA: Davies-Black.

Williams, G., Wilke, G. and Binney, G. (2004) *Living Leadership: A Practical Guide for Ordinary Heroes*. London: Financial Times/Prentice Hall.

Williams, R. (1965) *The Long Revolution*. Harmondsworth: Penguin.

Wilmot, J. and Shohet, R. (1985) Paralleling in the supervision process, *Self and Society: European Journal of Humanistic Psychology*, XIII(2): 86–92.

Winnicott, D.W. (1965) *Maturational Processes and the Facilitating Environment*. London: Hogarth Press.

Winnicott, D.W. (1971) *Playing and Reality*. London: Tavistock.

Witherspoon, R. (2000) Starting smart: clarifying goals and roles, in M. Goldsmith, L. Lyons and A. Freas (eds) *Coaching for Leadership*. San Francisco: Jossey-Bass.

Woodcock, J. (2005) *Can Work With Trauma Harm Psychotherapists?* Bristol: Centre for Psychosocial Studies, University of West of England.

Worthington, E.L. (1987) Changes in supervision as counselors and supervisors gain experience: a review, *Professional Psychology: Research and Practice*, 18(3): 189–208.

Yalom, I. (2002) *The Gift of Therapy: An Open Letter to a New Generation of Therapists and Their Patients*. New York: HarperCollins.

Yankelovich, D. (2001) *The Magic of Dialogue: Transforming Conflict into Cooperation*. New York: Touchstone.

Yerkes, R.M. and Dodson, J.D. (1908) The relation of strength of stimulus to rapidity of habit formation, *Journal of Comparative Neurology and Psychology*, 18, 459–82.

Zeus, P. and Skiffington, S. (2002) *The Complete Guide to Coaching at Work*. Sydney: McGraw-Hill.

Zinker, J. (1978) *Creative Process in Gestalt Therapy*. NY: Vintage Books.

Index